Digital Innovation and Entrepreneurship

The digital economy encompasses more than half the world, and in today's business market, those with a technology background have an advantage. This textbook provides students who already have digital expertise with a solid foundation in business and entrepreneurship in order to launch and run a business.

Using a logical, objective-based structure, the book guides students to a comprehensive and practical understanding of innovation and entrepreneurship. Chapters progress through the steps in creating a successful digital business: framing the business promotion and sales, delivery and operations, value capture, growth and scalability, intellectual property and protection, and leadership and structure.

Features include:

- Learning objectives, introductions, conclusions, tables and figures, highlighted key terms, and analysis and design exercises in each chapter.
- A wide range of real-world examples.
- A rolling case study of a hypothetical digital business that models the concepts covered in each chapter.
- Appendices of business terms, including those relating to product licensing, customer service agreements and customer delivery contracts, with key terms explained throughout.
- Supplementary online resources, including: a test bank, lecture slides and a teaching guide for instructors; and a business design template for student use.

Dick Whittington taught Business Innovation at the University of York and is an entrepreneur, business mentor and investor with over twenty-five years' experience. Co-founding a successful UK technology business recognised through three Queen's Awards, he was elected Fellow of the Royal Academy of Engineering in 2012. He is also an active mentor and angel investor within several London and regional technology accelerator programmes.

Digital Innovation and Entrepreneurship

Dr Dick Whittington FREng

CAMBRIDGE
UNIVERSITY PRESS

CAMBRIDGE
UNIVERSITY PRESS

University Printing House, Cambridge CB2 8BS, United Kingdom

One Liberty Plaza, 20th Floor, New York, NY 10006, USA

477 Williamstown Road, Port Melbourne, VIC 3207, Australia

314–321, 3rd Floor, Plot 3, Splendor Forum, Jasola District Centre, New Delhi – 110025, India

79 Anson Road, #06–04/06, Singapore 079906

Cambridge University Press is part of the University of Cambridge.

It furthers the University's mission by disseminating knowledge in the pursuit of
education, learning, and research at the highest international levels of excellence.

www.cambridge.org
Information on this title: www.cambridge.org/9781108470506
DOI: 10.1017/9781108643252

© Cambridge University Press 2018

First published 2018

Printed in the United Kingdom by TJ International Ltd. Padstow, Cornwall 2018

A catalogue record for this publication is available from the British Library.

Library of Congress Cataloging-in-Publication Data
Names: Whittington, Richard, 1958- author.
Title: Digital innovation and entrepreneurship / Richard Whittington, University of York.
Description: Cambridge, United Kingdom ; New York, NY : Cambridge University Press, 2018. |
    Includes bibliographical references and index.
Identifiers: LCCN 2018017446 | ISBN 9781108470506 (hardback : alk. paper) |
    ISBN 9781108454940 (pbk. : alk. paper)
Subjects: LCSH: Electronic commerce. | Entrepreneurship. | Information
    technology–Economic aspects. | Technological innovations–Economic aspects.
Classification: LCC HF5548.32 .W485 2018 | DDC 658.4–dc23
    LC record available at https://lccn.loc.gov/2018017446

ISBN 978-1-108-47050-6 Hardback
ISBN 978-1-108-45494-0 Paperback

Additional resources for this publication at www.cambridge.org/Whittington

For Sharon and all those who travel with, through and ahead of us, including those born in the midst of things

Contents

Contents

Foreword

There are countless books on business development, marketing and entrepreneurship, but many follow either a rather singular experience or a theoretical/academic pathway. Dr Dick Whittington has produced a deep and broad treatise on the full complexity, challenge and opportunity of entrepreneurial business development. He focuses primarily on the digital sector which he knows best, but most of the content of this book is more broadly relevant to many businesses in the plethora of sectors. Dick is unusual in having both an eminent academic career and an excellent track record as a successful serial entrepreneur. He is extremely well connected to international networks in both business and academia and as a fellow of the Royal Academy of Engineering has played an important role in the creation of the acclaimed Enterprise Hub. This hub has helped, guided and supported over fifty businesses from start-up, raising substantial investment and creating many new highly skilled jobs. The hub is also supporting over fifty established medium-sized businesses, assisting in their strategy development for growth and scale-up.

Dick's rich combination of experience over many years has given him deep insights into the complete life cycle of technology innovation, business creation, development, scale-up and maturity, which is rare. This business development process has great complexity and is certainly not linear. He addresses this complexity in a very clear and succinct step-wise manner with sharp focus on iterative review. The key issues of leadership, risk tolerance and management, core competence, value proposition, people, customers, partners, and asset and intellectual property protection are all treated in a systematic and very clear manner.

Within the UK over the last two decades there has been a significant amount of attention given to start-up businesses and venture funding, which has led to an emphasis on gaining investment and moving to exit at the expense of longer-term sustainable business growth, development and scale-up, and hence the UK has often missed out on the consequential economic benefit of retaining truly scalable and rapidly growing mid-sized business.

This book offers a rounded and complete recipe for full business development and scale-up which will help entrepreneurs consider a broader range of options than currently appears to be the case. Perhaps more will now choose the 'accelerated growth elevator' and not simply 'run to the exit'. I have no hesitation in commending this book for any budding entrepreneur, or even an established business leader, to help ensure that maximum potential is realized to fully develop the inherent value of business, assets and teams with genuine wealth creation.

Ian Shott CBE FREng
Founder and Chairman of the Enterprise Hub, Royal Academy of Engineering
Managing Partner of Shott Trinova Ltd

Preface

Motivation

After twenty-five years as an entrepreneur, mentor and investor in digital businesses, teaching business innovation in a UK university provided me with three insights:

One, students studying STEM disciplines readily spark at the opportunities offered by the fast-moving world of digital business, and are keen to apply their inherent analytical skills to business design and business realization.

Two, a significant majority of STEM students graduate with only the most rudimentary and anecdotal appreciation of how digital techniques, technologies and processes apply to business and entrepreneurship, despite a formal education which includes a wealth of relevant digital knowledge and skills.

And three, while there are many excellent books that address innovation and entrepreneurship, there is real need for a student textbook that specifically addresses today's digital economy for those planning to enter the technology sector.

This book bridges the gap between formal STEM education and the business world, and introduces innovation and entrepreneurship as core components of the modern professional's skillset in the digital economy.

It aims to enable and encourage the application of students' inherent digital computing knowledge, imagination and creativity to the activities of business innovation and entrepreneurship.

Focus

Peter Sondergaard, Executive Vice President of Research at Gartner, a leading market analysis company, famously stated that: 'every company is a technology company'. It follows, therefore, that if all businesses are digital, then all digital professionals should have business skills.

The success of global companies such as Amazon, Uber and JustEat has been founded on highly effective digital e-commerce platforms; nevertheless, their business models require and involve large numbers of people handling and processing physical artefacts, thus the modern digital economy entrepreneur needs to know more than how to create digital technology.

In this book, the digital world is assumed to embrace all of those businesses that produce digital products, or for which a digital platform is in some way essential to their fabric, and the approach taken to entrepreneurship embraces the wider range of subjects that need to be understood to succeed in business.

Approach Taken

While there are some aspects of business creation that are universal, such as the need for an identity and a legal structure, there are many aspects that need to be addressed as design decisions and which result in businesses differing in rich and surprising ways.

This book takes a business design-led approach to digital entrepreneurship. There are many decisions in the design and operation of a business that can be treated rationally, and which can make a real difference to its performance and success. This book logically sets out what these decisions are and how a successful digital entrepreneur would go about designing and implementing them for their own business idea.

Alongside this, however, it is important to recognize that those characteristics of a business determined by its design are layered over a matrix of assumptions, values and qualities that reflect the ethos of the founders or leadership, and which are beyond the remit of design: this is what gives a business its unique personality.

The Business Design Framework

The central chapters of the book are structured around a business design framework that has been synthesized from experience for the purposes of this book. It provides a broad logical structure for thinking about business design in a way that separates the diverse set of considerations involved and guides the sequencing of chapters. Presented throughout in diagrammatic form, the framework clearly and logically directs the student through the principal steps of business design.

Each chapter of the book guides the student through a collection of design decisions that are needed, using a methodical structure with an emphasis on defining and achieving business objectives. Useful techniques and evaluation approaches, such as ecosystem design and customer-journey mapping, are included to help consolidate students' understanding and application of entrepreneurship in the digital economy.

SportMagenta – a Rolling Case Study

A hypothetical business idea – SportMagenta – which provides a digital channel between sport clubs and their visitors – is used throughout the book to provide a rolling case study. The story of this venture's development unfolds with each chapter to illustrate to students the way in which a business can be designed and developed in concert with the business design framework.

Although hypothetical, the business is sufficiently realistic that the required design decisions provide useful examples of the working of the techniques introduced by each chapter, including considerations of ecosystem, routes to market and growth plan.

Intended Readership

The book has been written for STEM and business students, including undergraduate, postgraduate and beyond, to bridge the world of their studies with the digital business world.

The book recognizes that some of its readers will have ambitions to start their own businesses, others will intend to join existing start-ups, and yet others will plan to join larger organizations, possibly as part of a research and development function. Whatever their ambition, students need to understand how business works in the digital economy. Without this, a student's employability will be limited, as will be the contribution that they can offer to a prospective employer.

It can also be (and indeed has been) used to provide a concise and practical introduction to digital innovation and entrepreneurship for those who are studying a more wide-reaching business study programme.

This book gives students a thorough grasp of the fundamentals of business in one volume, without the need for a full-blown business curriculum. My experience of teaching the content and framework contained in this book has demonstrated it to be effective with students of many disciplines and situations, from first-year undergraduates through to research staff and those entering the world of business.

There are no assumed prerequisites, other than a broad appreciation of the digital world. Every topic is introduced, explained and illustrated. Where relevant, references are provided to sources for further research or learning.

Pedagogical Features

- A rolling case study of a hypothetical business developed incrementally throughout the book to illustrate the main points of each chapter.
- Diagrammatic illustrations and tables throughout to clarify important structures and concepts.
- Real-world examples from larger businesses such as IBM, Amazon and Google, and also from smaller businesses such as Bright Funds, Onlicar and Sorry as a Service are used to illustrate key points.
- Detailed case studies of digital businesses and successful business design, such as the example of Swift Comply in Chapter 3, which illustrates an innovative approach to scaling of promotion.
- A glossary that explains all of the business terms and jargon introduced by the book.
- A business design template to record and consolidate design decisions, introduced and illustrated in principle and provided as a resource for students.
- Learning outcomes at the start of each chapter.
- Analysis questions at the end of each chapter.
- A rolling design activity for students to complete at the end of each chapter.
- An accompanying website at [www.cambridge.org/Whittington] provides additional lecture and assessment materials, plus a downloadable version of the business design template.
- Each chapter addresses a collection of design decisions, structured so as to explain the options available, listing applicable considerations and, in many cases, describing a practical technique that can be applied, with examples.

- A comprehensive bibliography for further reading and research, including books, journal articles and business reports.
- Appendices providing more detailed coverage of the principal terms applying to licensing agreements, service agreements and delivery contracts.

Chapter Overviews

Chapter 1, About Innovation and Entrepreneurship, addresses innovation from the perspectives of process, ecosystem, types and implications, historical patterns, and the various classes of innovators and their motivations. It addresses the distinctions and interactions between innovation and entrepreneurship, and examines the principal ingredients for success, and the most common reasons for failure.

Chapter 2, Framing the Business, proposes a template for business design and outlines the hypothetical business case exercise to be used throughout the book. It introduces, applies and illustrates seven principal questions that together frame a business venture: the mission, the customer, the problem it solves, the technology offering, how performance will be measured, the key risks and the plan.

Chapter 3, Promotion and Sales, explains and illustrates the analysis of market size, structure and dynamics. It reviews options for creating visibility, branding, presence, influence, and the planning and costing of promotional activities. The management of sales is addressed in respect of methods for customer prioritization, stakeholder management, engagement, negotiation, piloting and the development of customer communities. A final section stresses the need to apply the innovative power of the business to its promotion.

Chapter 4, Delivery and Operations, addresses considerations and techniques for building and managing the supply chain, and for mapping and analysing the customer journey. The planning of development is covered in terms of requirement prioritization and product roadmap, and the need for continuing management and control of development and release is highlighted. Considerations and techniques for developing a channel strategy and routes to market are addressed, and a final section stresses the need to apply the innovative power of the business to the development and delivery of its offerings.

Chapter 5, Value Capture, highlights the need to set a value capture strategy, including objectives and a return-on-investment case. It recognizes the need for care when defining the option to be offered to customers and the importance of understanding the purchasing process. Creation and calibration of a pricing structure is addressed in terms of *what, who, when, how*, and *how much* to charge. Value capture should enhance business value, and hence methods for assessing the value of a business are described, including their driving factors. The chapter concludes with a section that stresses the need to apply the innovative power of the business to its value capture.

Chapter 6, Growth and Scalability, highlights distinctions between growth and scalability, start-up and scale-up, and innovation and entrepreneurship. It addresses the need to set a strategy for growth and scalability and illustrates the creation of a growth plan comprising financial projections, the required size and shape of team, and the design of a scalable organization. Funding options are addressed, including organic growth and investment readiness. Sources of investment are explained, as is the creation of a business plan in terms of required content and associated presentation materials.

Chapter 7, Intellectual Property and Protection, is about understanding the principal risks, requirements and means of protection. The protection of IP includes trademarks, design rights, patents and copyright, including open source, which are explained in an international context. The protection of confidential information and trade secrets is addressed, as is the need to protect against risky contracts. Three appendices provide detailed coverage of contractual clauses that can carry risk. Two further risks are addressed: the need to protect against damage and intrusion, physical and cyber; and the need to protect against non-compliance with legal requirements, including data protection and employment legislation.

Chapter 8, Leadership and Structure, subdivides into two parts. The first relates to the leadership and governance requirements of a business, explaining and differentiating the respective requirements, and highlighting the need for a balanced team. Financial planning and control is covered in respect of cash management, setting and balancing of budgets, monitoring of performance, and requirements for company reporting and taxation. The second part relates to structural and legal requirements, including company legal entities, and the contractual structures and agreements relating to people and shareholdings.

Chapter 9, Key Themes and Summary Points, collects and reflects upon ten key themes that emerge across the other chapters. For each theme, a brief narrative summarizes its applicable contexts and picks out the principal points to be noted.

Acknowledgements

I am grateful to a number of people and organizations that have provided useful input and feedback during the development of this text. These include the following:

- Max Kelly and the team at TechStars UK for inspiration and feedback on early ideas.
- Phil Stephenson, Patent Attorney at Bailey Walsh & Co., for technical input on IP matters.
- Peter Thomas from IBM for insights into intrapreneurship.
- Tristan Watson and the team at Ignite100 for lively encouragement and input.
- The fantastic teams behind those early-stage businesses that have shared their stories as case exercises, especially Onlicar, Reposit and SwiftComply.
- My students, mentees and business friends for a wonderfully wide tapestry of experiences and learning.

To the Student

Whatever your ambitions, you need to know about business in the digital economy – its language, assumptions, methods, the opportunities it offers, and what it is likely to expect from you in terms of knowledge, imagination and creativity.

Many people learn what they need to know through experience, which is invaluable; however, relying solely on experience takes time, usually involves repeating well-known mistakes and can lead to a patchy and anecdotal understanding. This book is a short-cut to a comprehensive and practical grounding in everything that you need to understand to succeed in the digital economy.

By following the components of the business design framework that is comprehensively examined from Chapter 2 to Chapter 8, you will learn about notions of product, platform and service, customers and ecosystems, markets and their dynamics, promotional and delivery channels, intellectual property and its protection, risk, finance, team-building and motivation, investment and legal requirements – and above all, about what is needed to create, grow and scale something of value.

The practical style of the book develops three threads which will help you gain a comprehensive understanding of business in the digital world:

- A wide range of real-world examples, including Apple's approach to managing its routes to market, IBM's categories of intrapreneurship, Onlicar's supply chain management and Reposit's redesign of the tenancy ecosystem, to illustrate approaches that are being applied effectively by businesses of all sizes.
- A rolling case study of a hypothetical digital business, SportMagenta, to illustrate how design decisions can be addressed in a coherent manner.
- Exercises at the end of each chapter, to provide an opportunity for you to apply your talents to business analysis and design.

The business world is rich in jargon and terminology, much of which will be alien to those without experience, and which needs to be understood and applied intelligently. The book introduces relevant terms with explanation where they arise, and provides a comprehensive glossary of more than 300 relevant terms.

1   About Innovation and Entrepreneurship

Learning Outcomes

After studying this chapter, you will:

- Appreciate the relationship between innovation and entrepreneurship.
- Understand the innovation process, its constituent parts and applicable risks.
- Appreciate the concept of ecosystem and why this is central to exploitation of innovation.
- Be able to assess the likely implications of an innovation on the basis of its type.
- Be able to contrast three of the principal historical frameworks of innovation trends.
- Understand the kinds of parties that drive innovation and what motivates them.
- Appreciate the ingredients for success and the most common reasons for failure.
- Understand much of the current terminology of digital business.

Introducing Innovation and Entrepreneurship

The world of digital business is rich, diverse and fast moving in ideas, structures and terminology. This book explains and charts paths through many of the underpinning concepts and techniques.

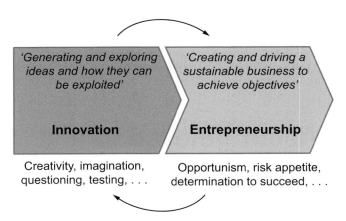

Figure 1.1 *Innovation and entrepreneurship*

This chapter sets the scene by introducing and contrasting innovation and entrepreneurship.

As illustrated in Figure 1.1, innovation is about ideas and how they can be exploited through product and service offerings. For an innovator, creativity and imagination are crucial aspects for success, as are questioning, testing and incisiveness. The term *enterprise* is sometimes used with the same meaning.

By contrast, an entrepreneur is someone with the talent, skill and determination to create and drive a viable business that transforms innovation into value. A central aspect of this is risk: the successful entrepreneur is continually identifying, assessing and working with a risk profile that ranges across people, technology, systems, the marketplace and the economic landscape. Knowledge, skills and connections with these domains must be built, hired and purchased for successful delivery of innovation.

The general term *business* is used here to encompass all kinds of ventures, including those whose objectives involve financial gain and also those *social enterprises* whose objectives are driven by social or cultural values.

Succeeding in the design, operation and growth of a business needs a blend of innovation and entrepreneurship, and the balance of this blend changes over time. An important element of the entrepreneur's risk profile is judgement of the degree of innovation that is currently sustainable. Too much innovation can mean that a business loses its focus, becomes distracted by continual internal change and presents a confused or chaotic picture to its customers. On the other hand, with insufficient innovation, a business may struggle to sustain competitiveness in the market and can lose the interest of its customers.

Some people are innovators and some are entrepreneurs. A third category are *operators*: these are people with talents that ensure effective delivery and performance of some business activity, such as product, sales or finance. The successful business achieves the right mix of these three kinds of talent through a team that has the motivation, experience, support and resources needed.

This chapter first addresses the broad topic of innovation, from five perspectives:

- The innovation process – how ideas become successful business offerings.
- The ecosystem – the importance of locating innovation in a market context.
- Types of innovation – including the market impact of different types.
- Historical context – with reference to three longer-term models of development.
- Innovators – including the different parties involved and their motivations.

It then returns to the subjects of innovation and entrepreneurship, addressing questions of the principal ingredients for success, and the most common reasons for failure.

This chapter concludes with an explanation of how the subjects of innovation and entrepreneurship will be structured and presented through the remaining chapters. This point is particularly important as the subjects embrace a wide range of interrelated topics. One of this book's principal contributions is a systematic framework within which all of those various topics can be understood and accessed.

Throughout the chapter, relevant business terminology is introduced and defined, including with reference to the Glossary. Examples are provided from the current world of digital business, and references are provided to sources of further detail.

Innovation and the Innovation Process

Innovation is more than a new idea.

A UK Government report 'Succeeding through innovation' provides a useful definition: 'the successful exploitation of an idea as a product or service offering' (DTI, 2004).

As shown in Figure 1.2, an idea remains just an idea until it is embodied within a tangible product or service offering, at which point it may be described as an invention. An offering is only considered to be an innovation when it is

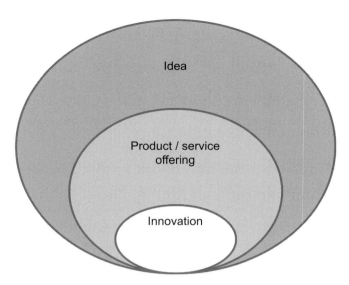

Figure 1.2 *Relationship between ideas and innovation*

successfully deployed and used by some community or market for which it delivers a benefit. The definition of success in this context depends upon the objectives that are set by those driving the initiative. This may mean widespread adoption of the innovation by a community of users, or it may mean meeting revenue-generation targets within a particular time-frame.

Putting this in an engineering context, a wide-ranging study carried out by Bhuiyan (2011) at Concordia University in Montreal, Canada found that for every seven new product ideas, about four enter development, one-and-a-half are launched and only one succeeds. Seven ideas yield one innovation.

In the current climate of fast-moving digital start-ups, it is more difficult to estimate the percentage of ideas that see the light of day, but it has been estimated by the journalist Erin Griffith (2014) writing in *Fortune Magazine* that 80 to 90 per cent of start-ups fail to succeed, principally because of lack of market need for their offering. Given that many of those ventures that do succeed are likely to have pivoted through several ideas, it is clear that the number of ideas needed to yield a single innovation in this sector is significantly higher than within more established sectors.

This factor underlines the importance of taking a systematic approach to the design of a business venture right from the outset to create confidence that an idea can be successfully exploited and deployed. Where this confidence proves elusive, the idea should be discarded before it consumes significant fruitless effort.

The Innovation Process

Building on these observations, innovation has usefully been characterized by Gee (1981) as a process through which a new product, technique or useful service is obtained from the generation of new ideas and their development. In their introduction to *The Oxford Handbook of Innovation*, Fagerberg *et al.* (2005) characterize this process as a 'systemic phenomenon resulting from continuing interaction between different actors and organizations'; hence the importance to innovation of a concept of *ecosystem*, which is addressed in more detail in the following section.

Innovation is treated throughout this book as a process that involves a range of participating players, or actors. Figure 1.3 shows its most general three-phase form, reflecting the elements in the definition introduced above.

An idea is exploited through an offering, which combines a product or service with a business model and a plan of action. As the plan executes, the market consumes, or absorbs, the offering and responds with indications of success. Based on this response, the offering, the business model and/or the plan may be reviewed and iterated. Alternatively, the idea itself may need to be reviewed or discarded.

This is succinctly expressed by Tonnessen (2005): 'innovation starts with the proposal and generation of new ideas and finishes with the use and commercial exploitation of the outcomes'.

In current parlance, a significant modification to the plan, or even a complete replacement of the idea, is referred to as a *pivot*. It is not uncommon for start-up businesses to pivot several times before investing significant effort in growing the success of an innovation.

In 2003, a start-up called Android had the idea to build an operating system for cameras. Its initial vision was an ecosystem of smart cameras connecting to

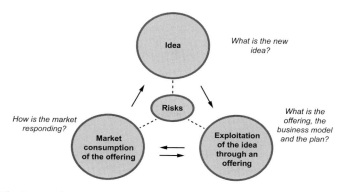

Figure 1.3 *The innovation process*

PCs and linked to Android-powered data centres that offered cloud storage for photos. However, the downward market trend of camera sales and the parallel growth in mobile device sales prompted the venture to make a significant pivot, which led to its acquisition in 2005 by Google for $50 million. Further detail of this case has been reported in TechCrunch by O'Hear and Lomas (2014).

Figure 1.3 also refers to risk associated with each phase of the process. The following sections address each phase in turn, including the principal applicable risks.

Ideas and Their Origins

An idea is the first milestone in the process of building a successful business. An idea is a thought. It can be expressed in words or diagrams, but its value is only potential until it is given tangible form through a product or service offering. From a single idea, many innovations may emerge. A web browser is a generic user interface for accessing content organized as hyper-text. The idea is attributed to Sir Tim Berners-Lee, currently director of the World Wide Web Consortium (W3C), which oversees the Web's continued development. The idea was significant because, up until that time, providing access to content usually involved some form of custom user interface. Berners-Lee's idea stimulated a first generation of browser offerings which inspired the development of families of increasingly widely used products that have enabled the development of the web economy.

Some authorities promote the view that creativity can be learned, applied and improved through the application of principles and techniques. Examples include the Strategyn 'outcome-driven innovation' method, and the 'idea hunter' approach proposed by Boynton, Fischer and Bole (2011). Methods such as these encourage a broad and structured approach to ideation.

Ideas can also emerge from the following:

Association – the bringing together of previously unconnected ideas to solve a problem or open a new market. There was a time when phones were used only to make calls and photographs could only be taken by a camera. The idea to associate these functions contributed to the now ubiquitous smartphone products.

Adaptation/analogy – the adaptation of an existing solution for a different purpose, potentially in a different situation. Platforms such as Uber underlie what is now called *collaborative consumption* or the *sharing, access* or *peer* economy. This approach is now being applied to a wide range of business situations to create platforms whereby consumers pay to access someone else's goods or services. Similarly, the notion of *software as a service* (SaaS) has been applied by analogy to all sorts of *x as a service* (XaaS) offerings, including infrastructure, analytics and even business.

Serendipity/chance – a new idea arises through random occurrence or acci-dent. A classic example of serendipity occurred in 1945, when Percy Spencer was working with magnetrons (electronic devices that create microwave radio signals). He noticed the melting of a chocolate bar in his pocket when he stood next to a magnetron. This observation led to the invention of the microwave oven. Another example comes from the early 1990s during the development of Acorn Computers' first Advanced RISC Machine (ARM) chip. During testing, a fault was preventing current from passing to the motherboard and ultimately to the chip, but the team noticed that the chip was still working. It was being powered by electricity leaking out of the rest of the circuitry (less than a tenth of a watt). This serendipit-ous discovery led to the chip's low power consumption becoming a key competitive advantage. And due to its outstanding efficiency, the descend-ants of this processor now run many of today's mobile computing devices.

Irrespective of how an idea has been inspired, it is important to recognize that many of the ideas underpinning successful digital businesses were originally prompted initially either by identifying problems worth solving – such as the need for improved internet search or lower-cost overnight accommodation – or by identifying market opportunities – such as for an online book store or a video streaming service. Unless one of these criteria is met by the idea, it is unlikely to form the basis of a sustainable business.

Two risks commonly apply to the development and evaluation of ideas.

The first of these is poor research, relating either to technology feasibility or to the expected market demand, both of which can encourage false confidence in the potential of an idea. Before investing in development and exploitation planning, this risk needs to be addressed through objective market research. In his book, Rob Fitzpatrick (2013) describes a series of *mom test* techniques which can be useful in this regard.

The second risk relates to weak expression or articulation of an idea, which leads to ambiguity around its implications and potential, and a difficulty in translating the idea into an offering. Research by Phadke and Vyakarnam (2017) identifies this problem as the first of three chasms to be crossed by a venture. In addition to clarifying the underlying idea, crossing this chasm requires a clear focus on the technology and the business model through which it will be exploited. This topic is addressed further in Chapter 4 in the context of development discontinuities and in Chapter 6 in the context of capabilities required for growth and scalability.

Exploitation of Ideas through a Product or Service Offering

This phase of the process is about the way in which an idea can be taken to market through some form of offering. An idea cannot be taken to market in its pure form: it needs to be wrapped into a product or service offering with an associated **business model**.

A business model is a set of propositions, analyses and design decisions that embrace all aspects of how an offering will be taken to market. A business model is embodied in and empowered by a business structure.

The components of a business model can be described under the following four headings:

Value creation – describing the value of the offering and the beneficiaries of this value.

The term *value* here relates to anything that can be perceived as beneficial to one or more customer communities, irrespective of whether such value can easily be quantified.

Value may relate to solving a problem, or saving time, or making money, or reducing a cost, or mitigating a risk, or enabling something that was not previously possible. In plain business speak, it has been said that value means 'either making more money or keeping out of jail', and it can be a helpful discipline to express any proposed statement of value against these criteria.

Typically, a business model will comprise several value propositions, each relating to a particular customer, or beneficiary. As a simple example, consider the idea behind *Westfield*, a smartphone app intended to help shoppers get the most out of visiting any of the company's shopping centres. A value proposition for retailers is that it enables shoppers to find what they want and hence increases their sales volumes. A second value proposition – this time for the shopper – is that it saves them time by enabling them rapidly to locate what they need.

Chapter 2 will show how multiple value propositions can be expressed and consolidated through a representation of the business ecosystem.

Common risks associated with value creation include assuming a value that does not really exist, and failing to recognize that the promised effect can be achieved by another means. Effective market research is the mitigation in both cases. Unless the value is real and distinctive, the offering will not succeed.

Value promotion – describing to whom the value proposition will be offered, and how.

This means understanding the *target market* in terms of its size, structure and dynamics, and constructing and executing a plan for achieving visibility and generating demand within that market. Such a plan will include activities to create visibility, build knowledge, engage with customers and other relevant parties, and develop beneficial partnerships.

Central to these activities is the notion of brand: value promotion is driven by the objectives of creating and establishing *brand image* and of growing *brand value*. And a significant contributor to both is a strong customer community.

A business model may address several target markets, sometimes aligned with geographic segmentation, and sometimes with other characteristics, such as industry sector. This topic is addressed further in Chapter 3.

Common risks associated with value promotion include targeting the offering at a customer base for whom the value proposition is unattractive or meaningless, adopting ineffective or overly expensive promotional approaches, and underestimating the effort needed and hence allocating insufficient resource to the activity. Each of these is mitigated through market research, planning, monitoring and having the agility to pivot in response to feedback and learning.

Value delivery – describing how the value will be made available to the beneficiaries.

This introduces the subjects of *supply chain, channel strategy* and *routes to market*. Decisions here combine considerations around technologies and processes for production and delivery with the development of relationships and partnerships through which materials can be sourced and the offering can be *channelled*.

Developing and managing value delivery mechanisms can be demanding. Whereas a simple consumer app might be delivered directly through an online app store, a more sophisticated enterprise software offering might need to be integrated and accredited onto a customer infrastructure by a network of competent and qualified partner companies, which in turn could be motivated to further promote the offering to other customers.

Global technology company Cisco, for example, uses many routes to market, including value-added resellers, independent software vendors, IT service providers and platform partners. In some cases, these relationships will be arm's length arrangements, in other cases they will involve co-creation of offerings for specific markets.

This area is addressed in greater detail in Chapter 4, along with the design of a *customer journey* and a roadmap for continuing development.

Many large organizations can and will only make purchases through licensed channels, which means that if an offering is targeting such customers, it needs first to achieve appropriate accreditation. This will be the case with many health-care and defence-related offerings, but can also apply to other sectors in which activities are regulated.

As with value propositions, a business model may comprise several value delivery mechanisms, aligning with the various value propositions and target markets.

Consider again the Westfield app introduced previously. In relation to the retailers, value delivery will involve a data integration activity whereby the stores' offerings and location will be made available to shoppers. For the shopper, it will involve creating app store listings whereby the product can be downloaded for the supported brands and models of smartphone.

Two risks commonly apply to value delivery. The first of these is failing to achieve an offering that can be deployed. The resulting delays will inhibit value capture ambitions, which may in turn affect the viability of the venture. Phadke and Vyakarnam (2017) identify this as the second of three chasms to be crossed by a venture. Crossing this chasm requires organization, talent and leadership to shape and package a market-ready product. This topic is addressed further in Chapter 4 in the context of development discontinuities and in Chapter 6 in the context of capabilities required for growth and scalability.

A second risk is that the offering is not accessible or usable by those for whom it is intended. This can result from an inadequate understanding of the requirements of customers, poor design of the associated customer experience or an ineffective delivery ecosystem. These subjects are addressed further in Chapter 4.

Value capture – describing how the business will benefit from exploitation of its offering.

Value capture is about how the customers' perception of value will be translated back into value for the business. This might take the form of financial revenue, market endorsement, community impact, brand awareness, enhanced visibility, reputational growth, demonstration of effectiveness . . . and in many cases some combination of these.

The decisions that underlie value capture drive licensing and pricing models, and have a strong influence on promotional and community-engagement activities and the branding of the offering.

Multiple value capture mechanisms may be established, aligned with value propositions and value delivery approaches. In the case of the Westfield app, value capture for the shopping centre includes enhanced rental income from retailers who are attracted and retained by the higher volume of sales.

The following common risks all follow from a poor understanding of the value created and therefore of the value that can be achieved from each beneficiary:

- Charging the wrong party, which can limit take-up and hence growth potential.
- Not charging an important beneficiary, which effectively reduces market size and threatens future sustainability.
- Under-charging for the offering, which will reduce both market size and revenues.
- Over-charging for the offering, which can limit take-up and reputation.

These risks can be mitigated by an analysis of the return on investment for each beneficiary, together with continuing market research.

Suppose, for example, that a decision was made to charge shoppers to download the Westfield app. This would be likely to limit take-up of the service, which would mean fewer additional sales by retailers, potentially leading to loss of rental income if retailers were to relocate. Likewise, charging retailers a fee is unlikely to yield significant revenues unless a clear return-on-investment case could be presented. A value-capture approach that addresses both of these risks would be to make the service freely available to both retailers and shoppers, and to capture value through growing rental income.

Combining value creation, promotion, delivery and capture to establish a business model for exploitation of an offering is central to the design of a business, and market success depends significantly on this activity.

This point can be illustrated by Bright Funds, a platform for charitable giving and volunteering that enables customers to manage a portfolio of funds directed at their favourite causes and non-profit organizations. The business captures value by charging processing fees for handling donations and credit card payments.

The initial business model targeted its value proposition at individuals with strong social consciences, offering an attractive platform which they could use to manage their donations to causes. This choice of customer proved expensive in terms of promotion, and limited in respect of value capture, because the donations were small; hence the business experienced slow growth. The business responded by pivoting towards corporate customers, offering a solution that can integrate into payroll systems, hence making it possible for businesses or teams to launch and manage larger charitable giving programmes. As a consequence of this change, promotional activities became more effective and the business now serves more than 30,000 charitable givers at more than twenty-five companies and organizations. This larger customer base has increased value capture, which has been recognized by a $1.8 million investment for the business's next phase of development.

Here, we note that the same idea exploited through a revised business model achieves greater success for the innovation.

Market Consumption of an Offering

The third phase of the innovation process is about interpreting and handling the market's response to an offering. A positive response provides evidence that the business model is working, and hence encourages more of the same. A negative or disappointing response may reflect badly on the idea, on the way that it has been wrapped into an offering, or on the business model adopted.

Understanding and interpreting market response is only possible if the required data is available. This means that, before launching an offering, thought needs to be given to the following:

- What data will best indicate market response? This may include, within a defined time frame, numbers of downloads, numbers of enquiries received, numbers of feedback requests and financial revenues achieved.
- How will that data be captured and recorded so as to support analysis and reporting? This may be possible directly through the planned value delivery mechanism, or may need additional data capture activities by the business or by a partner organization.

The answers to these questions may need to be reviewed after initial experience: if the emerging picture is unclear, then it may be necessary to identify additional measurable quantities, or to fine-tune the capture mechanisms, perhaps to include the behaviour of sub-groups of customers. Without such data, interpreting market response will be at best subjective and anecdotal, and hence any resulting pivot may take the business in the wrong direction.

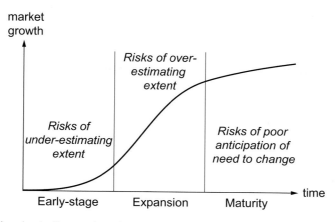

Figure 1.4 *The classic 'S-curve' market consumption model*

The classical shape for market consumption is the *S-curve*, illustrated in Figure 1.4, which shows the cumulative distribution of adoption over time. First proposed by Bass (1969), the model postulates market consumption occurring over three broad stages.

The growth plan for a business will usually assume something akin to an S-curve when plotting projected increases in revenues, profits or customer numbers over time.

It can be difficult to anticipate the time frame for progress through these stages for a new offering. Consequently, when looking at data collection and interpretation, it is helpful also to consider indicators of progression from one phase to another:

- Rapidly increasing levels of unsolicited orders can indicate progression from *early-stage* into *expansion phase.*
- A slowing down of new orders, or a reduction in requests for significant developments, can indicate progression into *maturity.*

Peres *et al.* (2010) analyse applications of Bass's work and Boretos (2012) summarizes the underlying economics of S-curves.

Another way to visualize market consumption is the *bell curve*, illustrated in Figure 1.5. This model was originally proposed by Everett Rodgers, an eminent communication theorist and sociologist, in 1962. Rodgers (2003), the fifth edition of his original work, is a definitive text on this subject.

Rodgers' approach adopts a psychographic categorization of five types of customer, from *innovators* through to *laggards*. This depiction can be used to inform a plan for growth based on the known characteristics of the categories of

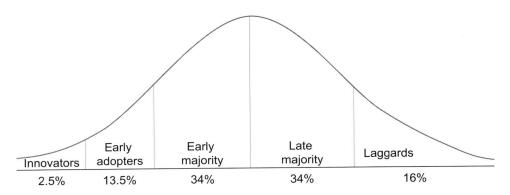

Figure 1.5 *Rodgers' bell curve of market consumption*

people that need to be engaged. The assumptions applied by Rodgers have been questioned in empirical research published by Phadke and Vyakarnam (2017), which shows much lower percentages of innovators and early adopters.

In his seminal book, *Crossing the Chasm*, Moore (2014) summarizes Rodgers' psychographic categories as follows:

- Innovators are enthusiastic in pursuing new technology products.
- Early adopters share this enthusiasm for new innovations and are comfortable with technology, but are not technologists themselves.
- The early majority are also comfortable with technology, but they are pragmatists that need to see any innovation working for others before committing.
- The late majority are also pragmatists, but unlike the early majority they are less comfortable with technology solutions and hence need to be confident of support from established suppliers.
- Laggards never purchase a new technology except when it is embedded within something else that they need.

The purpose of models such as those shown in Figures 1.4 and 1.5 is to support the development of a plan for growth. They do this by providing cognitive models for interpreting and plotting market response and trajectory to inform decisions of beneficial changes that can be made to the idea, the offering or aspects of the business model.

Decisions motivated by observations of market consumption may be incremental, such as price tuning for a particular group of customers, or may trigger a more radical pivot such as a move to a revised target market or delivery mechanism. This decision is represented by the sequencing of arrows between *exploitation* and *market consumption* in the innovation process depicted in Figure 1.3.

Three risks commonly apply to the achievement and management of market consumption. The first of these is failing to gain traction with a sufficient and expanding customer base. Limited market acceptance inhibits growth ambitions and can affect the viability of the venture. Phadke and Vyakarnam (2017) identify this problem as the third chasm to be crossed by a venture, which aligns with the chasm identified by Moore (2014). Crossing this chasm requires leadership to shape and motivate required talent, intense promotional and sales activities to validate and prioritize target customer markets, and a production and delivery organization that is capable of shaping and packaging a market-ready product. This topic is addressed further in Chapter 4 in the context of development discontinuities and in Chapter 6 in the context of capabilities required for growth and scalability.

A second risk is that the offering is not sustainable due to unforeseen costs or difficulties with supply of people, materials or services, which can seriously affect the venture's ability to support growing market consumption. It can result from a failure to plan for product scalability or an inadequate understanding of the supply chain requirements. These subjects are addressed further in Chapter 4.

The third risk is inadequate data capture or poor interpretation of that data. This can create a misleading picture of market uptake that leads to poorly focused investment of effort, over-resourcing or a need for unplanned investment to meet unanticipated demand.

Market Trends in Innovation

At any point in time, certain technologies and markets are more successful than others in attracting innovation. Those that are in vogue at any time tend to attract the lion's share of investment activity.

At the current time, the digital technologies that are viewed as being *hot* across Europe and the USA include the following:

- Virtual and augmented reality (VR/AR), especially in respect of their wider applicability beyond gaming and entertainment.
- Artificial intelligence and machine learning (AI/ML), especially in respect of applications relating to productivity enhancement or risk reduction.
- Big data and analytics, especially in relation to improved decision making and machine learning.
- Blockchain technologies, especially in relation to secure online transactions within distributed ledger networks and complex supply chains, and to document sharing and management.
- Cyber security technologies, including those that exploit AI techniques.

- Internet of Things (IoT) technologies, especially in relation to business transformation.
- Robotics, including industrial and domestic applications that exploit AI/ML and IoT.

Some of the current *hot* markets for innovation include:

- Manufacturing processes, materials and logistics, including automated vehicles – *Autotech* – and smart warehouses, with applications of technologies such as VR/AR, AI/ML, big data and analytics, cyber security, robotics and IoT.
- Smart, flexible and clean energy technologies, including batteries and demand response, with applications of technologies such as AI/ML, big data and analytics, cyber security and IoT.
- Financial and e-commerce –*Fintech* – including mobile payments, peer-to-peer lending and algorithmic trading, with applications of technologies such as AI/ML, big data and analytics, blockchain and cyber security.
- Digitization and improvement of procedures for property sales and rental management – *Proptech* – including platform offerings and smart data collection and analysis devices.
- Medical and health care –*Medtech* – including patient engagement and interoperability and smart devices, with applications of technologies such as AI/ML, big data and analytics, cyber security and IoT.
- Gaming and gamification, including social and industrial applications, with applications of technologies such as VR/AR, AI/ML, big data and analytics, and robotics.

Priorities and interests can change rapidly in response to economic and environmental factors. As an entrepreneur, it is important to understand current trends, as these can indicate likely levels of interest, both from customers keen to benefit from early adoption, and also from investors keen to be aligned with significant future advantage.

A related consideration is any alignment or dependence upon technologies that are themselves recent innovations. Gartner produces an annual 'hype cycle for emerging technologies' (Gartner, 2016) that is helpful for this purpose, in that it positions a wide range of technologies across a maturity time frame, as shown in Figure 1.6.

Although the published graph inevitably lags behind the current situation, and so can become overtaken by events (such as with Pokémon Go and its

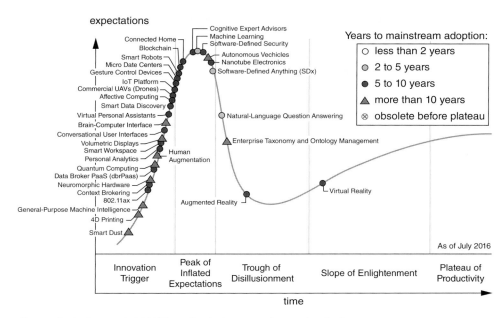

Figure 1.6 *Gartner's 2016 Hype Cycle for emerging technologies*

acceleration on the positioning of AR), it provides a note of caution to any venture that plans to develop an offering with direct or indirect dependence on an underlying immature technology.

The Ecosystem

The business model for an innovation cannot be developed independently of the market into which that innovation is targeted. The modern framing of this principle uses the term *ecosystem* to refer to the network of *parties*, *stakeholders*, *actors* or *players* – customers, suppliers, distributors, competitors, regulators, government agencies – that contribute, threaten or participate in some way in the exploitation of an offering.

Having a solid understanding of the ecosystem into which an innovation is planned to be introduced is critical to the success of the business model. There are two extremes:

- For an offering that assumes an existing set of market dynamics, the impact on the currently operating ecosystem may be minimal. Such cases require market research to validate the assumptions of current players, motivations and dynamics. This would be the case, for example, when Westfield introduces their app into a new shopping centre. The aim would be to fit in alongside existing technologies and practices with minimal friction.

- For a more radical offering that introduces a new technology or practice, there may be a need to redesign an existing ecosystem, or even design and create a new ecosystem. This would be the case, for example, when Uber launches its taxi platform into a new city. In this case, new players (such as Uber drivers) need to be established and enabled.

Ron Adner, a professor of strategy and entrepreneurship and also a speaker, consultant and business adviser, is a respected commentator on this topic. Adner (2013) stresses that, although technical focus on exploitation of an idea as a product or service offering is necessary, it may not in itself be sufficient for market success. His book focuses on two specific aspects:

Co-innovation – referring to those innovations that are required to be developed by other players, especially on the supply or enabling side of the ecosystem. Prior to the launch of the digital camera, new storage technologies and standards were required. Also, many wearable innovations require continual improvements in battery technologies.

Co-adoption – referring to the required adoption of the innovation by other players in the consumption or distribution side of the ecosystem. A product that assesses household energy usage requires that householders first adopt devices that will capture and share the data that is required to make the assessment.

These considerations need to be incorporated into the design of the business model. This can be achieved by creating a visual representation of the ecosystem as a tool for analysis of implications. Figure 1.7 shows a simple layout for a visualization approach.

Under the recommended approach, the business is positioned in the centre of its ecosystem, and the other involved parties are placed around the periphery. Directional links between parties signify a flow of value or service. In an initial representation, the arrows between the business and each of the parties can be labelled by considering the following questions:

What value does the venture offer to the other party?
This refers to the value creation component of the business model. Consider the case of a venture that introduces a new wearable technology into the health

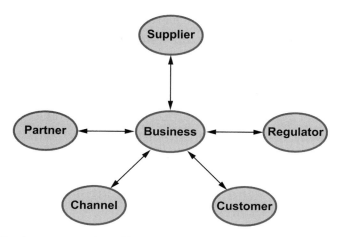

Figure 1.7 *Simple representation of business ecosystem*

and fitness market. The value to its users might be expressed as 'improved tracking of progress towards health outcomes', and the value to its subscribing health-care providers might be expressed as 'a reliable source of fitness data to inform future customer offerings'.

What value does that party offer to the venture?

This refers to the value-capture component of the business model. Continuing the example introduced above, this relationship would indicate which of the parties is expected to purchase the product. Depending on the business model, this might be the user or, perhaps, their employer or health-care provider.

What does the venture need from the other party?

This can refer to the value promotion and/or value delivery components of the business model, and also to any requirements for co-innovation, co-adoption or service provision. Using the same example, this might refer to the venture's needs for health-care providers or employers to endorse or recommend the product, and for retailers to stock the product together with accessories and replacement batteries.

What does the other party need from the venture?

This can refer to any requirements by another party for the venture to co-innovate, co-adopt, pay, provide a service or in some other way to contribute to that party's business model. Using the same example, this might refer to the need by retailers for sales of the product to deliver above a stated margin on sales, or the need by health-care providers for data to be made available in standard formats to enable analysis.

Chapter 2 addresses this topic in more detail and introduces a step-wise ecosystem design technique. This initial framing of the ecosystem is elaborated through continuing business design considerations that aim to elucidate the business model and maximize its potential to create value in the venture.

The topic of *open innovation* relates closely to considerations of the business ecosystem. It is not related to open-source licensing models. The word *open* in this context refers to the relaxing of traditional boundaries between organizations.

Traditionally, innovation within an organization occurred in the domain of its research and development (R&D) function. Those developments that met market-driven criteria would be launched by the organization as new or enhanced products and services.

The economics of the digital world has loosened this process in two significant ways:

- An internally generated innovation may be licensed or sold to a third party that is judged to be better placed to take the offering to market (*inside out*).
- Instead of sourcing all innovations internally, innovations may actively be sourced from third-party organizations (*outside in*).

Open innovation has increasingly been embraced by many large and successful companies, including Apple, Amazon and more recently Lego. In Apple's case, it has enabled the company to establish a vast community of app developers who work for free and contribute a percentage of their licence revenues back to Apple.

The progress of open innovation has been charted by Hossain *et al.* (2016) through a comprehensive literature analysis that covers both publication activity and the application of open innovation to different disciplines.

Types and Impact of Innovation

The identification and classification of types of innovation has been explored by many authors. Many of these, including the work of Boer and Gertsen (2003), Bessant (2005), Lok *et al.* (2005), Tonnessen (2005), Marin-Garcia *et al.* (2011) and Goffin and Mitchell (2016), recognize a spectrum of innovations from those that are incremental in impact to those that imply a radical change.

It is widely noted that innovation at the lower, more sustaining or incremental level needs no large investment, whereas more radical, disruptive innovation can produce a more drastic effect that has more impact on all parties involved. Research carried out at Michigan State University and reported by Garcia and Calantone (2002) identifies empirical evidence to confirm this correlation.

The model adopted here builds on these observations and extends the characterization of an innovation to cover the following four criteria:

- Is it sustaining or disruptive (how radical is it)?
- Is it a technology push or a market pull?
- Is its impact vertical or horizontal?
- Does its scope include a new product, a new process or a new paradigm?

Adopting these more specific criteria enables an analysis technique that is useful when exploring the likely market impact of an offering and its associated **business model**. This technique is described and illustrated later in this section, following a description of each of the criteria.

Sustaining versus Disruptive Innovations

Sustaining or *incremental* innovations offer improved performance within an established market. They may be radically new offerings within that market, but they do not change the nature or basic assumptions about how things work. Most new offerings are sustaining in nature. Obvious examples are new apps offered through an app store, and new, improved mobile phone handsets.

Disruptive or *radical* innovations bring to market a different and new kind of value proposition, which may have the effect of changing the market's assumptions around how things work. Although a disruptive offering may initially underperform against established products in some ways, it needs to be significantly preferable – some say an order of magnitude preferable – through being advantageous in price, size, performance, simplicity or convenience. The world of *collaborative consumption* – the Uber phenomenon – is notably disruptive to existing offerings in the markets to which it has been applied. Examples include the emergence of the digital camera, and the successive generations of computing devices, from mainframes through to mobile devices, and the Internet of Things.

Clayton Christensen, a professor at Harvard Business School, is credited with coining the term *disruptive innovation*. Christensen (2013) addresses the impact of disruptive offerings on existing market leaders and shows how their position can actually inhibit them from responding effectively to the challenge of disruptive entrants.

This happens because technology development by market leaders can progress faster than market demand. Driven by competitive pressure, suppliers often overshoot their market need by giving more than customers would be willing to pay for. Within such a context, the supplier of a disruptive technology needs only to deliver something that would be sufficient to satisfy its customers, so long as it also brings some other significant benefit that was not available through the established offerings. In such a case, established suppliers may be unable and unwilling to try to compete on similar lines, because to do so would mean a significant change and a substantial cut to existing profit margins.

For example, before the commercial emergence of the digital camera, leading camera and film suppliers competed through incremental improvements and pricing differentials. Early digital cameras entered the market in the 1980s with much less capability and performance than the current offerings, but with the significant benefit of offering an immediate digital image, thus removing the need for the sophisticated production and printing process associated with camera film. For existing market leaders, competing head-on would mean risking their current leadership positions and the margins that they were achieving through continuing high-end equipment sales.

Some of the leading suppliers, most notably Kodak, were casualties of this disruption and went out of business, or re-emerged as substantially reduced operations. Interestingly, as explained by Scott Anthony (2016) writing in the *Harvard Business Review*, this was despite Kodak investing billions of dollars in developing a range of digital cameras.

Introducing or responding to disruption involves not only new technology, but also acceptance of a new or changed paradigm, and this can be a significant consideration. Kodak failed to grasp the paradigm change away from cameras and printing of photographs and towards the merger of cameras with phones and the use of social media and apps to share images.

When introducing a disruptive offering, it is crucial to appreciate three things:

- What it is about the offering that is significantly preferable to established offerings. In other words, what is the disruption?
- In which ways may the disruptive offering be less attractive or capable compared with existing offerings?
- What paradigm shift(s) by other players in the market will be required for the disruption to succeed?

Innovations Based on Technology Push versus Those Based on Market Pull

An innovation based on technology push is driven by a research and technology idea that has been qualified as offering the potential to be developed as a successful market offering. The digital camera is a good example. From research in the mid-1970s came early products in the late 1980s, but it was not until the mid-1990s that sales flourished, and not until 2003 that digital cameras first outsold film cameras: a period of thirty years. The success of the technology depended on significant co-innovation in memory and battery technologies, and also in standards such as JPEG and MPEG. Introducing an innovation with this profile is a significant endeavour.

An innovation based on market pull, on the other hand, is driven by an observed need, problem or opportunity in a market. For example, in 2017, Facebook addressed the need – initially identified and satisfied by Snapchat – for images that disappear after a period of time. The resulting incremental functionality is a market-pulled innovation that is competitively motivated.

The difference between these approaches was famously expressed by Henry Ford: 'if I had asked my customers what they wanted, they would have said a faster horse'. Apparently though, this quotation is suspect, as there is no evidence that Ford ever said it.

Innovations based on technology push tend to be disruptive in nature, and market-pulled innovations tend to be sustaining, but this is not necessarily so: the Uber taxi service can be considered as a market pull, motivated by the cost and difficulty often experienced by people needing cabs in large cities. For the passenger, the paradigm is not significantly changed. Instead of hailing a cab in the street, they order one on their phone. The resulting experience of sitting in a car and paying for a journey is not significantly changed. In this example, the disruption is apparent in its effect on the wider ecosystem: the introduction of a new Uber driver role, and of a new and threatening competitor for existing cab drivers.

When introducing any innovation, and especially one based on technology push, it is important to consider:

- What are the implications of deploying any new underlying technologies? See the section above referring to Gartner's hype cycle, and the risk of dependence on an immature enabling technology.
- What are the implications on the ecosystem, including any implied demands for co-adoption or co-innovation to enable or sustain the innovation?

Vertical versus Horizontal Innovation

A vertical market refers to an industry sector, such as energy, education, retail or health care. Consequently, a vertical innovation is one that applies specifically to a particular sector. In many cases, vertical offerings involve integrating new and existing technologies or practices to achieve an improved performance or effect.

Vertical innovation is often sustaining and hence associated with more localized impact. An example in the health-care sector is 3D4Medical, an AR offering that helps medical staff to learn about anatomy without having to cut open a body. In the retail sector, an example is Shutl, a London-based fulfilment company that promises deliveries within 90 minutes or less. Now owned by eBay, Shutl uses an algorithm to determine the best courier for any delivery.

A horizontal innovation is one that addresses the needs of many industries. This includes innovations that address *horizontal markets* such as security, HR and finance management. It also includes technologies such as cloud or authentication services that provide a technical platform for a range of offerings.

Examples of horizontal innovation include Apple Pay and Google Wallet, which enable online payments within or across any sectors.

The following considerations apply to the characterization of an innovation as vertical or horizontal:

- For vertical innovations, what are the sector values, norms and standards with which alignment or integration is required?
- For vertical innovations, what are the dynamics of the established ecosystems and how will these be accommodated or disrupted?
- For horizontal innovations, which standards apply to the sectors that are spanned, and are there any consequences of pricing norms in different sectors?
- For horizontal innovations, will the plan include an initial market focus?

Scope of Innovation

Unlike the previous sets of criteria, which are each characterized by two options, there are three options for the scope of a proposed innovation, which draws upon the work reported by Bessant and Tidd (2011).

A **product innovation** is one that introduces changes in the things that are offered and/or in the customer experience of the offering. An example would be an improved encryption, search or analysis algorithm. These tend to be sustaining, but can lead to disruptive impact: remember that google was initially introduced as a new improved search technology.

A **process innovation** is one that brings changes in the way things are created, performed or delivered. An example is the introduction of secure online payment systems, and the continuing evolution of such mechanisms. These can vary in impact, from incremental, sustaining improvements within a vertical market through to substantial disruptions across markets.

A **paradigm innovation** is one that brings about changes in the underlying mental model whereby people think about how something is done. Examples include:

- The change from on-premise installation of software applications to cloud-based software as a service (SaaS) offerings.
- The change from specialist adviser functions to online self-service solutions such as chatbots.
- The change from dedicated black cabs to Uber drivers in their own cars.

Paradigm innovations tend to be disruptive and hence to imply the need for more radical ecosystem design.

Applying the Criteria to Characterize and Assess an Innovation

The four criteria described above underlie an analysis technique that can be useful when exploring the likely market impact of an offering and its associated business model. This exploration can help to inform the entrepreneur about likely levels of risk and the degree of impact and therefore effort that will be required.

The technique uses the range of options within each of the four criteria as a graphical framework. It works as follows:

Step 1: Establish the characterization framework
    This involves adopting the diagram shown in Figure 1.8 as a framework for recording the characterization.
    Each criterion provides a range of possible values against which the characteristics of the innovation can be plotted to give shape to its likely market impact.

Step 2: Characterize the innovation against each criterion

For each criterion, consider the nature of the innovation and assess its vertical positioning. The higher up each scale that an innovation is positioned, the greater is its assumed impact, as depicted by the increasing breadth of the triangle.

For example, an innovation that will significantly disrupt a market will be plotted at the top of the first criterion. Such an innovation is likely to have much greater impact that one which sustains a market. Similarly, an innovation that introduces a new product into an existing market process will be plotted at the bottom of the fourth criterion, and is likely to have a lesser impact than one that changes an existing paradigm.

Step 3: Interpret the characterization to inform market-facing activities

For innovations characterized by a low projected impact, the risk and effort are unlikely to be significant, and the existing ecosystem is unlikely to be significantly changed. Taking the innovation to market will primarily require a good understanding of the current market dynamics and the differentiation of the new offering.

The higher the projected impact of an innovation, the greater the risk and effort involved in taking it to market, and hence the need for imaginative design and testing of the business model and ecosystem to determine and plan for the changes that will be needed. The challenge in such cases can be

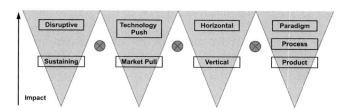

Figure 1.8 *Criteria for assessment of the impact of innovation*

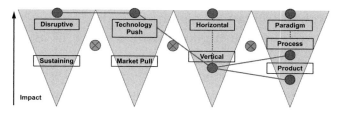

Figure 1.9 *Characterization of the digital camera innovation*

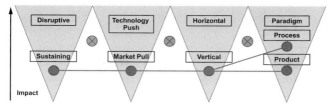

Figure 1.10 *Characterization of a typical new mobile device app*

exacerbated by the difficulty of conducting effective market research for an offering that will bring radical market change, or even introduce a new market.

As a first illustration, the technique is applied to characterize the introduction of the digital camera. The assessment is shown in Figure 1.9.

The digital camera was introduced as a disruptive technology. Clearly a technology push, the digital camera was initially deployed specifically into the photographic equipment sector, where it was introduced as both product and process innovation (the printing and replication processes were radically changed). Over time, the widespread adoption, exploitation and integration of digital image technologies across all markets has repositioned the innovation as horizontal in nature, and as the driver of significant paradigm change.

As indicated by the shape of the plotted characterization, this is a high-impact innovation, which has radically changed multiple markets and provoked redesign of the dynamics of several ecosystems. Not surprisingly, therefore, as detailed previously, its introduction involved significant development, planning and investment, from many organizations around the globe.

By contrast, Figure 1.10 illustrates the application of the criteria to characterize the introduction of a typical new mobile device app.

A typical new app, such as the Westfield app that was used as an example in the previous section, sustains an existing market by introducing a new offering that operates in a recognizable way. Driven by observation of a market opportunity, the app introduces a new product, and potentially a process change, into a targeted sector. In this case, the retailers' process is changed by the need to share relevant data with shoppers, and the shoppers' process is changed by the option to pre-plan their route through a shopping centre.

This profile indicates a much lower impact, and hence a lower cost and risk of introduction. Consequently, there are likely to be fewer dependencies and an assumption that the innovation will operate within the dynamics of an existing ecosystem.

Historical Perspectives on Innovation

Several historical frameworks have been developed to assist with analysis of trends in innovation over the longer term. These can provide a context for understanding the present environment, by comparison with and differentiation between previous situations. They can also, potentially, be used to predict likely future trends and resulting economic effects.

Three such frameworks are summarized here. By addressing them in the sequence chosen, it is possible to align the approaches through a coherent, top-down perspective.

The Three Waves of Civilization

Of the three frameworks addressed here, the broadest, longest-term and most globally applicable framing of innovation and development is that provided by Alvin Toffler (1981), an American writer and futurist.

As illustrated in Figure 1.11, Toffler's model starts at the point at which human beings first began to settle and to apply innovation around crop growing and animal management.

This is his first wave, which resulted in the agricultural era; the second wave broke in the late eighteenth century with the advent of water and steam power and factory-based manufacturing, initiating the industrial era; and the third

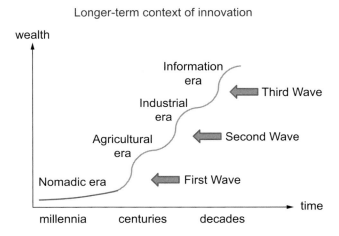

Figure 1.11 *Toffler's three waves of civilization*

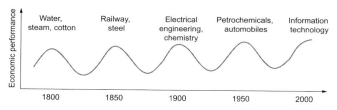

Figure 1.12 *Kondratieff waves*

wave arrived in the middle part of the twentieth century with the advent of digital computing, heralding the current information era.

Toffler associates each of these waves with a range of societal, political, economic, cultural and technological factors. The value of the model is primarily in its broad contextual pattern, the revealing of which is his main purpose.

Kondratieff Waves

In the early twentieth century, the notion of longer-term trends in technology innovation was a topic that exercised macro-economic researchers. The hypothesis was that such trends might indicate patterns, or cycles, in economic development that would provide useful tools for longer-term economic prediction.

A compelling outcome of this research was initially published in 1925 by the Russian economist Nicolai Kondratieff. Although he died in 1938, his work has since been translated and published in Kondratieff (1984). His research identified a series of long-term waves, or cycles, illustrated in Figure 1.12, that represent broad phases of innovation, from the age of steam-powered manufacturing in the late eighteenth century, through railway and steel industries in the nineteenth century, to electrical and chemical industries in the early twentieth century, and to petrochemical and automobile domination in the mid to late twentieth century. This sequence of cycles has been extended by more recent commentators, including the work of Freeman and Louçã (2001), to include advances in information technology.

Kondratieff noted that each wave of innovation proceeds through a similar series of phases, from rising prosperity into recession, then depression, finally yielding to improvements triggered by the rise of the next wave.

The term *Kondratieff wave* was originally coined by Joseph Schumpeter, an Austrian-born American, who introduced the term *creative destruction* to describe the innovative force that sustains long-term economic growth. Originally published in 1942, Schumpeter's *Capitalism, Socialism and Democracy*

(1994) is one of the most famous and important books on social theory, social sciences and economics.

The effectiveness of Kondratieff's observations as a predictor of economic activity has also been acknowledged by the British Marxist historian Eric Hobsbawm (1999).

Kondratieff's first four waves can be interpreted as a sector-specific elaboration of Toffler's industrial era, whereas the fifth wave in Kondratieff's sequence aligns with the introduction of Toffler's information technology era.

Industry 4.0

More recently, an industrially focused framework has been developed by Germany Trade & Invest (2014) to reflect the results of a European strategic project. Motivated by the need to characterize a new emerging generation of industrial technologies, referred to as Industry 4.0, or the *fourth industrial revolution*, the terminology and context of this framework has gained strong traction within Europe.

As with the approaches covered previously, this model identifies a developing series of stages. In this case, the stages are as follows:

- Industry 1: from the late eighteenth century and driven by water and steam-powered mass-production.
- Industry 2: from the early twentieth century and driven by electrically powered mass-production.
- Industry 3: from the late twentieth century and driven by the use of IT to automate production.
- Industry 4: from the early twenty-first century and driven by the use of cyber-physical systems to create smart factories.

This framework is motivated by the need for a useful characterization of the technological world into which we are now moving, to provide a basis for wider education and planning.

The alignment of this framework with those addressed previously is shown in Table 1.1. As the table shows, the three frameworks are compatible in their structures. The frameworks differ primarily in the terminology adopted and the intended purpose and audience.

The late twentieth century is significant across all the frameworks reviewed here. The paradigm shift that occurred at that time has been responsible for the explosion of technology innovation and entrepreneurship in the developed

Table 1.1 Alignment of Innovation Frameworks

Framework	Earlier times	Late eighteenth century	Nineteenth century	Early twentieth century	Late twentieth century	Early twenty–first century
Toffler's three waves	First wave: agricultural	Second wave: industrial			Third wave: information technology	
Kondratieff's cycles		water and steam power	railway and steel industries	electrical and chemical industries	information technology	
Industry generations		Industry 1: water- and steam-powered production		Industry 2: electrified production	Industry 3: IT automation	Industry 4: cyber-physical systems

world. Phadke and Vyakarnam (2017) highlight the role of venture capital (VC) funding as a key contributor to this paradigm shift.

The Innovators

Innovation is performed principally by companies, universities, individuals and teams, and business incubators and accelerators, each of which is motivated by different factors.

As these groups co-exist within national and international innovation eco-systems, it is helpful for an innovator working in any context to understand the principal drivers of the others.

Innovation by Companies

In a nutshell, companies of all sizes innovate either to enhance their performance or to reduce their risk profile. The implications of this motivation vary over time by sector and by company, but enhanced performance might be driven by any of the following target outcomes:

- Higher quality of service, enhanced reputation and brand value.
- Improved staff confidence and retention, and increased ability to attract new staff.
- Improved process efficiency and greater effectiveness of production.
- Increased revenues, improved sales margins, and increased cash generation.
- Growth in new customers, greater revenues per customer and increased market share.

A reduced risk profile might be driven by an objective to achieve any of the following:

- Reduced negative coverage in market publications.
- Fewer mistakes, accidents and delays through inadequately competent staff.
- Fewer errors, mistakes, faults and delays in production.
- Avoidance of unnecessary charges due to unanticipated cash shortfalls.
- Mitigation of dependence on a small pool of customers.

A comprehensive study by the management consultancy PwC (2013) found that 67 per cent of the world's most innovative companies believe that innovation is a competitive necessity, regardless of industry. This is illustrated in Hartmann (2014) through a series of case studies that show how established businesses are responding to a dynamic and global competitive environment by institutionalizing processes for radical innovation.

The term *intrapreneurship* was coined in the 1980s by Gifford Pinchot, an entrepreneur, author and inventor, to refer to the practice of entrepreneurship by innovators within large organizations. The similarities and differences between intrapreneurs and entrepreneurs principally follow from the benefits and constraints of working within an existing operation.

In this context, IBM, which invests significantly in innovation, recognizes three categories of intrapreneurship:

- *Incremental innovation*, which involves making logical extensions to existing offerings, usually exploited using existing routes to market. An example is the IBM Case Manager.
- *Breakthrough innovation*, which involves more significant innovation that introduces a new value proposition, potentially requiring the development of new routes to market. An example would be IBM Advanced Care Insights.
- *Market-making innovation*, which involves major innovation that will enable substantial new value. These may create new markets and ecosystems, and require new routes to market, as with, for example, IBM Watson.

The trend towards open innovation means that larger organizations in both public and private sectors increasingly contract their innovation through small and medium-sized enterprises (SMEs). There is a sizeable pool of SMEs that satisfy this demand.

National Incentives for Companies to Innovate

At a national level, it is critically important to governments that companies innovate to improve their productivity and hence their contribution to the economy. For the UK, where productivity lags significantly behind that of other advanced industrial nations, this is currently a high priority. According to a report by the UK Office for National Statistics (2017), output per hour worked in the UK during 2015 was 16.6 per cent below the average for other members of the G7 group of industrial nations.

For companies, innovation carries risk, because not all new developments succeed in the anticipated time frame, and the cost of change can be high. For this reason, governments make available a range of grant-funding initiatives and tax incentives to offset the risk.

Grant funding for UK companies is primarily provided by Innovate UK. In the 2016–17 tax year, Innovate UK distributed more than £550 million of public money to fund business innovation, including through its Smart and Launchpad programmes. Some grant-funding initiatives target specific technologies that are judged to be critical to national competitiveness, whereas others are open to any proposed innovation.

Grants are also available for European companies through the EU, mostly under the branding of Horizon 2020. These can be collaborative across companies and nations, or single-company projects. Within the wider programme, the *SME instrument* targets support for smaller companies, including through the *open disruptive innovation scheme.*

Almost all EU governments have an R&D tax relief scheme, but there is currently no harmonized EU offering. A UK scheme has been designed to motivate companies of all sizes to invest in innovation. Under the current scheme:

- For SMEs, tax relief on R&D is 230 per cent. This means that, for each £100 of qualifying costs, the company could have the income on which corporation tax is paid reduced by an additional £130 on top of the £100 spent. This can include a payable credit in some circumstances.
- For larger companies, tax relief on R&D is at the lower, but still significant, level of 130 per cent.

Other tax incentives are also available, including, in the UK, the *patent box* scheme, which enables companies to apply a lower rate of corporation tax to profits earned from patented inventions. The various types of incentive are mutually exclusive, which means that tax relief is not possible against grant-funded innovation.

Many other countries offer comparable schemes: these are summarized in Deloitte (2015) and OECD (2017). According to the OECD (2015), twenty-eight of the OECD (Organisation for Economic Cooperation and Development) countries offer incentives to encourage innovation and the total annual level of support is in the region of $50 billion worldwide.

The US version is *research and experimentation tax credit.* This scheme provides tax credits to businesses for which qualifying research expenditure exceeds a base amount. The applicable percentage varies according to factors such as the business's date of incorporation and its ability to collect required documentation.

Such schemes serve to mitigate the risks of innovation for companies of all sizes, with the wider strategic aim of stimulating productivity growth and hence contribution to the national economy. For companies, expert knowledge of the available schemes and benefits is highly recommended to enable full participation and benefit.

Innovation by Universities

In the developed world, universities usually fund between 20 and 25 per cent of national research and development in scientific and technical fields. Exploitation of this research occurs through two routes:

- University spin-outs (USOs): companies formed for the purpose of taking university-originated innovation to market.
- Licensing of innovative intellectual property (IP) for exploitation by external organizations.

According to research carried out by the European Research Council (ERC) and reported in Hewitt-Dundas (2015), UK universities have shifted their emphasis from licensing of university IP through to greater focus on spin-out activity. Research published by BEIS (2016) reports that 142 new USOs were created in the UK in 2014–15 and notes that the levels of investment achieved by these is increasing, which suggests that the commercial success of such ventures is improving.

The university body responsible for arranging and managing exploitation within a university is generally referred to as its Technology Transfer Office (TTO), and the dominant business model of USOs is around commercial exploitation of university-originated IP as a product- and/or service-based offering that targets some defined market.

The UK-focused research reported in the ERC paper covers 350 USOs (selected from more than 1,000 candidate companies) of varying ages, and reports that:

- 75 per cent of USOs are revenue-generating, with an average annual revenue of $250,000.
- On average, USOs employ four highly educated employees, with almost all (93 per cent) having a degree level qualification or higher.
- The majority of USOs have a founding team typically comprising three individuals.
- Average investment per USO is $375,000, with moneys coming principally from founders, venture capital (VC) funds, universities and angel investors.

Research by De Cleyn and Braet (2010) of factors influencing the success of spin-outs from European universities demonstrated the need for a TTO to have sufficient critical mass to support the spin-outs created. More recent research by the Royal Academy of Engineering (2016) confirmed that the talent and skill level of the TTO staff has a direct bearing on the quality of research commercialization, and noted also that a lack of understanding of the spin-out process by academic entrepreneurs can put the founders of a spin-out at a disadvantage when entering negotiations. The Academy believes that 'levelling the information asymmetry between the academic entrepreneurs and the university' is likely to improve the success of the spin-out process for all parties involved.

The USA is widely held to be the global leader in the formation of university spin-outs, but available data tends also to include businesses started by faculty, students and even alumni, even where these did not license any technology from the institution involved. China increasingly ranks alongside the USA for combined university–industry activity, in part because Chinese universities receive a relatively small contribution of national research funding, and are therefore motivated to work closely with government-controlled enterprises which receive the majority of China's R&D funds.

Innovation by Individuals and Teams

This has been referred to as the *garage* model of innovation, by reference to the initial development of businesses such as HP and Apple from within individuals' garages. It is interesting to note that the original garages of both HP and Apple are now managed as historic sites.

Individuals' or teams' motivation for starting a business tend to include one or more of the following:

- To make a living doing something interesting or personally rewarding.
- To create an independent lifestyle.
- To improve something about society.
- To gain the satisfaction of having taken an idea successfully to market.
- To generate a lump sum, potentially as the start of a series of innovations.

In the USA, the procedure for setting up a business (as a *C Corporation*) varies by state. Some states support electronic filing, and all states charge a fee, typically in the region of $200, for incorporation.

UK government agencies provide online advisory services and support for the creation of a limited company. Setting up a company online takes a few hours and can cost as little as $20.

According to Bello-Perez (2016), start-up formation in the UK increased by just under 5 per cent in 2015 with 608,100 new businesses created. In London alone, over 200,000 companies were created in 2015, due to its access to funding and strong entrepreneurial support. Palmer (2016) reports that, between January and June 2016, 342,927 new businesses were registered in the UK, indicating a continuation of the trend.

In the world of digital technology, getting started may not require significant investment. Where capital is needed, the usual funding options include:

- Fund it yourself, from what you have.
- Take a loan, from friends and family.
- Generate revenues from early sales.
- Raise funding, usually from a crowd-sourcing platform or angel investor.

Tax credit schemes have been devised by many governments to encourage early-stage investment in SMEs. In the UK, the Seed Enterprise Investment Scheme (SEIS) is an income tax relief scheme designed to help small, early-stage companies raise finance by offering tax relief to individual investors (UK taxpayers) who purchase shares in those companies. The investor would normally expect a company to gain prior approval of its eligibility for the scheme. More information about such schemes is provided in Chapter 6 in the context of raising growth capital.

As documented by the OECD (2016), most developed countries offer comparable schemes to stimulate investment in entrepreneurial businesses. A summary of available schemes in the USA (which operate at state level) and elsewhere is provided by the *Handbook of Research on Business Angels*, compiled by Landstrom and Mason (2016).

Innovation by Business Incubators and Accelerators

Business incubators, also known as start-up or seed accelerators, provide fixed-term, cohort-based programmes of education, networking, introduction and mentoring, typically culminating in a public *pitch event* or *demo day*.

The original accelerator was Y-Combinator, which started up in Cambridge, Massachusetts in 2005, and later moved to Silicon Valley. As of 2016, it had invested in more than 900 companies, including Dropbox, Airbnb, Coinbase, Stripe, Reddit, Zenefits, Instacart, Machine Zone and Weebly. The combined market capitalization of its alumni is over $65 billion.

A number of similar schemes set up in the USA shortly afterwards. The success of the approach has spread and there are now hundreds of programmes operating across Europe. According to BEIS (2017), more than 150 are active in the UK, supporting more than 3,500 new businesses each year. A common approach is for the accelerator to make a small financial investment in each participating company in return for a small equity stake, on average in the region of 7 per cent. Some accelerators take no equity, and instead use the programme as a form of due diligence for future investment decisions.

Accelerators are early-stage investors, run by small entrepreneurial teams that stimulate early-stage companies and share in their success. They are funded by a mixture of corporate and venture capital funds, plus public funding. Some focus on a market such as financial, technology or fitness. Most operate through an annual schedule of fixed-term (usually three- to six-month) programmes, each of which involves a cohort of a dozen or more start-up teams, some of which may already have funding or be revenue-generating.

Within an accelerator programme, in addition to the investment provided, start-ups receive a workspace, and – crucially – exposure to a lively ecosystem of mentors, investors, other start-ups and larger companies, entrepreneurs in residence and various interested parties. A common approach, which is applied by TechStars and Ignite100 in the UK, is for around a dozen small teams to progress through the programme, starting with an idea or early-stage development, and ending with a *demo day* that triggers serious discussions about future development and investment plans. The Entrepreneur First approach differs in that it attracts ambitious individuals at an early stage and encourages them to develop ideas and form teams through its process.

The UK's Royal Academy of Engineering brings together the most successful and talented engineers to advance and promote excellence in engineering. Its Enterprise Hub forms an important part of this commitment. The Hub has adopted a related but interestingly different approach that provides grant funding, training, mentoring and network access to support the development of a broad base of engineering start-ups and scale-ups, many of which exploit substantial technology developments. Programmes offered by the Hub have been designed to support students, start-ups founded by graduate engineers, university spin-outs and successful SMEs that need support to scale-up. The Academy's charitable status, strong international network and reputation contribute to the distinctiveness of these schemes.

Succeeding in Innovation and Entrepreneurship

Innovation fuels the engine of entrepreneurship, and entrepreneurship is the driving force for innovation. Although closely related, these topics differ qualitatively in terms of the ingredients needed for success.

Innovation is about ideas - creativity and imagination – whereas entrepreneurship is about drive, determination and risk appetite. Innovation can be an introspective process, whereas entrepreneurship must be outwardly focused, engaging, influencing and empathizing with people and organizations of many kinds. The innovator can be divergent in their thinking, identifying and exploring multiple approaches and options, whereas the entrepreneur needs to be convergent, focusing on exploitation of innovation through a resourced plan of activity.

These polemical contrasts are not literally true: they are intended to differentiate. As stressed at the start of this chapter, the design, operation and growth of a business needs a blend of innovation and entrepreneurship, and the required balance of this blend changes over time. The successful business achieves the right mix of these required talents through a team that combines the creativity, motivation, experience and resources needed. This topic is addressed further in Chapter 6 in the context of business growth and scalability.

Both innovators and entrepreneurs deal continually with uncertainty in their own domains. The way in which they handle this, however, differs fundamentally, and this differentiation helps to distil the ingredients for success in each.

Ingredients for Success in Innovation

Successful innovation requires a range of factors and qualities, most of which relate to team leadership, mix and capability. The ingredients listed below draw upon the experience and findings of several market commentators and researchers, including Govindarajan (2011) and Hewlett *et al.* (2013), both writing in the *Harvard Business Review*, and van der Panne *et al.* (2003) from the Delft University of Technology in the Netherlands.

- A diverse leadership profile. Companies with more diverse teams have been shown to be 45 per cent more likely to report growth in market share and 70 per cent more likely to capture a new market.
- A compelling vision that can carry the team and the people they need to influence in the market.
- An understanding of the business ecosystem and the marketplace drivers of innovation.
- A culture dedicated to innovation and explicitly recognizing its collective nature.
- A degree of learning from past experiences, both good and bad.
- A multidisciplinary team with a balance of technological and market-facing skills.

- Judgement in choosing and managing the timing of market introduction.
- An unconstrained openness to explore new ideas or business models.

For a more comprehensive coverage of the general topics of innovation and innovation management, including within larger and more established organizations, the reader is referred to Hartmann (2014), Trott (2016), Goffin and Mitchell (2016), Westland (2017) and to Tidd and Bessant (2013). Additionally, Schilling (2016) provides a comprehensive treatment of innovation within a technology context.

More specifically in relation to the innovation of services, the handbook compiled by economics professors Gallouj and Djellal (2011) from universities in France addresses the many theoretical and operational challenges.

Ingredients for Success in Entrepreneurship

Innovators tend to deal with uncertainty by applying reasoning to identify and explore ideas and their potential. Entrepreneurs, however, tend to be more opportunistic and to apply something more akin to what Saras Sarasvathy, a professor at the Indian Institute of Management in Bangalore, has termed *effectual reasoning.* Sarasvathy (2009) succinctly formalizes the ingredients for success through the following five principles:

- Entrepreneurs start with their means – the so-called *bird in hand principle.*
  When addressing an uncertainty of some kind, the successful entrepreneur starts by considering what they have, what they know, who they know and what they can do. From these answers, they develop possibilities.
- Entrepreneurs focus on downside risk – the so-called *affordable loss principle.*
  When assessing a risk, the successful entrepreneur considers what is the worst that can happen. They can then confidently set goals and actions to deliver the upside, even if the downside ends up happening.
- Entrepreneurs exploit whatever happens – the so-called *lemonade principle.*
  This means responding to any event, observation, surprise or disappointment as a stimulus prompting new opportunity. This principle has also been called *failing forward,* a phrase first coined by business author John C. Maxwell (2007).
- Entrepreneurs form partnerships – the so-called *patchwork quilt* principle.
  When assessing a risky or competitive situation, the entrepreneur seeks to build partnerships with relevant parties to reduce uncertainty and co-create a new market dynamic.
- Entrepreneurs control rather than predict – the so-called *pilot-in-the-plane principle.*

When creating a plan of activity, the entrepreneur focuses on activities within their control, because the future needs to be made rather than discovered.

To be effective, these principles need to be applied by an entrepreneur with the courage to expose themselves to risk, the ability to grow a network of relevant contacts and the judgement to invest in an offering that addresses a real need, or problem. Additionally, a successful entrepreneur has the determination to be undeterred by knock-backs, difficulties, disappointments, betrayals and complications.

As most successful entrepreneurs will tell you: 'the key ingredient for success is grit'. They will also tell you that your inherent talents need to be seasoned with a good dose of luck.

For a more comprehensive coverage of the concepts of entrepreneurship, including across a wide range of market sectors and geographies, the reader is referred to Barringer (2015) and to Burns (2016).

Most investors take the view that it is the entrepreneur and their team rather than the idea that matters, because a strong entrepreneur will test and tune ideas until they hit upon one that will succeed. This is evident in the priorities of the Techstars accelerator: team, team, team, market traction and idea.

Common Mistakes and Reasons for Failure in Entrepreneurship

Ultimately, a venture fails either because it starves – of people and/or cash – or because it drowns, in confusion and disaffection, which in turn leads to starvation. These outcomes can come about for many reasons, some of which have been addressed as risks earlier in this chapter, and which can be categorized under one or more of the following headings:

- Failure of the idea.
- Failure of the business model.
- Failure of the team.
- Failure of the plan.

The story behind every failed venture combines a unique collection of reasons, typically involving poor judgement, poor preparedness, lack of required abilities or even just bad timing. By analysing the range of reasons for failure, it is possible to distil some further critical qualities of entrepreneurship that enable such mistakes to be avoided, or at least to be recovered rapidly enough for the venture to survive and flourish.

Failure of the Idea

An idea can fail because it does not work: it may not be implementable, or deliverable, or sustainable, or there may simply be no demand for it. It can also fail if it cannot be expressed in a meaningful way – to the team and the market – or if it is too vague and ill-defined.

However good the business model, team and plan, if the underlying idea is poor, then the venture will not succeed. A good idea with a poor initial implementation can survive, with sufficient resource behind it, but it is a mistake to continue to invest money and effort into an idea that ultimately has no application.

The successful entrepreneur listens to feedback and learns from experience, openly recognizing and acknowledging a poor idea. Applying the 'lemonade' principle, they 'fail forward' by using the learning to invest effort in a new idea that offers a greater chance of success.

Failure of the Business Model

The business model can fail for a wide range of reasons, and these can be addressed using the four-part business model structure introduced earlier in this chapter:

Failure of value creation can occur because the offering does not address a real problem. A proposition can be developed with compelling language and conviction, but if it does not address something that is needed by a sizeable population of customers, then the venture will not achieve sufficient traction. It can also occur because of poor analysis of the ecosystem, which leads to incorrect assumptions of who is the beneficiary, or of which other parties need to be engaged for the value to be realized.

Failure of value promotion can occur because of poor knowledge of the target market, including customers, partners and competitors, or because of inadequate assessment of the effort needed to create visibility. In the first case, effort may be wasted through being invested in the wrong activities; in the second, not enough effort may be invested in the right ones. Consequently, the offering may never become visible or sufficiently attractive to its market, or it may become vulnerable to an aggressive competitor with the strength to cut the venture off before it gains a foothold.

Failure of value delivery and operation mechanisms can occur because of poor assessment or development of routes to market. This will limit scalability, and may also severely damage the venture's ability to respond to customer interest in an acceptable way. This can occur when the offering fails to meet required standards or regulations for deployment by the customer organization. This category of failure can also occur because of inadequate product development, leading to a poorly functioning or performing user experience.

Failure of value capture mechanisms can occur because the value capture/pricing model is wrong for the market, or because it is unclearly expressed to the customer, or because it is set at the wrong value (too high or too low). This will limit revenues, either because of poor market take-up or because the pricing is below what is achievable. Poor market take-up can also result from customers being unclear about what future commitments or internal resources will be needed to sustain their purchase.

The successful entrepreneur tracks progress closely to identify signs of trends towards any of these causes of failure. They respond rapidly and positively by making changes and then re-engaging the right market through the right channels with the resources needed.

Failure of the Team

The team can fail because it comprises the wrong people or because it is poorly composed, led or motivated.

The skills and personal qualities of those recruited are critically important, especially at the early stages of a venture. If the people responsible for development lack the skills needed, then the roadmap will be unachievable and customer confidence lost. If the market-facing individuals lack the market knowledge and personal qualities needed to empathize with and influence customers, partners, regulators and other parties, then the plan will fall short.

Even a team of people with the right skills, qualities, contacts and experience can fail if the mix is wrong. For each role filled there should be a consideration of whether the individual by nature needs to be an entrepreneur, an innovator or an operator: with the wrong mix the team can become overly driven and ambitious, overly creative and divergent, or overly operational and process-focused. In the first case, the venture risks tearing itself apart; in the second case it risks drowning in options; in the third it risks failure through inability to adapt rapidly to changing circumstances.

A strong team can also fail if it is poorly led by its founders and directors. A common cause of failure is lack of clarity across the team of the venture's proposition, ambitions and plan. This can lead to confusion – or even to overt conflict – across the team, to suboptimal decisions and to the inevitable communication of that confusion or conflict to the market, which will be damaging to reputation and revenues. Clear messaging across the team and through all engagements with the market are core to the success of a venture.

A related factor is the motivation of the team to perform. If people believe in a venture, are clear in their purpose within the team, are well rewarded and recognized, then they can be expected to perform their role effectively. If any of these criteria do not hold, then people will underperform and leave.

The successful entrepreneur leads the team by staying close both to recruitment decisions and also to current team performance and sentiment. Issues of the kinds outlined above need a rapid and open response. Sometimes, team-related issues can arise due to runs of bad luck – for example, losing multiple staff due to personal reasons – and such situations need to be borne with grit and the determination to survive what will be a short-term problem.

Failure of the Plan

The plan describes the set of actions over time by which a venture will be realized, established, developed and scaled, including the means whereby these actions will be funded and resourced. The plan can fail for a range of reasons, including:

- Running out of runway.
- Inability to scale.
- Inability to change.
- Malicious or accidental damage.

Running out of runway means running out of cash – starving. When this happens, it is difficult to sustain staff, accommodation and supplies. This can come about in a number of ways, primarily:

- Failure to raise investment in the required time frame. This can occur because of an inadequate investment case or poor preparedness for the effort required.
- Failure to correctly plan for required resources. This can occur because of poor planning, poor internal cost controls, over-optimistic cost, effort or revenue forecasts, or failure to anticipate an expensive eventuality.

The successful entrepreneur is closely aware of the financial situation and plan, and is realistic about time frames. Any surprises (positive or negative) are accepted as learning points that need to be incorporated in a revised plan, which bring the venture under their control.

Inability to scale can occur after a positive first phase of operation where insufficient effort has been invested to develop a plan that can achieve and manage greater scale, such as by opening new channels to market. Failure to respond to an opportunity for greater scale can disappoint customers, investors and staff, and can potentially overwhelm the venture's operations, leading to loss of confidence, cancelled orders, resignations and withdrawal of funding.

Inability to change is closely related to this. Business circumstances can change quickly and sometimes unpredictably, due to the entry of a new competitor, a new regulatory or standards regime, or a new pricing structure offered by an existing competitor. If the venture is not prepared for such changes, then the effects can quickly become very serious. This problem can also arise when moving into a new market, or even a new phase of operation within an existing market. Practices can differ widely in different markets or geographic regions, and failure to anticipate and plan for such differences can lead to delays and reputational damage in those markets.

The successful entrepreneur designs for scalability early in a venture, and closely tracks the ecosystem for potential or actual change. They expect the plan to change, and apply the 'pilot in the plane' principle of effectual reasoning to make changes proactively to achieve advantage, rather than waiting for negative effects to be demonstrated. They build a culture that is comfortable with and excited by change.

All ventures can experience malicious or accidental damage to their assets or resources. Acceptance of this brings a need to establish specific competencies and controls, together with a mature approach to the assessment and management of risk.

Concept and Structure for Addressing Business Innovation and Entrepreneurship

As will be apparent from the range of topics introduced in this chapter, business innovation and entrepreneurship are fascinatingly diverse and fast-moving subject areas that combine aspects of finance, legality, human psychology, team behaviour, project management, technology and imagination.

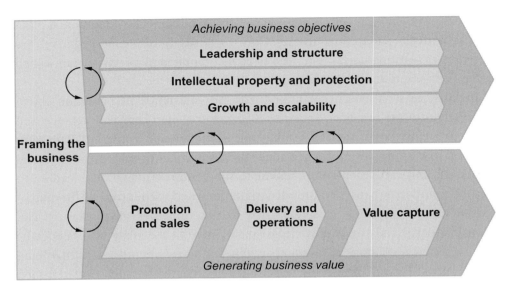

Figure 1.13 *The business design framework*

Having a logical structure within which to address the principal subject areas provides a conceptual framework for thinking about business design in a way that separates the considerations involved. Any structure will be imperfect and artificial because of the extensive inter-relationships between its component parts. The framework described below and adopted throughout this book has been developed, proven and tuned through its application to ventures of many kinds.

The framework is shown as Figure 1.13. It is based on the following principles:

Framing the business (addressed by Chapter 2) establishes a shared and constructive baseline for evaluating choices. It is about expressing a common high-level understanding that evolves with the business and contributes to the process of continuing development. Framing a venture involves defining its core value creation concept, its customer and market ecosystem, its business objectives and the key performance indicators by which success will be evaluated. The subsequent chapters elaborate upon the elements addressed initially during framing.

Generating business value (addressed by Chapters 3, 4 and 5) comprises a series of three core value-creating capabilities that address the respective needs to analyse, define and engage with the market; deliver a sustainable offering into that market; and capture value from the market to benefit the venture.

Although the framework conceptually represents these in a linear fashion, their application in practice is far from that: each event that occurs and decision that is taken by a venture triggers the execution of a series of iterating threads within and between these capabilities.

Achieving business objectives (addressed by Chapters 6, 7 and 8) addresses the capabilities needed for a business to achieve growth and scalability; to exploit its intellectual property and protect itself; and to adopt a leadership approach and structure that can succeed in delivering the defined objectives. These three capabilities parallel those responsible for generating business value. There is no implied sequence, and all three are equally critical to success.

The positioning of the capabilities responsible for *generating business value* at the bottom of the framework is intended to imply an analogy with the engine that drives the business. The generation of value makes it possible for a business to achieve its defined objectives.

The cyclic arrows are intended to imply the need for coherence across the framework. The initial framing of a business will inform and direct other decisions; these in turn might modify the initial framing, with consequent implications on other aspects of business design. Because of the interconnectivity between design decisions, those taken within any context may have important implications on other aspects of design.

Inevitably, circumstances change and 'stuff happens' that can prompt reappraisal of decisions. No limitation of agility or opportunism is implied by the framework.

The terms *business* and *venture* are used interchangeably throughout the book, although when referring to a business at its very early stage it is more natural to refer to it as a venture. Neither term is intended to limit the applicability of the material: it applies irrespective of whether the venture in question is public or privately held, whether it seeks to achieve financial gain or is a not-for-profit entity, or whether its offering is product or service based. The only assumption made is of a significant application of digital technology, either in the venture's offering, or in its operating platform.

Summary of Innovation and Entrepreneurship

- Innovation and entrepreneurship are complementary.
  - Innovation is about ideas and how they can be exploited through product and service offerings, whereas entrepreneurship is about turning an innovation into a sustainable business.

- o Succeeding in the design, operation and growth of a business needs a blend of innovation and entrepreneurship, and the balance of this blend changes over time.
  - o Some people are innovators, some are entrepreneurs, and some are 'operators' that ensure effective delivery and performance of some business activity. The successful business achieves the right mix of these three talents.
- Innovation is a process involving idea generation, exploitation of the idea through an offering and a business model, and market consumption.
  - o Ideas emerge through association or adaptation of existing ideas or through serendipity, or chance.
  - o A business model comprises four components: a value proposition, a notion of value promotion, a mechanism for value delivery and a plan for value capture. Each of these is critical to success.
  - o Market consumption can be interpreted as an 'S-curve' or a 'bell curve'. Understanding and interpreting market response requires planned data collection and analysis.
- A venture's ecosystem refers to the network of players, or stakeholder organizations, that are involved in the delivery of its offerings.
  - o Some innovations can be accommodated within an existing ecosystem, whereas others imply the need to modify or design a new ecosystem.
  - o Co-innovations are those innovations that are required to be developed by other players, especially on the supply or enabling side of the ecosystem.
  - o Co-adopters are those players that are required to adopt the innovation for it to succeed.
  - o All components of an innovation's business model can be developed, visualized and analysed in the context of its ecosystem.
- Innovations can be classified according to four criteria, and this classification is instructive in designing a business model, considering its likely market impact and planning for its release.
  - o A *sustaining (or incremental)* innovation is one that offers improved performance within an established market, whereas a *disruptive (or radical)* innovation brings to market a different and new kind of proposition.
  - o Innovations based on *technology push* are driven by a research and technology idea, whereas innovations based on *market pull* are driven by an observed need, problem or opportunity in a market.
  - o A vertical market refers to an industry sector, and a *vertical* innovation is one that applies specifically to a particular sector, whereas a *horizontal* innovation addresses the needs of many industries.

- ○ *Product* innovations introduce changes to what is offered or to the customer experience, *process* innovations bring changes to the way things are created or performed, and *paradigm* innovations bring about changes in the underlying mental model.
- Three historical frameworks have been described as ways of understanding and analysing trends in innovation over the longer term.
  - ○ Toffler's three waves are each associated with a range of societal, political, economic, cultural and technological factors. The value of the model is primarily in its broad contextual pattern.
  - ○ Kondratieff identified a series of cycles of innovation from 1800 through to the present day, each of which proceeds through a similar series of phases.
  - ○ The European Framework of Industry 1.0 through to 4.0 provides a useful characterization of the technological world into which we are now moving, as a basis for wider education and planning.
- Innovation is motivated by a range of factors and is performed principally by companies, universities, individuals or small teams, and start-up accelerators.
  - ○ Companies innovate to enhance their performance or to reduce their risk profile, and are motivated to do so by nationally designed tax incentives.
  - ○ Universities exploit innovation through spin-out companies and technology licensing agreements.
  - ○ Individuals and teams innovate for a variety of personal reasons and are supported by governments through attractive schemes to encourage investment.
  - ○ Accelerators are run by small entrepreneurial teams that stimulate early-stage companies and share in their success. They are effectively early-stage investors.
- Succeeding in innovation and entrepreneurship requires different ingredients.
  - ○ Successful innovation requires a diverse leadership profile, a compelling vision, an understanding of the marketplace, a culture dedicated to innovation, an experienced multidisciplinary team, judgement in the choice of timing for market introduction and a willingness to explore new ideas.
  - ○ The successful entrepreneur starts with what they have, what they know, who they know and what they can do; assesses risks by considering what they can afford to lose; responds to events, observations, surprises or disappointments as new opportunities; responds to competition by building partnerships that reduce uncertainty and co-create new markets; and creates plans that focus on activities within their control, and which create the future that is envisaged.

- A venture fails either because it starves of people or cash, or because it drowns in confusion and disaffection, which leads to starvation. These outcomes can come about for many reasons.
  - An idea can fail because it does not work: it is not implementable, it is not deliverable, it is not sustainable or there is no demand for it.
  - A business model can fail if any of its components are not viable or are poorly implemented.
  - The team can fail because it comprises the wrong people or because it is poorly composed, led or motivated.
  - The plan of activity can fail for several reasons, including running out of cash, an inability to scale or an inability to change.
- The chapters of the book have been designed to reflect a business design framework that permits each component to be addressed as a tractable, high-level capability that is needed for a business to succeed.
  - The centre of the framework comprises the business value chain of capabilities that generate value in the business.
  - The additional capabilities empower and scale the value chain and embed it within a legal and viable business structure.

ANALYSIS EXERCISES

The table below lists four digital businesses to be used as subjects for the exercises that follow.

Business	Focus	Website
Darktrace	Cyber security	www.darktrace.com
Fitbit	Health, fitness and performance	www.fitbit.com
JustEat	Online takeaway food	www.just-eat.co.uk
Snapchat	Social media	www.snapchat.com

On the basis of information available in the public domain, address the questions below for at least one of the businesses listed.

1. The underlying idea:
   (a) What is the inventive step that underpins the offering?
   (b) Has the idea come from association, adaptation or chance?

2. Exploitation of the idea through a business model:
   (a) What is the value proposition and who are the beneficiaries?
   (b) To whom is the proposition promoted and how?
   (c) How is value delivered to the customers?
   (d) What value is captured, and how?

3. The business ecosystem:
   (a) Who are the principal parties that participate in the business's ecosystem?
   (b) Are there any assumed co-innovators?
   (c) Are there assumed co-adopters?

4. The type of innovation:
   (a) Is it a sustaining or a disruptive technology?
   (b) Is it a technology push, or a market pull?
   (c) Is it a vertical or a horizontal market offering?
   (d) Is it a product innovation, a process innovation or a paradigm innovation?

DESIGN EXERCISES

This book uses a running case exercise that is introduced in Chapter 2 and developed through subsequent chapters. In parallel to this, the reader is encouraged to identify their own business idea to be developed incrementally through specific design exercises set in subsequent chapters of the book.

The following criteria are suggested:

- It must significantly exploit digital technology, either in its offering or its operations.
- It must be technically implementable using current methods and technologies.
- It must be commercially feasible in that it is viable in a current market.
- It must be sufficiently unique and distinctive, and not a small incremental improvement or development to something that currently exists.
- It must be achievable in that it can reasonably be addressed through the effort that is available.

These exercises may be performed individually or in small groups of two to four people.

Chapter 2 introduces a business design template that is available for download as a means of documenting and consolidating the design decisions relating to questions set in subsequent chapters.

2 Framing the Business

Focus of This Chapter

Figure 2.1 illustrates how the material addressed by this chapter fits within the framework of considerations for business design.

Framing a business provides a platform that informs and directs all aspects of business design.

Readers that are familiar with the usual method of piecing together a jigsaw puzzle might compare the framing of a business with completing the straight-line border of the puzzle. Subsequent chapters can then be compared to filling in the detail of the puzzle. Like all metaphors, however, this one has its limitations, because more detailed business design commonly provokes changes to the framing, and it is not uncommon for the entire structure to change and develop over time.

Although apparently simple, the questions posed by business framing can be surprisingly demanding. Team consensus on the answers is paramount.

Learning Outcomes

After studying this chapter, you will:

- Understand what frames a business, and be able to explain why each element is important.
- Understand the meaning of, and distinctions between, mission, objectives and measures.
- Be able to position customer relationships within the business ecosystem for a venture.

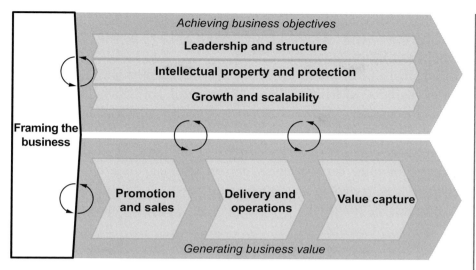

Figure 2.1 *Context of business framing*

- Be able to describe a value proposition in terms of the problem that it solves.
- Be able to frame a product or service offering.
- Be able to construct a balanced collection of relevant key performance indicators.
- Be able to create a risk register and know how to apply it to manage business risks.
- Understand the need for a plan of action and appreciate its principal components.

Introducing Business Framing

This chapter is about the importance of framing a business, and the elements involved.

Framing a venture at the outset or at any point in its development can make a real contribution to its value. It creates a shared and constructive baseline for evaluating choices, and gives clarity both to the team and to those with whom they need to communicate. That is not to say that the purpose of framing is about drawing lines in the sand: it is about expressing a commonly held, high-level understanding that will evolve with the business, and contribute to the process of its continuing development.

A poorly framed venture is likely to result from, and to exacerbate, confusion and division within the team. Ad hoc decisions will lead to continuing fragmentation, loss of focus and mounting stress.

The approach here follows a widely applied design principle known as *separation of concerns*, whereby distinct problem areas are isolated so they can be addressed separately, hence making a complex problem more tractable. Although each element of the business frame ultimately connects with all of the others, they are considered separately at the outset to enable each to be introduced in turn. Later chapters of the book elaborate upon the themes introduced here, including their interconnectivity.

A business is framed by the answers to the seven questions listed in Table 2.1.

Five of these questions correspond directly to those originally proposed in Drucker (2008) for use by any organization in assessing what it is doing, why it is doing it and what it must do to improve its performance. An influential thinker and writer, Peter Drucker is widely considered to be the foremost pioneer of management theory. Two additional questions have been added to his list due to their significance for ventures in the digital technology sector: *what is the problem that is solved* by the venture, and *what are the risks* that apply to its operations and threaten its success?

The sequence in which the questions are addressed by this chapter logically follows the sequence in which the questions are developed by the following chapters in the book. As noted in Table 2.1, the questions about mission and plan are implicitly developed by all chapters.

Table 2.1 Questions by Which a Business is Framed

Framing question	Chapter(s) by which the question is developed further
What is the mission?	All chapters
Who is the customer?	Chapter 3 – Promotion and Sales
What is the offering?	Chapter 4 – Delivery and Operations
What is the problem that is solved?	Chapter 5 – Value Capture
How will success be measured?	Chapter 6 – Growth and Scalability
What are the risks?	Chapter 7 – Intellectual Property and Protection
What is the plan to make it happen?	All chapters

Early in this chapter, a business idea is introduced to serve as the subject of a sample case exercise that is used for illustration throughout the book. In this and for many of the subsequent chapters, after introducing a consideration, the applicable options are applied and determined for the sample business. Its complete design is therefore incrementally completed as the book progresses.

A recommended template for business design is also introduced in this chapter as a vehicle for capturing, recording and managing the various aspects of business design, both in terms of adding increasing detail and recording changes over time. The template is introduced in its entirety in this chapter, and its use is recommended in the context of the design exercise that is set at the end of the chapter.

After briefly introducing the sample case exercise and the business design template, this chapter addresses in turn each of the principal questions associated with framing a business. Each question sets the scene for, and is further developed by, one or more of the following chapters.

The degree of rigour apparently recommended by this chapter may appear to be at odds with the entrepreneurial principles of effectual reasoning laid down in the previous chapter. An objection might be that in a venture's early days the team just needs to run with an idea and pivot when they encounter an obstacle. This assertion is countered as follows:

- Without some form of agreement of what the venture is, and of its value, the initial offering may be too unfocused to be scalable or sustainable, and hence any promise made is unlikely to be deliverable beyond the very short term.
- Without an agreement on the customer base to which the team will direct the offering, the effect is likely to be diluted and confused across several markets, each of which receives low confidence that the offering can be relied upon beyond an enthusiastic initial promise.
- Without some thought about what success would look like, and some consideration of the risks that might block this, the team cannot know whether their efforts are succeeding.

While recognizing that planning is not in itself a revenue-generating activity, these points argue for a degree of early investment of effort, usually through team workshops, to address the topics raised here, and hence establish a baseline position and plan to make it happen that will increase the likelihood of the team's efforts delivering on their objectives for the venture.

The story of CrowdMix, documented by James Cook (2016), technology editor at Business Insider UK, illustrates the importance of framing an early-stage digital business. The original idea behind the business was to use digital down-loads to create real-time, localized charts of popular music which could be used by the audience at a concert or festival to create lists of music being played. Using a highly optimistic assessment of its likely customer base and value, the founders succeeded in achieving a high valuation for the business, even though a limited, pre-release version was only ever used by a few thousand users, none of whom ever paid for the service.

With an ever-changing definition of its mission and product offering, between 2013 and 2016 the company spent $20 million of investor money hiring staff, equipping lavish offices and sponsoring extravagant parties. The company never succeeded in launching the more-elaborate offering some of its founders envisaged, its costs ran out of control, and in July 2016 it went bankrupt. Although the causes of failure are myriad in this example, the lack of any sense of framing a common understanding within the company and across its stakeholders clearly played a central role.

Case Study: SportMagenta

Introducing the Running Case Study

SportMagenta is an entirely fictitious business devised as a running case study for this book. Similarity with any actual business is unintended.

The founders Zara and Sonny are entrepreneurs with a few years' experience from earlier digital ventures, and who have now decided to team up to form a new business that successfully exploits their joint interests in technology and sport. Their idea is SportMagenta, a digital mobile service for members and visitors to sports clubs and gyms.

The story behind the name derives from the fact that the colour magenta is formed from an equal blend of red and blue. The business that the founders envisage will equally blend benefits to members of sports clubs with benefits to their clubs. Moreover, just as the colour magenta does not appear in the spectrum of colours, so will their business provide a unique and distinctive offering. Zara and Sonny also consider that adopting a vibrant and intriguing colour at the outset will enable them to develop distinctive and recognizable branding.

For a member or visitor to a sports club, the offering will ensure that they are able to make the most of the facilities available, including exercise classes, equipment, coaching and training, and social events. They will also be able to connect with local, club, minor league or college teams in their preferred sports, further enhancing their fitness profile and social engagement.

For a sports club, the offering will be a digital platform creating a communication channel with its members and visitors that can be controlled and updated in real-time to enable the club to better understand and connect with the interests and potential of its visitors. As a consequence of members' greater use of club facilities, they are likely to spend more money with their club than they have in the past. With analytics driven by data captured through the channel, the club will be able to tune the services and facilities that it offers to maximize its engagement and attractiveness to its users. Over time, SportMagenta will enable a sports club to build a substantial profile of its members and their communities, hence positioning it well to attract a higher proportion of their spending.

Zara and Sonny also recognize the potential to offer promotional opportunities for retailers whose offerings can be aligned with the interests of club members and visitors. This means that SportMagenta will also provide its users with access to special offers on sports-related purchases, such as trainers, specialist clothing, foods and home equipment.

A Template for Business Design

The complete design of a business includes many considerations that range from fundamental aspects of its mission through to detailed aspects of pricing, shareholding structure, revenue and margin projections, and investment ambitions. The purpose of the *business design template* is to provide a single repository for recording the principal assessments and decisions relating to these matters.

It is helpful to contrast the intended role of this template with that of the *business model canvas* first proposed in the late 2000s by Alexander Osterwalder, a Swiss business theorist, author and consultant. This is a widely used visual chart that helps ventures to assess options and trade-offs, and to align their activities.

By contrast, the template offered here, which is compatible with the business design framework adopted by this book, addresses a broader range of topics than does the canvas, and is intended to capture the considerations and rationale applied, in addition to the key decisions taken. It is not introduced as an alternative to the business model canvas, but as a complementary resource that can help to consolidate and document the design considerations and decisions, to enable continuing analysis and questioning as the venture develops.

The template is subdivided into seven blocks, corresponding to Chapters 2 through 8 of this book. The first block comprises a collection of rows that together consolidate the answers to the questions addressed by this chapter, as shown in Table 2.2.

Table 2.2 Business Design Template Entries for Business Framing

Business design template		
Framing	What is the mission?	
	Statement of business mission	
	Who is the customer?	What is the offering?
	Customer(s), value propositions and summary ecosystem	*Summary description of the offering and its unique differentiators*
	What is the problem that is solved?	How will success be measured?
	Statement of the problem solved by the offering and alignment with the value created for customer(s) and other beneficiaries	*Objectives and balanced list of measurable performance indicators*
	What are the risks?	
	Principal risks, including assessment and management decisions	
	What is the plan to make it happen?	
	Summary plan: required resources and key activities for the short and medium term	

As shown in Table 2.3, the blocks corresponding to the later chapters share a common two-part structure: the first part records the results of assessing and analysing the applicable considerations, and the second records the consequent decisions. The template prompts areas for consideration within each block, in line with topics covered in the relevant chapter.

What Is the Mission?

The mission of a business states its purpose, its *reason for being.* It is not about *what* it does, or *how* it will do it, but about the *why.* It states what the business wants to be famous for, or remembered for, and why the team will be proud to be associated with it.

The terms *mission* and *vision* are used variously, sometimes synonymously and at other times with specific differentiation. For simplicity, this book standardizes on the term *mission* and where necessary clarifies any specific use of *vision.*

Table 2.3 Business Design Template Entries for Subsequent Chapters

	Assessment and analysis	Decisions
Promotion and sales	*Market segmentation and sizing; market forces and implications; potential promotional channels; options for achieving visibility in the market; key stakeholders to be engaged; options for customer advocacy...*	*Business design decisions:* *1.* *2.* *3.*
Delivery and operations	Assessment and analysis	Decisions
	Routes to market; engagement channels and customer touch points; product viability and readiness, priority development requirements and roadmap; product scalability implications; procurement and management of materials and services...	*Business design decisions:* *1.* *2.* *3.*
Value capture	Assessment and analysis	Decisions
	Objectives for value capture; return-on-investment case; purchasing option and process; pricing structure and planned variations; business valuation and drivers...	*Business design decisions:* *1.* *2.* *3.*
Growth and scalability	Assessment and analysis	Decisions
	Exit ambitions; growth drivers; revenue, cost, margin and cash projections; scalability requirements for team, organization and funding; plans and business case for investment...	*Business design decisions:* *1.* *2.* *3.*
IP and protection	Assessment and analysis	Decisions
	IP exploitation and protection options; secrecy and confidentiality requirements; standard document types; insurance policies; physical and cyber protection requirements and options; legal compliance...	*Business design decisions:* *1.* *2.* *3.*
Leadership and structure	Assessment and analysis	Decisions
	Leadership and management team requirements; delegated responsibilities; team reward and motivation; budgeting process; monitoring of achievement towards business objectives; legal entities; contractual arrangements; shareholding structure design...	*Business design decisions:* *1.* *2.* *3.*

The value of explicitly constructing and expressing such a statement derives in part from the team focus and discipline involved in achieving consensus, and also from having a common way of explaining the business to those outside of the immediate team, including potential new recruits, customers, partners or investors.

A well-written mission should usually be:

- Short and sharply focused.
- Meaningful to all stakeholders – inside and outside of the business.
- Distinctive, in that it could not equally apply to other businesses.

And a well-written mission will:

- Say what the business does and does not stand for.
- Act as a test for decisions faced by the business.
- Guide what the business does and does not do.

Against these useful tests, it can clearly be seen that the lack of a mission statement, or a poorly expressed mission statement, will usually imply a lack of clarity or consensus within a venture.

Table 2.4 provides and assesses the mission statements of a sample of major technology companies.

Table 2.4 Mission Statements for Sample Technology Companies

Company	Mission or vision statement	Alignment with criteria
Amazon	*Vision*: 'to be earth's most customer-centric company; to build a place where people can come to find and discover anything they might want to buy online' *Mission*: 'we strive to offer our customers the lowest possible prices, the best available selection, and the utmost convenience'	Both statements are sharp and to-the-point, meaningful to anyone, and each clearly expresses the global ambition, breadth and reach of the world's largest online retailer.
Google	'to organize the world's information and make it universally accessible and useful'	Highly focused wording is used to express a distinctive and significant ambition.
Microsoft	'to empower every person and every organization on the planet to achieve more'	These statements express significant breadth and ambition, but lack distinctiveness. Arguably, either of these might equally be asserted by any other of today's major technology companies.
Cisco	'to shape the future of the Internet by creating unprecedented value and opportunity for our customers, employees, investors, and ecosystem partners'	

Case Study: SportMagenta

Mission Statement

Zara and Sonny recognize the need to form a mission statement that will apply equally to sports club members and to the clubs themselves, as it is important that the venture is designed to appeal to both communities.

Accordingly, they determine the mission for their business to be 'to enhance the engagement and active participation of visitors at sports clubs'.

These words have been chosen purposefully. With so many calls on members' and visitors' attention while at a sports club, the success of a new digital offering depends on its ability to engage peoples' interest. Taking this further, having engaged peoples' attention, the offering needs to fuel their active participation in, for example, subscribing for additional services, or choosing the club as the venue for a forthcoming birthday party.

This combination of engagement and active participation will lead to members and visitors encouraging their friends and relations to join up, hence achieving a *virtuous cycle* of endorsement whereby the more successful the club becomes, the better able it will be to attract ever more members, and hence grow its business. With a larger active population of people visiting the club and using the service, SportMagenta will be less vulnerable to any dampening effect from those less inclined to use technology while at the club.

This statement is distinctive to SportMagenta and will guide decisions in the forthcoming business design.

A venture's mission is achieved by the effective combination of all of the considerations addressed by this book, hence there is no specific chapter dedicated to its elaboration. It is the driving force behind all design decisions, and the notion by which they are held together.

Who Is the Customer?

The customer is the party – or set of parties – that values the offering of the business. Or, put another way, the customer is the party that must be satisfied for the business to achieve its objectives. These definitions recognize that there may be multiple types of customer for a business, which is the case for many modern digital ventures.

Although realizing value for customers is necessary for business success, it is not in itself sufficient. There are other ways that a business can fail. It may let its costs run out of control, or fail to find a way to *monetize* the value realized by its customers, or it may simply be a question of unfortunate timing.

This point can be illustrated by the experience of Springpad, a start-up founded in 2008 that offered a mobile organizer for recipes, films, home improvement projects and interior design projects. At its peak in 2014, the company had an international customer base of 5 million users, for whom the business clearly realized value. The problem was that the business failed to agree on how to monetize that usage, and the company closed in June of the same year. Speaking of the experience, co-founder Jeff Janer said: 'we built a heck of a product, but we didn't build the business'.

The Ideal Customer

To help focus and clarify customer understanding ahead of more detailed considerations, it can be useful to consider the characteristics of the *ideal customer*.

Depending on the nature of the offering, the ideal customer may be an individual, a business or in some cases either:

- Businesses that sell direct to individual consumers are called business-to-consumer (B2C) businesses. For these, the ideal customer may be characterized by some combination of age, gender, location, budget, situation or lifestyle and preferences.
- Businesses that sell to other businesses are called business-to-business (B2B) businesses. For these, the ideal customer is more likely to be characterized by size (financial and/or number of employees), market, maturity, culture, geographic spread, spend pattern, purchasing process and seasonality, plus other more market-specific attributes such as security, reliability or compliance requirements.

Although there may be similarities in their underlying technologies, the ideal customer for an ancestry discovery offering is likely to be very different from that for a festival foods application; and the ideal customer for a business offering a small business accounting product is likely to be very different from that for a business that offers an enterprise resource planning system. For some businesses, including LinkedIn, there may be separate profiles for the ideal individual customer and the ideal business customer.

The Business Ecosystem

The concept of a *business ecosystem* can be central to business design. It refers to the network of organizations – suppliers, distributors, customers, competitors, government agencies and so on – that are needed in some way to participate in the delivery of an offering into a market.

There are many potential ecosystem designs for any venture, depending on its decisions relating to customer market(s) and delivery approaches. An ecosystem can be designed to disrupt a market, or to fit within and enhance existing parties and relationships. When Apple first launched iTunes, the company created a new ecosystem that included an online music store, a diverse supply chain, and value propositions for both artists and consumers. By contrast, the Westfield app, a personal shopping assistant offered by Westfield shopping centres, has been designed to fit squarely within its existing ecosystem, with no disruptive impact.

Ecosystem design is central to the framing of a business. Over time, any ecosystem will change as new customer groups or routes to market are identified, new regulations are introduced or relationships are modified in response to a new competitor. A well-framed ecosystem representation is a great asset in exploring alternatives, both at the outset and as the business and its markets develop.

Every venture's ecosystem involves a range of parties, some of which may usefully be referred to as customers, some as partners, others as suppliers, regulators, distributors, competitors and so on. And it is not uncommon for a party to behave simultaneously as customer, partner and competitor to a business, hence the recent coining of the term *coopetition* to refer to the situation where businesses both cooperate and compete, especially in the development of new mutually beneficial offerings.

Consider IBM as an example. The company sells software and services, including to major technology businesses such as Oracle, Microsoft, Google and Cisco, and also to management consultancies such as Accenture. It also purchases a range of products and services from many of the same companies. At the same time, it competes with these companies in a range of markets: with Oracle in the database space, with Google and Microsoft in the cloud hosting and analytics spaces, and with Accenture in the technology services market. IBM and Cisco have recently announced a partnership arrangement to maximize joint strengths in the areas of

Internet of Things (IoT) analytics and cloud offerings. Hence many of the major businesses listed above are, at the same time, supplier, customer, partner and competitor. Furthermore, as companies such as Accenture provide a significant aspect of the route to market for the offerings of many technology businesses, further significant ecosystem relationships become apparent.

For this reason, the tags assigned to ecosystem players can be difficult and unhelpful. What matters is the set of value propositions that sustain the various relationships in the ecosystem. If these are not in balance, then the ecosystem will not function properly. For example, if a distributor, or route to market, is not sufficiently incentivized, then it may not perform as required, resulting in a loss of confidence by customers.

Although it is necessary to understand the drivers across the whole ecosystem, and to design the business within the perspective of the wider picture, it is always the customer connections and relationships that are central: unless it can realize value for its customer(s), any venture will ultimately be unsustainable. Applying the terminology of management consultants and authors Don Peppers and Martha Rogers (2016): it is only by gaining a 'deep understanding of this critical dynamic' with the customer that a business becomes able to drive revenues and increase margins.

Building a representation of the ecosystem is a good early step in the design of a business.

Here is a suggested technique.

Step 1: Establish the business and its relationships

Place the business in the centre of the diagram, and surround it with all other parties, or types of party, with which relationships are envisaged to be required. If there are obvious subdivisions within some parties, such as corporate and individual customers, represent these as separate elements. Indicate the relationships between the business and each of the other parties using bi-directional links, as shown in Figure 2.2.

Step 2: Explore the business relationships

The direction of a link on the ecosystem map indicates a flow of value, and so the bi-directionality of links implies an exchange of value between parties. Consider in turn each link with another party and annotate the implied or required value exchange by answering the following questions:

- What value does the business offer to them? This may refer to a value proposition.

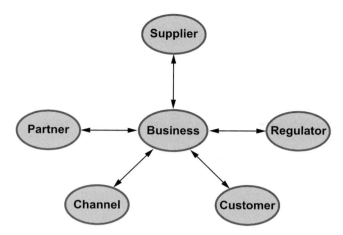

Figure 2.2 *Initial ecosystem representation*

- What value do they offer to the business? This may refer to a potential for value capture.
- What does the business need from them? This may relate to co-innovation, co-adoption, value promotion, value delivery, or the provision of goods or services.
- What do they need from the business? This may relate to co-innovation, co-adoption, value promotion, value delivery, or payment for goods or services provided.

In answering the questions at this point, no design decisions should be taken, and no untested assumptions should be made. The intention here is simply to express in one diagram the principal value propositions and any other known, obvious or potential dependencies and interactions.

Relationships between the other parties in the ecosystem can be significant to understanding their motivations and requirements. In such cases, these should also be annotated for completeness of capturing the market dynamics.

It is important to be confident of all assumed relationships with and between parties of the ecosystem. For example, if it is assumed that regulation or certification of some aspect of the offering will be required, then this assumption will need to be checked and confirmed in respect of required activities and implied constraints.

Step 3: Identify questions requiring further analysis

Complete the representation by annotating question marks against all those relationships that are not fully understood and which require either market research or design decisions.

It is quite normal at this point to acknowledge uncertainty about what can or should be expected in return for delivery of value to a party. It is useful to be able to see the remaining collection of unknowns, which can then be addressed in a balanced and systematic way.

Two further steps of the technique are suggested in the later section that addresses the question of *the problem that is solved.*

Case Study: SportMagenta

Business Ecosystem

The founders decide to locate their business within and across existing market structures and players. Their initial ambition for disruption is limited to the operations of sports clubs, rather than the wider market in which they operate. Consequently, applying the above steps yields the following representation of an initial ecosystem for SportMagenta.

The founders identify the involvement of four classes of customer: sports clubs, sponsors, club members and visitors, and local leagues. They formalize the wording of the intended value propositions for each, without at this stage making any assumptions of value capture.

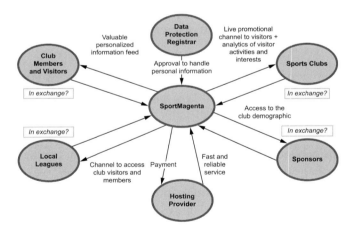

Additionally, they acknowledge the need for a commercial relationship with a provider of hosting services for the offering, and a potential dependency on a data protection registrar, the specific requirements of which will be determined as business design progresses. Finally, the outstanding questions of balancing the value exchanges with key parties are noted as points for further analysis.

The framing of the customer is elaborated further by Chapter 3, which addresses techniques for further qualification and analysis of the market, for achieving visibility within that market and for engaging and achieving advocacy with customers. Chapter 4 progresses this further by addressing the implications of delivering the offering to the customer.

What Is the Offering?

This question is about describing the offering in terms that will be meaningful in relevant contexts. It is important that everyone in the business can articulate this, at least at a high level, as it has implications for all aspects of the business model.

The following considerations guide the kinds of descriptive forms that are needed:

- What is the technology: in a nutshell, what actually is the offering, expressed in terms that will enable the business to be understood by its various stakeholders?
- What is unique about it: what other offerings can it be compared with, and what distinguishes and differentiates it?
- What type of innovation is it, and what are the implications of this?
- What implications are there for innovation within the business's ecosystem – especially considering requirements or assumptions of co-innovation or co-adoption?

Each of these questions can yield useful, generative material for business framing.

What Is the Technology?

The way that this is written depends on the intended target audience, which means that several framings of the technical description may be needed. Some of these apply to all businesses, others depend on the ecosystem:

- For any business, the team needs a common way of describing the offering – at least at a high level of technical detail – to enable planning, consistent communications and informed decisions around risk.

- For a B2B offering, those people responsible for its sale, deployment and support need a detailed description, potentially including network integration, security and access control, and licence management.
- For those contracted to distribute or channel the offering into a market sector, detailed sales and deployment understanding will be needed to promote, sell, distribute and support the offering.

Technical descriptions to meet these needs must be managed in parallel with continuing product and business model development. A common problem with early-stage ventures is incomplete, poorly written, unclear or out-of-date documentation, all of which introduce avoidable risks that can make the offering fall short of its potential value.

Case Study: SportMagenta

The Underlying Idea

The founders agree to the following forms of words as their source of *elevator pitch* summaries.

The product is designed to be used by members and visitors to sport clubs. Distributed as a smartphone app, for IOS and Android, it provides its users with useful information about their club and the facilities available, plus other relevant information relating to local leagues, catering and special offers, plus social events. It enables opinion sharing through social media links.

It connects the sports club with its visitors and members, and provides a unique digital channel that enables the club to focus its services, and to introduce real-time special offers. It also provides targeted sponsorship opportunities for providers of products and services relating to sport, health and fitness.

It is hosted within a private cloud for control, scalability and access to analytics to drive and inform the club's future plans. The software is integrated into the club's management systems to enable it to accumulate a rich picture of its members and visitors to enable effective targeting of services.

What Is Unique about the Offering?

A sense of uniqueness, or differentiation, is an essential aspect of a venture's messaging and communications. As with the technical description of the underlying idea, this will be needed for all stakeholders in the ecosystem. In many cases, however, the same messaging will suffice.

A unique selling point or proposition (USP) should be a succinct statement of what differentiates the offering or what makes it better than its competitors. This can refer to a product feature or to its price, availability, accessibility, security, quality, speed or responsiveness, breadth, focus, ease of use, reliability, connectedness ... or to the level of local support available, or its social or community credentials, or some combination of these.

Case Study: SportMagenta

Unique Selling Point

The founders recognize that they will need to appeal to both individual users of the offering and to the clubs that will adopt and deploy it. Consequently, they frame two USPs, one for each kind of customer.

For club members and visitors: the *only free way* to keep up to speed with everything you need to benefit from your club and local sporting interests.

For the club: *a personalized digital channel to your members* driving enhanced loyalty and participation in the services offered.

Turning to potential sponsors, a third USP is framed as: *the most targeted high-value channel* for promoters and distributors of sports and fitness products.

A differentiation can sometimes be expressed by alignment or comparison with other, more widely known services. For example, everyone is now familiar with Uber as a collaborative consumption platform that provides a taxi service. A venture that applies a similar approach for the provision of car parking spaces, therefore, might use the short-hand 'like Uber for car parking'. In this case, customers will quickly understand how this might work, and infer its likely benefits in terms of improving utilization of available free space. Likewise, everyone is familiar with Experian as a financial credit rating service, so a venture that describes itself as 'like Experian for cars' will quickly communicate the idea of a rating assessment for cars to guide potential buyers.

As with any simile, this approach can be efficient in helping customers or distributors to grasp a proposition quickly, and to envisage its benefits.

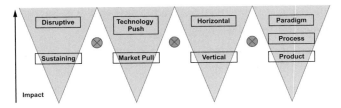

Figure 2.3 *Criteria for assessment of likely impact of innovation*

However, it may not necessarily provide a replacement for a distinctive USP, as there may be multiple offerings that claim the same comparison.

Another approach can be to differentiate an offering by stating what it has that its competitors do not have, as in, for example, 'like X, only twice as fast', or 'like Y, but at a fraction of the cost'. Again, this approach has the useful property of enabling people quickly to grasp the essential nature of what is being offered.

What Type of Innovation Is Offered?

Chapter 1 introduced a four-part classification framework for innovation. That scheme is illustrated here as Figure 2.3, repeating the previously used figure for convenience.

The consideration here is: how is the offering classified, and what is the likely market impact of each aspect of its classification?

As explained in Chapter 1, the higher the projected impact of an innovation, the higher the risk – and usually also the potential rewards – and hence the greater the need for imaginative business design and judicious planning.

In general, the higher the innovation scores on the impact scale, the greater the effort needed in expressing its description, because there will be fewer existing *hooks* on which to hang it. For example, an offering described loosely as 'like Uber for car parking' may be disruptive in the vertical market for car parking solutions, but will benefit from a market pull for the economies of such offerings, and will imply no paradigm change. Consequently, the work needed to describe the proposition and its operation will be more limited than was required for the original Uber offering.

As shown in Chapter 1, plotting an offering across the framework can be helpful in assessing the likely degree of effort required to achieve market understanding of the offering.

Case Study: SportMagenta

Innovation Type

The founders classify the offering as shown in the figure below.

It has disruptive elements in that it offers a new value proposition for sports clubs: a digital channel for direct communication with members and visitors through their mobile devices, to generate greater revenues by enabling real-time tuning and promotion of services. It also offers a new promotional channel for sponsors.

It is a market pull, driven by demand from visitors for improved information services, and by the desire of clubs to extend revenues from catering and merchandising options, and by local leagues that are ambitious to identify new talent.

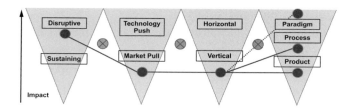

It is a vertical offering in that it specifically targets members and visitors at sport clubs. There may be future opportunities to extend the offering to other comparable environments, including live sports and entertainment.

For visitors, it is a product innovation, incremental to their existing online information sources and services. For clubs, though, it is a process innovation – and possibly a paradigm innovation – that transforms the way in which a club can engage with its members, and the way in which it can design, market and tune its offerings.

Sonny and Zara recognize that the disruptive and process change aspects of their offering imply a need to invest effort with sports clubs to gain their trust and confidence that the benefits will more than offset the need for increased process and communications effort.

This also feeds into considerations of recruitment by implying the need for help in building an understanding of clubs' current operations and motivations, to inform a plan for engaging clubs with an attractive pilot offering.

The market pull and vertical market aspects of the classification feed into development priorities by implying that the customer experience must be intuitive and unsurprising, compatible with the normal technology platforms and usage conventions of those that join and visit sports clubs.

What Are the Implications of the Ecosystem?

No innovation can be launched independently of the dynamics of the target market. Focus on excellent exploitation of an idea is necessary, but may not in itself be sufficient for market success. This is because it is also necessary to consider two classes of assumptions:

Co-innovation: these are the innovations assumed to be provided by other players, especially on the supply, or enabling, side of the ecosystem. For example, the development of electric vehicles is crucially dependent upon co-innovation of battery technology to enable long-distance use without the need for frequent recharging.

Co-innovation can occur by choice where two or more suppliers decide to collaborate for mutual advantage. An example described in Griffith (2017) relates to Pulse, a technology business that supplies enterprise resource planning (ERP) solutions specifically suited to mining companies. When developing a solution for Centennial Coal, an Australian mining business, the company worked closely with business intelligence and analytics company Birst to create the required new functionality much more quickly than it could have done if either company had worked independently.

Co-adoption: this refers to adoption assumed by other players on the consumption, or distribution, side of the ecosystem. For example, IoT technologies are often dependent on users' prior adoption of sufficient network bandwidth or connectivity. This assumption applies from home entertainment systems through to offerings for smart energy management.

Low-impact innovations are unlikely to include any significant assumptions for either of these considerations. For example, introducing a new consumer app that helps people to choose a restaurant or fashion outlet might safely assume that the technology required to source the required data and host the app is established and mature; likewise, it might confidently assume that its target customers and data providers already possess the required technologies.

On the other hand, for a business that plans to introduce a disruptive security device aimed at professional services businesses, it would be necessary first to investigate the price-performance trend of required components, and also to establish whether existing IT providers to such businesses would be prepared to distribute and support such technologies.

Case Study: SportMagenta

Co-Innovation and Co-Adoption Requirements

The founders assess the venture's impact on the market in respect of its requirements for co-adoption and co-innovation. Their conclusions are as follows:

The ecosystem assumes adoption by members and visitors to sports clubs. If this does not happen, then there will be no demonstrable response to the club's new value propositions, and hence no new value to the club. Consequently, the product must be readily acceptable to its users.

The ecosystem assumes co-innovation by three parties:

1. By clubs, to exploit the new service by promoting additional facilities and offers to visitors. If the club does not make such changes, then it will achieve no new value.
2. By sponsors, to exploit the new promotional channel. Again, if they do not take advantage of the offer, then they will achieve no new value.
3. By local sports leagues. If they do not adopt the opportunity to promote themselves to the wider community, then they will see no new interest; and hence will achieve no value.

Together, these assumptions mean that these stakeholder groups must be successfully disrupted – engaged, influenced and supported – through product launch and early operation, with the effectiveness of change tracked through key performance indicators (KPIs).

The framing of the offering is elaborated further by Chapter 4, which addresses techniques for managing the required supply chain, designing the customer experience, planning and managing continuing development and release, and delivering the offering to customers.

What Is the Problem That Is Solved?

The primacy of the customer relationship is the rationale for this question being factored out from the broader considerations of ecosystem design.

Framing the Problem

This question prompts the need for additional detail about the venture's value proposition(s) to its customer base, and in doing so it opens the related question of what customers will pay for it, which in turn introduces preliminary options for value capture.

It is useful to frame the customer value question in terms of a problem that is solved, because this creates focus on something that is testable through market research. If there is no evidence that the business solves a real problem, and that customers will pay in some way for a solution to this problem, then further business development is likely to be fruitless. It can be helpful when framing the problem to explore how else the problem might be solved, and at what cost.

The history of AirBnB provides an interesting illustration of the need for a business to solve a real problem. In 2007, two of the company's founders, Joe Gebbia and Brian Chesky, were entrepreneurs working for different ventures and who needed money to pay the rent. By letting out space on airbeds in their flat, they earned enough to keep going and, significantly, learned that there was a real need for low-cost overnight accommodation, and that this need could be met through a collaborative consumption platform that enables people with underutilized space to offer accommodation to those who need it. By switching focus to developing a solution to this problem, and bringing in a third founder, Nathan Blecharczyk, they built a business now valued at $31 billion. At the time AirBnB was established, there was no way to identify available accommodation other than approaching individual venues.

Using statements expressed in the customer voice, the problem and the corresponding solution can be aligned with relationships on the ecosystem diagram. This gives rise to less formal and more workable – and testable – statements, such as:

- 'It is inconvenient to carry around multiple payment cards and cash, so I welcome being able to pay for purchases with my smartphone.'

- 'We lose money every time a customer leaves us, so it is a real benefit to have a service that can retain their loyalty, even after we failed to deliver the service they expected.'

Any assumed value, and the way in which this is expressed, needs to be tested, and a venture's principal value proposition needs continually to be validated by evidence. In cases where there are current active customers, this can be achieved through a continuing programme of customer surveys. In the early days of a venture, before *live* customers are available, collecting evidence usually means designing surveys to test the needs and attitudes of prospective customers. These surveys can be executed either by online questionnaires, or by targeted interactions with individuals or groups. Although this process can be time-consuming, it is much less costly than a failed promotion of an offering into a market, followed by its subsequent retraction.

The *mom test* techniques suggested in Fitzpatrick (2013) can be relevant to early-stage market research, to avoid overly optimistic assumptions that derive from *feel good* conversations. For a more comprehensive treatment of the topic of evaluation within the context of proposition design, the reader is referred to Osterwalder *et al.* (2015).

The results of this analysis enable a further step in the ecosystem mapping technique that was introduced in an earlier section in the context of framing the customer.

Step 4: Describe the problems solved and value created

For each problem that is solved, annotate the relevant ecosystem element with a statement of the problem and a summary of the associated value proposition. These should be expressed informally using the customer voice, and supported by evidence. There should be at least one value proposition for each customer role in the ecosystem.

Case Study: SportMagenta

Problems Solved by the Innovation

Using their friends and networks, Zara and Sonny conduct online market research across a representative sample of individuals from each of the principal stakeholder parties. As a consequence of the learning gained, they are able to re-express the customer value propositions of the business using the customer voice as shown below.

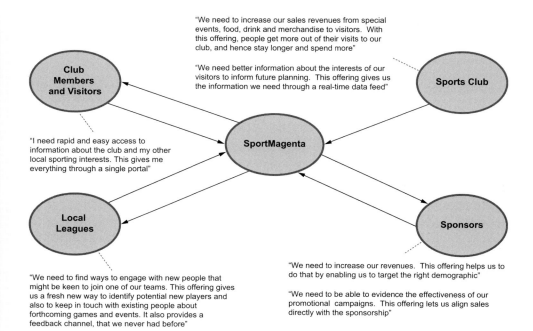

"We need to increase our sales revenues from special events, food, drink and merchandise to visitors. With this offering, people get more out of their visits to our club, and hence stay longer and spend more"

"We need better information about the interests of our visitors to inform future planning. This offering gives us the information we need through a real-time data feed"

"I need rapid and easy access to information about the club and my other local sporting interests. This gives me everything through a single portal"

"We need to find ways to engage with new people that might be keen to join one of our teams. This offering gives us a fresh new way to identify potential new players and also to keep in touch with existing people about forthcoming games and events. It also provides a feedback channel, that we never had before"

"We need to increase our revenues. This offering helps us to do that by enabling us to target the right demographic"

"We need to be able to evidence the effectiveness of our promotional campaigns. This offering lets us align sales directly with the sponsorship"

The figure elaborates upon the set of validated value propositions offered by the business to the relevant parties, each expressed in terms of the problem solved, and written in the customer voice. With this greater understanding of the potential value offered to each party, questions of value capture can be addressed more confidently.

Considerations of Value Capture

Gaining a more confident assessment of the value offered to customers opens the opportunity to consider how the business might benefit from delivering that value to those parties.

This topic is addressed in more detail in Chapter 5, but can usefully be given early consideration within the framing of the business.

Value capture can take many forms. In some cases, the value captured will be financial, through licence or subscription fee, or charge per use. It can, however, take other forms.

- Public or market endorsement of the venture, where a customer contributes material for a promotional video or case study, or agrees to participate in or speak at an event.

- Market validation or information to inform pricing, positioning or functionality prioritization, such as through customer agreement to a pilot programme that will enable the venture to collect useful data to inform its plans for approaching similar businesses.
- Product integration, to demonstrate technical and market confidence, or adherence with standards.

This is an opportunity for creative thought. Whenever a venture provides value or meets a need of another party in the ecosystem, there is an opportunity to capture value, financial or otherwise, back into the venture. In assessing the value capture options, questions that can usefully be asked include:

- What would be the cost to the customer of solving the problem without using the offering?
- What would be the most compelling and least-risk proposition for the customer?

The results of this activity enable a fifth and final step of the ecosystem mapping technique introduced earlier.

Step 5: Complete and balance all assumed value exchanges
Annotate provisional value capture intentions to complete the initial design of the proposed set of value exchanges. For each party in the ecosystem, assess the balance of the proposed exchange for being feasible and reasonable.

Case Study: SportMagenta

Value Capture Options

The venture offers value propositions to visitors, sports clubs, local leagues and promoters; therefore, the founders address the question of value capture from each of these parties. They start by asking what would be the most compelling and least-risk proposition in each case. Their logic is as follows.

Club members and visitors are the end-user customers. They offer significant value in terms of creating and promoting visibility of the product across the market, and through offering product feedback. Furthermore, unless they adopt and engage with the service, there will be limited potential for value creation with other players. Charging them a download or subscription fee would be a high-risk option, as this may limit their inclination to use the service.

Clubs offer significant value in terms of revenue potential, plus market endorsement and visibility. Charging them a fee also risks inhibiting take-up, even though they may be able to recover their costs through offering premium services to their members and visitors.

Although charging clubs a fixed fee may initially be difficult, due to the initial lack of any quantified return-on-investment data, charging them a share of the additional revenues generated may be a more compelling and lower-risk option.

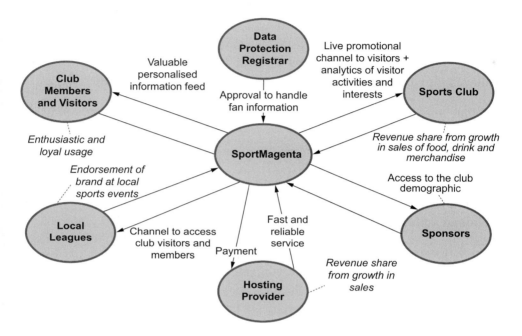

Although this approach will need to be renegotiated as the relationship develops, it provides an attractive starting point and may help to develop a credible return-on-investment case for future negotiation.

Charging promoters a fee may again be difficult at the outset, but offering a service in return for a share of additional revenues is again likely to be compelling.

These initial preferences for value capture are now added to the ecosystem to produce the representation shown, which is now complete from the perspective of framing the business.

The framing of the problem solved is elaborated further by Chapter 5, which addresses techniques for defining what will be offered for purchase and for designing and calibrating a pricing structure. It also addresses approaches for assessing the value of a business and the factors that contribute to its growth.

How Will Success Be Measured?

A venture's mission helps to differentiate it and set its broad direction and values. A clear statement of mission also has value in guiding the definition of a set of specific objectives for the business which translate – in measurable terms – what the mission means in terms of achievement and outcome.

Three factors align to give coherence to a business concept:

- *Mission* drives *key objectives*, which are measured using *KPIs*.

The strength of this alignment is that KPIs can be measured periodically (monthly, quarterly, annually) to indicate achievement of objectives, which in turn indicates successful delivery of the business mission. Through the dynamics of this process, the measured achievements will prompt questioning of objectives (too demanding, too lax, too unadventurous . . .), which may in turn challenge the mission.

The approach described here is similar to that used effectively by successful technology companies, including Google and LinkedIn, under the branding OKR: Objectives and Key Results. This topic is widely addressed in the management literature, initially by George T. Doran, a consultant and former director of corporate planning for Washington Water Power Company (Doran *et al.* 1981), and more recently by, for example, Hersey *et al.* (2012).

Designing Good Objectives

The widely described technique of defining *smart objectives* is helpful in setting good targets. Although the acronym *smart* is defined variously by different sources, the following interpretation is recommended for business design:

- 's' – specific: focusing on a particular subject, such as customer satisfaction or revenue.
- 'm' – measurable: amenable to quantification, such as monthly revenue from sales.
- 'a' – aligned: coherent with the business mission.
- 'r' – realistic: given the current state of the venture and market, and the available resources.
- 't' – time-related: acting within a specific time envelope, such as monthly or annually.

As there are many possible smart objectives for any mission, and each one adopted has associated costs of data capture and calculation, it is necessary to select a manageable set of around half-a-dozen *key objectives* that together provide balance across the aspects of business achievement, and which are judged likely to be the most informative.

It should be noted that not everything worth achieving is measurable, at least at the outset, and also that not everything that is measurable is worth capturing and reporting. It is useful to consider, for each objective, how the results would be used: what action might be taken, depending on the measurement produced? For example, if a customer satisfaction objective shows a decreasing trend, would further effort be invested in development or customer engagement? If there is no good answer to this question, the objective should not be adopted.

Case Study: SportMagenta

Key Objectives

The mission statement set by Zara and Sonny was 'to enhance the engagement and active participation of visitors at sports clubs'. They now elaborate this by setting the following set of key objectives:

Key objectives
To achieve regular monthly usage by more than 75 per cent of members and visitors at targeted clubs.
To achieve availability on 95 per cent of smartphone products used by members and visitors.
To demonstrate greater than 5 per cent increase in monthly revenues from sales of services, food and merchandise by targeted clubs.
To demonstrate greater than 5 per cent increase in monthly revenues by sponsoring businesses to targeted club members and visitors.
To achieve recurring revenue growth of more than 200 per cent year on year for each of the first three years.
To achieve gross margin growth of more than 150 per cent year on year for each of the first three years.

This set of smart objectives will evidence the extent to which the offering is *engaging* and encouraging of *active participation*. Together, they define the targets that the founders reasonably seek to achieve through the combination of value propositions they envisage for visitors, clubs and sponsors. The objectives also establish initial growth targets for the business in anticipation of a potential need to raise investment for scalability. Performing above or below any of these objectives will trigger a review leading either to an increase in the level of ambition or a plan for remedial activity.

Designing Good Key Performance Indicators

To be effective, each key objective needs to be associated with one or more key performance indicators (KPIs) by which it will be evaluated. As with choosing objectives, selecting good KPIs is important to enable objectives to be tracked effectively, without unnecessary waste of effort in capturing and evaluating data.

It is helpful to think of measures as being either *leading* or *lagging*:

- *Leading measures* look forward towards achievement of objectives, and so are sometimes referred to as *performance drivers*. Examples of leading measures include customer satisfaction, development productivity and revenue growth trends.
- *Lagging measures* look backwards at what has been achieved, and so are sometimes referred to as *outcome measures*, or *rear-view mirror*. Examples of lagging measures include revenue generated per employee, year-to-date sales and number of downloads achieved.

Some measures have aspects of both lead and lag; for example, the number of downloads for an app is a lagging measure that might also serve as a leading measure by indicating the potential for future use. When designing a set of KPIs, it is important to create a good mix of leading and lagging measures, so that achievement can be reviewed both in terms of forward-looking considerations, and also the actual performance that has been achieved.

Another useful guideline for choosing measures is provided by the balanced scorecard approach. Originating from Harvard and first published in Kaplan and Norton (1992), the method has since been reviewed and developed further by several academics and management consultants, including, for example, Olve *et al.* (2004), Kaplan (2010) and Braam (2012). The approach suggests four perspectives to be measured, which encourage a mix of financial and non-financial considerations:

- *Customer* measures – for example, relating to satisfaction or retention.
- *Financial* measures – for example, relating to revenue mix or margin.
- *Process* measures – for example, relating to development productivity or the time taken for new staff to become productive.
- *Learning and growth* measures – for example, relating to employee satisfaction or information availability.

The set of perspectives adopted can depend on the nature of the business: in service delivery organizations in the public or private sector, it can be useful to include a **service** perspective that measures delivery volumes, quality levels, unit costs of delivery, and time or cost of developing a new service.

Combining multiple perspectives with a balanced mix of lead and lag measures provides a robust framework with which to monitor and evaluate progress towards achieving key objectives.

Case Study: SportMagenta

Key Objectives and Aligned KPIs

On the basis of the chosen set of key objectives, the founders apply the guidelines recommended above and determine the following set of associated KPIs and targets.

Key objectives	Key performance indicators	Target	Perspective	Lead/ lag
To achieve regular monthly usage by more than 75 per cent of members and visitors at targeted clubs	Percentage user satisfaction with product	100%	Customer	Lead
	Percentage of user base downloads	95%	Customer	Lag
	Percentage of customer feedback requests satisfied per month	80	Learning	Lead
To achieve availability on 95 per cent of smartphone products used by members and visitors	Percentage of relevant platforms supported	95%	Process	Lag
	Time required to support new platform (days)	3	Process	Lead
To demonstrate greater than 5 per cent increase in monthly revenues from sales of services, food and merchandise by targeted clubs	Percentage revenue increase by targeted clubs	5%	Financial	Lag

Key objectives	Key performance indicators	Target	Perspective	Lead/lag
To demonstrate greater than 5 per cent increase in monthly revenues by sponsoring businesses to targeted club members and visitors	Percentage revenue increase by sponsors	5%	Financial	Lag
To achieve recurring revenue growth of more than 200 per cent year on year for each of the first three years	Recurring revenue growth month on month	10%	Financial	Lag
	Recurring revenue growth year on year	200%	Financial	Lag
To achieve gross margin growth of more than 150 per cent per annum for each of the first three years	Gross margin growth month on month	5%	Financial	Lag
	Gross margin growth year on year	150%	Financial	Lag

Each key objective is associated with at least one KPI, and the complete set of KPIs covers all four perspectives of the balanced scorecard, and includes a mix of leading and lagging measures.

The inclusion of multiple KPIs for the first two objectives reflects the critical need by the business for visitors to increase engagement and participation in club events, and hence the importance of their having access to the product and being satisfied with its use. The measures established will enable the team to track uptake at a level of detail that will permit rapid remedial action where required.

The framing of this aspect of business design is elaborated further by Chapter 6, which addresses techniques for achieving the objectives set for growth through a scalable organization.

What Are the Risks?

A risk, or threat, refers to the possibility of something untoward or negative that may happen. It is important that risks are correctly articulated in terms of the threat that they pose. For example, the introduction of a new regulation may not in itself pose a risk, but the introduction of a new regulation that renders the venture's offering illegal in its target market would constitute a risk. In other words, it is important that the description of a risk expresses the negative implication on the business.

Risks apply at all levels, from the global assessment published by Jeschonnek *et al.* (2016) through market-specific assessments such as those provided by EY (2016), to those relating specifically to a business. It can be important to consider all levels when assessing those risks that pose the most significant threats at any time.

Much of the recent risk-based research, such as that published by Aven (2016), aims to establish broader perspectives on the conceptualization, assessment and management of risk. Such perspectives apply especially to vulnerability and probability, with an emphasis on knowledge, the treatment of uncertainty, impact on robustness and resilience, and the importance of managerial review and judgement in risk management.

It is important to appreciate that the aim is not to minimize risk, but to understand it, and to manage its impact on the business. This sometimes means establishing mitigation strategies, and at other times tolerating the possibility that a bad thing happens, and then reacting if it occurs.

The risk register is the usual technique for expressing and managing the risk profile of a business. This is a tabular structure that identifies, characterizes and defines risks, gives an assessment of their potential for business impact, and defines the business's planned response to the occurrence of each risk.

Expressing the underlying concepts more formally:

- A risk (or threat) has a likelihood of occurring, usually expressed as a probability, and if it does so, then there will be a negative consequence on the business, which can be scored in terms of its degree of impact.
- The occurrence of a risk will be detected by an indicator, and in that event a response may be specified.
- Assessment of each identified risk will determine whether it will be tolerated, mitigated or transferred.
- Any intention to mitigate or transfer a risk will be associated with a pre-action that performs the mitigation or transfer.
- From a management perspective, every risk identified has an owner, a log of when it was last assessed and a diary date for when it should next be reviewed.

Risk management involves three phases. These are reflected in the following recommended form of risk register, comprising three blocks of columns here divided, for convenience of presentation, across Tables 2.5, 2.6 and 2.7.

Table 2.5 Identification of a Risk

Risk identification		
Identifier	**Consequence**	**Type**
An indicative name for the risk	How the business could be negatively affected by the risk	Business/Technical/ Environmental

Table 2.6 Rating of Severity of a Risk

Risk rating		
Probability	**Impact**	**Score**
The risk's likelihood of occurring (0–1)	The severity of the risk's impact (0–1). A severity of 1 would imply a catastrophe	Probability × impact, to give a score for ranking of risks in the register

Table 2.7 How a Risk Will Be Managed

Risk management						
Indicator of occurrence	**Current assessment**	**Pre-action**	**Response when detected**	**Risk owner**	**Date last assessed**	**Date for re-assess**
How the occurrence of the risk will be detected	Tolerate/ mitigate/ transfer to another party	Mitigation or transfer activities to be performed	Action to be taken when the risk is detected	Who is accountable for managing the risk	When the risk was last assessed	When the risk should next be assessed

Risk identification is about assessing the nature and consequence of a risk. Although it is helpful to have an indicative name for reference, the principal field in Table 2.5 is that which describes the damage that would be inflicted on the business should the risk occur.

Risk rating is about assessment of likelihood and impact. The sequencing of risks in the register usually takes account of their *score*, such that those risks with the highest combined likelihood and impact are listed at the top of the table. In some cases, in place of numbers between 0 and 1, a relative scheme is more appropriate, using symbols H (high), M (medium) and L (low). Where this approach is used, risk scores usually take the form HH, HM, LL.

The principal value of a register is its role in making decisions about how to handle the risks that have been identified and rated. For each risk, a decision must be taken as to which of the following is to apply:

- Tolerated – no action will be taken to avoid or head off the risk. A response (or recovery) activity may be prescribed. For example, a risk that system performance falls below expected bounds may be tolerated and recovered by compensation or relationship activities.
- Mitigated – a prescribed action will be performed, either to reduce the likelihood of the risk, or to reduce its impact on the business. As with tolerated risks, a response activity may also be prescribed. For example, a risk that monthly revenue falls below projections might be mitigated by issuing warnings to interested parties and dedicating sales effort to the closing of deals that offer short-term revenue potential.
- Transferred – the risk is judged to be too serious, and so a prescribed action will be performed whereby it will be *sold* to some other party. For example, a risk that *lumpy* cash collection endangers payment of monthly staff salaries may be judged too serious to accept, and too difficult to mitigate, and so might be transferred to a credit factoring company which offers to smooth cash availability in exchange for a percentage of the amount invoiced.

A further consideration is to question whether an identified risk presents any opportunities to the venture. A severe risk can support a case for change, and a risk that applies more broadly within a market may present opportunities for collaboration.

It is important to give attention to all three phases of the process. If a risk is not identified, or is poorly expressed or inadequately rated, then a poor decision may be taken that exposes the business to unacceptable damage.

Risk management is a continuing process: new risks emerge and existing risks modify and disappear. It is therefore important to review the register periodically to sustain a strong current understanding of the current risk profile and the required mitigation and transfer activities.

Case Study: SportMagenta

Risk Register

Zara and Sonny focus their risk analysis on those catastrophic threats that could destroy or seriously damage their business. As entrepreneurs with some experience, they are aware of the central need to realize value for the customer, and hence they consider how this might be threatened.

	Risk identification				Risk rating			Risk management						
	Risk description	Identifier	Consequence	Risk type	Probability	Impact	Score	Indicator	Current assessment	Pre-action	Response	Risk owner	Date last assessed	Date for re-assess
	Sports club fails to respond to opportunity offered by the service	Failure to generate new revenues	Usage by visitors does not yield increased purchasing, leading to loss of confidence by clubs	Business	0.6	0.8	0.48	lack of content provision by club	Mitigate	Engage club management to mitigate likelihood by promoting benefits	Engage with club management with offer of assistance	CEO	May 2017	June 2017
	Connectivity problems inhibit service performance within sports club	User connectivity problems	User frustration hits product reputation, leading to reduced usage, leading to loss of confidence by clubs	Technical	0.5	0.8	0.4	% dropped or slow connections	Tolerate	Test bandwidth available ahead of live operation	Assist club to increase available bandwidth	CTO	May 2017	June 2017
	Members and visitors use the service to communicate inappropriate content	Inappropriate or illegal content	Company is exposed to legal action leading to reputational damage, leading to loss of confidence by clubs	Business	0.35	0.7	0.245	Complaint from club or other visitors	Transfer	Include club liability for content of messages transmitted in standard agreement	Close service and report abusive individual(s)	Club manager	May 2017	June 2017

This train of thought leads them to identify as a key risk the club's unwillingness or inability to make the necessary changes to its processes and communications to take advantage of the potential offered by SportMagenta. A further risk is identified by consideration of potential technical issues that could inhibit the usefulness or availability of the service to its end-users. And an additional key risk is identified in relation to the way in which the service might be used by visitors to a sports club, and in particular, to the consequences of becoming associated with malicious or illegal activity.

These three key risks populate the risk register shown above. As shown in the register, the founders decide to mitigate the first risk, to tolerate the second and to transfer the third. These decisions define the *risk envelope* of the business, and indicate the extent of the founders' joint risk appetite. Making decisions such as this is a good test of founders' compatibility; even if they initially disagree, it is necessary that they are able to reach and commit to a decision.

The framing of risks is elaborated further by Chapter 7, which addresses techniques for assessing and determining mitigation and transfer options in relation to generally applicable risks relating to the venture's IP, confidential information and trade secrets, contractual obligations, unwarranted intrusion and requirements for legal compliance.

What Is the Plan to Make It Happen?

There is always at least one assumed plan for taking a business to market, even though it may not be articulated or expressed, and it may not be agreed by all concerned. An agreed plan directs and prioritizes the team's activities, and guides trade-offs between alternatives. However uncertain its consequences might be, it is important that the broad detail of an initial plan is agreed to complete the framing of the business.

Conflicts are likely to occur unless a clear plan has been communicated and agreed across the team. These can be provoked by issues such as the prioritization of development effort against promotional effort, or whether to accept an offer of tangentially related work, or the priorities for hiring a new team member. Such decisions can be difficult, and the results suboptimal, if resolved in isolation, without a plan of activity. Even where a plan has been agreed, these kinds of decisions may cause it to be questioned, changed or re-expressed. There is a military expression that says, 'no plan survives contact with the enemy'.

This applies equally to business, where *the enemy* corresponds to the real world and the events that occur within it.

An initial plan of activity will complement the various other considerations introduced in this chapter to define:

- The immediate requirements for people, partners, communications and resources, and an assumption of how these will be satisfied.
- The activities to be performed over the short, medium and longer term. In the short term, this should include activities relating to development, promotion, market engagement, recruitment and risk mitigation or transfer. For an early-stage venture, 'short term' might mean three to six months, 'medium term' might mean up to a year, and 'longer term' might stretch to three years.

A simple plan that addresses these points can provide the basis for light-touch management and coordination of team activity. It will be continually reviewed and iterated with the team as the business develops. In the event of a need to pivot, the plan will provide useful clarity over the nature of the proposed change: is it a change of time frame, of the nature of the offering, of the market to be addressed or of the planned means of approaching the market?

Case Study: SportMagenta

Plan to Make It Happen

The founders recognize immediate requirements to supplement and complement their own talents and abilities by recruiting the following:

- A small initial development team of three technically able people with experience of working in early-stage ventures, to build and deploy the initial product.
- A partner individual or company with knowledge, experience and contacts within sports clubs, to open doors and inform the business on integration requirements and engagement approaches.

And they establish a plan of short-term activity, including:

- Starting in the UK, targeting large sport club chains with the intention of securing between one and three pilot projects to prove the offering and confirm details, including benefits achievable, required functionality, customization effort needed, pricing model, competition and risks.
- Deploy a minimum viable product and drive development iterations from pilot feedback.

In the medium term, extend this activity:

- From pilot success, roll out the offering across clubs within the targeted chains to gain market share, generate profitable revenue and prove scalability.
- Following proven success in one chain, access other chains with a well-evidenced return-on-investment case.
- Develop channel partners in the UK and other territories.
- Qualify additional use cases for wider application, and hence build the longer-term plan.

The framing of *the plan to make it happen* is elaborated further by Chapters 4, 6 and 8. Chapter 4 addresses techniques for design of the development roadmap, including alignment with business objectives. Chapter 6 addresses techniques for creating a growth plan and for designing a team, an organization and the funding sources whereby this can be achieved. Chapter 8 complements these considerations by addressing techniques for the structuring of the venture, for establishing leadership and motivation and for financial control.

Case Study: Reposit – Disrupting the Property-Letting Ecosystem

Background to the Company

Reposit – www.getreposit.uk – addresses the problem that paying a tenancy deposit is expensive and wasteful for the 5 million UK households that belong to *generation rent*.

The company's motivation was to provide an alternative approach based on trust, automation and financial innovation, to reduce cost and to make moving and living easier and more affordable.

The Innovation

The property rental ecosystem in the UK requires a tenant, at the outset, to pay a large financial deposit to the agent, to cover the case that they default in some way on their tenancy. This deposit is usually lodged with an external scheme, as illustrated in Figure 2.4.

Paying this deposit is a burden for trustworthy tenants that would prefer to have continuing access to their money. It also adds to the administration load of the agent, and delays the process for the landlord.

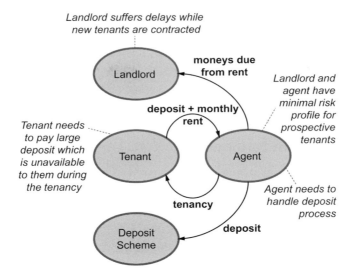

Figure 2.4 *Ecosystem without Reposit*

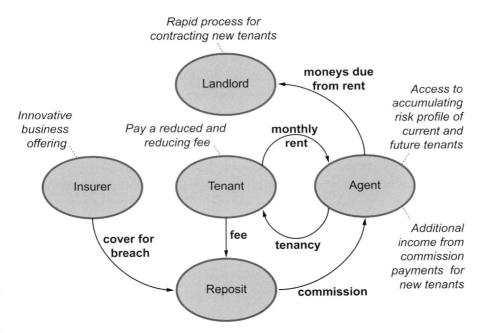

Figure 2.5 *Ecosystem including Reposit*

As illustrated by Figure 2.5, Reposit's customer proposition redesigns the ecosystem to benefit all parties. Instead of paying a large deposit, the tenant pays a small fee to the Reposit platform, to cover the cost of an insurance policy, which underwrites the risk of default.

The process is simplified, the effort and time to let a property reduces, and so both landlord and agent also benefit. As a further innovation, the tenant's performance is tracked, with good behaviour being rewarded with a reduced fee on their next tenancy. The accumulating data on tenants' risk profiles – their rental passport – means that agents and landlords can pre-screen tenants, saving costs and delays of viewings, and de-risking tenancy offers.

The Plan and Actions Performed

On the basis of market research, Reposit decided to focus in London due to the high levels of rental property and the very real problem faced by young people in paying the high levels of deposit required. Consequently, the team's initial plan was to engage letting agencies with properties in London, with the intention of securing a small number of pilot projects with early adopters of their minimum viable product offering. In parallel to this, they secured the required insurance underwriting and legal wording.

Having succeeded within the first year in demonstrating value with early adopters, and with confidence in their ability to scale the platform, they extended the plan to cover a wider geographic area, initially remaining within the UK, but with a parallel intention of qualifying additional markets in the USA and Europe.

The experiences of their initial activities taught the Reposit team that disrupting the UK market would likely take longer than had originally been planned, hence requiring the early phase of the plan to be extended. They also learned, however, that by minimizing changes to established processes, technology development can be made less demanding than initially anticipated, which speeded up their ability to deliver enhanced services to early customers, and enabled development of a more resilient platform upon which to scale their operations during the medium and long term.

Outcomes

The success of the business in transforming the market is evidenced through the following KPIs:

- Several hundred letting agencies have signed up and are actively using the service.
- A large insurer with a household name across Europe is now engaged and operational.
- Several hundred tenants have subscribed to the scheme, so far with no defaults.
- A strong revenue stream has been generated, consistently growing at 30 per cent month on month.

- Rental passport data has been accumulated – 'Experian for tenants' – offering value for all parties.
- The recent emergence of competition indicates the strength of market take-up.

The team have plans for expansion to other geographies, especially the USA and Europe, drawing on evidenced success in the UK.

Learning

In summary:

- It is difficult for a small player to disrupt an established market, even where there are evident current problems. Significant progress was achieved when a major insurer agreed to engineer a new product under the framework of a corporate innovation scheme.
- To succeed, the redesign of the ecosystem must build a case for change that benefits all parties.
- The design of a new technology platform can benefit from retaining existing processes and conventions where possible, reworking only those that need to be changed or replaced.
- Exploiting the potential of data collected can be a significant additional benefit of digital transformation. This contributes to a *smart letting* innovation that will benefit all stakeholders, including rewarding good behaviour by tenants. Through this, the current 'cottage industry' of property rental can be transformed into a high-performing digital operation.

Summary of Business Framing

Framing a business involves addressing the seven important questions covered by the principal sections of this chapter. Each section has discussed relevant considerations, suggested useful techniques, provided a range of real-world examples and illustrated approaches using a running case study. Each of these questions has been aligned with relevant subsequent chapters by which material addressed during framing will be elaborated.

The key points addressed are summarized below.

- It is important that the principal elements of a business venture are defined for common agreement and clarity of direction.

- o These elements and their natures have been introduced through a framework of seven questions comprising the 'five most important questions' relating to mission, measurement, customer, problem solved, and plan, supplemented for digital businesses with aspects of product and risk profile.
  - o A running case study has been introduced as a vehicle for general illustration of topics covered throughout the book.
  - o The business design template has been introduced in terms of its purpose, structure and intended usage.
- A mission statement provides a powerful means of focusing the purpose of a venture. A clear mission provides guidance for business design decisions.
  - o The purpose of a mission statement has been elaborated and illustrated.
  - o The qualities of a good and useful mission statement have been elaborated to provide design criteria.
- Building an understanding of the customer and the value offered by the business is central to its success.
  - o A technique to design a representation of the business ecosystem has been introduced, incorporating the customer relationships and also those of other key players, including partners, suppliers and regulators.
  - o The importance of analysing and balancing the value exchanges between ecosystem players has been stressed as a powerful consideration underpinning many design decisions.
- For a venture exploiting a digital innovation, it is important to have a clear way to express the nature of that offering from a range of perspectives, both internal and external to the business.
  - o Approaches to the framing and differentiation of a product or service offering using clear words, and from multiple perspectives, have been suggested and illustrated.
  - o The innovation that underlies any offering can be characterized using the framework introduced in Chapter 1. This can be helpful in determining its likely market impact, which in turn informs the required planning activities.
- Any business must create value for its ecosystem partners, and especially for its customers. A good test of this is to express that value in terms of the problem that it solves.
  - o The framing of an innovation as the solution to a problem has been discussed and illustrated, including the need for market research to test assumptions.
  - o The use of an ecosystem representation to express the underlying problems and solutions has been illustrated, including its application to inform the identification and assessment of options for capturing value back into the business.

- Measuring business achievement enables tracking of progress towards the mission.
  - A method has been introduced to relate mission, objectives and measures. This has been applied to show how to produce a collection of *smart* objectives for a business, together with KPIs whereby achievement of each can be tracked.
  - In establishing a set of key performance indicators, it is important to design a balanced and economic collection of lead and lag measures. This consideration has been elaborated and illustrated.
- Risk is inevitable. It is not inherently bad, but it needs to be understood and managed, and this can be a fast-changing aspect of the landscape.
  - The importance and scope of risk management have been elaborated, and the principal elements in the definition of a risk have been described.
  - A risk management technique involving the creation of a risk register has been introduced and described, including its application to the management of different kinds of business risks.
- The structural aspects of business framing need to be complemented by a plan of activity to make it happen. An initial plan provides focus on the key activities needed to set things off on the right footing.
  - The need for an outline plan has been stressed, even – and especially – in fast-moving markets where agility is needed. Lack of a plan can result in uncoordinated activity and waste of effort and resources.
  - The principal components of an initial plan have been elaborated, including required resources and a map of activity in the short, medium and longer term.

ANALYSIS EXERCISES

The table below lists six digital businesses to be used as subjects for the exercises that follow.

Business	Focus	Website
Darktrace	Cyber security	www.darktrace.com
Fitbit	Health, fitness and performance	www.fitbit.com
JustEat	Online takeaway food	www.just-eat.co.uk
Reposit	Property rental	www.getreposit.uk
Snapchat	Social media	www.snapchat.com
Sorry as a Service	Customer service and retention	www.sorryasaservice.com

Using information available in the public domain, address the questions below for at least one of the businesses listed.

1. The mission:
   (a) If the information available on the company's website includes a mission statement, how well does this align with the criteria suggested earlier?
   (b) If the information available does not include a mission statement, what would you suggest as a good mission for the business?

2. Measuring success:
   (a) What collection of smart objectives might be used to track achievement of its mission?
   (b) What would be a good balanced set of measures to evidence achievement of objectives?

3. The customer(s):
   (a) How would you characterize the ideal customer (person or organization) for the business?
   (b) Who are the principal players in the business's ecosystem?
   (c) What are the principal value exchanges with these players?
   (d) You may choose to answer parts (b) and (c) using an ecosystem representation.

4. The problem solved:
   (a) What problem(s) does the business address, for each of its principal customers?
   (b) How does it solve those problems?
   (c) How might the customer(s) express the value of having a solution to these problems?

5. The offering:
   (a) How would you phrase the offering's unique selling point?
   (b) Does the nature of the offering imply any co-innovation or co-adoption requirements?

6. Risks:
   (a) What would you say are the business's three principal risks?
   (b) Create a register of principal risks and proposals for how these might be managed.

7. Plan:
   (a) What do you think was the shape of the initial plan for the business?
   (b) What principal activities might the business consider for its future development and advancement? These may relate to technology, market, geography or a mix of these.

DESIGN EXERCISES

The design exercise at the end of Chapter 1 encouraged identification of a business idea to be developed incrementally by specific design exercises through subsequent chapters of the book. You are now equipped to begin framing the selected business idea using the elements introduced in this chapter.

1. The business design template is available for download from the companion website.
2. If you choose to use it, you can make a copy to document the design of your business.
3. For each of the seven elements of business framing, address the considerations recommended in this chapter, and document your decisions in the appropriate cell of the template.
4. Review the completed framing for consistency and completeness.
5. Capture separately any of the following:
   (a) Key points learned from the exercise.
   (b) Outstanding issues or uncertainties.

3 Promotion and Sales

Focus of This Chapter

Figure 3.1 illustrates how the material addressed by this chapter fits within the framework of considerations for business design.

The considerations addressed here elaborate upon the decisions made during business framing in the context of the question *who is the customer?*

These decisions made will guide and inform the considerations that apply to delivering and operating the business and to all of those relating to *achieving business objectives*. It is important that consistency is achieved and sustained across the decisions made in relation to each component of the framework.

Learning Outcomes

After studying this chapter, you will:

- Be able to assess market segmentation, size and landscape, to inform promotion activity.
- Be able to analyse the market forces that affect competition, collaboration and negotiation.
- Be able to analyse, prioritize and plan promotional activities that align with objectives.
- Appreciate the need for stakeholder management, value exchange and customer communities.
- Understand the need and benefit of applying innovation to promotional activities.

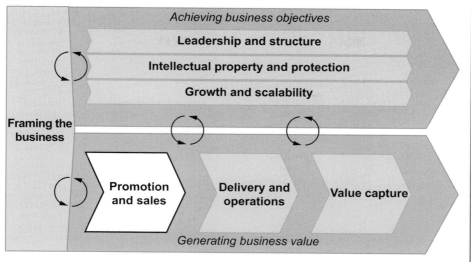

Figure 3.1 *Context of promotion and sales*

Introducing Promotion and Sales

Promotion, also referred to as marketing, or demand generation, is about establishing an attractive, distinctive and accessible position within a *targeted market*. It is also about doing this effectively, using methods that are affordable and which avoid the need for remedial activity to correct mistakes.

Sales is about enhancing the value of the venture through an exchange of value with a customer. At the *point of sale*, a contract is enacted whereby possession, or licence of a good or property, or the entitlement to a service, is exchanged for money, or for some other value. It is also about building communities of customers that enhance the venture's future development.

Whereas promotion is about opening the right kinds of opportunities, sales is about closing these into deliverable and value-creating contractual agreements. Although closely related, these activities involve different considerations and techniques, and require different talents. Effective synchronization of promotional and sales activities drives growth by establishing a beneficial feedback relationship by which each activity enhances the other.

Figure 3.2 shows the material covered by this chapter in the form of a value chain.

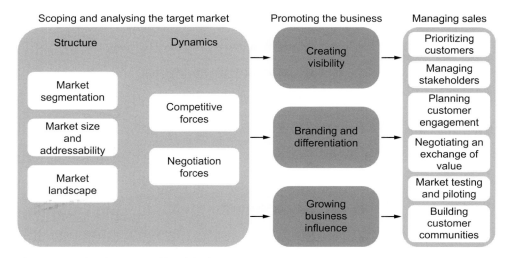

Scoping and analysing the target market   Promoting the business   Managing sales

Figure 3.2 *Topics covered by this chapter*

The considerations addressed embrace what is needed to generate and satisfy customer demand to achieve the defined objectives:

- *Scoping and analysing the target market structure* is about defining, quantifying and understanding the customer communities to which promotional activities must be targeted.
- *Scoping and analysing the target market dynamics* is about assessing the opportunities and threats implied by the market's competitive, negotiation and collaboration forces.
- *Promoting the business* is about creating visibility and building brand value and influence in the market, taking account of costs and benefits.
- *Managing sales* is about converting opportunities into value for the venture by managing customer stakeholders, planning customer engagement, negotiating fair exchanges and building communities of advocates that will contribute to the feedback loop of continuing development.

For each topic, this chapter introduces and illustrates relevant considerations and techniques, and the SportMagenta case study introduced in Chapter 2 continues as a rolling example.

A final brief section stresses the importance of applying the innovative capability of the venture throughout all promotional and sales activities.

Although logically sequential, business framing, promotion, delivery and value capture overlap in respect of some of the considerations involved. This means that a decision made during the design of the delivery or value-capture approach may prompt a review of the original framing or promotional decisions. The point was illustrated by the example of Bright Funds, introduced in Chapter 1. In the case of that venture, the initial framing assumed that the customer was an individual with a social conscience. The promotional approach followed suit and defined a plan for identifying and engaging such people. However, value capture considerations demonstrated that a corporate customer framing would be more effective, hence prompting a review of the original framing, with consequential changes to promotional and delivery-related decisions.

Scoping and Analysing the Target Market Structure

As shown in Chapter 2, the design of a business ecosystem involves making assumptions about who is the customer. Through that activity, business framing indicates a broad *target market* to which the proposition will be promoted. Effective promotional and sales activities, however, need greater focus and qualification of the customer, especially in terms of:

- *Segmentation*: how the market subdivides, and what interest across segments the venture will assume.
- *Size and addressability*: quantifying the extent of the market, including determining how best to express this, and assessing how much of the market can or will be addressed by the venture.
- *Landscape*: characterizing the nature of the market in terms of its maturity and the existing players, and assessing the implications of this on the venture.

Market Segmentation

Segmentation is about dividing a wider heterogeneous market into more homo-geneous subsets that have common needs, preferences and priorities. For example, 'white males aged between 30 and 55 with gross annual income between $100,000 and $250,000' is a segment, as is 'European businesses that employ more than 250 people and have a turnover in excess of $20 million'.

Having identified a broad customer proposition, the purpose of market seg-mentation is to create focus for promotional activities. Different segments can have different requirements and hence may need to be addressed differently, and it can be necessary or advantageous to address segments in a particular sequence. Deciding on initial and subsequent segments to be targeted enables promotional activities to be planned on the basis of specific needs and preferences.

Segmentation can apply to any of the following non-mutually exclusive criteria:

- *Geographic*: relating to subdivision by country or region. Due to the widespread application of geographic segmentation, several standard segment identifiers have emerged, including NA (North America), UK&I (the UK and Ireland), EMEA (Europe, Middle-East and Africa), EMEIA (Europe, Middle-East, India and Africa) and APAC (Asia Pacific).
- *Demographic*: relating to subdivision based on qualities such as age, gender, occupation or education. Examples of demographic segments include 'young professional females' or '18–34 year olds with degree-level education'.
- *Behavioural*: relating to subdivision based on qualities such as attitude, readiness or loyalty. Examples of behavioural segments include 'early adopters of sports wearables' or 'current account customers who have stayed with the same bank for more than 10 years'.
- *Psychographic*: relating to subdivision based on qualities such as lifestyle, including activities, interests and opinions. Examples of psychographic segments include 'regular users of multiple social media channels' or 'frequent attenders of car auctions'.

It can be a useful discipline to apply these dimensions to identify and evaluate alternative possible segmentations for the customer communities identified in the business ecosystem. Evaluation of possible target markets requires market research across segments.

Case Study: SportMagenta

Market Segmentation

In their framing of the venture's business objectives, the founders initially assume the target customer segment for initial promotional focus to be geographically limited to the UK and to include the larger chains of sports and fitness clubs such as Virgin Active, Pure Gym and Fitness First. Market research confirms that there are around ten chains currently within this segment.

The founders make this choice because, in their judgement, it opens the most likely route towards achieving rapid widespread usage of their offering. Additionally, this decision enables the venture to exercise the existing knowledge and experience within the team and avoids the costs and risks involved in building an international capability early in the life of the company.

This decision enables Zara and Sonny to assess the market size for their venture. It will also inform the approach to be adopted when engaging with customers, as these are likely to share the common interests and problems of running large chains of fitness clubs. End-users – or consumers – of the offering will be UK members and visitors to chains of sports clubs. Research shows that these fit the following segmentation:

Demographic – 18–60 years of age, mid-income and above.
Behavioural – positive attitude towards technology.
Psychographic – lifestyle – club members tend to be sociable and gregarious.

In terms of future market development, options will need to be evaluated. For example, the next segment could be selected to extend geographic focus by targeting chains in Europe or the USA. Alternatively, the founders could choose next to address a different psychographic segment, such as stadia sports or music events. These could potentially be adopted in parallel if the business has the marketing and delivery capacity.

Market Size and Addressability

When assessing market size for a business, it is important first to distinguish and clarify the market segmentation assumptions. The worldwide market size for a security device will be significantly larger than that for a specific geographic region, and the market size for such a device will also differ depending on whether it targets large, medium or smaller businesses.

A useful technique is to distinguish three different levels of addressable market, as illustrated in Figure 3.3.

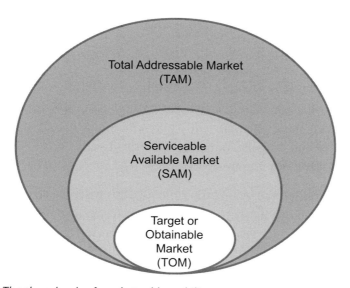

Figure 3.3 *The three levels of market addressability*

- The *total addressable market* (TAM) is the total potential demand for an offering, assuming the whole available market can be achieved.
- Within the TAM, the *serviceable available market* (SAM) is that part of the market that can realistically be served by the business taking into account factors such as competition, available routes to market and product or regulatory constraints.
- Within the SAM, the *target or obtainable market* (TOM) is that portion that can practically be obtained by executing the current plan.

Assessing the Total Addressable Market for a Business

There are many approaches to assessing the TAM, and various ways in which it can usefully be expressed. The following examples illustrate some TAM formulations:

- According to Gartner, worldwide spending on information security will reach $75 billion for 2015, an increase of 4.7 per cent over 2014.
- It has been estimated by Statistica that, by 2017, there will be almost 2.6 billion smartphone users in the world.
- According to Spil Games, more than 1.2 billion people are playing games worldwide, and of those, about 700 million play online games.

The units in which market sizes are expressed can be significant to a plan or investment proposal, and so must be chosen with reference to the nature of the offering and the economics of that market.

Behind this point is the crucial importance of choosing the right market to measure. For example, a venture that plans to launch a new online computer game to improve the teaching of grammar in schools might potentially use any of the following as the basis of the TAM:

- The number of computers in schools.
- The number of school children with online access.
- The number of school children that currently play online games.
- The number of people that currently play online games.
- The current spend on educational computer software.
- The current spend on grammar teaching.

The choice depends on the value proposition. In this case, the answer will depend on whether the proposition is to enable schools to compete better, or to enable parents to provide greater assistance to their children, or to support a government policy relating to enhanced teaching of grammar. This illustrates the importance of first framing the business before addressing considerations of promotion.

Wherever possible, the chosen measure for the TAM should be checked from multiple angles, to give greater confidence to the business and greater credibility to any case for investment or support.

The TAM for a business can be calculated or it can be asserted with reference to external sources. Clearly, caution needs to be applied regarding the independence or otherwise of any external market assessment that is to be adopted, but a recent and reasonably independent source is usually the preferable basis for this measure, especially if it is to be used within an investment proposal.

Where no market source is available, and so market size needs to be calculated, one of two common approaches can be chosen:

Bottom-Up (or Demand-Side) TAM Calculation
Compute the TAM based on the following three questions:

• Who needs the offering, can afford it and find it? In other words, what is the target segment?
• How many of these kinds of people or organizations exist today? In other words, what is the extent of that segment?
• How much does, or could, each of these spend every year solving the problem addressed?

Top-Down (or Supply-Side) TAM Calculation
Compute the TAM by addressing the question: what is the annual cost to the market of solving the problem that is addressed by the offering?

The world of cybercrime can illustrate a top-down calculation. According to Hiscox (2017), cybercrime cost the global economy over $450 billion in 2016. This gives the annual cost of solving the problem, hence the TAM for an offering that purports to address the problem. Clearly, such a number does not give a realistic indication of the likely sales of a product, but it shows that the market into which the offering will be launched provides significant capacity.

Assessing the Serviceable Available Market for a Business
This is usually calculated by considering what proportion of the total can be achieved within a particular time period for the targeted segment(s) of the market, taking account of a range of factors, including: the likely effectiveness of the available routes to market, any inherent latency in take-up (perhaps due to regulation requirements), the likely proportion of users that can be expected

to adopt the offering, the impact of any competitive activity and other con-straining factors.

When calculating the SAM for an offering, the approach used to calculate the TAM can again be applied, although in a qualified way:

- Within the target segment(s), how many customers can realistically be accessed by the business?
- Of those that can realistically be accessed, how much does, or could, each of these spend every year solving the problem addressed?

Cautionary points when calculating SAM:

- Be wary of simply assuming that an arbitrarily small percentage can be achieved of a very large TAM. This can lead to overly ambitious and indefens-ible numbers. It is difficult and time-consuming to achieve even a small percentage of a very large market.
- It is important to factor into the assessment the impact of other things that are happening in the market, including competitive developments and disrup-tive forces, as well as in respect of assumed co-adoption or co-innovation trends.

When asserting a SAM, it is important to make explicit all the applicable assumptions, and to continually check these against market knowledge and experience.

Assessing the Target or Obtainable Market for a Business

Whereas the SAM defines the totality of the market that is achievable by the business with the assumed routes to market, the TOM for a business defines that proportion that is practically achievable by the current business plan. This may be the whole of the SAM, a shorter-term subset, or a portion that is obtainable through executing only limited routes to market, or by deploying only a limited form of the offering.

Importantly, where the TOM is applied within an investment proposal, it is important that it is credible and achievable. This means that all assumptions are clearly expressed, and that tracking of progress can be established.

For disruptive offerings, the latency of change should not be underestimated. This point has been addressed by Martin Gladwell (2002), author and staff writer at *The New Yorker*, where he refers to the difficulty of 'getting past the tipping point'.

Case Study: SportMagenta

Market Size Assessment

In their framing of the business, the founders assumed that they could achieve a proportion of the additional revenue available to sports clubs and promoters of relevant products and services. This is the quantity that needs to be assessed to define the venture's market size.

There is no available independent market data for the specific market, but the founders are able to find relevant data on the components needed to make a reasonable calculation. Using this data, the TAM can be assessed at being in the region of $18 billion per annum, applying a bottom-up approach as shown in the table below.

Illustrative TAM Calculation for SportMagenta

(a) worldwide sports club membership	150m
(b) average monthly spend by visitors on non-membership products and services	$50
(c) average monthly spend by visitors on promoted products and services	$25
(d) annual non-membership revenue by clubs ((a) × (b) × 12)	$90bn
(e) annual potential revenue from promoted products and services ((a) × (c) × 12)	$45bn
(f) assumed potential to increase club non-membership revenues	15%
(g) assumed potential to increase promoter's revenues	10%
TAM (((d) × (f)) + ((e) × (g)))	$18bn

The founders apply a similar approach to quantify a UK-specific SAM that disregards inactive users of clubs, as these are unlikely to contribute any enhanced value. This market is calculated to be in the region of $825 million per annum, as shown in the table below.

Illustrative SAM Calculation for SportMagenta

(a) UK sports club membership	9m
(b) active users of sports clubs	5m
(c) average monthly spend by visitors on non-membership products and services	$75

(d)	average monthly spend by visitors on promoted products and services	$25
(e)	annual non-membership revenue by clubs ((b) × (c) × 12))	$4.5bn
(f)	annual potential revenue from promoted products and services ((b) × (d) × 12))	$1.5bn
(g)	assumed potential to increase club non-membership revenues	15%
(h)	assumed potential to increase promoter's revenues	10%
SAM (((e) × (g)) + ((f) × (h)))		$825m

For the TOM, the founders calculate a number in the region of $25 million per annum, which takes into account active members within a single chain of UK clubs, as shown in the table below.

Illustrative TOM Calculation for SportMagenta

(a)	target sector membership	250k
(b)	active users of sports clubs	150k
(c)	average monthly spend by visitors on non-membership products and services	$75
(d)	average monthly spend by visitors on promoted products and services	$25
(e)	annual non-membership revenue by clubs ((b) × (c) × 12))	$135m
(f)	annual potential revenue from promoted products and services ((b) × (d) × 12))	$45m
(g)	assumed potential to increase club non-membership revenues	15%
(h)	assumed potential to increase promoter's revenues	10%
TOM (((e) × (g)) + ((f) × (h)))		$24.75m

Market Landscape

Describing the market landscape of a business involves addressing multiple facets. Each of these in its own way can have a bearing on many aspects of business design, including decisions around promotion.

Three facets need to be understood and considered:

- The division of market share.
- The impact of dominant players.
- The maturity of the market.

The Division of Market Share

Market share can be measured either by value or by volume, and these are not necessarily aligned.

For example, according to Statistica, more than 268 billion mobile apps will have been downloaded by 2017. Comparable figures show that 130 billion apps have been downloaded from Apple's App Store to 2016, suggesting that, by volume, Apple has approximately 50 per cent of the mobile app market. However, according to Digi-Capital, in terms of revenue generated for app providers, the market share is more strongly dominated by Google.

In cases where value and volume shares appear to be out of alignment, it is important to consider which of these is most important to the venture's value proposition.

And it can be important to understand this from both supply and demand perspectives: knowing the respective market share (and hence stability and level of ambition) of potential suppliers can be as important as knowing it for potential channel partners and customers.

The Impact of Dominant Players

Markets can be classified as follows:

- *Perfect competition*: many companies, freedom of entry for buyers and sellers.
- *Monopoly*: one seller and many buyers – for example, utility providers in some countries.
- *Oligopoly*: a small number of sellers and many buyers – for example, mobile networks.
- *Monopsony*: one buyer and many sellers – for example, government defence procurement.
- *Oligopsony*: a small number of buyers and many sellers – for example, some commodity markets.

In general, as a market matures, the effect of consolidation tends to establish a small number of significant players, as in the case of mobile technology platforms, banks or mobile service providers. Designing a business to address the players in such a market can mean taking quite a different approach than in the case where there are myriad medium and smaller players. In the latter case, it is more important – and can be more difficult – to target those that are most likely to grow in significance.

Consequently, it is important to appreciate how market share is currently divided across existing players in the target market: whether there is a single dominating player, a small number of significant players or an absence of any dominant player.

When designing a venture to address a market with a small number of large players and many smaller players, an important decision needs to be taken about whether to focus on the large, the small or potentially both. There can be good reasons for adopting either of these, but the decision must be based on a clear rationale. Furthermore, this decision may have an impact on the choice of sources of supply and on channel partners; an offering that targets providers of mobile platforms might benefit from selecting an independent hosting provider.

Market landscapes are not inherently good or bad for a venture: the important point is to understand the landscape of the target market and to take informed and rational decisions about how to succeed within it.

The Maturity of the Market

This overlaps with the previous facet in that newer and less mature markets are likely to have myriad players on both supply- and demand-sides. When operating in such markets, a venture continually faces the risk of 'backing the wrong horse'. An apparently good decision can prove disastrous if, say, an unsupported standard is mandated, or a significant consolidation occurs between other players.

In less mature markets, the risks can be higher, but so can the gains. If a new market grows rapidly in value and the business has positioned itself well, the benefit can be substantial. Consider YouTube, for example. The business was set up in 2005 by three founders working for PayPal. The online video-sharing market at the time was very immature with many players, including Google Video. YouTube positioned and promoted itself so well that during the summer of 2006 it was one of the fastest-growing web-based businesses. In November 2016, the company was acquired by Google for $1.65 billion. Google judged that it could not afford to miss out on the growing popularity being achieved by YouTube in a market that clearly offered enormous future potential.

One helpful consideration by way of external perspective is the position of the market on Gartner's *hype curve for emerging technologies* (introduced in Chapter 1), where this is relevant to the technology used by the offering. In general terms, the further to the right the market appears on the curve, the lower the risk of unpredicted change in the market dynamics. Those markets to the left of the curve tend to be highly dynamic in terms of the emergence of new players, and the intensity of mergers and acquisitions, hence posing a higher risk/reward ratio for new entrants. For example, the market for gesture-controlled devices is at an early stage, whereas that for virtual reality offerings is consolidating with the emergence of large players.

A principal consideration for business design is therefore whether the venture's risk appetite is consistent with the degree of risk that is inherent in the current maturity of the market landscape, on both supply- and demand-sides.

Scoping and Analysing the Target Market Dynamics

This is about anticipating the likely dynamics of interactivity with the principal other players in the ecosystem. The value of analysing dynamics in this way is that it enables a venture to identify its strengths, weaknesses and vulnerabilities, and hence informs a plan for how best to capitalize on opportunities and to mitigate or avoid risks.

A useful workshop tool for identifying and analysing market dynamics has been developed by Michael Porter, a Professor at Harvard Business School.

Porter (1979) proposed a *five forces* model that combines the related considerations of competition and negotiation into a single framework. That original model is extended here to include a sixth force, *collaboration*, so that the model better reflects entrepreneurial principles and current business practices. The resulting *six forces* model is shown in Figure 3.4.

Of these six forces, those presented horizontally relate to competition, and those presented vertically relate to negotiation. The central forces –*industry rivalry* and *collaboration* – relate to both.

The application of this model to the analysis of market dynamics is here presented with reference first to competition, and then to negotiation.

Competitive Forces

Competitive forces can impact the ability of a business to fully execute its plan to deploy an offering into a market. The effect of such forces is to drive a need for clear differentiation of the offering, and to influence the style of messaging used. These forces can also encourage collaboration with other players. If the

Figure 3.4 *Porter's market forces model – modified to recognize collaboration*

applicable forces can be exploited advantageously, then the offering can be deployed successfully into the market; if not, the traction achieved can be limited and the venture may be forced to accept a change in its planned approach.

As collaboration applies universally across the model, it is addressed across the coverage of each of the other forces, rather than in isolation.

Industry Rivalry

The central competitive force is referred to as *industry rivalry*. This relates to the impact on the business of other offerings that claim a similar, comparable, overlapping or otherwise related value proposition.

The existence of other rival offerings can be positive in demonstrating the liveliness and desirability of a market. In many situations, customers like to have optional products from which they can choose. It is important to understand all rival offerings and to be able to differentiate the venture's offering from each of them in terms of approach, benefits and disadvantages. It is also important that rival companies and their offerings are treated with respect.

Steve Denning (2012), a business consultant, author and market commentator, writing in *Forbes online*, observes that: 'The business reality of today is that the only safe place against the raging innovation is to join it. Instead of seeing business ... as a matter of figuring out how to defeat one's known rivals and protect oneself against competition through structural barriers, if a business is to survive, it must aim to add value to customers through continuous innovation and finding new ways of delighting its customers'.

Accepting Denning's observation, it is important to appreciate the impact on rivalry of inherent differences between disruptive and sustaining innovations in a market. A disruptive offering that is introduced into a market is likely to be less performant in certain respects to its rivals, but is equally likely to be significantly different and advantageous in others. For the venture that introduces a disruptive offering, the principal challenge is to communicate effectively the benefits of the disruption that is being offered, and to address any concerns about areas of lower performance. This is also important to mitigate the attention that the disrupter is likely to draw from the existing players, who may collaborate in some way to protect an existing market dynamic.

One instance of the force of collaboration is where existing players (even competitors) work together to block a new entrant by jointly agreeing to a price reduction or by joining forces to mount a negative publicity campaign. This can be seen in the collaboration of existing taxi operators and the Hailo app to combat the entrance of Uber into their marketplace.

Other applications of collaboration can include an overt approach by a business to one or more rivals to collaborate to the mutual benefit of the players involved, and to the disadvantage of others. This may relate to joint agreements within a particular market segment or to some form of product integration to yield a more powerful joint offering against specific rivals.

There are many examples of this kind of collaboration, especially in the technology sector. The enterprise platform initiative formed by a collaboration between Intel, Microsoft and Cisco has been analysed in detail by Gawer and Cusumano (2002). Three significant examples emerged in 2017: IBM and Cisco announced a collaboration in the context of threat intelligence; Apple and Accenture formed a collaboration to challenge Microsoft's position as the default operating system within enterprises; and Amazon and Microsoft announced Gluon as a new machine intelligence library designed collaboratively to make it easier for developers to create machine learning-enabled applications.

Threat of New Entrants

The *threat of new entrants* applies to a business that has established a degree of market presence, including competitive and collaborative relationships with other players, and is therefore likely to be inclined to resist the entry of new players into the mix.

In some cases, a new entry might be seen as a friendly ally against existing rivals, in which case another application of collaboration can be brought into effect to disadvantage other current players. For example, Toyota has encouraged Microsoft to enter the *autotech* market through a collaboration that is delivering new in-car internet-connected services for its vehicles, while at the same time disadvantaging those rivals who do not have access to the same technology base.

Some markets have inherent *barriers to entry* or *exit*. A barrier to entry is a specialist requirement for a business to be able to operate in a particular market. This can be the need for accreditation or licensing, for specialist skills or knowledge, or for support for an established standard. Because stringently enforced barriers to entry deter new entrants, existing players – potentially acting collaboratively – tend to be assiduous in ensuring that the necessary criteria are rigorously applied to putative new entrants.

A barrier to exit is an obstacle that limits the ability of a business to leave or to be displaced from a market. This often relates to a long-term contract or commitment. Barriers to exit can be positive or negative: on the one hand, they make it difficult for a business to be displaced by competitors; on the other hand, they can limit the ability of a business to pivot away from an undesirable market.

Understanding inherent barriers is an important aspect of market understanding, and can help to inform a range of activities, including competitive response. For example, a business that addresses a health-care, defence or security market is likely to need to invest significant activity to overcome barriers to entry ahead of achieving any significant traction.

Timing is always important. In a market with major players, large procurement activities can attract new entrants who see the activity as a way to enter a market. Conversely, missing out on such activities can lead to significant weakening of market position. This means that it becomes a competitive imperative to be aware of large forthcoming events and to invest effort – potentially collaborative – to establish a strong competitive position. This applies particularly to large government procurement activities.

Threat of Substitutes

A substitute is an offering from another party that, although differently packaged and presented, can nevertheless produce the same or similar effect as that being offered by the business. For example, the market for digital cameras has been disrupted by the increasingly high-quality cameras embedded within mobile phones. In many cases, substitutes can be more difficult to anticipate and to mitigate against than new entrants to a market.

In many recent cases, substitutes have emerged through horizontal market offerings from the *sharing economy*, illustrated through the various Uber-like services that are now available for accommodation, car parking and so on. Mitigating against substitutes usually involves strengthening the business case for adopting a specific market offering rather than a more generic platform, and collaborating with like-minded rivals to establish a powerful market response.

Collaboration between existing players and disruptive substitutes can suit both parties, especially in the fintech sector, where an established player can protect its core market by developing innovative partnerships, such as that which has been established between Santander with Kabbage, a US-based small and medium-sized enterprise (SME) lending platform that helps small business customers to gain access to capital.

Negotiation Forces

The market forces of negotiation can have a significant effect on the framing of a venture and on its pricing. It can also encourage new forms of collaboration, including those that can help to control the costs of purchases.

As above, because collaboration applies universally across the model, it is addressed across the coverage of all other forces, rather than in isolation.

Industry Rivalry

As with competitive forces, industry rivalry is the central force affecting negotiation. In this context, it relates to the impact on price and performance of other comparable offerings.

The implications of competitive forces on pricing are addressed comprehensively in Chapter 5, so are not elaborated here.

An interesting case occurs when a disruptive offering is introduced into an existing market where it will compete with a collection of existing rivals. Because the experience offered to customers by the new disruptive innovation may differ radically from that of familiar offerings, it is important that the venture invests focused promotional effort to overcome any inherent resistance, perhaps by offering a very attractive initial pricing model or by collaborating with an existing well-known player to give confidence. This is the approach that was adopted by Reposit, the disruptive *proptech* business that was described in the case study in Chapter 2. In that example, the business overcame the natural caution of both tenants and agencies by offering significant financial advantages and partnering with a household name insurance player.

Bargaining Power of Suppliers

For ventures that need a specialist or high-cost supply chain, the negotiating power with suppliers can be a major driver of profitability, and hence viability and success in a market.

Ventures that have sophisticated supply requirements may be faced with few options, and hence their suppliers' negotiating position may be strong. Although it is unlikely to be in a supplier's interest to charge a price that makes their customer unviable, it is in their interest to charge as much as the customer can sustain. It is important in such cases to anticipate this requirement at an early stage and hence to prioritize the need to identify substitute suppliers to increase negotiating power.

A business can increase its bargaining power with suppliers by collaborating through a supply agreement or joint venture. Either of these can create a barrier to entry for other suppliers, and also a barrier to exit for the chosen supplier. Longer-term arrangements can mitigate the risk of unexpected price hikes, or the loss of supply due to an exclusive arrangement with a rival.

Another collaboration approach that can strengthen negotiating power involves providing a channel to market for a range of supplier offerings through a *white labelling* approach. This involves providing a branded and reputable platform for promoting and selling suppliers' offerings. Ticket Evolution is an example of a business that has adopted this approach by offering close integration with suppliers of tickets. The inventories are aggregated and promoted to individuals and brokers. Customers purchasing tickets are aware only of the Ticket Evolution brand, and the business's growing market reputation and strength helps to protect its bargaining power when dealing with ticket suppliers.

Bargaining Power of Buyers

As with supply dynamics, the negotiating power of a business decreases with the availability of comparable alternative offerings. This means that the specific benefits of an offering need to be articulated to sustain a price differential. A strong approach is to demonstrate a *return on investment* (ROI) to the customer that is expressed in their language and that cannot also be claimed by rivals.

Sorry as a Service is a business that works with corporate customer service operations. Their proposition is a promise to improve customer retention and value by creatively recovering from mistakes or bad experiences. Their success has been driven by their promotion of an evidenced ROI that uses customer service language to express benefits such as 'up to 50% after-complaint churn reduction' and '+13.4% NPS improvement'. The latter benefit relates to the *net promoter score*, a customer loyalty measure based on likelihood that a customer would recommend an offering to a friend or colleague.

This strong and confident ROI strengthens their bargaining power when negotiating with corporate customers.

The *price sensitivity* of an offering can be a critical determinant of the negotiation power of the venture:

- Offerings with closely comparable competitors tend to be price sensitive: if the price is increased, then the customer is less likely to purchase.
- Offerings that can demonstrate an evidenced ROI relating to customer financial benefit or proven reduction of risk can be less sensitive to price, and hence increase bargaining power with customers.

Just as collaboration with suppliers can help to reduce the cost and risk of supply, collaboration with customers can help to build loyalty and encourage repeat business, hence increasing bargaining power. Customer collaborations can include event sponsorships, joint research and development, longer-term or exclusive arrangements and mutually beneficial joint ventures.

Case Study: SportMagenta

Analysing Market Dynamics

The founders' market research confirms that industry rivalry is currently low: the SportMagenta offering is breaking new ground in the sport club marketplace.

They recognize, however, that their success is likely to provoke new entrants, some of which might be *copycat* offerings launched by other chains of clubs or their software partners. Accepting that this cannot be avoided, the founders decide that the best mitigation is likely to be through creating strong and loyal collaborative relationships with chains of clubs and their memberships, to create relationship-based barriers to entry. This will include a programme of sponsorships and special events to continually enhance the SportMagenta brand across clubs.

To strengthen this further, Zara and Sonny decide to explore options to collaborate with a range of suppliers of digital services into clubs, including options for *white labelling* of additional services directly to visitors through the SportMagenta app, both in currently served clubs and in others. This might include, for example, league management software that is currently used by sports clubs, but which could also be *white labelled* for individuals to use across their own communities. Such initiatives would again build barriers to entry for new entrants.

It is acknowledged that a potential substitute could emerge through clubs exploiting the increased interactive capabilities of digital display panels. The founders decide to tolerate this risk and to ensure that their development programme prioritizes the value of a personalized mobile service.

External hosting services are the principal supply requirement for SportMagenta. As there are now multiple reliable and performant suppliers of such services, with low barriers to entry or exit, price performance will be the sole criterion for choice.

The founders have decided upon a pricing model based on revenue sharing with both clubs and sponsors. This means that the way to strengthen the venture's negotiating position for a higher share of revenues will require demonstrating a substantial ROI that is uniquely attributable to SportMagenta. Conversely, the venture's bargaining power will weaken if additional revenues are not forthcoming.

Consequently, the founders are aware of the need to collaborate closely with clubs to ensure that the offering is established and supported as an effective channel to increase visitors' spend at the club.

Together with collaborative initiatives to build loyalty so as to frustrate new entrants, this is the principal dynamic that needs to drive business decisions.

Promoting the Business

The very wide range of promotion methods can be double-edged. On the one hand, it has never been so easily possible to reach so many people so rapidly at so little cost; on the other hand, it can be difficult to capture peoples' attention when they are continually bombarded with messaging.

This section is about identifying and qualifying approaches for attracting the attention of customers and other significant players within the targeted market segments, taking account of their likely relative effectiveness, costs and benefits. The approaches explored are grouped into the following categories:

- Creating visibility and customer awareness.
- Branding and differentiation.
- Growing business influence in the market.

Creating Visibility

This section focuses on two important questions:

- To whom does the business need to be visible?
- How will the business most effectively make itself attractive to those parties?

The first question relates to the business ecosystem, and the principal parties involved. First and foremost, visibility is required across the chosen segment(s) of the customer market to create the right kind of awareness around the offering, its applications and benefits.

Additionally, and depending on the nature and priorities of the business, visibility may also be needed across other parties identified in the business ecosystem, including:

- Channel partners: offering routes to market.
- Development partners: offering product integration or support services for financial transactions, communications, security or access control.
- Investors: offering future funding options.
- Recruiters: offering access to wider pools of talent.

Clearly, the messaging offered to each of these players will differ, although – as per the branding considerations addressed below – it is important that brand image is consistent across all communications activities.

There are myriad promotional methods and channels by which a venture can appeal to parties of all types and sizes. For clarity, these are grouped here into several categories. The expertise and networking capabilities of PR agencies provide an alternative to in-house management for any of these.

Proactive Communications
These include generic mailshots, purchased or compiled contact lists, and targeted approaches to identified individuals. Contact can be by email, phone, text or face-to-face.

Website
This is the venture's shop window, possibly accessed through multiple domain names to establish related names and provide options for differently focused campaigns. The website may simply offer an introduction to the business and its offerings, or it may provide a comprehensive online portal for customer engagement, transactions and support.

Search engine optimization and sponsored links or pay-per-click adverts can be invaluable in ensuring that the website can easily be found by interested parties.

Mutual links with partners, ambassadors and other parties with a strong online profile can be significant in driving web traffic towards the site.

Where a site has been designed to operate principally as an introduction to the business, it is important to encourage continuing contact with relevant visitors. A common technique for doing this is to encourage the visitor to express their specific needs or interests, or to offer attractive resources or services in exchange for contact details. This latter point relates to the need for business collateral such as white papers, technical summaries, case studies, brochures and flyers, which can also serve to demonstrate the venture's maturity and competence.

Other Online Communications

These include a wide range of services and tools, such as:

- Social media networks, including LinkedIn, Facebook, Twitter, Google Plus and YouTube, which should be used proportionately and with sensitivity to the culture of the target communities.
- Viral giveaway competitions that encourage people to promote the message across their networks by offering an enhanced opportunity to win an attractive prize.
- Blogging and online communities, which give an opportunity to be provocative and drive interest to the venture's website or to specific individuals.
- Search engine local directories, such as Bing, Google Local, Yahoo!Local or Yell, in cases where a local physical presence is important to the business.
- Catalogues, including app stores, for listing and advertisement of offerings, and also in most cases as a delivery and payment mechanism.

Partner or Channel Relationships

Relationships with partner organizations can provide positive and extensive market promotion. Three kinds of partnership are addressed here by way of illustration.

Compatible-product partnerships apply where a venture's offerings are compatible or potentially closely aligned or integrated with those of another business operating in the same market. In such cases, it can be mutually beneficial for each business to promote the others' offerings to enhance both brands through association. In some cases, jointly branded market solutions might also be developed through joint activity.

An example of this is the IBM and Cisco plan to collaborate in the development of threat intelligence solutions. Another example is the joint activity between the Indian IT services and outsourcing business Wipro and the US-based enterprise services business DXC Technology (formed by the merger of HPE Enterprise Services and CSC) to exploit the compatible technology and skills bases of the two businesses to deliver consumption-based IT infrastructures. Both initiatives were announced in 2017 and in both cases the participating businesses judge that the combined power of the partnership will provide increased competitiveness and market advantage.

Complementary-product partnerships operate between ventures that promote non-competing offerings that have the potential to be complementary within some market. By exploiting the complementary nature of their offerings, both ventures benefit through enhanced market access and potentially through an aggregated brand value. The Starbucks Digital Network agreement between Starbucks and Yahoo provided a tailored package of Yahoo web content that was delivered over Starbuck's free Wi-Fi network to both parties' advantage. Similarly, Walt Disney and YouTube jointly agreed back in 2011 to invest in an original video series to be produced by Disney and delivered over a co-branded channel on both Disney.com and YouTube.

Complementarity can also apply on a geographic axis, as in the case of the 2015 announcement of a tie-up between the US ride-sharing company Lyft and its Chinese equivalent, Didi Kuaidi.

Karray and Sigue (2016) analyse this partnership approach and conclude that the decision by a venture to enter into such an arrangement depends on evidence of a positive *spillover effect* on its product portfolio; in other words, the joint promotional effort must have the effect of enhancing the attractiveness or demand for both ventures' offerings.

Channel partners are businesses that deliver the offerings of others. They may or may not have offerings of their own. These include sales agencies, catalogue providers, distributors, value-added resellers, retailers and businesses that brand *white labelled* offerings. In all cases, a channel partner is motivated to promote the venture's offerings by the offer of a commission, royalty, finder's fee or other reward. When promoting a business through such channels, the resulting customer enquiries and purchasing requests may be handled either by the partner or may be referred directly to the venture.

An example of a value-added reseller in the UK software and services market is SBL. The company offers quality and security accreditation and an ability to provide access into many large public and private sector organizations. Ticket

Evolution is an example of a US business that offers a promotional channel specifically for ticket vendors. In this case, the company also handles sales and payment through a *white labelling* approach.

In any kind of promotional partnership, it is crucial to be clear about the messaging to be used for market communications, the expected customer engagement process, and the responsibilities and motivations of the parties involved. These topics are addressed further in Chapter 4 in the context of designing routes to market and the customer journey.

National and Local Media

Producing copy for the media, including TV, newspapers, magazines and radio, can be effective for some ventures in reaching a wide audience.

Two approaches are available:

- The venture purchases space (or airtime) for an *advertorial* – a piece of content that combines commentary, or *thought leadership*, with promotional material.
- The venture produces a true piece of commentary that is of sufficient interest to be accepted by the media. This approach can be more effective, as it carries the implied endorsement of the media channel, but it needs a story that is acceptable to the channel. With national-level media, journalistic freedom implies that the final wording may not be amenable to revision by the venture, and there is a risk that the publisher or broadcaster chooses to tell the story differently from that which is preferred by the venture.

When using media of any kind to promote a venture, it is important to be aware that there may be little control over adjacent material, which may be over-shadowing or undesirable.

Networking Events

Events can provide an opportunity to meet a range of useful contacts in a social environment. The promotional and sales value of a specifically organized event depends on getting the right people to it and on using the right structure and messaging to create the required effect.

To be effective, an event needs a clear purpose, such as:

- To mark a launch, anniversary or celebration of achievement.
- To introduce individuals from customer or partner organizations at a particular level of seniority.

- To address a market or technology, offering an opportunity to learn about or discuss a topic such as cyber security or AI.
- To provide an informal gathering aligned with a sports or cultural activity.

A good way to frame an event is to set objectives and KPIs for what will be achieved in terms of, for example, opening new contacts, learning about market problems or needs, or progressing specific sales opportunities. The purpose and objectives should help to determine the invitees, the kind of venue and an appropriate form for the event.

All planned events need to be designed with care to enhance the reputation of the business. They also need to be conducted with professionalism and respect for all participants. A well-conceived and organized event can be powerful in establishing the business at the centre of a wider market initiative that enhances credibility and hence business value. On the other hand, a poorly designed or chaotic event can have a very negative effect on a venture's reputation.

Wider public events such as national or international subject conferences or local business gatherings can also provide useful promotional opportunities. Any of these can provide the opportunity to enhance business credibility and visibility, especially where independently endorsed material is being presented.

Although organization or participation at an event does not usually lead directly to new sales, the venture's presence and performance can have a powerful effect in reinforcing the confidence of existing customers and partners, which feeds into enhanced value through greater likelihood of future business. For this reason, calculating ROI for event attendance is notoriously difficult.

A stock of relevant business collateral can help to broaden dialogue and extend contact with interested parties.

Costing the Effectiveness of the Techniques Applied

Each of the promotional approaches addressed above involves effort and cost, and some will inevitably be more cost-effective than others. Consequently, it is important to plan and monitor the effectiveness of the approaches explored and adopted, as follows:

- Using planning horizons of three months, six months and a year, decide upon the set of approaches to be considered.
- For each horizon, assess the implications of the decisions in terms of effort (how much and by whom) and cost.
- Determine which data will be captured to enable a cost-benefit analysis to be performed on the relative effectiveness of each technique that has been applied.

The cost per acquisition (CPA) is a widely used measure of effectiveness. It measures how much it costs to acquire a new customer, or to achieve a sale to a customer using a particular approach. The data required to assess CPA varies between approaches and markets, but having an approximate value can help avoid less-productive spend. It can be helpful to include internal spend on effort and external spend on services within the calculation of CPA.

In the specific case of adopting pay-per-click advertising to promote an offering, the cost per click (CPC) can be a useful measure of the cost to the business of each online interaction.

It can be difficult to separate the effects of different techniques, because there can be a valuable aggregate effect where a customer responds to one approach because of positive reputation achieved through another. This points towards a balanced approach of adopting multiple techniques that will together consolidate and reinforce the venture's messaging and ensure that customers and partners receive regular, consistent and intriguing communications from multiple sources.

Case Study: SportMagenta

Creating Visibility

Zara and Sonny understand the need to promote SportMagenta to each principal ecosystem party, and recognize that a range of lively and novel approaches are likely to be effective with the kinds of communities involved. They decide upon the following:

A personalized initial mailshot will be sent to each of the targeted chains of sports clubs. This will align the offering with that chain's current profile and interests. The mailshot will request a face-to-face meeting to demonstrate the capability and discuss its implementation. Independent recommendations will be sought from market professionals to add weight to the approach. A professional brochure will be produced and sent to the targeted clubs together with the mailshot. This will present the offering's benefits using the language of the specific chain, and outline a return on investment case. Having established contact, the founders know that they need to keep alive the promotional channels with each targeted club. This will be achieved through invitations to locally organized networking events involving sports personalities and industry commentators, plus intense social media activity, provocative blogging and advertisements in sporting magazines.

A similar approach will be used with promoters, although the sources of recommendations will be individuals that are known in the sports retail sector, and the brochure will focus on the enhanced retail opportunities that the offering presents.

For club members and visitors, the principal promotional approach will be endorsement and recommendation from clubs and sponsors, both of whom will be motivated to promote the offering. The messaging used by clubs will be echoed in the relevant app store entries for the service. This approach will be reinforced continually by a sporty and fresh design for the SportMagenta website together with the blogging and advertisements in sporting magazines. Wider interest from individuals will be attracted by search engine optimization, word-of-mouth recommendation from existing users, and mutual links with prominent vendors and accessory retailers.

Promotion to local leagues will be through sports clubs and their members and visitors. Zara and Sonny decide to encourage leagues to come to them for support rather than investing proactive effort developing relationships.

The founders set a budget of $10,000 for the first three months, a further $8,000 for the following three months, and $12,000 for the six months after that, to contain the spend that these decisions will entail. They also budget for an initial 2.5 days per week of Sonny's time to be spent on promotional activities. They decide to track performance of each promotional technique using CPA, which will require surveying stakeholders for their opinion on the effectiveness of each approach adopted.

Branding and Differentiation

A business's brand is what distinguishes it from everyone else. The outside world knows a business by its brand. A brand may refer to both company and product, although some businesses choose to develop, or acquire, multiple brands. A brand usually has an associated logo, and everything about the brand should reinforce the customer value propositions.

This is a much-published subject in its own right, and for more detail the reader is directed to Millman (2011), Wheeler (2013) or Wind and Findiesen Hays (2016). The principal concepts are as follows:

Brand image is the psychological association that a business builds through all of its various activities. This can have a very strong impact on customers' and partners' responses to an offering, beyond its specific technical merits. Creating a poor, inappropriate or confusing image can lead to long-term disadvantage or the need for expensive recovery activity. On the other hand, a positive brand image – such as is currently held by Apple or Amazon – encourages customer loyalty to existing offerings and guarantees acute interest in new developments.

Brand experience relates to peoples' actual experience of engaging in some way with the business or its offering, including the handling of enquiries, delivery and installation, configuration and integration, and continuing support and extension. Consistency of experience and alignment with the expectations set by the brand image are important so as not to undermine valuable and expensive reputation-building activities.

Brand management is about building *brand recognition* within a target market, and growing *brand value* through positive *image* and *experience*. Effective brand management can benefit multiple offerings associated with a brand.

Consequently, branding and brand management need to be factored into the design of all aspects of the business, from its recruitment advertisements and its various communications activities, to the design, delivery and protection of its offerings and all associated interactions with parties in its ecosystem. This topic is addressed further in Chapter 4 in the context of customer journey design, and in Chapter 7 in the context of intellectual property protection.

Many guidelines have been proposed to direct brand design. The following simple rules provide a checklist:

- The brand name and graphic should be *compatible with the business and its offerings*. The brand must fit culturally with the customer base.
- The components of the brand should be *coherent* in that any graphic imaging fits easily with any wording and font.
- The brand should *not be similar or comparable with another in a related market*. In addition to causing confusion, this may also attract legal action, as addressed in Chapter 7.
- The brand should be *easily identifiable at a distance*, including on presentation slides or on wall posters, and against different background colours. The latter point may require alternative colour versions with different backgrounds.
- The brand should *work at different sizes*, including when blown up large on a banner or welcome screen, and when rendered small, such as on the screen of a mobile device.
- The brand should *work both in colour and in greyscale*, as material may be printed in black and white. Some authorities also suggest that no more than two colours are used, in addition to black and white.
- In general, complex text or graphics should be avoided. *Simple and minimal designs* can be more effective.

Several commentators and publishers create annual lists of top brands by value. Although global, each listing tends to have a geographic bias. For example, the lists published by BrandFinance, Forbes and Interbrand take a US perspective, whereas that from B&T takes an Asia-Pacific perspective. All listings for 2017 show the two top global brands to be Apple and Google, with the Apple brand assessed at being worth well in excess of $150 billion. At least 50 per cent of each of the principal lists of top ten global brands are technology companies.

Brand value can contribute significantly to business value, which in turn contributes significantly to investment valuation and attractiveness, and to the willingness of people to join and stay with the business. With brand management, success breeds success.

Growing Business Influence

Influencers are individuals and organizations, recognized and respected by a market, which have the power to influence the way in which the market responds to a new initiative or venture. Understanding who and what these are and how they can be engaged to positive effect can help to catalyse customer interest and build confidence in an innovation.

Four types of influence are addressed here: customer advocacy, awards, accreditations and market analysis.

Customer Advocacy

Customer advocacy can be a powerful promotional and sales tool: it communicates the confidence that someone has successfully deployed the offering. It can also demonstrate a degree of experience within the venture to mitigate any risks of implementation or deployment. The more respected and reputable the customer, the more powerful the impact of their advocacy. Examples are provided below:

- A positive quote from an existing customer on the venture's website or as part of a case study that demonstrates benefits.
- A joint press release that explains the customer's requirement, the reason for their choice and the benefits achieved, using language that aligns with the venture's value proposition.
- An offer to act as a reference point for other customers.

- A news item, written by an independent journalist or blogger, that positions the customer and the offering within an interesting wider market perspective.
- A generally applicable letter of support that stresses the venture's innovation and reliability.

Customer advocacy arises from effective synchronization of activities. This is a core aspect of the positive feedback loop that was referenced in the introduction to this chapter.

It is important that the topic of advocacy is discussed explicitly with a customer at a level sufficient to achieve approval for wider publication. It can also form part of a negotiation with a new customer, potentially in exchange for a special financial arrangement.

Awards

Association with awards and prizes can be attention grabbing and can provide powerful opportunities for creating visibility and differentiation within a market. The benefits of building associations with awards and award presenters include the following:

- Enhanced brand image and brand value through independent endorsement, as in: 'our award-winning product has been commended for its unique . . .', or 'finalist for the award for . . .'.
- Morale boosting and confidence building for the team.
- In some cases, valuable prize money.
- An opportunity to participate in a celebration event to which prospective customers and partners can be invited, and at which team members can be recognized.

Awards and prizes are broadly of the following three kinds:

- National awards: in the USA, the American Business Awards (the *Stevies*); in the UK, the Queen's Awards for Enterprise and the National Business Awards. The application effort for such awards can be substantial, and this is in proportion to the reputational advantages of winning. Other national awards, such as Deloitte's Technology Fast 500, relate to business performance and require only data to evidence a compelling rate of growth or export activity.
- Local awards, such as local business of the year, or fastest-growing local business. The relevance of locality will depend on the nature of the business and its geographic focus.

- Industry-specific awards, such as Edison Awards or, in the UK, the MacRobert Award from the Royal Academy of Engineering.

A venture should be aware of the awards and prizes that may be applicable to their offering and market focus, and to the relevant time frames for submission.

The effort involved in preparing, submitting and promoting an application can be substantial for a small business, and so it is important that provision is made for this when deciding whether to participate. As with promotional activities in general, the in-house load can be reduced by outsourcing, at a cost, the application writing and event handling to an external person or agency.

Accreditations

An accreditation is a certification by a recognized body of competence or conformity in some aspect of business practice or operation. Accreditation bodies include national and international organizations such as the American National Standards Institute (ANSI), the British Standards Institute and the International Standards Organization (ISO), and also industry bodies such as The Open Group or the Better Business Bureau.

Although not competitive in the same way as awards, accreditations can enhance a venture's reputation and give reassurance to customers.

Some customers require certain accreditations. Many UK public bodies require accreditation to the ISO 9001 quality standard and to the Cyber Essentials standard. Even when not required, accreditations demonstrate that a business is serious and committed to the market.

Achieving any accreditation requires effort and may imply a need for operational changes. Specialist service providers can be engaged to reduce the internal resources required.

Analysts and Commentators

Some markets include highly influential expert commentators and analysis bodies. For businesses operating in such markets, investing in a relationship with the relevant parties can significantly assist both visibility and reputation growth. In the business intelligence market, for instance, Gartner publishes an annual *magic quadrant* review, and Forrester publishes an annual *wave* report, each of which applies a distinctive proprietary methodology. Analyst bodies such as these regularly publish influential analysis and commentary on important trends and key suppliers in this and other markets.

Large purchasers of technical products and services take advice from analysts. Consequently, promoting to such players can be assisted by prior engagement with appropriate analysts to ensure their awareness of the venture, and also to reinforce and tune the key messaging. It can be damaging to underestimate the influence of market analysts.

Many market analysis organizations can also be commissioned to produce product reviews. Although less independent than market commentaries, such reviews can provide respectable alignment with current market trends and perspectives.

Engagement with technical news publishers, reviewers, bloggers and online commentators can also open opportunities for endorsement by respected market authorities. Such parties can provide wide market visibility for the launch of an interesting new product or market development. Organizations in this category include mainstream online technical magazines such as *Wired* and *TechCrunch*, plus technical and business commentators such as TechMarketView, LinkedIn and BusinessInsider.

As with awards, the effort involved in producing content and managing relationships with such organizations can be disproportionately high for smaller businesses, but for some offerings this is a cost that must be absorbed to achieve wide visibility and credibility.

Managing Sales

This section marks the progression from promotional considerations that focus on defining and establishing a position within a market, towards those considerations that are oriented towards engagement, negotiation and closing sales to customers.

Contrary to a widely held view, making a sale is not generally about aggressively securing a deal through coercive or manipulative behaviours. In most cases, a sales activity involves negotiating a win-win exchange whereby the customer gains a solution to a problem or opportunity, and the venture achieves something that enhances its value. Many large organizations will not be sold to, but will expect a negotiation around mutual value. Confidence, creativity and transparency are important aspects of any sales approach, and these must be rooted in an understanding of the customer's ecosystem and ambitions. In this context, a conversation about money need not be difficult.

The wider subject of sales is well addressed by works such as Pink (2014), Shultz and Doerr (2014), and Dixon *et al.* (2015). The focus here is on techniques that support the key activities of prioritizing customers, managing stakeholders, planning customer engagement, negotiating an exchange of value, market testing and piloting, and building customer communities.

Prioritizing Customers

Prioritizing target customers can be a significant consideration, especially with B2B and B2G ventures, because the sequence in which customers are engaged can affect the likelihood of success. Furthermore, the cost of engagement can be high, and each customer organization tends to have a particular appetite for innovation and risk. Prior research is important.

One consideration is whether there are advantages of any particular prioritization. This might include existing contacts, geographic benefit or some commonality of interest that can be leveraged.

In general terms, any organization that meets one of the following criteria can be a good candidate for early engagement:

- One that promotes itself as a market leader, and which is therefore likely to be keen that any innovation is used for its advantage.
- One that promotes itself as being innovative and receptive to new ideas. Such organizations tend also to be willing to serve as reference users.
- One that promotes itself as being hungry and ambitious, looking for advantage, and which is therefore likely to have an appetite for a promising innovation.

Having understood the structure and dynamics of the market and prioritized the customer organizations to be engaged, it is possible to create a plan for how best to use the market's influencers to create advantage when engaging customers.

Engaging B2B and B2G customers requires an understanding of who, how and when to go about it.

Managing Stakeholders

A stakeholder is any person in a target organization that is in some way significant to a sales campaign. This can include decision-makers, purchasers, operators, technical advisers, influencers, implementers or any other role needed to secure a successful exchange of value.

This consideration is especially important for B2B and B2G ventures, where the management of stakeholders is a necessary competence for those engaging with customers. However, the ecosystems of many B2C offerings require effective engagement with partner organizations to establish promotional, supply or distribution channels, and the principles and considerations covered here also apply to engagements with market influencers, regulators and authorities.

Stakeholder management requires both analytical and networking abilities. The following four-step method provides a framework. Executing these steps usually involves a mix of online research and engagement with personnel in the organization. The latter may be achieved by cold-calling personal assistants and switchboard operators or – preferably – by developing contacts within the organization.

Step 1: Identify the key stakeholders

For a target customer organization, it is necessary to identify those roles that need to be engaged in some way for the offering to be purchased, delivered, implemented (where this applies) and successfully operated such that the customer achieves at least the expected benefit. It can be helpful to consider the following questions:

o Who are the decision-makers with the power to agree to the sales objectives?

o What are their current priorities and concerns?

o Which other roles may be influential and hence also need to be engaged at some point (including for technical viability or procurement)?

o Which roles will benefit from the offering, and hence can be encouraged to recognize and attribute the benefit?

Identifying relevant roles, and the individuals concerned, can be difficult and time-consuming, as decision-making structures can vary across organizations. Persistence and creativity may be needed. Furthermore, this analysis can bring into scope a wide cross-section of an organization, from senior decision-makers through to technical specialists and operators.

Step 2: Locate the key stakeholders on an organization chart

Although not all stakeholders may need to be engaged personally, it is important to identify who they are and where they fit within the organization, including to whom they are responsible. In general, it is a useful guideline that a business should always build a good relationship at least one level up from any key stakeholder. This gives resilience to changes in personnel, and can also open other opportunities elsewhere in the organization.

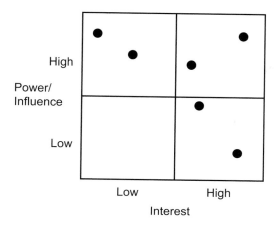

Figure 3.5 *A power/interest grid for stakeholder analysis*

Step 3: Assess each key stakeholder

This should categorize each stakeholder's interest in the proposed offering alongside their power and influence, as illustrated in Figure 3.5.

Such a grid provides a useful means for prioritizing those stakeholders that are especially significant to any campaign: those that are marked high in respect of both interest and power/influence.

Step 4: Create a plan for engaging prioritized individuals

The activities of identifying, locating and prioritizing stakeholders provides significant knowledge about an organization's structure and roles. This knowledge now needs to stimulate a process of creative thinking to determine how best to access and engage those individuals that will be needed to commit and act to enable a successful purchase of the venture's proposition.

Planning Customer Engagement

The approach taken when engaging key stakeholders within a targeted organization can be critical to the success of a sales campaign. There are two principal considerations:

- What outcomes are needed from each planned engagement?
- For the individuals to be engaged, how will contact be made and sustained?

Approaching someone who has no role or interest in whatever is needed by a venture is a waste of valuable effort and can cause confusion within the organization. The four-step method described previously should avoid this. More dangerous, however, can be approaching someone who is important, but doing it in the wrong way or with the wrong conversation. Again, this is wasteful of effort, as the approach may need to be repeated, but the impression conveyed can potentially be much more damaging to the venture's reputation. A repeat approach may not be invited. Consequently, the above questions deserve careful consideration before effort is expended.

What Outcomes Are Needed?

The questions of who to engage and how to engage them depend on what needs to be achieved from the engagement, so this is the place to start.

Driven by an understanding of the significance of the individual to be engaged (as collected using the stakeholder management method), it is useful to consider the following:

- What would be a *great* outcome from the engagement?

  Describe a great outcome in terms of ambitious objectives such as a commitment to a high-volume order, or an agreement to co-innovate and establish a joint marketing team. It is useful to consider such options so as to be prepared for questions such as 'what would you want in exchange for an exclusive arrangement?', or 'help me to understand how pricing would work at high volumes'.
- What would be a *good* outcome?

  Although less advantageous than a *great* outcome, a good outcome would nevertheless provide a basis for good business, and so should be described using objectives such as an agreement to a paid pilot programme, or an initial purchase and deployment within a specific part of the organization.
- What would be enough?

  This is a definition of the required backstop; anything less would present a problem. It is useful to have such options in mind in case things do not go as well as hoped. Objectives in this category include an agreement to talk further within a particular time frame, or a warm introduction to another key stakeholder.

Outcomes and their constituent objectives need to be considered ahead of making contact. Failure to do this can lead to meetings being poorly framed or performed by people who do not understand or cannot offer what is needed.

How Will Contact Be Made and Sustained?

The way in which contact is made with a targeted individual can be critical to the success of the engagement. A poorly executed or inappropriate approach can ruin or disadvantage future approaches, and even damage the venture's reputation.

In general, a warm introduction is always preferable. It is highly beneficial to find a common contact, either through social media or from someone elsewhere in the organization or the market. A highly desirable approach is where a recommendation from a reputable source, such as an existing customer advocate, prompts the contact to make the first move by inviting a meeting. For a cold contact (an approach out of the blue), it is particularly important to align the purpose of the contact with a known current priority.

The engagement channel (face-to-face meeting, email, telephone ...) is important, as is the style of the approach made: the language used, the formality and the brevity. In deciding this, it is important to consider the culture of the organization and, as far as it is known, the nature of the individuals concerned. This may mean that in one organization the right way is a formal approach to a personal assistant requesting a meeting with the Chief Financial Officer to talk about an option to cut fuel spend, whereas in another, the right way might be a one-line text message to an individual offering to call by later today.

Likewise, it is important to consider the messaging that is applied. This needs to be consistent with the known priorities of the contact, the value proposition that will be offered and the supporting collateral that will be needed to support the engagement. The latter point relates to any reports, financial models or presentations that will be helpful in achieving the targeted outcomes. Retaining the focus on outcomes should avoid the danger of spoiling a good opportunity by delivering an inappropriately long or tedious presentation. If it does not align with a required outcome, do not do it.

It is important to have a plan for 'staying above water' with senior decision-makers. What follows is a common scenario, especially for smaller and less mature ventures:

A first meeting with a customer decision-maker leads to a good outcome around some initial work, together with an introduction to a relatively senior technical role who will be responsible for the activity on behalf of the customer. As work commences, the senior technical role delegates responsibility downwards, and the activity progresses under the sponsorship of a relatively junior person within the customer organization.

At some point during the activity, the technical team is reorganized in such a way that there is no longer any obvious point of contact, or the customer's priorities change in a surprising way that negates the purpose of the activity, or a powerful competitor emerges. Any of these eventualities would threaten the whole relationship with the customer.

This kind of scenario constitutes a very real risk. It is mitigated by making an effort from the outset to keep regular contact with the original senior contact. This will mean that any impending changes in priority will be understood and may be navigated, and that any reorganization can be anticipated and addressed in terms of continuity of an important piece of work.

Unless the engagement plan includes continuing connection with the role(s) that is (are) needed to evidence the benefit of the offering, it will always be difficult to sustain and grow a customer relationship.

Case Study: SportMagenta

Customer Engagement

The founders agree that Sonny is to be responsible for planning and engaging sports club chains with the aim of securing a pilot activity with at least one chain.

From online research and conversations with friends and contacts, Sonny learns that chains of clubs vary in the management roles that are responsible for making decisions about introducing new technology offerings. Some have a director of digital media, whereas others include such matters within the finance director's remit, taking advice from technical staff. Consequently, it will be necessary for him to identify the relevant individuals from websites and contacts. Applying the four-step method described previously, Sonny identifies the key stakeholders that need to be engaged within each of the target chains.

He knows from experience that as he begins to engage individuals, he will be able to build and use the growing network of contacts to get warm approaches to other key stakeholders within and across organizations. Asking for introductions, even to competing organizations, need not be such a big ask, as clubs are likely to welcome endorsement from others that they are doing the right thing. Consequently, he decides to start by engaging the responsible director within the chain with which he has the most knowledge.

Each of the senior decision-makers will be approached through their administrators, with a request for a face-to-face workshop to explore an option to pilot an interesting new approach for additional revenue generation. Ahead of each approach, Sonny will research the particular priorities of the chain and learn about any relevant current activities.

For the initial workshop session, Sonny decides that a great outcome would be a commitment to operate a paid pilot, sponsored at board level, and with strong support for involvement of relevant other parties, including members, local leagues, and existing suppliers of software and infrastructure services. A good outcome would be an agreement to set up a further meeting with all relevant parties, at which the venture would be invited to present its case. An agreement to canvass opinion ahead of a follow-up call before the end of the month, together with introductions to relevant individuals in other chains, might be good enough.

Ahead of the first session, he will produce a small number of jointly branded slides that explain succinctly the business case being offered to that particular chain and how the proposed pilot activity would work. He plans to take hard copies of these to put on the table at the workshop.

In the event of gaining agreement to progress, Sonny's intention will be to arrange a follow-on meeting with the director as soon as possible to conclude details of the arrangement and to plan for any required technical integration. In any case, he will continue to keep in touch with the director through sending invitations to relevant industry events and interesting market insights, plus updates on results from SportMagenta activities. He knows that sustaining a positive relationship will be critical to the success of any shared-value initiative, whether this happens in the short term or at some point in the future.

Negotiating an Exchange of Value

A customer order might be a paid purchase for a product, service or project; an unpaid loan, download or trial; or an agreement to a pilot or co-development activity.

Early sales build and test relationships and products. They also set precedents and provide an environment in which the parties learn how to do business together, and determine whether they wish to continue to do so. When engaging a large organization, this can sometimes be arduous, but is always necessary.

In the first instance, irrespective of the nature of the order, it is crucially important to negotiate a balanced value exchange, a win-win. The customer expects to achieve value from the offering and should therefore commit to something in return. This need not involve money, but it is highly desirable that at least some money is paid by the customer early in a relationship. Other than money, a value exchange might involve a commitment by the customer to promote, encourage, review, evaluate or integrate the offering. Whatever the nature of the exchange, it needs to be negotiated openly and fairly to build trust and establish the language and mechanisms needed for future transactions.

In the context of early sales, it is important to be aware of the risks associated with offerings that may be pre-viable, hence the attractiveness of market testing with the customer through a pilot, trial or proof-of-concept project.

It is also important to consider the scalability of any offer made to secure an early sale. If an initial offer is too generous, then it may be difficult at a later time to increase this to a level that is sustainable for the venture. There is a high chance that other customers will learn the details of the offer and expect similar treatment. This can be mitigated by developing a clear rationale for the generosity of the initial offer, including other contributions or risks that were accepted by the customer, or by identifying specific aspects of the customer that argue for its special treatment. On the other hand, a high-valued initial sale can also provide scalability problems if other customers do not share the valuation achieved. This can mean a need to reduce the price to secure later sales, which is likely to upset the initial customer.

Market Testing and Piloting

Live deployment of an offering within a customer organization can pose significant risks. On the one hand, the much-quoted maxim of 'be happy, be snappy – fail fast and recover' is compelling, but launching too early, with a product that may be sub-viable (see Chapter 4), can be costly in terms of the effort involved and the potential damage to reputation and credibility. On the other hand, being overly cautious in going to the market can lead to missed opportunities or consumption of too much *runway*.

A common way to sidestep the risks of these extreme positions is by running a limited pilot or trial operation in a customer organization or limited segment of the market. Ahead of its operation, it is important that a pilot activity is designed and agreed across participating parties, with a shared statement of each party's objectives. The venture's objectives will usually focus on a combination of relationship building and the collection of information about the customer organization, the product and business model, and the dynamics and opportunities offered by the market.

The terms of the pilot are usually expressed either in a formal contract or memorandum of understanding signed by the participating parties. This will lay out the parties' objectives, responsibilities and agreements around the handling of costs.

In situations where the customer is expected to benefit from the pilot, the venture may charge a fee, usually at a fixed cost. Where a pilot activity is deemed to be of mutual advantage, it is normal for each party to carry its own costs. A midway approach involves the customer paying for the pilot against an understanding that some portion of the cost will be reimbursed from future orders.

Case Study: SportMagenta

Pilot Project Design

Sonny succeeds in his bid to gain a pilot project with five clubs within a large chain of UK sports clubs. His offer is to provide the SportMagenta software to their members and visitors for a period of three months in exchange for a share of increased revenues achieved by those clubs as a consequence of the service. At the end of the period, either the chain and the business will negotiate terms for roll-out and operation, or the arrangement will terminate. Ahead of the pilots, the chain will capture baseline data on revenues from retailing for each of the nominated clubs, to enable computation of beneficial impact.

SportMagenta's full set of objectives from the pilot are set out as follows:

Customer-related objectives

- To involve all the key people who will be needed to enable the success of future roll-out.
- To understand likely levels of demand by the customer over time.
- To confirm the working of the customer's purchasing process for future roll-out.
- To explore the reaction of other parties in the customer's ecosystem.

Product-related objectives

- To assess product usability for club staff and members.
- To analyse the performance of the offering and any implications.
- To optimize the customer journey from expression of interest through to delivery, operation and support.
- To inform prioritization of forward development requirements.
- To understand and cost the integration requirements with the club's existing systems.

Business-model-related objectives

- To collect feedback on the current framing, promotion, delivery and pricing of the offering.
- To calibrate the likely effectiveness of alternative promotion methods.
- To gain an indication of how much clubs might be willing to pay for the offering, and to inform the choice of value capture options.

Market-related learning objectives

- To confirm the assessment of market size.
- To analyse end-user response to the offering and any implications for market segmentation.
- To assess the competitiveness of the offering, including learning about direct and indirect competition.
- To understand any unanticipated regulations or special requirements that apply to the offering.

These objectives are summarized within a signed memorandum of understanding that also includes the following set of responsibilities:

For SportMagenta:

- Provide the software to the piloting club, its members and visitors for a period of three months.
- Ensure continuing availability of the service offered throughout the pilot.
- Customize the offering with club-specific branding.
- Achieve revenues both for the clubs and for the venture to demonstrate the effectiveness and potential of the venture.
- Monitor the operation of the service closely and act to resolve any unintended consequences.

For the club:

- Integrate the offering with relevant existing systems to enable effective provision of attractive new services over a live digital channel.
- Actively promote the software to its members and visitors.
- Actively encourage users to provide feedback on their experience.
- Report on revenues achieved during the pilot activity, for comparison with the baseline.
- Survey a focus group of members to collect and discuss more detailed feedback.
- Inform SportMagenta of any third-party interest or approach received.

Building Customer Communities

The relationships that are developed with customers and other ecosystem players can provide a wealth of opportunity. In addition to the benefits of repeat and extension business, well-managed relationships can open access to wider markets and help to identify and test desirable improvements. For many ventures, the effort invested in community building will be repaid many times over.

Maximizing the effectiveness of relationships means thinking about early adopters and special relationships, customer retention, user groups, and building team knowledge and confidence.

Early Adopters and Special Relationships

Early customers often get privileged deals. In many cases, this involves a heavily discounted price as part of a special agreement that recognizes the risk that will be carried by the customer. Special relationships with early adopters can extend through the life of a venture, with customer expectations of a continuing special status. This can mean that the profitability objectives which apply to later customers need to be relaxed for these customers.

In some cases, the partnership with an *early adopter* will give them privileged influence and access to new product plans in exchange for a continuing advocacy role. In all cases, however, it is important that the venture recognizes and respects that loyalty cuts both ways. A crude attempt to bring a special customer into a regular pricing framework may be interpreted as a betrayal of understanding and trust, with damaging consequences. Consequently, any proposals for changes to a special relationship need to be handled with sensitivity and recognition of past and future contribution.

Chapter 6 returns to this subject in the context of considerations around *crossing the chasm* between *early adopters* and a larger *early majority* customer base that comprises differently inclined customers. This can require the development of additional reference customers of a more pragmatic nature. The same can be necessary when a venture moves into a new market or segment. Consequently, over time, multiple groups of special customers may need to be sustained, each enjoying particular benefits in exchange for an advocacy role across other customers of their type.

Customer Retention

A loyal customer base is a great source of repeat business. If this can be quantified in a confident projection of future sales, then it can contribute positively to the value of a venture.

There are several kinds of repeat business, including:

- Continuing *recurring revenue* for a service – for example, consumer payments for a Netflix monthly subscription.
- *Renewal business*, where a customer extends their commitment to a product or service agreement for an additional period – for example, a business's renewal of a multi-year software update and support agreement with Oracle.
- *New business with an existing customer*, involving purchase of a new or enhanced offering, or additional purchases by other parts of the customer organization – for example, an existing Oracle business customer purchasing additional licences to extend its user base, or a new purchase of Oracle software by a different department within that business.

Repeat business can cost significantly less than the development of new business – according to many commentators, between six and ten times less. Consequently, investing in continuing promotion to existing customers can yield a higher profit than investing in the development of new customers.

Against this, however, is the risk of becoming dependent on a small number of customers: an effect that will reduce negotiating power. Furthermore, growth levels can be limited for ventures that rely only on their existing customer base. This has been analysed by the business coach Paul Lemberg (2016), who argues that to achieve growth levels above 20 per cent per annum, it is necessary also to invest in the development of new customers.

Consequently, there is a balance to be struck between retaining customers and achieving repeat business, and winning new business with new customers. The desirable balance will depend on many factors, including typical customer size, the venture's ambitions, the nature of the market and the time taken for a new customer to become profitable.

To help manage this balance, two useful and related measures are *customer retention rate* (CRR) and *customer lifetime value* (CLV).

- CRR measures the *churn rate* of customers: it is a measure of how well the venture is performing in terms of keeping customers that it has gained. Many formulae have been suggested for CRR calculation. This text adopts the following:

  ((number of customers at period end – number of customers acquired during period) / number of customers at start of period) × 100

  This approach calculates the percentage of customers retained over the course of a period (month, quarter or year). A CLV of 100 per cent

implies that no customers have churned (been lost), whereas a CLV of 0 per cent would imply that all customers have been lost.
- CLV measures the average value (revenue or profit margin) achieved by the venture from a customer over the lifetime of their relationship. This measure can be calculated and tracked as an aggregate across all customers, or across all customers within a segment, or by a specific customer, to enable the comparison of relative values.
- In its simplest form, it is calculated using the formula:

(average order value) × (average number of purchases in a period) × (average number of periods over which a relationship is retained).

As with any measurement, unless these metrics can be aligned with business objectives and will usefully inform decision making, any effort expended capturing data and producing reports will simply be wasted. Where possible, market norms for such measures should be collected for reference.

Case Study: SportMagenta

Calculation and Analysis of Customer Retention Rate (CRR) and Customer Lifetime Value (CLV)

During the framing of the venture, the founders set objectives of achieving recurring revenue growth of more than 100 per cent per annum and gross margin growth of more than 150 per cent per annum for each of the first three years. These ambitious objectives mean that CRR and CLV will need to be tracked and managed closely.

Knowing that churn rates of up to 20 per cent are widely reported in the sports sector, the founders set a target CRR of at least 85 per cent during the venture's roll-out phase. A scenario along the following lines is anticipated:

- At the start of a month, suppose that forty clubs are actively using the offering.
- During that month, suppose that another fifteen sign up.
- At the end of the same month, suppose that there are fifty active clubs.

Consequently, the CRR for that month would be $((50 - 15) / 40) \times 100 = 87.5$ per cent.

On the basis of market research, the founders believe that a target CLV of at least $150,000 from each club should be achievable during the venture's roll-out phase. A scenario that will achieve this level of CLV is as follows:

- Suppose that SportMagenta is able to negotiate annual contracts with clubs.
- Suppose that these contracts can be sustained for an average duration of three years.

- Suppose also that the venture can achieve on average $5,000 per month from each club with which it contracts.

On these assumptions, the venture's CLV would be ($5,000) $\times$ (12) $\times$ (3) = $180,000.

Sonny performs the following analysis on the implications of these targets:

- A customer base of fifty clubs each producing $180,000 revenue will provide Sport-Magenta with $9 million.
- If, in the scenario adopted, the customer base had been fifty-two rather than fifty, then the value of the customer base would be $9.36 million: an increase of $360,000 by reducing customer churn.
- Achieving that would require increasing the CRR by five percentage points to 92.5 per cent ((52 − 15) / 40).

Consequently, based on the numbers assumed, each percentage point increase in CRR could be worth $72,000 ($360,000 / 5) to the venture. This analysis is helpful in demonstrating the importance of effective customer relationship management.

Sonny decides to calculate both CRR and CLV each month and to track their trajectories. These trends will provide useful leading indicators of how well the venture is satisfying its customers' needs and monetizing its relationships, both of which will be necessary to achieve the ambitious financial objectives. If either trend shows a worsening pattern, then immediate customer activity will be required to bring the venture back on track.

Sonny also decides to calculate the rolling CLV separately for clubs within each chain that is successfully contracted. This will enable comparison of the relative benefit being achieved from each chain, and hence inform decisions around prioritization of sales effort.

User Groups

A user group can be a powerful mechanism for building loyalty, gathering feedback, identifying new opportunities, demonstrating future enhancements and testing ideas.

These can be pitched at various levels from actual end-users of an offering to senior decision-makers in customer organizations. It can be advantageous to run multiple parallel groups at differing levels and with differing objectives. Clearly, the agendas and styles of meetings will vary between such events.

Events can be hosted by the business if it has suitable space, or in a reputable hired location, such as a hotel or professional society. A third option is to invite customer organizations to take turns in hosting. This latter approach can have additional benefits in terms of implied advocacy and a shared objective for the event to be a success.

Another option is to host user group meetings virtually, as webinars. Although attractive in terms of time and cost, this approach can be less effective in respect of achieving the networking benefits of physically engaging a community of people with mutual interests.

As with any business event, and irrespective of the way in which the event is to be hosted and arranged, professional management is critical to success. A shabby or disorganized user group event is likely to reflect badly on the business and on the value of its offering.

It can be beneficial to invite prospective customers or influential market players, such as analysts, to join user group events. An analyst may be positioned as a key note speaker, to set the tone for the event in terms of current market priorities, and hence to give later speakers an independent point of reference.

Importantly, a user group event is not an opportunity for overt selling, and any specific opportunities forthcoming should normally be handled by arrangements for future specific meetings.

Following an event, it is usually beneficial to publish a high-quality output, distributed as a link to a relevant web page providing presentation materials used, links to participating organizations and a brief commentary that consolidates the key messages to be conveyed.

Building Team Knowledge and Confidence

Customer organizations usually welcome an opportunity to meet competent new team members from the venture, and can also be generous in providing market education and training. Consequently, it can be important to invest effort to ensure that a balance of customer exposure is achieved across the team.

If this is not recognized, then a venture can get into a situation where it is overly dependent on a small number of individuals for customer-facing activities. This can increase the venture's risk profile. Furthermore, resentments can grow within the team between those who seem to get all the interesting front-line work and those who are expected to stay behind the scenes. Interestingly, with some technical roles, the opposite can also apply, where it can be important to encourage less confident people to develop a balance of customer-facing skills.

Bringing Innovation to Promotion and Sales

As with all aspects of business design and activity, effective business promotion and sales demands innovative qualities such as alertness to opportunity and imagination in identifying options.

Every engagement or event with an existing or a new customer, or with some other player in the market, gives opportunities to enforce the venture's brand value and to extend its visibility and reputation.

The following situations illustrate the principle:

- When agreeing a product integration arrangement with a technology partner, an innovative approach would be to suggest a jointly-branded promotional video that describes the specific competitive benefits of the venture's offerings and how these will be enhanced through integration.
- If a customer confirms that an offering or activity has performed better than expected, then an innovative response would be to seek agreement to add their quote to the website, or to jointly develop a promotional case study around the experience.
- When demonstrating a new product release to a customer, an innovative approach would be to suggest producing a joint video of the benefits from the new release. This will be a valuable promotional tool, and will also help the customer with in-house communication and education.
- When agreeing an extension to an order or a piece of new business, an innovative approach would be to suggest a joint press release, which could also be useful to the customer to demonstrate their innovation and activity.
- Following a successful implementation or project, an innovative approach would be to arrange a market event at which the customer will present the success achieved to an invited audience of other market players.

Applying innovation to promotion and sales activities means maximizing the opportunities available in situations such as the above. In some cases, this will mean anticipating such situations and agreements, and therefore including them in the objectives that are set in the preparation of an event. In other cases, where unexpected opportunities arise, it is important to be alive to the possibilities presented, and imaginative – and courageous – in creating additional advantage.

Case Study: SwiftComply – Scaling Promotion across Large Communities

Background to the Company

Modern city authorities need to protect the health of their city at a cost that is affordable both to themselves and to local businesses. This includes the need to regulate fat, oil and grease (FOG) handling across large and growing numbers of food outlets. Regulation is important because uncontrolled *fatburgs* behave like cholesterol in cities' sewer systems; however, it is expensive to all parties involved: restaurants globally spend more than $200 billion per annum complying with regulations.

This is the problem addressed by SwiftComply – www.swiftcomply.com.

This venture has been chosen to illustrate the material addressed in this chapter due to its innovative promotional approach. Its approach also illustrates the value of ecosystem analysis and design, which were addressed in Chapter 2.

The Innovation

Across the cities of the developed world, FOG control requires authorities to set and administer regulations that can be understood and satisfied by food outlets. For these to be implemented effectively, providers of compliance-related services need to engage with the large and growing volumes of outlets to position and sell their services. As illustrated in Figure 3.6, all three parties bear a heavy burden.

SwiftComply brings to market the first real-time platform to automate the whole regulation process (see Figure 3.7). The platform notifies outlets when a service is due, enables online booking and payment for the required activities, with automated generation and transmission of a compliance certificate for the authorities.

The innovation redraws the ecosystem map to benefit all three stakeholders: the city no longer needs to operate an expensive regulation process; outlets no longer need to invest

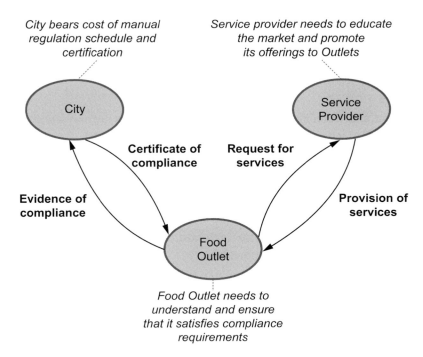

Figure 3.6 *Ecosystem without SwiftComply*

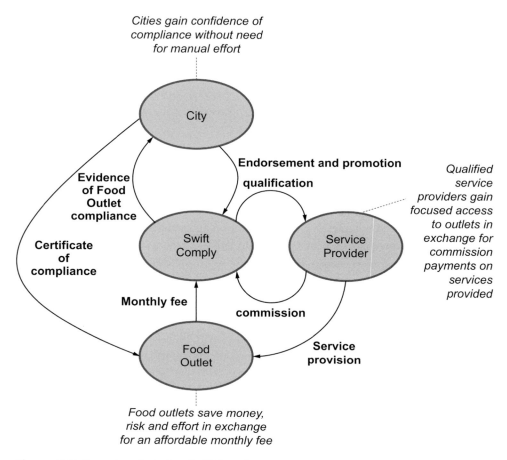

Cities gain confidence of
compliance without need
for manual effort

Figure 3.7 *Ecosystem including SwiftComply*

valuable effort understanding and planning what they need to do; and service providers position their offerings against well-defined requirements.

The approach was initially proved in Dublin, working with 3,500 restaurants.

Promoting the Offering

The challenge initially faced by the venture was how to promote their innovation to a worldwide market without bearing the high cost of engaging with large volumes of individual food outlets and service providers.

The solution adopted has been to promote the offering to city authorities, offering SwiftComply as a trusted partner that can reduce cost and effort through a reliable and business-friendly solution. This approach uses city authority regulators as powerful promotional channels into the food outlets and their service providers, who will be required to pay for access to the service. Early successes in the USA, including in

Mammoth Lakes in California, Fox Metro in Illinois and Gresham in Orlando, confirmed the viability of the approach.

The Plan and Actions Performed

Bringing this innovation to the FOG regulation market required the following key actions:

- Designing and executing a promotional plan to prioritize cities and marshal the resources needed.
- Educating cities in the feasibility and benefits of automating their current regulatory processes.
- Ensuring early-adopters achieve the benefits of the platform.
- Calibrating the subscription level for food outlets and the commission levels for suppliers to ensure their buy-in to the new ecosystem.

Outcomes

The business is achieving scale through its innovative promotional approach. The success of the business in transforming the market is evidenced by the following achievements:

- More than ten cities have now adopted SwiftComply.
- More than 8,000 food outlets are now regulated through the platform, and this number is growing rapidly.
- Generation of a strong revenue stream for the business, growing more than 10 times year on year.
- Plans for rapid growth and expansion to cover six countries and over 100,000 restaurants within twelve months.

Learning

The following learning points have been reported by the SwiftComply founders:

- Building a business that involves promoting multiple value propositions to different stakeholders can be a complex activity. An ecosystem with two major players is tough. Handling a third player that is also a governmental agency is really tough.
- It is easy to underestimate the operational challenges of moving from a strong concept to actually meeting customers' delivery expectations.
- The value propositions for different parties may need to be expressed in very different terms. The proposition and language for cities differs significantly from that for restaurants. It is important to get both right.
- Scaling a business in multiple countries at the same time can be very challenging, and there is a risk of losing control if growth occurs too quickly.

Summary of Promotion and Sales

Promotion and sales are about growing business value through market-facing activities and engagements. It is important that these retain alignment with the framing of the business, including its messaging, ecosystem and objectives, and so develop a strong outward-looking face for the business model. Applying the considerations and techniques described in this chapter can help to avoid undue remedial or repeat work from mistakes or confusion, and to contain costs within affordable limits.

The key points addressed are summarized below.

- **Scoping and analysing market structure** enables the venture to define and quantify those communities to which promotional activities must be targeted:
  - Segmentation is about analysing the subdivisions of the market to determine the venture's preferred interest and focus across segments.
  - Size and addressability is about quantifying the extent of the market and assessing how much of this can or will be addressed by the venture.
  - Landscape is about characterizing the nature of the market in terms of its maturity and existing players, and assessing the implications of this for the venture.
- **Scoping and analysing market dynamics** enables the venture to build awareness of its strengths, risks and potential for collaboration:
  - Porter's original *five forces* model has been extended to include a sixth force, *collaboration*, to better reflect entrepreneurial principles and current business practices.
  - Competitive market forces *threat of new entrants, industry rivalry* and *threat of substitutes* drive a need for differentiation of the offering and influence the style of messaging used. They can also encourage collaboration with other players.
  - Negotiation market forces *bargaining power of suppliers, industry rivalry* and *bargaining power of buyers* can have a significant effect on the framing of a venture and on its pricing. They can also encourage new forms of collaboration, including those that help to control the costs of purchases.
- **Promoting the business** is about establishing a position and creating demand in the target market. Each promotional approach involves effort and cost, and some will be more cost-effective than others, hence it is important to plan and monitor the effectiveness of approaches adopted:
  - Creating visibility means determining those parties to whom the venture needs to be visible and attractive, and how it can most effectively achieve this.

- o Branding and brand management need to be factored into the design of all aspects of the venture, from its recruitment advertisements and communications activities to the design and delivery of its offerings, and all interactions with parties in its ecosystem.
- o Some individuals and organizations have the power to influence the way in which the market responds to a new initiative or venture: understanding who these are and how they can be engaged can catalyse customer interest and confidence.
- **Managing sales** is about engaging effectively with customers, negotiating fair exchanges of value and building communities of advocates to maximize the power inherent in the venture's relationships:
  - o A stakeholder is any person in a customer organization that is significant to a campaign: decision-makers, purchasers, operators, technical advisers, influencers or implementers. Key stakeholders need to be identified, located and prioritized, to enable engagement planning and relationship management.
  - o Successful customer engagement requires setting of desired outcomes and assessment of how best to make and sustain contact.
  - o A sale builds and tests the relationship with a customer: any exchange of value needs to be transparent, so as to build trust and establish the language and mechanisms for future transactions.
  - o Relationships developed with customers and ecosystem players provide a wealth of opportunity; effort invested in community building can be repaid many times over.
- In performing each of these above, it is important to apply the **innovative power of the business.**
  - o Innovation can be applied to the way in which the team thinks about the business and its market, and the way it engages with that market.
  - o Innovation can make a significant contribution to the growth of business value.
  - o Some companies succeed through investing in product, and others through investing in promotion and sales; addressing both with equal vigour and creativity gives the greatest chance.

ANALYSIS EXERCISES

The table below lists a collection of digital businesses to be used as subjects for the exercises that follow.

Business	Focus	Website
Darktrace	Cyber security	www.darktrace.com
Fitbit	Health, fitness and performance	www.fitbit.com
JustEat	Online takeaway food	www.just-eat.co.uk
Reposit	Property rental	www.getreposit.uk
Snapchat	Social media	www.snapchat.com
Sorry as a Service	Customer services and retention	www.sorryasaservice.com
SwiftComply	Regulation and compliance	www.swiftcomply.com

On the basis of information available in the public domain, address the questions below for at least one of the businesses listed.

1. The business's customer(s):
   (a) Who is the customer(s) for the proposed innovation?
   (b) Who are the principal players in the business ecosystem?
   (c) What are the principal value exchanges with these players?

2. Segmentation and market landscape:
   (a) What criteria might be applied to segment the business's customers?
   (b) Which segments do you think offer the greatest potential for revenue generation, and why?
   (c) How would you assess the business's market in terms of its maturity, the current division of market share and the impact of dominant players?

3. Market size calculation:
   (a) What units would be most appropriate to express the market size (for example, $ per annum, user population ...)?
   (b) How would you assess the total addressable market, and what value does this suggest?
   (c) How might you assess the serviceable available market, and what value does this suggest?

4. Analysis of market forces:
   (a) Which of the competitive forces is most likely to dominate, and what are its likely implications for the business?
   (b) Which of the negotiation forces is most likely to dominate, and what are its likely implications for the business?
   (c) What kinds of collaborations may benefit the business, either competitively or in terms of negotiating power?

5. Promoting the business:
   (a) Which approaches are most likely to be cost-effective for the business to promote its offerings?
   (b) In which ways are the business's brands used to differentiate its offerings, and in what way are these distinctive?
   (c) What measures would it be useful to compute to assess the relative effectiveness of the promotional approaches adopted?
6. Managing sales:
   (a) How might the business go about prioritizing the customers that it engages?
   (b) Which roles are likely to be the key customer stakeholders that need to be engaged by the business?
   (c) What is (or are) the exchange(s) of value that occur(s) during a sale by the business?
   (d) What evidence is there for an active community of the business's customers?

DESIGN EXERCISES

The design exercise at the end of Chapter 1 encouraged identification of a business idea to be developed incrementally by specific design exercises through subsequent chapters of the book. That activity commenced in Chapter 2, with the framing of the selected business idea using the elements introduced in that chapter.

Extend that framing through the following tasks:

1. For each aspect of business promotion and sales covered in this chapter, perform an assessment and analysis of your business. If using the Business Design Template, summarize the resulting considerations in the left-hand cell of the *promotion and sales* section.
2. Extract from your considerations the set of key decisions relating to the promotion of your business. If using the Business Design Template, document these in the right-hand cell of the *promotion and sales* section.
3. Review the extended design of your business for consistency, and address any issues that arise.
4. Capture separately any of the following:
   (a) Key points learned from the exercise.
   (b) Outstanding issues or uncertainties.

4   Delivery and Operations

Focus of This Chapter

Figure 4.1 illustrates how the material addressed by this chapter fits within the framework of considerations for business design.

Building upon decisions in the context of promotion and sales, the considerations addressed here elaborate the framing of the business in the context of the question *what is the offering?*

The decisions made will guide and inform the considerations that apply to value capture and to those relating to achieving business objectives. It is important that consistency is achieved and sustained across the decisions made in relation to each component of the framework.

Learning Outcomes

After studying this chapter, you will:

- Be able to identify and assess supply options for a business.
- Be able to map and analyse a customer journey in terms of touch points and channels.
- Understand technology-readiness levels, and be able to construct a product roadmap.
- Be aware of the key considerations of managing release and deployment.
- Understand the need for a channel strategy, and the principal considerations involved.
- Appreciate the need for, and value of, innovation in business delivery and management.

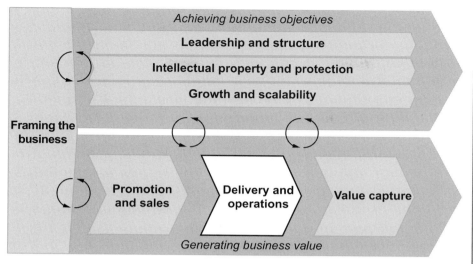

Figure 4.1 *Context of delivery and operations*

Introducing Delivery and Operations

Driving objectives for scalability and growth while managing continuing development can be a demanding mix. On the one hand, the myriad elements involved need careful consideration and planning, and on the other, the various decisions need innovation and courage. This chapter is about achieving that balance.

The nature of the activities and decisions involved varies with the type of offering, and especially according to the levels of complexity and risk involved in any manufacturing process. Consequently, the focus throughout this chapter is to offer generally applicable principles and techniques.

Chapter 2 addressed considerations around what the venture will offer, and the ecosystem in which it will operate. Chapter 3 addressed considerations around the size and structure of the market, and how the venture can establish a position for itself and engage its customers. This chapter builds on these by addressing:

- How required services and materials will be sourced through the *supply chain.*
- How the desired customer experience will be achieved through the design of *a customer journey.*
- How *continuing development* will be prioritized and planned.

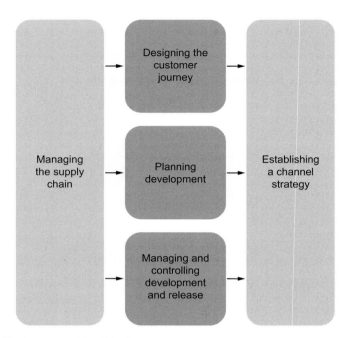

Figure 4.2 *Topics covered by this chapter*

- How development and release of the offering will be *managed and controlled*.
- How the offering will be delivered to customers, including through a *channel strategy*.

Figure 4.2 illustrates the coverage of this chapter in the form of a simple value chain that connects considerations of supply through design, development and release to customers through market channels.

For each of these topics, relevant principles, considerations and techniques are introduced and illustrated using a collection of real-world examples and the SportMagenta exemplar.

Many of the subjects introduced in this chapter are large and sophisticated. Out of necessity, therefore, the approach adopted is structured and presented at a level to serve the principal needs of the entrepreneur.

Managing the Supply Chain

In its most general interpretation, this is about managing the flow of goods and services from their point of origin to the point of consumption. A software-only venture that uses online services for delivery may have very little to concern

itself with in this regard, but a venture that deals in part with physical components may need to make decisions on a range of considerations, including:

- The movement and storage of raw materials, finished goods and spares.
- The delivery of finished goods to the end-user, through whatever channels
  are supported, including mechanisms for handling damaged goods and returns.
- For each required transaction with a supplier of materials, the point at which
  title and moneys transfer between the parties involved.
- The management of risk across the production process, including clarity over
  the venture's liabilities for faulty goods and damage or injury to customers or
  distribution partners.

This is a large and complex subject in its own right. More detailed coverage is
provided by, for example, Chopra and Meindl (2006), Rushton *et al.* (2014),
Christopher (2016), and Mangan and Lalwani (2016).

Traditionally, supply-chain management (SCM) was modelled as a linear
structure across relevant participating parties, as illustrated in Figure 4.3.

Under its simplest implementation, the parties involved are loosely connected
with each other, and multiple independent systems are used to manage information flows and goods movements along the chain. Such an approach can be
unresponsive to rapidly changing circumstances, and can potentially lead to
delays, surprises and high costs of management.

The recent trend has been towards an increasing focus on digitization to
create systems that are more connected, intelligent, automated, scalable and
rapid, both in delivery and in response to change. With such systems, the parties
involved can be closely aligned around common objectives.

The use of standards continues to be a major driver towards this end. The
supply chain operations reference (SCOR), managed and developed by APICS,
provides a process reference model endorsed by the Supply Chain Council as a

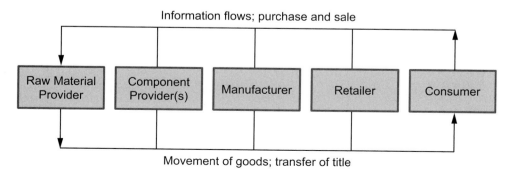

Figure 4.3 *Traditional formulation of a supply chain*

standard, cross-industry tool for supply chain management. It provides a wealth of process definitions and metrics to enable participating organizations to synchronize their respective responsibilities and systems. Whereas the detail is unlikely to be of interest to the entrepreneur, the terminology adopted can be helpful as a useful cross-industry reference.

Another cross-industry standard is the Global Data Synchronization Network (GDSN) from GS1. Widely applied within the retail, health-care and food-service industries, the standard underpins a network by which subscribing trading partners can share product data through automated data exchange.

Industry-specific standards also play a significant role in enabling today's connected world. For example, in the financial services sector, the International Standards Organization (ISO) currently provides twenty-seven standards covering information exchange for financial services, covering topics such as interchange message specifications and mobile payments to businesses.

Adoption and adherence to standards can be critical to product acceptability within a sector, in addition to providing resilience and opportunities for integration and collaboration.

In-Source, Outsource, or a Mixture of the Two?

A venture with a non-trivial supply chain needs to decide upon its ambition and appetite for managing aspects of that supply chain. The process can be outsourced, in whole or in part, either locally within the venture's geographic base, or internationally. This decision can have a significant impact on the applicable risk profile.

At one extreme, the whole process is outsourced to partners that manufacture the product under licence from its owner. In such cases, the venture receives revenues from licensing its intellectual property without incurring the associated risks of manufacturing.

This approach has been used very successfully by British semiconductor and software design company ARM, which outsources the manufacture and distribution of its architectures and designs for processor chips to producers of mobile phones and other devices. Its customers include Apple, Nvidia, Qualcomm and Samsung, each of whom pays an upfront licence fee plus royalties on sales of manufactured chips.

At the other end of the scale, the venture retains responsibility for scheduling and executing all of the relevant activities: in SCOR terminology, these would be referred to as *plan, source, make, deliver* and *return*. Intermediate options involve the venture outsourcing certain of its more well-defined, or commodity, supply requirements, but retaining in-house responsibility for those that require the venture's specialist competence, or which cannot be trusted to an external party.

The risk profile of outsourcing aspects of the supply process differs considerably from that of managing the process in-house. When reviewing options, especially for outsourcing to a different geography, it is important to consider the implications of factors such as:

- Costs of language translation and currency exchange.
- Required security measures for materials or personnel.
- Applicable regulatory regimes and trade tariffs.

Contracting with Suppliers

For all supply requirements, whether these relate to outsourced services, component parts or materials, there are three broad approaches that can be taken, and the choice made can have a significant impact on business operations:

1. Identify and source materials from the open market, as and when required.
2. Build and manage a network of approved suppliers, placing orders with these as and when required.
3. Invest in an integrated, and potentially automated, purchasing system with a single preferred supplier.

In making this choice, there are several relevant considerations, including:

- Does the venture have a requirement for any special branding or configuration of a supply?
- Does the venture have a requirement for time-criticality of supply, and what would be the impact if supply were delayed?
- Is the supply price-sensitive to the venture's economics, and what would be the impact on the venture if supply costs were to increase or decrease?
- What about management of quality, and what would be the impact on the venture of varying quality or reliability of supply?
- What about any limitations on scalability, in respect of speed, volume or cost of delivery?
- What would be the implications for business performance of needing to handle under- and over-achievement of supply requirements?

Table 4.1 characterizes and contrasts each of the options by aligning each with the above considerations.

Given a characterization of a venture's supply requirements expressed in the terms of the above list of considerations, Table 4.1 can be applied to assess the relative merits of each option.

Table 4.1 Characteristics of Principal Supply Options

Supply option	Contract	Characteristics (typical)
Identify and source materials from the open market, as and when required	Transactional association with suppliers: arm's-length relationships	• Flexibility to respond to market opportunities • Low risk of becoming locked in to poor agreement • Negotiating power (including price) determined by market forces • Low potential for configuration/rebranding, unless inherent to product • Likely need to accept standard licensing, delivery, warranty and payment terms
Build and manage a network of preferred suppliers, placing orders with these as and when required	Contracted arrangements, with negotiated terms	• Negotiated terms on pricing, payment, quality, performance and delivery arrangements, with potential for longer-term commitment • Special product branding/configuration can be included in the supply agreement • Less flexibility to change suppliers • Potential for joint planning and management of scalability projections • May be locked in by purchasing commitment, with penalties in the event of needing to change
Invest in an integrated, and potentially automated, purchasing system with a preferred supplier	Close partnering arrangement, with commitment and dependence	• Negotiated terms on pricing, payment, quality, performance and delivery arrangements, with expectation of longer-term or exclusive commitment • Special product branding/configuration can be included in the supply agreement • Potentially highly scalable to match business need • Joint planning and management, with visibility of process and performance • Mutual dependence (double edged) – high cost of changing supplier • Mutual commitment to future plan, potentially punitive in the event of needing to change

Onlicar is a venture that produces a smart device that connects to a vehicle's engine management system and sends location and performance data about the vehicle to the cloud. Analysis of this data is used to deliver value propositions for fleet operators and vehicle purchasers. The venture's supply requirements include a custom-designed physical device plus a collection of software modules for data collection, storage, communication and analysis.

Suppose that Onlicar decides to develop its software in-house to retain control over its core algorithms, but determines to outsource manufacture of the hardware devices. The sourcing requirements for those devices can be characterized using the considerations listed above, as follows:

- Devices need to be branded with the venture's logo and design marks.
- Supply is time-critical because orders are placed by customers through a close relationship with the Onlicar sales team, and any delay would damage this.
- The cost of the device is highly price-sensitive because customer pricing is on a per-device basis. Furthermore, price levels are defined within sales and marketing materials, and can be subject to sales discounts at volume. Any variation of supply cost must be within a very small margin.
- Consistency of quality is essential as customers have no tolerance for failed devices, and this applies throughout the period of the service. Any failure would damage the venture's credibility.
- There must be no limitations on scalability: whatever volume is required must be available under the same conditions, or under conditions and time frames previously agreed for stepwise increases in order volumes.
- The implications on business performance of needing to handle supplier failure or underachievement are likely to be severe because customers' confidence would be lost. Over-supply would not be particularly advantageous.

This characterization of supply requirement can now be aligned with Table 4.1 to assess Onlicar's options. The open market option does not apply due to the bespoke nature of the required device and the need for volume production at a pre-set price. Consequently, the choice is between building and managing a network of preferred suppliers or contracting with a single integrated supply partner.

The business currently opts to manage a network of preferred suppliers because it cannot tolerate the risk of a single point of failure during an aggressive growth phase. This option is feasible because the device specification had been standardized. Each supplier adopted works to the same terms with regard to time, cost, quality and scalability.

Case Study: SportMagenta

Supply Requirements

The founders recognize that their supply requirements include software products for the B2B and B2C components, data integration services for deployment within sports clubs, and a reliable, performant and scalable hosting service.

Their assessment of these requirements is as follows:

- The software components are the venture's core intellectual property. Their design will evolve with experience. It is necessary that these are handled by a competent in-house team.
- Similarly, experience with data integration will be a core competence, and will involve working closely with sports clubs. Again, this requirement will be met by an in-house team that builds experience.
- The hosting service could be developed in-house or outsourced. If it is to be outsourced, then this could be from the open market, from a selected network of preferred suppliers or from a single integrated supplier.

From their technical and market experience, the founders know that hosting services have become a commodity offering from a number of reliable and competing suppliers, including Amazon, Google and Microsoft. Consequently, they decide that their requirement can be met by sourcing the service on the open market from whichever of the current service providers offers the best deal on price performance.

An implication of this decision is the need for a standard interface within the design of the product architecture to enable easy transfer to a different hosting service provider without disruption to the customer, as and when market or price-performance conditions change.

Designing the Customer Journey

The Acela Express is an Amtrak service between Washington DC and Boston. Launched in 1999, the service was designed jointly by Ideo Product Development in California and an Amtrak in-house team. That project first coined the term *customer journey*. The concept was expressed as a technique for designing a seamless customer experience across all *touch points* with the service, from initial awareness and enquiry, through service use, and into continuing relationship management and support.

The technique has since been used widely by businesses in all sectors to design the customer experience that is required to maximize the value achievable from a product or service.

Mapping the Customer Journey

Customer journey design usually involves a mapping technique. A range of techniques have been suggested, each of which in some way plots the experience of customers as they progress through a range of possible touch points, to test the coherence of the business design. It is important to note that the approach applies irrespective of the nature of the offering and the range of channels through which it is made available.

The motivation for this analysis is to ensure that there is no inadvertent confusion, frustration, inefficiency or inconsistency in the design of the various channels by which the customer engages in some way with the venture or its offering. This can easily come about through making several decisions, each of which are rational in themselves, but which together provide the customer with differing price structures or branding, depending on where or how they look for information.

A simple mapping approach can be set out as shown in Figure 4.4, which is illustrative and not recommended. The columns of a journey map list the series of engagements that are anticipated between the venture and its customers in relation to the offering, from the way in which customers first become aware of its existence, through negotiation, purchase, delivery, deployment and use of the offering, continuing through to exploring the potential to engage the customer as an advocate for future promotion.

The rows list the set of touch points relating to the supported channels by which a customer can interact or engage with the venture or its offering. Where multiple channel partners (see the later section) are supported, the map should be extended to list each of these separately to enable analysis of potential conflicts.

The cells in the table indicate the touch points that are planned for each type of customer engagement. Consequently, according to the journey design illustrated in Figure 4.4:

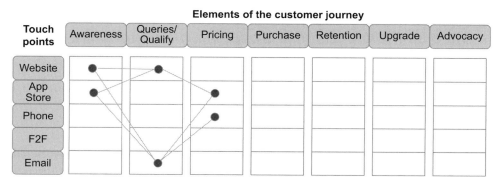

Figure 4.4 *Mapping the customer journey*

- Customers are expected to become aware of the offering either through the venture's website or as a result of browsing an app store. There is no expectation that telephone, email or face-to-face contact will be used for promotional purposes.
- Having become aware of the offering, customers are expected to engage either by using a website enquiry form or by email to pose any questions.
- Although pricing will be available on the app store, it is planned also to offer a telephone service by which customers can ask for this information.

The connecting lines between planned touch points can be used to show expected customer journeys through the anticipated types of engagement. So, according to the design illustrated in Figure 4.4, a customer who becomes aware of the offering through the venture's website, and who subsequently expresses interest through that channel, will be directed to the app store for relevant pricing information. However, a customer who expresses interest by email will either be directed to the app store or contacted by telephone to discuss pricing. If this choice depends on an applicable condition, such as the size of a potential order, then this should be annotated on the journey map.

Analysing the Customer Journey Map

As will be apparent from the simple and incomplete example used above, the mapping of the set of potential journeys can be a non-trivial task, but its value as a tool for the team in expressing and validating the effectiveness of the business design in terms of promotion and delivery can be significant.

The act of working collaboratively to create a journey map can be a valuable activity in creating a common understanding around assumptions and requirements. As the map is created, design decisions will be taken, assumptions will be questioned and validated, potential inconsistencies will be exposed and avoided, and requirements for new types of engagement or touch points will be identified.

There is no *right* and *wrong* with journey design, but there are some helpful considerations that can be applied to question the business design. These are of two kinds: structural and motivational, as shown in Table 4.2.

Detailed Process Mapping for the Customer Journey

Depending on the nature of the offering and the process by which it is deployed and used, it can sometimes be useful to map the process involved to a greater

Table 4.2 Considerations for Analysis of Customer Journey Maps

Type	Indicator	Considerations
Structural	*Channel hopping* This is where the journey changes channel between successive engagement types. Examples: a telephone response to an email request from the customer, or an unsolicited email to the customer after a telephone enquiry.	Can be irritating as it may change the customer's preferred tempo or style of working, which can result in losing their enthusiasm or attention. It can also lead to fragmented documentation of a dialogue.
Structural	*Splitting* This is where the customer is given the choice to respond through one of several channels. Example: a promotional email invites the customer to phone or email their requirements, or to contact one of the venture's agents.	Can be confusing – might the outcome differ depending on the option chosen? Can also lead to the customer pausing to decide how to respond, which may demotivate or lose their attention.
Structural	*Merging* This is where the customer is given one choice of touch point, irrespective of the channel(s) through which they have been engaging. Example: pricing information is only available through face-to-face meeting following validation of the customer and their requirement.	Can be irritating if the experience up until that point has been conducted consistently through one channel. That can make the customer question the venture's attitude towards its customers, and whether it really cares about their individual interests and requirements.
Motivational	*Encouragement to proceed* This is about keeping the customer moving to the next step of the engagement. Examples: availability of the required service is limited, or a time-limited offer of a special arrangement.	Having attracted a customer's attention, it is important to consider how they can be motivated to progress and endure the process steps that are needed to achieve the desired outcome.
Motivational	*Barriers that inhibit progress – 'pain points'* This is about any structural, legal or temporal factors that can inhibit the customer from proceeding to the next step of the engagement. Examples: time lag in responding due to limited team capacity or need to contact a third party to clarify a technical or commercial point, or need for the customer to provide detailed technical data.	In some situations, time delays are unavoidable, and these should be explained to the customer with clear expectations set and satisfied. Where the customer is required to provide data, it is important to make this as easy as possible. To sustain momentum, ensure that the customer knows what is expected and why, and hence avoid the risk of an erroneous or misleading response that introduces further delay.

Type	Indicator	Considerations
Motivational	*Uncertainties* This is about the existence of any ambiguity or lack of clarity in the process or its wording. Examples: the pricing structure on a partner's website differs from that on the venture's own site, or multiple email addresses are suggested for further contact.	Any perceived uncertainty can cause the customer to delay proceeding through the planned engagements, or to re-evaluate their opinion of the business. The customer may be minded to devise a plan to exploit apparent inconsistencies to get a better deal.

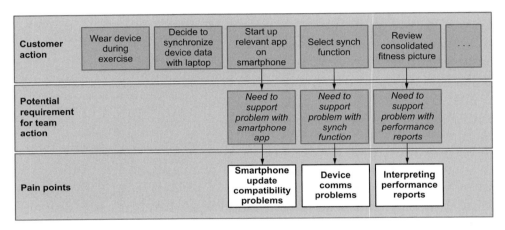

Figure 4.5 *A tactical map fragment for a sports wearable*

level of detail to test its coherence and design implications. Sometimes referred to as *tactical maps*, these usually have a different structure to the journey map shown previously.

Figure 4.5 illustrates a tactical map for a sports wearable such as a Fitbit or Garmin Vivofit pedometer or heart-rate monitor.

This technique can be helpful to identify and anticipate likely areas needing customer support.

As shown in Figure 4.5, tactical maps can also be helpful in identifying *pain points* to be addressed by continuing development. Such maps need to be continually tested and modified during trials and live operation of an offering.

Case Study: SportMagenta

Customer Journey

The founders work together on the journey map, as this will surface assumptions and implications for both promotional activities and technical requirements. They recognize that the B2C and B2B components of the offering will have different journeys, but find a useful way to plot both journeys on the same map, as shown below.

The B2B journey reflects the assumption that initial contact with clubs may be made by phone or email, depending on the assessment of the best means of approaching key stakeholders within the club. It is also possible that a club may proactively approach SportMagenta after reviewing the venture's website. Irrespective of how contact is made, the aim is to achieve a face-to-face meeting to make the business case, and to retain the relationship with key stakeholders through that channel. It is recognized that the venture's website will also play a role in retaining the club's interest by providing a continual stream of interesting material and offers.

The B2C journey reflects the assumption that the end-user of the app will be motivated and encouraged by those clubs that have been engaged. App stores will be used as channels for delivery of the app, but all other activities will be driven through sports clubs as the primary promotional channel to end-users.

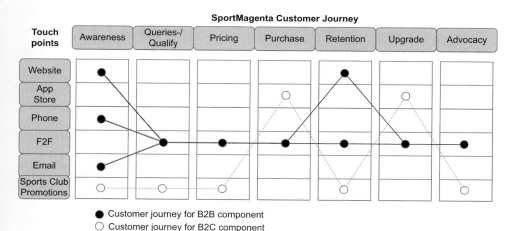

SportMagenta Customer Journey

● Customer journey for B2B component
○ Customer journey for B2C component

These simple journeys imply only that the venture's website and app store entries remain consistent with each other and with the messaging used with clubs. The founders recognize that so long as this is achieved, there will be minimal risk of confusion, irritation or ambiguity for either class of customer.

Planning Development

A venture's offering is central to its ability to gain traction with customers and hence to enhance its value. The offering is also crucial to its reputation, its brand value, and hence to any case for interest or investment, whether of effort or finance. This means that the forward plan for developing the offering is critical to a venture's success.

This section addresses the key aspects to be considered when forming this plan:

- Assessing product viability.
- Calibrating technology readiness.
- Prioritizing requirements for development.
- Developing and managing the product roadmap.
- Development velocity and discontinuities.

Assessing Product Viability

When the concept of *minimum viable product* (MVP) was first proposed by entrepreneur and blogger Eric Ries (2011), it was defined as: 'that version of a new product which allows a team to collect the maximum amount of validated learning about customers with the least effort'. In other words, Ries's intention was to use an early demonstration-oriented version of a product primarily to gather market feedback to inform true product development.

Since that time, particularly in the world of software products, the interpretation has broadened, and the term is now used also to imply an early release of a product within an agile development process. Consequently, a widespread current interpretation is that an MVP will evolve into a mature sustainable product, rather than informing the requirements for subsequent development of such a product.

For a product to be truly *viable*, in addition to its required user functionality it needs to meet a range of other architectural, operational and commercial requirements, including:

- Security and access control.
- Performance and reliability over target infrastructures.
- Resilience to customer operation and network effects.
- Scalability across user communities, including licence management.
- Stability of architecture to accommodate change without loss of integrity.
- Openness to integration with relevant third-party services.

- Sustainable cost of development to meet requirements for configuration, variation, integration and modification.
- Transparency of component licensing and implications for cost and access.

If an early prototype version of a product has the potential to evolve to satisfy such wider requirements, then an agile process can effectively be applied whereby successively more viable products are produced and delivered into customer use.

If, on the other hand, a *proof of concept* or a *demonstration version* has been developed principally to create impact or elicit customer feedback, then this assumption needs to be accepted by the team, and communicated clearly to customers and other parties. Successive iterations of agile development from such a starting point may not be sufficient to deliver a scalable and sustainable product.

A common mistake in early ventures is for an MVP that was initially intended for use as a demonstration in controlled situations to be promoted as a viable product by other members of the team. This can lead to damaged reputation and high costs of remedial activity. A product that is sub-viable needs to be contained within its boundaries.

Another interpretation of MVP is the minimum functionality product that can deliver the value proposition, and hence potentially contribute to value capture. Again, the same principle applies: both the team and the customer need to be aware of the early product limitations. These will usually be reflected in a special *pre-release* or *pilot* agreement that acknowledges and factors in the risk to the customer. Excessive pre-release deployments can be expensive to the venture if subsequent development requires additional retraining of early adopters and migration of customer data.

The important point is for the team to reach agreement over the chosen interpretation of viability, the current state of the offering and the forward plan, and for every member to act in accordance with this.

Calibrating Technology Readiness

Technology readiness levels (TRLs) provide a useful framework for describing and assessing product maturity. Originally developed by NASA, several variants are currently used to reflect the terminology used within sectors such as Oil and Gas or Aerospace. The general interpretation of levels is common across all sectors. The wording used below is from the general-purpose European Commission version, which is sector-neutral:

actual system proven in operational environment	TRL9.
system complete and qualified	TRL8.
system prototype demonstration in operational environment	TRL7.
technology demonstrated in relevant environment	TRL6.
technology validated in relevant environment	TRL5.
technology validated *in the lab*	TRL4.
experimental proof of concept	TRL3.
technology concept formulated	TRL2.
basic principles observed	TRL1.

Note that the terms *technology* and *system* need to be interpreted in the context of the offering involved. For example, the technology may correspond to the functionality of the native offering (product or service) itself, and the system may refer to the offering when customized, integrated, populated and deployed within a customer environment.

These levels are used by research functions to plan research programmes and hence determine which initiatives to fund. They are also used by investors to characterize their appetite and target balance of risk. Consequently, being aware of the current TRL of an offering, and aligning increased levels with development activities, can be useful planning disciplines.

Set in this framework, MVPs tend to be somewhere between TRL3 and TRL7, where the lower bound reflects the use of an MVP for demonstration of concept and collection of feedback, and the upper bound reflects the interpretation whereby the MVP is an early release of a minimally deployable product.

Prioritizing Requirements for Development

The topics of requirements engineering and management for software systems have been addressed substantially by, for example, Kotonya and Sommerville (1998), Bass *et al.* (2013) and Chemuturi (2013), and so are not developed further here in their own right. For the entrepreneur, the principal consideration is prioritization of requirements against the business proposition. The challenge is: which of the myriad potential functionalities and characteristics of a product are the necessary or *key requirements* needed to deliver the value proposition?

This again underlines the importance of explicitly defining the venture's value proposition and associated USPs, as these provide a checklist for key requirements, both of any proposed MVP, and also of the future product roadmap.

This applies more broadly than the user functionality that is provided by the product, as there are usually a range of non-functional requirements implied either by the target market or by the assumed routes whereby delivery will occur. These typically include:

- Required compatibility with standardized or mandated data or process structures.
- Required operating platforms and network infrastructures.
- Required interfaces to external services or data.
- Required levels of security authentication, data protection or safety.
- Required operating or performance conditions, or training needs.

All requirements originate from the business model, and a venture cannot fully succeed in generating value from its offering unless it aligns its development priorities accordingly. This can lead to contention between a sales mindset, which may be keen to respond to customer-specific demands, and an investor's mindset, which retains focus on the business proposition beyond a current *flavor-of-the-month* customer. Clearly, this can go too far, and lead to the team doggedly persisting with the wrong proposition. Working through such tensions can be valuable for developing team maturity and clarity of purpose.

Developing and Managing the Product Roadmap

A development roadmap is a plan that matches short- and long-term business objectives with the development activities by which they will be achieved. Usually represented using a block diagram, such as that illustrated in Figure 4.6, a roadmap is not a detailed project plan to be used for resource scheduling and dependency analysis, but a more strategic tool that connects the roles across the business, and potentially also roles external to the business, to sustain a common understanding of priorities, activities, required investment and planned achievements.

Without a roadmap, a venture risks descent into chaos, with poor understanding of who is doing what, or why, and of when anything will be achieved. An investor or close partner organization will usually expect to see a thoughtfully laid-out roadmap that aligns clearly with achievement of business objectives.

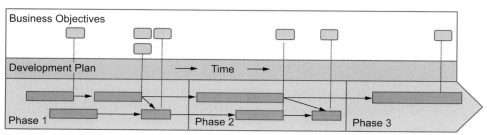

Figure 4.6 *A sample development roadmap*

The usual planning horizon for a roadmap will be relatively detailed for three to six months, with a larger-canvas view thereafter, potentially over the next one to three years, depending on the maturity of the business. The roadmap will often be accompanied by a more detailed project plan for near-term activities, to enable development managers to schedule resources. All plans need to be kept synchronized and up to date to reflect achievements and changes.

Case Study: SportMagenta

Development Roadmap

Zara constructs the venture's roadmap over three phases: the first describes development activity required during the forthcoming quarter, leading up to the time at which pilot projects will commence; the second relates to development during the pilot activity planned over the following quarter; and the third relates to further development in the six months following initial pilots.

Zara's roadmap blends development activities with the promotional activities to be performed by Sonny, so as to synchronize responsibilities across the team.

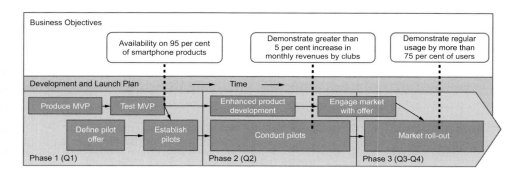

The roadmap also indicates the points on the plan when the business objectives defined during the venture's framing will be demonstrable. For example, during the first quarter, the plan is to meet the objective of achieving availability of the product on 95 per cent of the smartphone products used by club members and visitors.

Development Velocity and Discontinuities

Development velocity is a planning method associated with agile development. It describes the amount of development that can be completed in a time interval. For measurement purposes, development is usually quantified using notional *units of work.* Calibrating this measure enables a more objective assessment of the development effort required to achieve a roadmap activity, so long as the proposed activity can be accurately assessed in terms of the unit of work that it will require.

Tracking improvements in velocity as the team and product mature can be a useful indicator of preparedness for more rapid growth. Conversely, a poor or decreasing velocity would indicate a prior need for remedial action.

Through empirical research, Phadke and Vyakarnam (2017) identify two widely experienced discontinuities, or chasms, that need to be crossed in respect of development activity.

Chasm one is the challenge of developing an idea into a working prototype: achieving TRL3, an experimental proof of concept. Crossing this chasm requires a focus on the technology within the framing of the wider proposition for the venture. Resource requirements are not acute, but what is important is 'a culture which nurtures the talent required to invent new ideas and innovate to create new value'.

Chasm two is the challenge of creating a fully functioning product or service offering with a sustainable business model: achieving TRL8, a system that is complete and qualified. Crossing this chasm can be the most complex and risky part in the development of a venture; it requires organization, talent and leadership to shape and package a market-ready product. The cost of these activities can prove difficult, because many investors are unwilling to invest ahead of this phase, due to its high-risk profile.

These chasms, and a third, are addressed further in Chapter 6 in the context of growth and scalability. The purpose of introducing the first two chasms at this point is to highlight the need for realistic planning and management of development, and the intense risks that can be implied. An awareness of achievable development velocity, and a reasonable assessment of the work required, can inject realism into what will be required.

Managing and Controlling Development and Release

Whatever the nature of the product or service offering underpinning a venture's value proposition, there are a number of aspects that need to be considered to ensure the offering and its development process will be sufficiently robust to support business growth and scalability:

- Designing the production environment.
- Controlling development and variation.
- Governing the use of third-party components.
- Controlling access to source code.
- Managing release and deployment.

Designing the Production Environment

This is about the materials and resources needed to produce the offering, and the implications of these on the cost base and on delivery into the target operating environment.

This is an area that diverges significantly according to the nature of the offering. For a simple software-based offering, the implications will be much less onerous than for a multi-component product such as a cyber physical system (CPS), or for a product that needs volatile or expensive materials, or regulated processing. For this reason, this section limits its attention to general principles. Specific and more detailed coverage of the subjects of production planning and control is provided by, for example, McLean (2017) and Ramachandran *et al.* (2017).

Here, the concern is on the assets required for production, including specialist skills, environmental conditions, equipment, materials and accommodation, or plant. It is critically important to understand what is needed to achieve production and to consider how this will be sourced and managed for the projected levels of required output.

This means identifying the assets needed together with sources of supply and respective costs. The following questions can then be addressed:

- How does production scale, and what are the economics of production?
  - o Do costs scale with volume in a linear manner or otherwise?
  - o Does this limit scalability beyond an economic limit and so would there be benefit from outsourcing production?
- What risks are associated with production at different levels of scale, taking into account supply, storage, safety, control and security?
  - o What are the implications for insurance?
  - o Would there be benefit from outsourcing to transfer the risks of production?
  - o What would be the implication of sudden changes – upwards or downwards – in demand?

- Are there regulatory or security requirements that affect the product or its production process?
  - If so, then does the environment or the people working within it need to be registered or inspected periodically?
  - What does this mean for training and production schedules?
  - Do these pose limitations on staff that can be employed?

The question of regulatory requirements applies strongly to ventures that plan to offer medical devices.

In the USA, the Food and Drug Administration (FDA) has defined Good Manufacturing Practices (GMP) for device manufacturers. These dictate the measures required to ensure quality systems and processes are in place. Manufacturers are also required to implement controls, including audits, system validations, audit trails, electronic signatures, and documentation for software and systems involved in processing certain classes of data.

In the UK, ventures are required to ensure compliance with the conformity and CE (Conformité Européene) marking procedures, and may also need to follow the Medical Devices Regulations 2002. Furthermore, there are additional requirements to notify the relevant competent authority before carrying out any clinical investigation of the device.

A common mistake when planning production is to overestimate the speed of market take-up, and hence to scale too soon. This can lead to the venture bearing a high cost of over-capacity of people and assets, which can severely damage investor and team confidence, and even threaten the venture's viability. Understanding how to scale, and potentially bearing a short-term cost for accelerating this beyond the plan, is a preferable policy.

When planning the production environment, it is also necessary to consider the implications of the environment into which the offering will be delivered:

- The production environment needs to be planned with the customer in mind. This means anticipating requirements for compatibility with normal market expectations, including levels of required resilience, security, portability, ease of assembly or deployment.
- The environment also needs to be designed with consideration of the customer's operating infrastructure, including any network, manufacturing or branding process into which the product will be delivered. Compatibility and integration need to be tested against projected levels of production.

A useful approach when addressing these points is to consider the customer journey or tactical map and its impact on brand image from the point of order through production, dispatch, delivery, assembly/integration, training and operation. Will each stage of the journey reinforce the value proposition and enhance the brand value? If not, then the environment needs to be redesigned to avoid potential delays and costs.

Controlling Development and Variation

Agile development of software products or software components of products is well supported by a range of tools and available third-party components. One effect of this is the potential for very rapid development of code; another is the potential for loss of control; and a third is the risk of encumbering the business with unexpected future cost, or technical debt.

Achieving scalability demands the early implementation of a method for configuration and version control. However trivial this may be in the early stages, it can be beneficial to introduce such a scheme at the outset to ensure the team and the artefacts scale in a controllable way.

This is particularly relevant where the venture intends to support customized versions, or product variants for customers or markets. Managing a coherent code base avoids messy future problems involving product enhancements or fixes. Even with such management, there will always be a cost of supporting multiple variant offerings, and this should be questioned in terms of its value, cost and best method of handling. Although the additional cost overhead may be tolerable against a small set of early customers, it is important to consider how these costs will scale with business growth, and the burden that will be placed on the future cost of development.

If customer-specific variation can be limited to stylistic changes, then the future development cost will be significantly lower than if deeper functional differences had been tolerated.

Governing the Use of Third-Party Components

It can be very compelling to incorporate a hardware or software component or library that directly offers required functionality, and which therefore removes from the team the responsibility of developing and maintaining that functionality or effect. This advantage can become negative, however, unless the applicable licensing terms are reviewed in terms of:

- What are the provisions for redistribution of the component for commercial purposes?
  - Do these include a payment and, if so, who will bear this cost: the venture or the customer?
  - How do the provisions scale to higher usage volumes?
- If the licence belongs to an open-source family (see also Chapter 7), then what are the implications for the wider product offering within which the component will be embedded?
  - Does the licence simply require an acknowledgement of its provenance?
  - Or does it require that the entire product be offered under the same licence?

From the earliest stages of development, a schedule of third-party components used, together with relevant licensing terms, must be reviewed and managed. This can be a significant area of interest to an investor during the process of assuring the future security of a venture.

Controlling Access to Source Code

For open-source offerings, source code may be published under a GNU General Public Licence, making it available for access, use and modification by customers, integrators and other eco-system players.

For non-open-source, or proprietary, offerings, the licence agreement will usually limit source code access, typically using forms of words such as:

- '[The Venture] grants the User a non-exclusive, non-transferable, licence to install, load and use the object code only of [The Offering].'
- 'The user may not reverse engineer, decompile, disassemble or otherwise reduce any component of [The Offering] to its source code or otherwise access, use copy or load ... source code.'

In such cases, management and control over access to source code is a critical security and resilience requirement for the business. External access to sources, or their loss or damage, can lead to breach of contract with customers and significant business disruption. Due to the severity of the impact of such a failure, it is incumbent on the venture to establish and implement a strong policy.

In some sectors, a software escrow agreement may be required. This is an agreement to periodically deposit copies of the software source code with a third-party escrow agent, to provide the customer with an ability to maintain the software in the event that the business fails or becomes incapable itself of doing so. Such a request is more likely in a B2B environment, as some large organizations make software escrow a mandatory aspect of their software purchasing.

In addition to satisfying a customer requirement, establishing an escrow arrangement can lead to a useful software management discipline, where a coherent back-up of all sources are periodically generated and stored offline.

Managing Release and Deployment

This is an area that is easily underestimated in terms of its scope and required effort.

As with the various considerations addressed so far in this section, the focus here is not on the specific techniques or technologies that are available, but on the applicable principles, considerations and decisions needed by the team.

Releasing a product for live use by a community of customer and partner organizations means addressing the following:

- Testing at all levels, from individual components through to the whole offering, including within its intended operating environments.
- Development of required communications, including brochures that affirm the offering's value to the customer; user documentation; installation and integration information; and details of new features and upgrade support for those with earlier versions.
- Mechanisms, automated and manual, for technical delivery and integration, potentially including customization, transportation and specialist configuration.
- Training at multiple levels, online and face-to-face, including training for relevant classes of user and also establishing administrative procedures for user management, access control, back-up and performance tuning.
- Establishing support facilities, including multi-channel helpline arrangements and facilities for usage and technical enquiries, potentially including cover for out-of-hours service, and a multi-level offering with a combination of in-house teams and third-party organizations.

These considerations need to be addressed such that the venture's brand image is coherently sustained and enhanced through every encounter. This means that every customer touch point must be anticipated and considered in terms of what it communicates to the customer or partner about the competence, commitment and reliability of the business.

These activities will typically involve a wide range of team roles, and so it is necessary for everyone in the venture to be considered as potentially customer-facing, and hence trained and equipped to deliver a positive impact. Involving bright and motivated technical staff in joint activity with customer roles through a well-planned deployment process can go a long way towards establishing trust in the business and its offering. This trust can translate into an inclination to be understanding and forgiving in the event that things go wrong at some point.

Establishing a Channel Strategy

A channel strategy describes the way(s) by which a product or service will be promoted, ordered, delivered and deployed by the end customer: will it be downloaded and installed by the end customer, or will it be delivered and installed by an in-house team, or by one of a collection of contracted agents?

The terms *channel* and *route to market* are normally used synonymously: a channel partner provides a route to market. It should be noted that some commentators use the term *channel* to refer specifically to a promotional function or partnership, and the term *route to market* to refer specifically to a function or partner by which product ordering and delivery are handled. The terms *distribution channel* and *channels to market* are also sometimes used, adding to the variations. This book uses the terms interchangeably. Where it is helpful to differentiate, the specific terms *promotional channel* or *delivery channel* are used.

Just as an offering may target multiple segments of customers, so there may be benefits from supporting multiple channels. In some cases, each distinct customer segment will warrant a dedicated channel; in others, many channels may be established, all directed at the same customer group. In the case of the latter approach, it is important to ensure consistency, so as not to sow confusion of branding, pricing or terms offered.

Visually, the respective value chains can be expressed as shown in Figure 4.7, where the upper sequence denotes a direct channel to the customer and the lower depicts the intermediary role of a channel partner.

When considering channel strategy, it is important to consider the implications of the venture's position in the resulting value chain:

- To whom will the venture be promoting its offering – its customer or a network of partners?

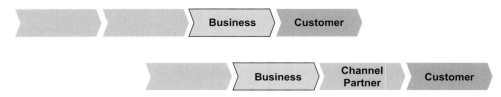

Figure 4.7 *Value chain depictions with and without a channel partner*

- What will be the implications for intellectual property protection and branding – will the customer perceive the venture to be the originator of the offering?
- What will be the implications for control – which organization will be responsible for the time and manner of delivery to the customer?
- What will be the implications for relationships with the customer decision-makers – which organization will be responsible for managing key customer stakeholders, ensuring repeat sales, pursuing wider opportunities and building user communities?
- What will be the implications for reputation – if there were a problem or complaint relating to delivery or operation, who would the customer deem to be responsible and who would perform any required remedial action?
- What will be the implications for risk – including those relating to delivery, payment, intellectual property protection and support?

At one level, channel strategy is about determining the kinds of channels to be developed and operated for delivery to customers; at another, it is about the method that is applied when selecting and managing the specific channel partner organizations. The latter topic is addressed afterwards, as it builds upon the choice of types of partner needed.

A more comprehensive coverage of this subject is provided by Raulerson *et al.* (2009) and also by the 'field guide' produced by Coughlan and Jap (2016).

Determining Routes to Market

This is about identifying the routes to market that will enable a venture to motivate and enable its customers to find, order, receive, deploy and use its offering.

In broad terms, there are three non-mutually-exclusive options:

- *Online platform*: orders will be placed through the venture's website. Delivery may be handled using the same site or via some other mechanism. If the offering is associated with training or customization, then these may be handled as separate, related offerings.

- *Direct team*: the venture builds and manages a team of employees or contracted agents for taking orders, arranging delivery and supporting deployment and use.
- *Distribution channel*: a third-party service provider, reseller, distributor, catalogue provider or other kind of channel partner is engaged to perform some combination of order handling, delivery, deployment and support.

Many permutations of these options are possible: a direct team might be used to process sales in one territory, with local channel partners responsible for handling orders from elsewhere; or orders might be placed through an online product catalogue, with delivery and deployment services provided by a service partner.

Apple, for example, delivers products directly and through a large number of sales and distribution channels, while sustaining both retail and online stores. A complex channel strategy such as this requires serious planning and management to ensure that the various potentially competing routes to market all contribute to Apple's value and that all remain motivated to promote and deliver products in line with the company's strategy. Apple balances its strategy by not discounting sales through any of its direct channels, and by consistently applying strict controls over its reseller arrangements: small margins, no volume discounts, and no variability in the terms offered for each product.

Choosing routes to market that fit the needs of the venture means first considering each of the following:

The Nature of the Customer
A venture can be categorized according to the following:

- Business-to-consumer (B2C), where the customer is also the user or consumer of the offering. Examples include businesses that offer smartphone apps or consumer electronics products.
- Business-to-business (B2B), where the customer is an organization, and therefore an order may be placed by the user or consumer or by a purchasing function. Examples include businesses that offer enterprise software solutions or network infrastructure components.
- Business-to-business-to-consumer (B2B2C), where there are two connected types of customer: a business service provider and the consumers of its services. Associated offerings are promoted to each, and orders are placed by each. Open Table is an example of a B2B2C business, as it offers a reservation platform for restaurants and an associated table booking service for diners.

- Business-to-government (B2G), where the customer is a national or local government body, and therefore likely to apply procurement rules and standards. Examples include providers of online citizen services or medical devices.
- Business-to-knowledge or affinity-based groups (B2K), a term coined by Phadke and Vyakarnam (2017), to refer to situations where the end-user is a professional knowledge-worker who uses an offering purchased by an organization. Global Data is an example of a B2K business; its clinical trials database is offered for purchase by pharma companies and investors and for use by researchers. B2K and B2B2C businesses are similar in having two connected types of customers.

The Planned Promotional Channels

Decisions around business promotion (addressed in Chapter 3) focus on creating awareness and demand for the offering, including through identification and development of partners that offer promotional channels into the market.

Where such partners also provide a delivery capability, it may be desirable for the venture to align its promotional and delivery channels, to achieve consistency of operation and customer experience. Two contrasting examples illustrate this:

Suppose that the promotional partner is a business that offers a complementary product, and a mutually beneficial joint marketing arrangement has been established. In this case, each business will establish its own routes to market, with the expectation that both will benefit through the joint promotional activities.

Alternatively, suppose that the promotional partner is a *channel business*, a reseller offering to generate demand and to provide access into the targeted market. In this case, the partner's promotional activities will naturally flow into handling of customer interest through order, delivery, usage and upgrade, and it will be important for consistency of the customer journey that the same channel applies throughout.

In some business models, it is inherently important that promotional and delivery channels are aligned. This is particularly the case with those B2B2C offerings where the business customers can also provide promotional and delivery channels to the end customers of the offering.

The Nature of the Offering

The kind of offering produced by the venture can have implications for applicable routes to market:

- Is the offering a packaged, off-the-shelf product or service, or does it involve customization of some kind? For example, a SaaS offering for expense handling may be offered as a packaged service, whereas a system integration capability is more likely to be offered as a service with its scope and outcomes agreed jointly with the customer.
- It is useful to distinguish *collaborative customization*, where a business works jointly with its customers to determine the precise requirement, from *adaptive customization*, where a standard product is adapted by the customer, perhaps by purchasing additional extra features, or through further development or integration activity. A further and less common kind is *transparent customization*, where an offering is pre-customized for a customer.
- Does the offering fit with a fixed and transparent pricing model, or will the market expect to negotiate on terms? In more competitive markets such as electronic payment services, larger customers may expect to be able to negotiate their own terms.
- Is the offering amenable to electronic delivery, or does it contain physical components? Offerings that include physical elements require some form of fulfilment process for physical delivery. This may be handled by an in-house team or by an external partner.

The Required Customer Experience

What experience must be created to build and reinforce the customer value concept?

- How important is it to provide speed of order, receipt and deployment? For example, this is very important with many B2C offerings, but less so with more process-based B2B and B2G offerings.
- How important is it to provide ease of order, receipt and deployment? Again, this must fit the customer profile. It can be important to consider whether the technical competence of the customer can be assumed to be sufficient to deploy and use the offering without the need for further assistance.
- What are the requirements for packaging and physical delivery of materials? If the offering comprises physical components, then the packaging design must reinforce the customer value concept.

The Scalability Ambitions

What are the scalability implications on both demand- and supply-sides of the business?

Table 4.3 Criteria for Assessment of Routes to Market

Route to market	Characteristics (typical)	Order handling			Delivery implications	Deployment implications
		B2C	B2B	B2G		
Online (own website)	• Cost of set-up can be high • Low variable cost of operation • Highly scalable • Rapid and easy to use	Offerings without collaborative customization	Especially XaaS offerings	Especially XaaS offerings (e.g. UK G-Cloud)	May need fulfilment solution and partner	May need additional offering or arrangement for training/technical activities
Direct (in-house or outsourced, e.g. telesales)	• Fixed costs of sale can be high • Control over process, terms, customer journey	Customized or high-value offerings	High value offerings, or collaborative customization, or negotiable terms	High-value offerings, or collaborative customization, or negotiable terms	Integrated order handling and fulfilment	Can control and take responsibility for complex or high-risk activity
Distribution channel (partners, app stores, catalogues, distributors, online stores, service providers, resellers)	• Cost of set-up, including agreement over branding, control and relationships • Highly scalable • Low variable costs • Can provide integrated promotion • Can lack process flexibility	Offerings without collaborative customization	• Offerings without collaborative customization • Can lower the barrier to entry (with approved channels) • Opportunity to white-label with recognized brand		• Integrated order handling and fulfilment • Need to ensure quality, performance, and brand / reputation protection	• May need additional offering or arrangement for training / technical activities • Need clear responsibility over deployment risks

- In terms of required capacity and cost scaling on the demand- or customer-side, what capacity is anticipated to be needed in terms of order and delivery volumes, and what limitations and risks apply?
- In terms of required capacity and cost scaling on the supply-side, what capacity is anticipated to be needed in terms of material volumes and timeliness, and what limitations and risks apply?

Evaluation of Options

Based on these considerations, the fit of the possible routes to market can be assessed using Table 4.3.

The application of the table is illustrated by the following examples:

Zmodo Greet is a smart doorbell. The user is informed by their phone when someone rings the doorbell. This is a B2C offering that is promoted by the company's own website and by online retailers, including Amazon. It is a fixed-price, off-the-shelf product that has physical components which need to be installed by the user. It is reasonably important that this product can be delivered within a few days of being ordered. Sales volumes need to be flexible to cope with fluctuating demand.

As shown by Table 4.3, candidate routes to market for Zmodo Greet include an online channel operated by the business and distribution partners, including online retailers. In all cases, a fulfilment partner will be required to deliver the product to its purchaser, and there may be demand for local service partners to assist with installation.

The Westfield app was used as an example in Chapter 2. It integrates with the retail outlets in a Westfield shopping centre to provide shoppers with 'less searching, more shopping'. This is a B2B2C offering comprising a B2B information platform that integrates with outlets and a B2C mobile app for shoppers. The B2B component requires adaptive customization to integrate outlets' data, and is less time critical. The B2C component is off-the-shelf and its delivery to shoppers is time-critical.

As shown by Table 4.3, candidate routes to market for the B2B component of Westfield include a direct channel that provides customization services for retail outlets, or Westfield's own online channel if such customization can be automated. Routes to market for the B2C component of the product include the Westfield website and the relevant app stores from which shoppers can download the app for immediate use.

Case Study: SportMagenta

Routes to Market

The founders recognize that SportMagenta is a B2B2C business, combining a B2B offering for sports clubs with a B2C app that will be used by members and visitors to clubs.

Their assessment of the implications of the offerings is as follows:

For the B2C component, the user experience must be fast, easy and self-branding. There must be no limitations on the distribution of software to those who wish to use it.

For the B2B component, the offering demands direct, face-to-face engagement, because of the need for significant effort and market knowledge, plus the likelihood of needing to negotiate terms individually with each club, or chain of clubs. Furthermore, a degree of collaborative customization will be needed for each club in relation to their existing software and data assets.

On the basis of these assessments, the founders agree to the following routes to market:

- Build a direct channel to support engagements into the B2B market, with the capability to cover all aspects of the customization and integration process. This channel will also be responsible for enabling clubs to operate as promotional channels into their membership bases.
- Use online distribution channels for distribution of the B2C app to members and visitors. These will include relevant app stores and also the online channels provided by the sports clubs.

The founders recognize that the use of app stores for online distribution will imply commission payments, if the B2C component has an associated charge, and also that certain licensing rules will apply. The consequences of the latter are addressed in Chapter 7.

The founders anticipate benefits in the future from building and managing a network of resellers or service partners, each bringing market knowledge and connections in additional markets or geographies.

Managing Relationships with Channel Partners

It is important to put in place a process to identify, qualify, establish and manage relationships with partner organizations to establish the required routes to market. Such a process involves the following steps for each required partnership:

1. Identify and qualify candidate partner organizations and select those that best meet business requirements. This may involve making proposals,

inviting bids or conducting interviews, according to the nature and dynamics of the market. It will conclude with an agreed set of terms for doing business, including responsibilities, liabilities, pricing, cost handling, commissions, intellectual property ownership and performance.

2. Establish and enable the selected partner(s) to operate as a channel for the offering. This may include training of personnel, equipping with materials and joint agreement to a plan for promotional activity.

3. Operate the channel, including measuring and tracking its performance and assessing this against targets and commitments.

4. Conduct periodic reviews of the relationship in terms of performance and expected benefit. Such reviews may lead to commitment for a further term, for amended terms or for termination.

Failure to establish such a process with channel partners can result in damage to the reputation of the venture or its offering, a need for additional unplanned remedial effort or costly legal action to resolve a dispute.

Bringing Innovation to Delivery and Operations

As noted in Chapter 3, all aspects of business design and activity benefit from innovation.

Innovation in supply means questioning the potential value and risk to the venture of every supply requirement. Buying things on the open market can be quick and easy, with minimal future commitment, but it can be useful to consider options whereby supply arrangements can be used to enhance the venture's reputation, perhaps by alignment with a respected and trusted partner.

Although outsourcing the supply chain can initially be attractive in enabling greater focus on delivery, it can also mean lost opportunities for resilience and breadth through creating new kinds of relationships with a wider range of suppliers.

Applying innovation to development relates not only to product design and build; it can also relate to the way in which customers are engaged within the process and given access to the roadmap. It can be advantageous to open the doors to a competent customer who can bring market experience to check assumptions, and who might play an active and educational role in testing and deployment planning. Any such approach needs to be handled carefully to avoid any claim of ownership over the product or the venture: underlying any customer conversation, there is always an implied and assumed contract. The offer to the customer might be framed in terms of equipping their own team to be able to exploit the potential of the offering ahead of the market.

The analysis of routes to market and implied customer journeys can benefit significantly from thinking beyond the obvious options and patterns. Useful questions to consider include:

- Who else does the customer purchase from?
- Which other similarly valued things does the customer currently purchase?
- What process does the customer expect to follow when they make a purchase?

The answers to such questions can indicate opportunities for novel routes to market, including through suppliers of complementary offerings, potentially bringing efficiencies for the customer in addition to useful recognition and partnership relationships. If the answers to any of these questions are not known, further research is needed.

Risk underlies all of these considerations: the risk of becoming locked into a punitive supply contract that is not needed because sales growth is slower than projected; or the risk of damaging an important customer relationship by losing their trust in the venture's ability to deliver its roadmap; or the risk of reputational damage through failure of a channel to market. Such risks can only be handled effectively if the various decisions are approached with innovation, with a good knowledge of the market and its dynamics, and with a clear focus on the venture's objectives.

Summary of Delivery and Operations

This chapter has addressed the principal considerations relating to the delivery, operation and support of a venture's offering into its market so as to create an effect that will meet its defined objectives.

These considerations are very wide-ranging, from the sourcing of required services and materials, through to the intended customer experience, the plan for continuing development and the means by which development and release will be managed and controlled, through to the need for a channel strategy to provide routes to market for the venture.

Many of the subjects addressed here are significant topics in their own right, with an associated research base, literature and market of supporting products. Each has here been addressed from the perspective of the entrepreneur, prompting the questions and options that need to be considered, and describing principles and techniques that can enable decisions to be approached rationally and with innovative intent. Examples of real-world businesses have been used, and the SportMagenta exemplar has been extended. References to a range of specialist texts have been provided to enable the subjects to be addressed in further detail.

The key points addressed are summarized below.

- **Managing the supply chain** is about managing the flow of goods and services from their point of origin to the point of consumption by the venture's end-users:
  - A venture with a non-trivial supply chain needs to decide whether to outsource this in whole or in part, locally or internationally.
  - Either identify and source from the open market as and when required, or build and manage a network of approved suppliers, or invest in an integrated, and potentially automated, purchasing system with a single preferred supplier.
- Designing the **customer journey** addresses the need to create a customer experience of a single seamless journey across all *touch points* with the venture, from the way in which the customer becomes aware of the offering, through to the management of retention, upgrade and customer advocacy:
  - Customer journey design ensures that there is no inadvertent confusion, frustration, inefficiency or inconsistency in the design of the channels by which the customer engages in some way with the venture or its offering.
  - The map can provide a valuable analysis tool to validate the effectiveness of the business design in terms of promotion and delivery.
  - It can be useful to create tactical maps to analyse the processes involved to a greater level of detail to test their coherence and design implications.
- The **plan for continued development** of the offering is critical to a venture's success:
  - There are many interpretations of MVP, from a feedback mechanism through to an early release; importantly, the team needs agreement over their chosen interpretation.
  - TRLs provide a useful framework for describing and assessing product maturity and are used by some investors to characterize their risk appetite.
  - An offering has both functional and non-functional requirements, and all of these originate from the business model: the venture cannot succeed in generating value from its offering unless it aligns its development priorities accordingly.

- A development roadmap is a plan that matches short- and long-term business objectives with the development activities by which they will be achieved.
- Whatever the nature of a venture's offering, its **development must be managed and controlled** for robustness, sustainability and scalability:
  - The design of the production environment needs to address the materials and resources needed and to assess their implications.
  - Scalability requires early implementation of a method for configuration and version control.
  - It is important from the outset to maintain a schedule of third-party components used.
  - For non-open-source offerings, management and control over access to source code is a critical security and resilience requirement for the venture.
  - Release and deployment of an offering must ensure that the venture's brand image is coherently sustained and enhanced through every customer encounter.
- A **channel strategy** describes the way(s) by which a product or service will be promoted, ordered, delivered and deployed by the end customer:
  - Determining routes to market is about identifying mechanisms such as an online platform, in-house teams and partner relationships that together will enable the venture to motivate and enable its customers to find, order, receive, deploy and use its offering.
  - Establishing and managing relationships with channel partners is about establishing a process to identify, qualify, establish and manage relationships with chosen channel partners to establish and sustain the required routes to market.
- For each of the above, it is important to apply the **innovative power of the business:**
  - Innovation in the analysis of potential routes to market can deliver efficiencies for the customer or additional recognition and partnership relationships for the venture.
  - Innovation in the way in which customers are engaged within the development process can enhance the additional market experience available to the venture.
  - Innovation in supply chain management can lead to enhanced reputation through alignment with a respected and trusted partner.

ANALYSIS EXERCISES

The table below lists a collection of digital businesses to be used as subjects for the exercises that follow.

Business	Focus	Website
Darktrace	Cyber security	www.darktrace.com
Fitbit	Health, fitness and performance	www.fitbit.com
JustEat	Online takeaway food	www.just-eat.co.uk
Reposit	Property rental	www.getreposit.uk
Snapchat	Social media	www.snapchat.com
Sorry as a Service	Customer services and retention	www.sorryasaservice.com
SwiftComply	Regulation and compliance	www.swiftcomply.com

On the basis of information available in the public domain, address the questions below for at least one of the businesses listed.

1. The business's customer(s):
   (a) Who is the customer(s) for the proposed innovation?
   (b) Who are the principal players in the business ecosystem?
   (c) What are the principal value exchanges with these players?

2. Managing the supply chain:
   (a) What are the principal supply requirements of the business?
   (b) Recommend preferred options for managing two of these requirements, in terms of whether they should be handled in-house or outsourced, and what kind of supply arrangements would be preferable.
   (c) Which characteristics of the business and its supply requirements drive your recommendations?

3. Customer journey:
   (a) Construct a customer journey map for one of the business's offerings.
   (b) What assumptions underlie the proposed map?
   (c) Give two suggestions to improve the effectiveness of the customer journey.
   (d) Would a tactical map be helpful with any aspects of the journey?

4. Planning development:
   (a) Recommend three priority areas for further development of the offering.
   (b) To which of the business's assumed objectives do each of your recommendations apply?
5. Management and control of development:
   (a) Which aspects of its offering might imply scalability or sustainability challenges for the business?
   (b) How might these be addressed by the business?
6. Routes to market:
   (a) Recommend the three routes to market that would be most effective for the business.
   (b) Which characteristics of the business drive each of your recommendations?

DESIGN EXERCISES

The design exercise at the end of Chapter 1 encouraged identification of a business idea to be developed incrementally by specific design exercises through subsequent chapters of the book. That activity commenced in Chapter 2, with the framing of the selected business idea using the elements introduced in that chapter. This was extended in Chapter 3, with the addition of considerations and decisions relating to business promotion and sales.

Extend your current design through the following tasks:

1. For each aspect of business delivery and operation covered in this chapter, perform an assessment and analysis of your business. If using the Business Design Template, summarize the resulting considerations in the left-hand cell of the *delivery and operations* section.
2. Extract from your considerations the set of key decisions relating to the promotion of your business. If using the Business Design Template, document these in the right-hand cell of the *delivery and operations* section.
3. Review the extended design of your business for consistency, and address any issues that arise.
4. Capture separately any of the following:
   (a) Key points learned from the exercise.
   (b) Outstanding issues or uncertainties.

5   Value Capture

Focus of This Chapter

Figure 5.1 illustrates how the material addressed by this chapter fits within the framework of considerations for business design.

Building upon decisions in the contexts of promotion, sales, delivery and operations, the considerations addressed here elaborate upon the decisions made during business framing in the context of the question *what is the problem that is solved?*

The decisions addressed by the material covered in this and previous chapters relate to the generation of business value. These decisions guide and inform those relating to achieving business objectives, addressed by the following chapters. It is important that consistency is achieved and sustained across the decisions made in relation to each component of the framework.

Learning Outcomes

After studying this chapter, you will:

- Understand the need to consider value capture in the context of business objectives.
- Be able to identify and qualify options for the commercial packaging of a product or service.
- Be able to qualify, assess and calibrate the possible pricing structures for an offering.

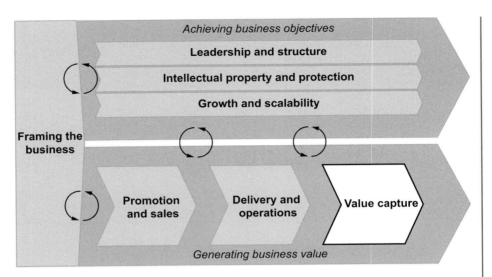

Figure 5.1 *Context of value capture*

- Understand the principal methods used for assessing and calculating business value.
- Appreciate the importance of applying innovation to considerations around value capture.

Introducing Value Capture

A business meets its objectives by creating value, both for its customers and for itself.

Chapters 2, 3 and 4 have focused on generating value for the customer. This chapter is about the corresponding process of capturing value back into the business, to enable its sustainability, development and growth.

As with all aspects of business design, there are myriad considerations and these need to be addressed rationally, with a clear focus on target objectives, while being driven by an open and innovative ethos.

As illustrated by the simple value chain in Figure 5.2, this chapter subdivides into four principal sections:

- The first section addresses the setting of a strategy for value capture, including defining objectives, assessing the implications of current market forces and creating a return-on-investment (ROI) case.

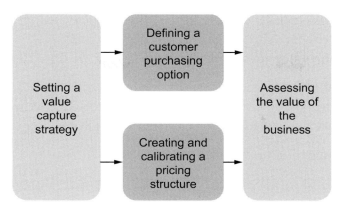

Figure 5.2 *Topics covered by this chapter*

- The second is about defining what it is that will be offered to the customer for purchase, including assumptions about how the customer's purchasing process will operate.
- The third is about creating and calibrating the details of the pricing structure to be applied.
- The fourth section takes a wider market perspective by addressing the drivers of business valuation and the principal methods that are used to assess business value.

For each of these topics, relevant principles, considerations and techniques are introduced and illustrated using a collection of real-world examples and the SportMagenta exemplar.

Many of the topics introduced in this chapter are large and sophisticated subjects and so the coverage is filtered to align with the principal considerations of the entrepreneur. A more comprehensive coverage of pricing and its relationship with business value is provided by Baker (2006), and more recently by Schwartz and Kim (2016). The works of Baker (2010) and Macdivitt and Wilkinson (2011) address the topic from the specific perspective of value-based pricing.

Setting a Value Capture Strategy

The pricing approach adopted by a venture has a significant impact on the market response to its offering, and hence on its performance. A venture with a strong offering that is under- or over-priced, or which expects payment from the wrong party, is unlikely to meet its objectives. Consequently, designing an effective strategy for value capture is critically important.

A strategy for value capture has three parts:

- A statement of the objectives that drive value capture.
- An assessment of the implications on pricing of the effective market forces.
- The case that can be made to the customer for an ROI.

These are addressed in turn below.

Setting Objectives to Drive the Pricing Approach

As with all business design decisions, the approach to pricing – including what, who, how and when to charge – must be driven by business objectives; consequently, the starting point for consideration of pricing must be the question of what the venture wants to achieve from its pricing.

The value capture objectives for a venture may include one or more of the following:

- To meet targets for revenue or profit margins, either in the long or the short term, to achieve and demonstrate financial strength and viability.
- To maximize the value created for the customer, to deliver societal benefit or to achieve the recognition and respect of a community.
- To maximize repeatable revenue growth over a particular time frame in order to demonstrate scalable potential for future cash generation.
- To maximize market share within a particular time frame in order to demonstrate potential for future profitability and market dominance.
- To maximize the reputation for quality in order to establish the potential of the brand as a high-end market leader.
- To maximize the volume of materials or services handled in order to demonstrate scalability and potential for significant future growth.
- To maximize impact on the market so as to establish a strong reputation as a disruptor or innovator.
- To achieve and sustain a financial status quo whereby the venture can continue to operate at a stable level.

The value capture objectives for a venture may equate to some of the key objectives defined during business framing, or they may be sub-objectives that are implied by others. As with all aspects of business design, value capture objectives can change over time in response to experience, change of plan or market events. When this happens, the implications on all aspects of value capture need to be assessed.

In some cases, the nature of the offering can imply specific considerations that influence the objectives that apply:

- For B2C offerings, a demonstration of increasing Customer Lifetime Value (CLV) can have a strongly positive impact on the valuation of the venture.
- For B2C and cloud-based software offerings, the demonstration of an increasing recurring revenue (typically monthly recurring revenue – MRR) tends to be viewed as a strong indicator of business value.
- For ventures that provide an e-commerce platform across a marketplace, gross merchandise value (GMV), measuring the total value of merchandise sold through the platform over a given period of time, can be a strong indicator of success.

Assessing the Implications of Market Forces

Chapter 3 introduced a *market forces* model as the basis of a technique for identifying and analysing ecosystem dynamics to inform considerations of business promotion. This model can also be useful in the context of value capture to analyse the pricing implications both of competitive pressures and of the negotiating, or bargaining, power of the venture.

Although these two aspects overlap, they can be addressed sequentially in terms of the market forces involved and the effect that each can have on pricing considerations. The pricing approaches initially introduced here are each explained further in a later section of this chapter.

Assessing the Competitive Implications of Market Forces

It is important to understand the implications of the three competitive market forces when considering pricing options. Figure 5.3 (which repeats Figure 3.4 for convenience) highlights the effective forces.

For a venture that is fortunate enough to gain access to a market with few or no existing competitors, there is an opportunity to exploit *first-mover advantage* to combat the *threat of new entrants*. This can be achieved by adopting one of the following approaches to create *barriers to entry* for would-be competitors:

- Apply a *penetration pricing* approach by setting a low initial price to capture a significant market share and hence establish a dominant position and reputation ahead of additional players.

Figure 5.3 *Forces with competitive implications on pricing*

- Apply a *skimming* approach by setting a high initial price to benefit from the lack of competition. This price can be reduced to enhance competitiveness as new entrants arrive.

Where first-mover advantage applies, the choice of which approach to adopt will be driven by the value capture objectives that have been set.

Barriers to entry for new entrants can also be created by exploiting collaborations with existing market players. Suppose, for example, that a venture is introducing a new sensor technology into the sports-wearables market. Establishing exclusive arrangements with leading manufacturers of wearable devices would create an effective barrier of entry for other businesses attempting to launch a comparable sensor offering. Limiting competitive access to the market gives an opportunity to review pricing levels to meet business objectives.

Combating *industry rivalry* – direct competition with existing players in the market – typically involves *competition-based pricing*, whereby the price is set with reference to the pricing offered by other players. This can imply the use of one of the following approaches:

- Where the competing offerings present equivalent value to the customer, either the price can be set to undercut the competition (and so offer 'better value for money'), or a *bundling* option can be offered to reduce the unit cost to the customer, while building greater customer commitment.
- Where the offering is distinctive or disruptive in some way that enhances its ROI relative to the competition, then there are two options: either set a higher

price ('you get what you pay for'), or set the same price as the competition ('more for the same'). Clearly, the ROI case will need to be compelling.

In either case, the important point is to know and track the pricing policy of the competition.

Industry rivalry can also be addressed through collaboration, along much the same lines as illustrated above to combat the threat of new entrants.

Assessing the *threat of substitutes* can be difficult because the potential competitor can be a very different kind of business: traditional taxi companies did not expect to be threatened by a substitute in the form of Uber.

The threat of substitutes can be mitigated through a combination of the following approaches:

• Build and evidence a highly compelling business case and ROI for the offering to defend the value for money offered.
• Monitor potential threats and quantify the switching costs that would be involved, to make a strong case for 'sticking with what you have'.
• Build brand loyalty, underpinned with contractual barriers to entry, such as exclusivity clauses with longer-term commitment, attractive enterprise-wide offerings and special one-off deals.

The above analysis of forces and implications underlines the importance of understanding the target market in terms of current and potential competitors and collaborators. A useful way to capture this is through the venture's risk register, which should be kept up to date with potential threats and mitigating activities. The old maxim applies: 'keep your friends close, but your enemies closer'.

Assessing the Negotiation Implications of Market Forces

The pricing implications of a venture's negotiating or bargaining power relate to both supply- and demand-sides of the business, as illustrated in Figure 5.4 (which repeats Figure 3.4 for convenience).

On the supply-side, the *bargaining power of suppliers* affects the venture's cost base, which may in turn affect the range of pricing options available. A cost increase by a supplier needs either to be absorbed by the venture, reducing its margins, or to be passed on to the customer as a price increase.

Cost increases may originate from factors in the supplier's own cost base, or from an ambition to increase its revenues or margins. Understanding and questioning the underlying rationale is a reasonable response in any case.

Figure 5.4 *Forces with negotiation implications on pricing*

In cases where a *cost-plus pricing* approach is applied (which is required in certain government contracting environments), the customer price is calculated by adding a profit margin to the cost of production and distribution, and so increased costs may automatically be absorbed by the customer.

However, with other approaches, increased costs, or even the risk of this, can be damaging financially and so will need to be addressed, usually through one of the following approaches:

- Create increased competition for the supplier by identifying plausible equivalent or substitute suppliers. This will be more feasible and incur lower switching costs if the need has been anticipated in advance by standardizing on generic or standard specifications or interfaces. The identification and adoption of such standards can provide a longer-term mitigation for this risk.

- Where there are distinct advantages of staying with an existing supplier, new benefits can be offered into the relationship, including partnership deals with mutual investment to create longer-term commitment aligned with beneficial costings. Where this fails, a more aggressive approach can be adopted, including threats to cancel current orders and terminate all plans for future business. Clearly, the effectiveness of this depends on the respective bargaining powers and the wider market conditions.

- Seek collaborations with other market players to enable purchase of supply in larger volumes, hence achieving greater economies of scale. Such collaborations may be with competitors or with other organizations that share comparable supply requirements. This applies particularly to commodity requirements.

On the demand-side, the *bargaining power of buyers* influences, and may limit, the pricing levels that can be achieved. Central to this are the effect of current and prospective competition, and the power of the ROI: the value that the customer believes is achievable from the offering.

A venture's negotiating power with its customers can be increased by the following approaches:

- Invest in high-level sponsorship within customer organizations. Senior roles have access to greater budgets, and can endorse higher spend against initiatives that they believe offer significant business value. They can also apply a longer-term perspective that can overcome short-term technical limitations in favour of the 'bigger story'.
- Invest in loyalty-building programmes across the customer organization to enhance the perception of value. This might include analysing the benefits of selected case studies to enhance confidence in the value that is being achieved, and hence to support the pricing applied.
- Offer partnership deals that involve mutual investment, potentially offering preferential pricing in exchange for longer-term commitment. Such arrangements can provide a good base of data to support future ROI cases to reinforce the value achieved, significantly raising the bar for competitors.

As with the implications of competitive forces, this analysis underlines the importance of understanding the target market in terms of current and potential suppliers and collaborators, and of tracking for changes in pricing or delivery approach by other players. Such implications can highlight both major risks and significant opportunities against which the venture needs to act fast and innovatively.

Creating a Return on Investment (ROI) Case

The essence of an ROI case is: for the buyer, the price of the offering must align with their perception of the value that it creates.

It is important to have a credible ROI case for each party in the ecosystem from whom some level of investment – financial, effort, risk, reputation – is required. An ROI may be presented as a financial model with evidenced assumptions, or it may be a series of compelling claims of qualitative benefit, supported by anecdotal evidence or general market analysis. In many cases, ROIs combine aspects of both.

For a simple financial value proposition, where an offering is promoted on the basis that it delivers a predictable financial benefit, the following formula can be applied to assess the ROI of an offering:

$$\text{ROI} = (\textit{benefit from the purchase} - \textit{cost of the purchase})/\textit{cost of the purchase}$$

In other words, the ROI measures the amount of benefit achieved relative to the purchase cost. The result is usually expressed as a percentage or a ratio. In simple cases where benefits can confidently be predicted, the formula allows respective offerings to be compared side by side. Such simple cases are uncommon, however, and the effect of time can seriously muddy attempts at comparison using this approach. For this reason, higher-value ROI calculations tend to be more complex, with predicted benefits plotted over time, and the use of discounting formulae to recognize the present value of future benefit.

Case Study: SportMagenta

Return on Investment

The founders understand that for a club or chain of clubs to accept the proposition, any fees payable to the venture, and any associated cost of change and management, must be more than compensated by the expectation of additional revenue generated.

Over time, Zara and Sonny expect to be able to offer an evidenced financial ROI model that references the positive experience of deploying the service across clubs of varying sizes. For early customers, however, the founders appreciate that the decision to purchase is likely to require a mix of credible financial return with a range of other likely benefits, such as enhanced retention through new channels of communication with members and visitors, and the competitive advantage of being able to showcase an exciting new technology platform to potential new members.

As a first-cut, the founders create an indicative ROI to support initial engagements with key decision-makers within clubs. They adopt the following reasoning:

From their market research, the founders know that each member or visitor to a club spends on average $75 per month on retail purchases within that club. A club with 1,000 members and visitors will therefore currently receive something in the order of $75,000 revenue per month from its non-membership services.

If the product can increase this retail purchase level by 5 per cent, then the gain from the club's investment will be $75,000 × 0.05 = $3,750 per month.

If, under the agreed revenue share, SportMagenta takes 12.5 per cent of this increase, then the cost of the investment to the club will be $3,750 \times 0.125 = \$469$ per month.

Consequently, the ROI for the club will be $((3,750 - 469) / 469) = 7$.

In effect, the founders will offer an ROI that multiplies the club's investment seven-fold, with no downside risk to the club, because if there is no increased revenue, then no payment will be made to SportMagenta. The equation presented here is very broad brush as it does not take account of any of the club's costs of promotion or data integration, but the founders consider that such a case will be sufficient for their initial purposes.

A promotional approach used by some businesses involves offering an ROI model to their customers together with an invitation to 'fill in the blanks and see how much you can save with our product'. This makes for a powerful statement of confidence, but suffers the downside that the model is likely to be explored also by competitors, with a risk of unintended consequences. A lower-risk approach involves presenting a custom ROI model specifically to each customer under a confidentiality arrangement to limit the chances of losing control over the model and its usage.

Where the benefits of the value proposition are more easily expressed in qualitative terms, such as *enhanced quality of life* or *greater opportunity*, creating an equation along the above lines demands more imagination and research. In such cases, it may be necessary to look for *proxies* that can serve as indicators for the benefits claimed. For example, *enhanced quality of life* can be measured through an increase in hours of sleep per night, a decrease in the number of sick days incurred, or by alignment with an accepted well-being measure for which market norms exist and against which a ratio of improvement can be calculated.

Where the case for a financial ROI is not strong, the search for such proxies can be crucial to the ability to articulate and demonstrate the value of an offering.

Different market segments may require different ROI cases, due to cultural or other differences. If so, multiple cases may need to be constructed and communicated. In all cases, customer evaluation of ROI cases is likely to be influenced by the messaging used and by current trends.

A comprehensive coverage of ROI models is provided by Phillips and Phillips (2006), and an approach that applies to open-source hardware is provided by Pearce (2015).

Defining a Customer Purchasing Option

Before considering details of the pricing structure to be adopted to meet the specified objective(s) within the context of the strategic considerations addressed above, it is instructive first to consider the following factors:

- The nature of the proposition that will be offered to the customer for purchase.
- The process by which a customer purchase will occur.

Defining What the Customer Will Purchase

A product or service offering can be packaged in many ways for customer purchase. The packaging approach is here referred to as the *customer purchasing option*. This can have a significant effect on the customer's willingness to purchase, the process whereby a purchase is made, and on the revenues and margins that are achieved.

For example, an ancestry investigation application could be packaged and offered as an *on-premise* product under a perpetual software licence that is purchased and installed by the customer, with periodic enhancements offered at additional cost. Alternatively, access to the same functionality might be packaged as a cloud-based, software-as-a-service (SaaS) offering that is charged either by time (a monthly fee) or by the number of searches conducted, with updates provided automatically at no extra cost. The choice that is made will have a bearing on the price that is charged, and on when payments will be made, and hence will influence the likelihood of purchase by customers within the target market.

Having identified a set of objectives to be achieved, a range of customer purchasing options can be evaluated. The decision taken on this matter can be highly significant for a venture, not only in terms of revenue achieved, but also in terms of securing customer commitment and repeat business. The current trend towards SaaS packaging for software means that a very strong case would need to be made for adopting an on-premise packaging of a new offering.

In broad terms, the available options fall into the following classes.

Licensed Offerings

The customer is invited to purchase a licence to *own* or to *use* a product, which may be physical or software, or a combination of the two. Any licence offered will have associated terms that state whether:

- It is *perpetual* – applies indefinitely – or whether the licence applies for a limited period of time.
- It is *exclusive* to the purchasing customer or whether the same licence may be purchased by many customers.
- It can be *resold* or *transferred* by the customer to another party, and if so, then under what conditions.
- In the case of an *open-source* licence, under what conditions the product may be used, modified and shared.

A *closed-source* proprietary software product or consumer electronics artefact will usually be offered to its users through a licence that is perpetual, non-exclusive and which offers no transfer rights.

Within the terms of the licence, the pricing approach might adopt any combination of the following approaches:

- Individual user licensing, where a licence is purchased for each person who will use the product. Under some approaches, individual users are named; in other cases, a licence is transferable across individuals within a customer organization.
- Concurrent user licensing, where a licence is purchased for a user community and the number of users at any point in time is bounded by the applicable concurrent community.
- Enterprise licensing, where a licence is purchased for the entire user population within an organization or function.

Chapter 7 returns to this topic and provides more detailed guidance on the clauses within a licence agreement.

When choosing an approach, a venture needs also to consider implementation implications; offering concurrent licensing requires either the ability to track usage at any point in time, or a level of trust that the customer can and will govern licence use.

Service Offerings

The offering is packaged into a service offering to which the customer is invited to subscribe. This may be charged by time, by usage, or by achievement of some deliverable or output. An Internet-of-Things (IoT) device for tracking energy consumption may be charged quarterly; a business enquiry service may be charged based on the number of queries submitted; and a lead-generation service may be charged by the level of interest or value generated.

A service is offered subject to terms and conditions that explain the nature and operation of the pricing rules. These terms are important for protecting the integrity of the venture, and so need to be defined explicitly. This topic is addressed further in Chapter 7.

As with licensing options, when choosing an approach, the venture needs also to consider implementation implications; the choice of a usage-based approach implies an ability to measure and track usage, and the choice of an approach based on achieving a predefined deliverable implies a need to verify the user's success with the service.

Payment for Access to a Specialist Asset

The customer may be invited to pay for access to, or usage of, a specialist asset such as a studio or manufacturing facility that provides equipment and skilled support staff.

Applicable terms will define what is provided – and what is not – under the price charged, and also the liabilities in the event of failure, damage or injury. Access to a specialist facility may be priced either for a period (per month), or to produce a particular output, such as an engineering calibration, a video or sound recording. In either case, an insurance arrangement will usually cover the cost of any mishap during usage.

Payment for Commitment

The customer – or competitor – may be invited to pay the venture in exchange for a commitment such as a promise to avoid or exclude promotional activity in a particular market for an agreed period of time. Such schemes are usually established entirely on the basis of negotiation.

Understanding the Purchasing Process

This is about understanding who will actually be purchasing the offering, and the process through which the purchase will be completed.

With a simple B2C offering, this question may seem relatively straightforward, but it is not necessarily so. Even for consumer offerings, the person paying may be a relative, a friend or even an institution. For example, a transcription service requested by a disabled student may actually be provided by a college and paid for with government support funding.

With B2B and B2G offerings, the purchasing process can be complex, and understanding how it will work may require detailed market research. The following two commonly encountered situations illustrate this point:

The first is where customer orders are processed through a procurement function that makes purchases on behalf of the organization. Any purchase will be made in response to a purchasing request from an authorized person within the organization, and will usually need to be aligned with a defined budget code. When someone in the HR department agrees to purchase a new service, then, depending upon the cost and commitment involved, authorization may first be needed from a more senior role. At that point, the request may be passed to a central legal team that is charged with reviewing and negotiating the terms of any associated agreements. Finally, the procurement function would check budget availability for affordability against existing commitments and then, if content, place an order for the service.

If the process and applicable rules are known in advance, then there will be an opportunity to prepare the request accordingly, and hence mitigate the various risks that can cause the process to fail or be delayed unnecessarily. The pricing approach adopted can make a material difference to the smooth running of the process, and a clear ROI case can be very helpful.

A second situation is where a customer order will be processed through a project or departmental budget. Within an organization, an individual will usually be authorized to spend up to a defined financial limit, the magnitude of which depends on their seniority within the organization. The rules need to be understood beforehand, as there may be limitations on the total value of repeat business, or on the level of commitment to a single supplier. In such cases, there may be an important decision to be made about whether to make an initial sale to a specific function, and then to engage a central procurement function for future purchases, or whether to secure a more central strategic commitment at the outset.

With B2G customers and some larger businesses, it is also normal for competitive tendering rules to limit the organization's ability to procure goods or services above a certain value without running a market competition against a published requirement. These rules can also limit the aggregate amount that can be purchased over time from a single supplier. Understanding the applicable rules is crucially important, as it can be very frustrating to invest effort in identifying and expressing a requirement, and promoting a solution, only to be outbid by a competitor.

Capex versus Opex Purchases
For higher-valued offerings into B2B customers, the treatment of the purchase as a capital or operating expense can become significant, as it can affect both

the customer's options for cost recovery through taxation, and also the shape of its balance sheet.

With a capital expenditure (*capex*) purchase, the cost to the customer is depreciated – or amortized – by being spread over its useful lifetime (which may be five to ten years). An operating expenditure (*opex*) purchase, however, is accounted entirely during the current financial year, and hence will attract any tax benefits relating to the same period.

When facing the decision of whether to package an offering as a capex or opex purchase, the following considerations usually apply:

- A customer organization may have a distinct preference for the treatment of a purchase and, if the relationship is sufficiently trusting, may be willing to share this.
- A perpetual licence will usually be considered as a capital purchase, whereas a subscription purchase will be treated as an operating expense.
- Capital purchasing decisions often involve more diligence and take more time.

Consequently, it is important to appreciate the implications and corresponding options, and to factor these into any presentation of pricing.

Payment Timing and Terms

The timing, or scheduling, of payments is a negotiable pricing variable that requires consideration. Options available include:

- Request full payment upfront, which is quite normal for a perpetual licence.
- Request payment by usage for time-based services. Such payments can be requested in advance of the service or following successful delivery. It is normal to charge for customer support in advance, by comparison with insurance premium payments. Payment on delivery can mean long periods between making a sale, delivering the service and receiving payment.
- Request staged or negotiated arrangement where an upfront part-payment is followed by a subsequent profile of payments at agreed points in time or on the achievement of agreed outputs or outcomes. Such schemes are sometimes used to balance the risk profiles of the respective parties in the situation where payment on delivery is requested by the customer.

The venture's pricing strategy should include a preferred scheduling for payments, together with acceptable negotiable bounds.

Payment terms relate to the length of time between invoice and payment. This can sometimes be significant during a customer negotiation, especially where customer year-end or quarter-end results are affected. The flexibility that can be offered needs to be assessed against the venture's cash flow projections. In situations where cash flow is projected to be tight, it may be attractive to both parties to negotiate a reduced purchase price in exchange for earlier payment. This kind of offer, however, carries a risk of setting a pricing-level precedent that may be difficult to avoid in future.

Creating and Calibrating a Pricing Structure

Choosing a Pricing Approach

The principal pricing approaches currently applied are detailed below. The choice of an approach should take account of those topics addressed by the preceding two sections: the value-capture objectives, the implications of the applicable market forces, the strength of the ROI and the nature of the customer purchasing option and process.

Some of the approaches to pricing have been referenced earlier in the chapter, in the context of market forces. Most approaches apply irrespective of the nature of the offering.

Cost-Plus, or Open-Book, Pricing

Under the cost-plus, or open-book, pricing approach, the price charged is calculated by adding a defined profit margin to the cost of production and distribution. In some B2G situations, this form of accounting is mandated by the customer. For example, the US government uses cost-plus contracts with companies that develop new technologies for national defence.

The effort involved in implementing and reporting such a scheme can be non-trivial, and the allowable profit margin is usually small, making this approach unattractive. It does, however, have the advantages of predictability and of mitigating margin erosion from increasing costs.

Demand or Value-Based Pricing

With this approach, the price is set with reference to the value delivered to the customer: for an offering that saves the customer $10,000 per month in charges, the price might be set at any value less than this to offer an attractive ROI. The approach is widely adopted in most markets.

Its effectiveness depends on a sufficient ROI case to justify the value delivered against the price. Although an ROI case may not be fully quantified at the outset, the expression of the value proposition will need to be sufficiently convincing. Over time, the value delivered will need to be evidenced by customer experience to sustain the customer's willingness to pay.

When adopting value-based pricing, it is important to consider the implications across market segments, because differing ROI calculation or competitive forces can affect the applicable pricing levels.

Dynamic Pricing

Dynamic pricing is driven by variables that change over time. It is becoming increasingly widely used by businesses that have the ability to exploit available data, both personal and environmental. For example, Uber's taxi fares are dynamically priced such that the price offered to a rider is based on a range of factors, including the number of riders and drivers currently using the service. This approach can cause fares to temporarily increase – the so-called *Uber surge* – to encourage more drivers to head to those areas where demand currently outstrips supply of drivers.

Many businesses have benefited significantly from this approach. For online retailers, the exploitation of available data to introduce dynamic pricing has increased both sales volumes and margins. Amazon, for example, has invested strongly in building a strong competence in data analysis at the centre of the business.

This approach can be adopted by any offering that can align supply and demand, and an increasing awareness of its successful use by large players is making the approach more widely applied. Interestingly, the approach is becoming associated with notions of fairness: if the customer is aware of the factors affecting pricing, then they can change their behaviour to benefit from it.

Competition–Based Pricing

With this approach, the price is set with reference to competitors' pricing.

As noted in an earlier section, the impact of competition on pricing depends on whether the competing offer(s) are directly comparable or not:

- Where the offerings compete head-to-head, and there is little difference in value terms to the customer, then the usual options are either to set the price so as to undercut the competition, or to create innovative volume-pricing options that reduce the unit cost to the customer, while at the same time securing their commitment for a larger volume.
- Where the offering is distinctive or disruptive in some way that enhances its ROI relative to the competition, then the usual options are either to set the same price or to set a higher price than the completion. The latter option is

sometimes called *premium pricing*, which can be used to exploit a strong brand value. Clearly, for either of these approaches to be effective, the ROI case needs to be compelling.

Skimming

This approach converts *first-mover advantage* into revenue by setting a high initial price and then reducing this over time as competitors emerge.

With skimming and penetration (see below) pricing, there is an important relationship between pricing and the intensity of promotional activities.

To be effective, skimming needs to happen rapidly, which requires high-intensity promotion, as illustrated in Figure 5.5.

A slow skimming approach is unlikely to succeed because competitors have the opportunity to gain access to the market before first-mover advantage has been secured.

Penetration Pricing

As with skimming, this approach exploits first-mover advantage, but in this case the strategy is to set a low (or even zero) initial price to achieve rapid market share ahead of the emergence of competition. This approach converts first-mover advantage into market share rather than short-term revenue, hence the choice of this approach over the previous one would depend squarely on the objectives that drive the pricing decision.

Figure 5.5 again applies, as the advantage can quickly be lost without commensurate promotional activity to enable rapid penetration.

| | Intensity of promotion activities | |
	High	**Low**
High	Rapid skimming	Slow skimming
Low	Rapid penetration	Slow penetration

Level of pricing (vertical axis label)

Figure 5.5 *Relationship between pricing and promotional intensity*

To benefit from starting with a very low – or zero – initial price, it is necessary to have a plan for exploiting the achieved market share to the venture's advantage. The following approaches can be applied:

- Introduce a charging scheme from a pre-announced point in time. This approach can succeed if the value of the offer is *sticky*, and hence there will be a customer appetite to start paying for it.
- Use the market share achieved to generate revenues from sale of data or analysis insights achieved, or from advertising or other promotional arrangement.
- Use the market share achieved to attract investors or acquirers with interest in achieving influence in the market.

Freemium Pricing

This approach has become ubiquitous across B2C software offerings: an entry level of functionality is offered free of charge, with options to pay for an upgrade to a premium or professional-level offering that provides enhanced features, data or functionality.

The great attraction of the approach is its low-risk offer to the customer of a way to try out the offering and get started. For it to succeed, however, there are some important considerations:

- The freely available offering must be good enough. As per the points made regarding criteria for minimum viable products in Chapter 4, the offering must not be so minimal that it irritates and frustrates the customer, and hence spoils its own reputation.
- The freely available offering must not be too good, otherwise there is no incentive to upgrade.
- The offering must encourage *stickiness* of usage in the sense that the customer will lose out or miss something if they can't continue to use the offering.
- The premium offerings available must add real value to the freely available proposition, and not simply add *bells and whistles*: there must be a simple and obvious reason for the customer to choose to upgrade.

The Eventbrite product illustrates the approach. A freely available offering allows customers (event organizers and promoters) to promote free events at no cost. This has a useful penetration aspect due to the wide range of relevant types of event. However, to promote a paid event, the customer must pay a percentage of the ticket price. This charge can be passed to the customer. In this case, charging brings no functional enhancement, only the right to apply the offering to a wider range of applications.

SurveyMonkey takes a slightly different approach. In this case, a freely available offering allows customers (those wishing to conduct online surveys) to create and deploy simple surveys to a limited number of recipients. Paid extras – through multiple levels of paid offering – include access to additional design facilities to support the creation of more impactful surveys, the rights to extend the numbers of recipients, and enhanced reporting and analysis.

Free and Open-Source Pricing

Despite being very different approaches, free and open-source pricing are here treated together in order to highlight the important difference between the two.

In respect of both hardware and software, the term *free* is ambiguous: it can mean something for which the cost is zero, or it can mean something, irrespective of its cost, that may be used, modified and distributed without limitation (i.e. *freely*). Clearly, these have very different business implications. For this reason, the term *free* is not generally helpful in this context.

An offering may be made available at zero cost for a variety of reasons, including:

- As part of a penetration pricing approach, as addressed above.
- As part of a freemium pricing approach, as addressed above.
- As an altruistic gesture, whereby an offering is made available to a community within the context of a value system.
- As part of an open-source arrangement.

Open source does not necessarily mean zero cost: an open-source product may or may not have an associated cost. With open-source software and hardware, the design of the product is made publicly accessible so as to enable modification and sharing by a community of users who, therefore, in the words of the Free Software Foundation, have the freedom to 'run, copy, distribute, study, change and improve' the offering. In the context of the open-source world, *free software* means software that in some way gives freedom to its users.

The topic of open source versus closed source is addressed in more detail in Chapter 7. For the purposes of this chapter, it is important to appreciate that this is an important distinction to be made by any venture as there can be severe consequences from taking an ill-informed decision. It is possible to combine open and closed source versions of a product, but such an approach needs careful management, both of technology and of licensing.

An example of successful *dual licensing*, where both open-source and proprietary (or *closed source*) versions of an offering are made available, is Oracle's MySQL database. In this case, a *community version* is available at zero cost under an open-source licence, alongside a range of more functionally extensive, commercially licensed offerings.

Offering both zero cost and commercial licences under a dual approach is one value-capture approach available to ventures deciding to make aspects of their offering available under a zero-cost, open-source licence. Other approaches include:

- The sale of subscriptions to associated support services such as training, configuration or consultancy, as offered by Red Hat.
- Funding from a corporation that has interests in the offering, such as Google's funding for Adblock Plus.
- The sale of ancillary merchandise in cases where brand image and value commands sufficient power, such as with Mozilla.
- Requesting voluntary donations from supportive individuals or organizations, as applied by Wikipedia.
- Crowdfunding by a sympathetic community.
- The sale of proprietary extensions to a zero-cost, open-source offering, such as with Microsoft's offerings for Skype add-ons and Voice over IP (VoIP) calls.
- The practice of so-called delayed open-source offering, whereby historic versions of an offering are made available under a zero-cost, open-source licence, and only the most recent version is offered on a commercial basis.

Additional Pricing Options

The collection of pricing approaches listed above covers those currently encountered. Additional to these is a collection of options that can usefully be applied alongside a chosen approach. As shown by Table 5.1, most of the additional options described below can be applied together with any of the pricing approaches.

Introductory Discounts

Special discounts for early customers or for initial orders from new customers can be offered. This can have the effect of *seeding a market* by enticing early adopters at a time when the ROI may not be well evidenced, and hence where customers may be sceptical about value.

Table 5.1 Applicability of Additional Options with Pricing Approaches

Pricing approach	Additional pricing options				
	Introductory discounts	Trial periods	Bundling	Volume-based or banded pricing	Optional feature pricing
Cost-plus pricing	N	N	N	N	Y
Demand or value-based pricing	Y	Y	Y	Y	Y
Dynamic pricing	Y	Y	N	N	Y
Competition-based pricing	Y	Y	Y	Y	Y
Skimming	Y	Y	Y	Y	Y
Penetration pricing	Y	Y	Y	Y	Y
Freemium pricing	N	N	Y	Y	Y
Free and open-source pricing	N	N	Y	N	Y

Care needs to be taken with such offers to ensure that they do not set a precedent that is difficult to escape in future. Any such offers need to be clearly explained, and it can also be helpful to set a reasonable expectation for likely future pricing.

It can be useful to offer a discounted price together with an agreed contribution of some other value, perhaps in the form of access to data or a shared case study or market reference. This has the advantage of retaining a more representative value exchange, albeit expressed in multiple currencies, which provides a strong response in the event that a later customer requests similar treatment.

Trial Periods

The offering of a trial or approval period is a widely offered option to de-risk a customer's purchase decision. As with the freemium approach, however, it is important that during any trial period the offering encourages *stickiness* of usage, such that the customer will gain a real sense that they will lose or miss something if they don't continue to use it after the end of the period. This can be achieved by encouraging integration with existing regular practices or by encouraging the customer to build useful artefacts that will be lost without continuing access.

Bundling

Bundling can be used to encourage an *up-sell* whereby the customer purchases more than they originally intended. Under this option, a collection of related offerings is packaged together under a single offering, for which the perceived value is higher than the sum of the parts. The purchase price for a product might be bundled with training, multi-year support, future upgrades and associated services, in such a way that the customer is persuaded to purchase the full bundle and hence gain greater value.

It can also be used to assemble a special-purpose offer to meet a particular situation. One common case is with a pilot or proof-of-concept project offered by purveyors of B2B and B2G offerings as a low-risk entry point to a customer. A bundled offer typically comprises a judicious mix of product and required services to demonstrate effectiveness in a limited and priority area of application. In many cases, a fixed price is set to ensure sufficient commitment on the part of the customer, and sufficient cost-cover on the part of the business.

Bundling can also be useful in cases where the customer has more financial freedom at the present time than they expect to have in the future, and hence may be inclined to pay for as much as possible in the short term. In such cases, special bundles can be assembled, ideally through joint activity with the customer.

Volume–Based or Banded Pricing

The use of volume-based pricing – also known as *price bands*, or *tiers* – can play a valuable part in negotiation. Under this option, a single unit of the offering is priced at one value, whereas a discounted price applies to the purchase of multiple units; effectively 'buy two, get one half price'. A typical approach is to use price bands, where the price for a single unit is x, the unit price of purchasing between two and five units is y, the unit cost of purchasing between six and fifteen units is z, and so on, where $z < y < x$.

When adopting this approach, a choice needs to be made about whether the bands are to be applied cumulatively: when the customer determines to order twelve units, will the first be priced at *x*, the next four at *y*, and the remaining seven at *z*, or will all twelve be priced at *z*? This can make a significant difference on larger-volume orders.

The design of the bands to be offered needs to be chosen and analysed carefully to ensure that they encourage the desired customer purchasing behaviour, and also that they do not lead to pricing anomalies. The latter can occur where poorly defined bands lead to higher volumes costing less in total than lower volumes. For example, suppose that the customer is offered a unit price of $750 for purchasing between twenty and thirty-five units, and a unit price of $500 for purchasing between thirty-six and ninety-nine units. This would mean that the total price for thirty-five units would be $26,250, whereas the total price for forty units would be $20,000. One way to avoid such anomalies is to use the cumulative calculation approach; another is to plot a graph showing the price curve for the whole range of volumes available.

Consistency and coherence with brand experience is a further consideration affecting the structuring and naming of bands. Customers are likely to be familiar with terms such as *regular, expert* and *professional,* and support services commonly use terms such as *bronze, silver, gold* and *gold-plus* to describe service levels available. Straying beyond these normal terminologies can be differentiating, but also potentially confusing unless applied with deliberate conviction.

Optional Feature Pricing

Under this option, certain features of the offering's functionality are omitted from the normal pricing package and treated as paid extras. This can be a useful approach where some features are either specialist in nature, and hence their absence allows discounting for a wider market, or where such features can be offered as a future up-sell. This option is commonly used to package functionality that may be of little interest at an initial sale, but for which requirements are likely to emerge following successful wider-scale deployment of an offering.

An example is the approach adopted by those printer manufacturers who sell printers at an affordable level and generate their margins by offering replacement toner cartridges at a higher price.

Calibrating the Pricing Structure

For most of the pricing approaches described previously, there remains the question of choosing a pricing level, which usually means judging what will be achievable by way of a balanced value exchange between parties.

According to the pricing approach adopted, the pricing level may be calibrated on the basis of an evidenced case demonstrating its value, the condition of the current market, competitive market forces or a market access plan designed to exploit first-mover advantage.

Whichever of these applies, it is important to have a clear statement that justifies the price being asked. It is perfectly reasonable for a customer to ask why the price is set as it is. A business with no good answer will give a poor impression of its integrity, which will in turn damage its reputation and hence reduce the likelihood of a customer order. The justification may be against an ROI case, a market alignment with other products or an indication of applicable costs and effort. The important point is that there must be a clear answer, consistently expressed.

In some cases, it is advantageous to offer pricing levels specific to particular market segments and situations, including geographic regions, student, research or educational use. For this to work, it needs to be aligned with a broader promotion plan that takes account of any implications of segmented pricing. For example, if a specially priced educational offer is to be made, then consideration needs to be given to any additional training and support implications for students and institutions, and of how students will be validated as such, especially after they leave education. Such an offer might also impose additional security considerations.

Whenever determining to adopt a segmented pricing scheme, it is also important to consider possible future side-effects on other related customer communities, and any ways by which the scheme may be circumvented by unscrupulous customers.

Case Study: SportMagenta

Pricing Structure

The founders determine that their value capture objective is to maximize revenue generation. This is compatible with their key objective of achieving recurring revenue growth of more than 100 per cent per annum for each of the first three years.

To achieve this objective, they recognize the need to move fast with a compelling offer to key chains of clubs and so to penetrate the market ahead of new entrants and substitutes. They are aware that enthusiastic and public feedback from existing users, plus an increasingly well-evidenced ROI case, will strengthen their negotiating power with customers.

The founders have decided that sports clubs and promoters are the parties that will be charged, and that pricing will align with increased revenues achieved from additional sales by clubs. They accept that it is likely that the specific mechanism adopted by each club or club chain will need senior approval through a contractual arrangement. They intend that payment will be invoiced monthly after calculation of revenue increase against an agreed baseline level.

On the basis of learning gathered during early engagements, Sonny determines that a bundled, fixed-price pilot offering will initially be made to build relationships, gather relevant baseline costing data, and de-risk integration and other introduction costs. The price payable for a pilot will be negotiable, with an expectation of the club paying something in the range of $20,000 to $25,000 for a three-month pilot.

Following such a pilot, the pricing structure decided by the founders is a value-driven approach based on a share of increased revenues generated by clubs and sponsors. They would also aim to secure an initial fixed fee to complete customization and integration. They recognize that the value of this will need to be negotiated within the contract, and anticipate that some customers may request a refund of any such fee after SportMagenta has earned a certain level of revenues. The founders also recognize that they will need a mechanism for setting pricing in future years, when the initial baseline ceases to be relevant. They determine during the first year to create an evidenced ROI to support a robust value-based approach for future years.

The founders have no plans for price variation by segment: wherever the offering is promoted, a similar pricing level will be applied.

Assessing the Value of the Business

The value captured by a venture is evidenced by the growth of its market value.

Consequently, it is important to understand those factors that are most influential in generating such growth. This introduces the topic of how businesses are valued, and the several different approaches that are used depending upon the reason for the valuation.

There are several circumstances in which an assessment of the financial value of a business may be required:

- To frame an investment, acquisition or disposal of the business.
- When creating, assigning or selling shares or share options.

- When recruiting a new senior employee, engaging in a partnership venture or negotiating a loan.

A variety of valuation approaches have been developed to support these requirements. In many cases, multiple approaches will be applied and compared to give a balanced indication of the fair and reasonable value of a business. In such cases, the weighting given to the various approaches will depend on the reason for the valuation.

The factors that drive the valuation of a business depend on its nature, its market and the reason for valuation. A valuation for the purposes of creating a new class of share options is usually driven by the criteria that will be applied by the taxation authorities, whereas a valuation for the purposes of securing investment funding is more likely to be driven by a desire to gain the best value for existing shareholders.

Ultimately, however, irrespective of the assessed value, fair market value is the price that a willing buyer will pay and a willing seller will accept.

Almost without exception, business valuation is a technical activity that is embedded within the tax environment of the relevant geography. For these reasons, the coverage given here is limited to high-level, indicative considerations.

The valuation approaches and respective drivers are summarized below.

Accounting Valuation

This is the approach usually adopted when valuing a business for the purposes of creating or reorganizing share classes. In such circumstances, a valuation is needed so that the tax authorities can assess the taxable nature of a share issue, or of any later transaction – such as an acquisition – involving those shares.

Matters relating to shares and options, including accounting-oriented approaches taken to business valuation, are addressed in more detail in Chapter 8, together with other topics relating to business structuring.

Asset Approach

This approach to business valuation is usually driven by an acquisition interest. It is an attempt to assess the value of a business to a potential acquirer on the basis of the likely cost of recreating the same benefit without acquisition. In other words, it is about answering the question 'what it would cost the acquirer to create an offering with a comparable value proposition?'

The answer is likely to include at least two parts: how much and how long to do it. The latter point may be critical, because during that time the business in question is likely to be building market share and reputation, and evolving its own offering. Furthermore, there may be significant limitations to redevelopment due to existing patents or design rights.

For these reasons, an asset approach usually involves hypothetical calculations of effort and risk, which together suggest an approximate value.

Case Study: SportMagenta

Asset Valuation by a Potential Acquirer

Although the SportMagenta founders do not know it, a leading digital media business is assessing the option of acquiring the venture and adding its offering into their existing portfolio. A benefit to the acquirer would be the ability to use existing routes to market to promote and deliver the SportMagenta service across multiple geographic regions.

To assess the value that it would be prepared to offer for SportMagenta, the business considers the cost of replicating the service using its own resources.

It applies the following rationale:

- From its contacts in the market, the business learns that the SportMagenta team has so far engaged two developers and has spent around two years developing the current product.
- The effort needed to replicate the current SportMagenta functionality, based on a technical review of the current product, is assessed to be about three working years, which would cost the business something in the region of $500,000.
- This activity would take at least one elapsed year to accomplish, due to the need for team composition and management, design, development and testing.
- Over the course of that year, SportMagenta is likely to have exploited first-mover advantage to secure several major customers, and their current development productivity is likely to have significantly improved the offering.

Consequently, the business might be prepared to acquire SportMagenta for a valuation in the region of $750,000 to $1.25 million. If the company's founders demand a valuation significantly higher than this, then the business might consider creating its own version and entering into direct competition.

Market Approach

This approach is usually driven by an interest in investment or acquisition of a venture. Commonly applied considerations include the following:

- Recent valuations of similar businesses, or of other businesses in the same market. This is comparable to the approach usually applied when valuing property.
- The current intensity of interest in the relevant market or technology, indicated by the number of comparable businesses that have recently been acquired, or which have secured investment.
- The degree of differentiation offered by the business, taking account of significant patents or design rights that give the business advantages over its competitors.

A number of market agencies, including Beauhurst, Duedil and Regent Partners, track financial transactions within and across markets and provide useful input to such analysis.

The factors that drive business value from this perspective are alignment with high-value markets and technologies. Current examples of these are provided in Chapter 1.

Performance Multiples

A performance-based approach to valuation is usually applied alongside a market approach, so that each can give a cross-check for the other.

This approach aims to assess the likely economic benefits to the investor or acquirer, and the time frame over which these are likely to be realized. The principal considerations underlying the approach are past business performance and projected future performance.

The approach applies multiples of widely used performance measures. Its simplicity enables direct comparison of different businesses, regardless of any differences in capital structure. An important decision is around which numbers to use: the current year, the most recently reported year or the projection for the forthcoming year. Forward-looking multiples are often more accurate predictors of value than historical multiples.

The measures adopted depend to some extent on the nature of the business, but typically involve some combination of sales and profitability. For publicly listed companies, a much wider range of data is usually available, including price/earnings (P/E) ratios. For private ventures, and especially for early-stage businesses, the available data is more often patchy, hence the attractiveness of taking multiple parallel approaches.

Sales Multiples

This approach applies only to businesses that are generating revenues from sales, so may not be applicable to very early-stage ventures. It is a crude measure as it takes no account of costs involved, and businesses with comparable revenues may have wildly differing profitability.

Sales multiples are, however, easily calculated and so this approach is widely applied within active markets where transactions are tracked and trends are reported to enable business valuation as a multiple of annual sales.

The applicable multiples vary over time. For example, according to research in 2017 by Regent Partners LLP, valuations within the European technology, media and telecom (TMT) sector were in the region of 1.4 × annual revenues. This multiple was a decrease on what had been observed in the years immediately prior to that.

The factor that drives business value from this perspective is top-line revenues, or sales, especially well-evidenced future sales projections. This explains the current focus by technology businesses on demonstrating increases in monthly recurring revenues.

Profit Multiples

There are several measures of profit. Two that are commonly used for the purposes of valuation are *earnings before interest and tax* (EBIT), and *earnings before interest, tax, depreciation and amortization* (EBITDA). These two measures are similar in value for businesses with low depreciation and amortization expenses, such as consulting companies that have little by way of capital purchases.

EBITDA is a proxy for the cash generated by a business, and so is one of the most commonly used valuation metrics. Research by Regent Partners in the European TMT sector reports EBITDA multiples between 9 × and 10 × for 2016 and 2017.

A summary of the range of EBITDA multiples that apply within different sectors has been provided by Aswath Damodaran, Professor of Finance at the Stern School of Business at New York University. Professor Damodaran uses data from early 2018 to report a very wide range of multiples: from 6.5 × in the Air Transport sector up to 32 × in Online Retail.

The factor that drives business value from this perspective is the margin achieved on sales, especially from well-evidenced future sales and cost projections. This underlines the importance to a venture of achieving scalability (addressed in detail in Chapter 6) such that its costs increase at a lower rate than its revenues, and hence its profitability increases proportionately higher than its revenues.

Strategic Valuation

A strategic approach to valuation applies where the acquirer is motivated not by any predictable economic benefit, but by a stronger market-driven ambition. The strategic valuation of a venture tends not to adopt any of the empirical methods described above, but to apply a negotiated assessment of value.

The normal scenario for a strategic valuation is where a larger business believes that it can generate much higher earnings, or secure a powerful market position, through absorbing and incorporating a venture. This often occurs when the potential acquirer is in a strong position to scale its acquisition rapidly alongside other offerings, potentially yielding significant earnings ahead of its own competitors.

This can be illustrated by some recent examples of strategic acquisitions:

- In November 2016, Oracle acquired NetSuite with the strategic intention of 'bringing together the reach of NetSuite's cloud ERP solutions for small to midsize businesses with the breadth and depth of Oracle's enterprise-grade cloud solutions for the back and front office'.
- In September 2016, Google acquired Apigee with the strategic aim to 'accelerate our customers' move to supporting their businesses with high quality digital interactions'.
- In June 2016, Microsoft acquired LinkedIn with the strategic objective to 'accelerate the growth of LinkedIn, as well as Microsoft Office 365 and Dynamics as we seek to empower every person and organization on the planet'.

Where a strategic acquisition seeks to secure access to a specific technology, an asset-based approach might also be considered to evaluate a *buy or build* decision. The choice would then rest on the effort, risk and time assessed as being required to *build*. However, many strategic acquisitions involve much more than simply a technology solution such as, for example, Microsoft's decision to acquire LinkedIn.

The factors that drive business value from this perspective are having an offering that could be exploited strategically by a major player, and being visible to relevant players in the marketplace. One way of attracting potential strategic acquirers is to secure strong customer endorsement for achievements that meet their strategic aims.

Bringing Innovation to Value Capture

Like all other aspects of business design, the approach for capturing value into a venture, whether by way of revenues secured or by demonstrating a beneficial impact within a community, benefits from creativity and innovation.

This point is well made by Hinterhubera and Liozub (2014): 'Few companies treat innovation in pricing as seriously as product innovation or business model innovation. However ... our research suggests that innovation in pricing may be a company's most powerful – and, in many cases, least explored – source of competitive advantage.'

Some examples of innovative trends can illustrate the point.

Pricing based on a balance of risk and reward is achieving wide traction across businesses in many sectors. Under this approach, rather than charging a fixed price for an offering, the business aligns its application directly with its value to the customer, and charges a proportion of this amount. This approach can be considered for any offering with a quantifiable ROI. It is widely offered by personal legal companies as a *no win, no fee* deal.

The prospect of needing to agree detailed goals and a commensurate risk/reward structure can be off-putting both to those developing the scheme and also to those to whom it is offered. This difficulty can be mitigated by taking a much less granular approach, and instead offering a banded approach whereby if achieved benefits are within a certain range, then the reward will be set at a particular level. This may be expressed in the form of a bonus, charged in addition to a fixed price that is below the market norm. Applying such an approach can bring an additional benefit by way of a strong, shared interest in making things work.

Another useful approach is to differentiate by pricing counter-culturally. For example, if comparable offerings are currently charged at a certain level, then the market's attention will be captured by pricing at a much lower or even zero level, as part of a package that makes a periodic charge for usage. This innovation can be especially relevant where it changes the profile of a purchase from a capital spend into an operational spend. The opposite can also be applied, where a single upfront cost is applied to package together a competitively priced multi-year service agreement. When designing such options, however, it is important to consider all consequences, including any risk of motivating customers to avoid usage to reduce costs.

The pre-sales costs of many offerings (meetings, demonstrations, mock-ups, business cases and presentations) can be punitive, especially for early-stage ventures. Where this is the case, it can be useful to consider how far such costs can be passed on to the customer, either upfront or recovered through future sales. One option is to offer the customer a fixed-price pilot or demonstration project ahead of a more significant commitment. Such projects give an opportunity to understand the relevant decision-making processes and to determine the most effective pricing approach. Another option is to offer a packaged analysis service that likewise assesses and evidences future value. The cost of any such option can be associated with a discounted initial order price.

The above examples are not exhaustive. Their purpose is to indicate the kinds of innovation that can be applied in respect of pricing approach, and to highlight the importance of designing and continually reviewing the venture's value capture strategy.

Summary of Value Capture

This chapter has stressed the importance of a venture designing its value-capture approach on the basis of a clear strategy; relevant considerations and techniques have been described. Underlying all of the various considerations addressed are the needs to retain focus on the business objectives, and to be continually innovative in the design and continuing development of value capture mechanisms.

Through its structured approach, this chapter makes the decisions tractable and contributory to a coherent business design.

The effectiveness of a venture's value capture is reflected in its growing value. Consequently, this chapter has also reviewed the drivers that affect business value, and summarized the principal valuation techniques that are used.

The key points addressed are summarized below.

- **Setting a value capture strategy** for a venture is important because the approach adopted can have a significant impact on the market response to its offering, and hence on its performance:
  - The strategy needs to be driven by the business objectives to be achieved through value capture, including revenues, profits, market share reputation and community recognition.
  - The strategy needs to be developed within the context of market dynamics, including current and future competition, the negotiating landscape and collaborative opportunities.
  - It is important to have a credible ROI case for each party in the ecosystem from whom some level of investment – whether financial, effort, risk or reputation – is required.
- **Defining a customer purchasing option** is about deciding how a product or service offering will be packaged for customer purchase:
  - Options include licensing, service offerings, access to assets and special commitments.
  - It can be critically important to understand the customer purchasing process, including who will actually pay, the conditions that will apply and when payment will be made.
- **Creating and calibrating a pricing structure** is about choosing an approach that takes account of value-capture objectives, applicable market forces, the strength of the ROI and the nature of the customer purchasing option and process:
  - Eight widely used approaches have been described with reference to their applicability and special considerations that apply.
  - A collection of five additional options have been elaborated that can be applied to augment most of the approaches.
  - Choosing a pricing level for a chosen approach usually means judging what will be achievable by way of a balanced value exchange between parties, and what will be justifiable to the customer.
- **Assessing the value of the business** recognizes that the value captured by a venture is measured by the growth of its market value, and therefore it is important to understand those factors that are most influential in generating such growth:
  - An accounting valuation is usually adopted when valuing a business for the purposes of creating or reorganizing share classes.
  - An asset approach to valuation is an attempt to assess the value of a business to a potential acquirer by assessing the likely cost of recreating the same benefit without acquisition.

    ○ A market approach to valuation reviews recent valuations of similar businesses, or of other businesses in the same market, blended with a perception of the current intensity of interest in the relevant market or technology.

    ○ A performance multiples approach to valuation aims to assess the likely economic benefits to an investor or acquirer, and the time frame over which these are likely to be realized: multiples can relate to revenues and/or profits.

    ○ A strategic approach to valuation applies where an acquirer is motivated less by predictable economic benefit than by a stronger market-driven ambition.

● When designing a value-capture approach, it is important to apply the **innovative power of the business** because research suggests that innovation in pricing may be a venture's most powerful – and, in many cases, least explored – source of competitive advantage.

ANALYSIS EXERCISES

The table below lists a collection of digital businesses to be used as subjects for the exercises that follow.

Business	Focus	Website
Darktrace	Cyber security	www.darktrace.com
EventBright	Event promotion and management	www.eventbrite.co.uk
Fitbit	Health, fitness and performance	www.fitbit.com
JustEat	Online takeaway food	www.just-eat.co.uk
Reposit	Property rental	www.getreposit.uk
Snapchat	Social media	www.snapchat.com
Sorry as a Service	Customer services and retention	www.sorryasaservice.com
SwiftComply	Regulation and compliance	www.swiftcomply.com

On the basis of information available in the public domain, address the questions below for at least one of the businesses listed.

1. The business's customer(s):
   (a) Who is the customer(s) for the proposed innovation?
   (b) Who are the principal players in the business ecosystem?
   (c) What are the principal value exchanges with these players?

2. Value capture strategy:
   (a) What are the likely value-capture objectives for the business?
   (b) What competitive forces apply and what is their likely impact on value capture?
   (c) What negotiation forces apply and what is their likely impact on value capture?
   (d) What collaborations are in play, and which others may be advantageous?
   (e) How might an ROI be constructed for the business's principal offering?

3. The customer purchasing option:
   (a) What does the business charge for?
   (b) Consider the business's customers: who pays, and what is the likely procurement process?

4. Pricing structure:
   (a) How does the business structure its pricing?
   (b) Does it make use of any of the additional pricing options?
   (c) How might the business have approached the calibration of its pricing levels?
   (d) Are there any apparent innovations in the pricing approach?

5. Valuing the business:
   (a) Under what situations might the business be valued?
   (b) For each situation suggested, how would valuation be approached?

DESIGN EXERCISES

The design exercise at the end of Chapter 1 encouraged identification of a business idea to be developed incrementally by specific design exercises through subsequent chapters of the book. That activity commenced in Chapter 2, with the framing of the selected business idea using the elements introduced in that chapter. This was extended in Chapters 3 and 4 with reference to the addition of considerations and decisions introduced.

Extend your current design through the following tasks:

1. For each aspect of business value capture covered in this chapter, perform an assessment and analysis of your business. If using the Business Design

Template, summarize the resulting considerations in the left-hand cell of the *value capture* section.

2. Extract from your considerations the set of key decisions relating to value capture by your business. If using the Business Design Template, document these in the right-hand cell of the *value capture* section.

3. Review the extended design of your business for consistency, and address any issues that arise.

4. Capture separately any of the following:
   (a) Key points learned from the exercise.
   (b) Outstanding issues or uncertainties.

Postscript to Chapters 2, 3, 4 and 5

With reference to the business design framework illustrated in Figure 5.1, this chapter concludes the part of this book that addresses those capabilities that contribute to the generation of business value.

Chapter 1 introduced and described a business model as having four parts:

- **Value creation**, expressing a value proposition for its beneficiaries plus other relevant parties across the business ecosystem. This component is addressed as a significant component of business framing in Chapter 2.
- **Value promotion**, defining the target market for the offering in terms of its structure, dynamics and size, together with a plan for achieving visibility, generating demand, engaging and building that market. This component is the principal subject of Chapter 3.
- **Value delivery**, incorporating the supply chain whereby the offering will be sustained, the roadmap whereby the promised value will be realized, developed and scaled, and the *routes to market* whereby the value proposition will be delivered to the customer. This component is the principal subject of Chapter 4.
- **Value capture** – determining how the venture will benefit from the value proposition through decisions of packaging and pricing structures, and how these will contribute to growth of business value. This component is the principal subject of this chapter.

Chapters 2, 3, 4 and 5 are logically sequential: a value proposition needs to be expressed ahead of determining, scoping and engaging the market. The offering then needs to be delivered and sustained, and value needs to be captured back into the business to enhance its worth. Within this logical sequence, the matrix of activities involved and the relevant considerations that apply to any particular venture inevitably iterate and overlap.

The following chapters move beyond the consideration of the core business model to address three additional, and equally critical, capabilities that build on the business model to provide a sustainable and scalable vehicle by which business objectives can be delivered:

- Chapter 6 addresses considerations around growing and scaling, including financial projections, growth strategy, team and organization building, and investment.
- Chapter 7 addresses considerations around valuing and protecting the venture's assets and reputation, including its intellectual property, trade secrets, contractual framework, security and legal compliance.
- Chapter 8 addresses considerations around leadership, management and governance, financial planning and control, and the legal, team and shareholding structures to be adopted.

6 Growth and Scalability

Focus of This Chapter

Figure 6.1 illustrates how the material addressed by this chapter fits within the framework of considerations for business design.

The considerations addressed are driven by the mission and objectives set within the framing of the business and by those decisions taken in respect of *generating business value.*

This chapter is about designing a business capable of achieving both growth and scalability such that it can progress from *start-up* to *scale-up* and beyond. The considerations involved provide a lens through which to view what is needed for a venture to grow beyond its population of early adopters and to scale beyond its initial domain and structure. The decisions made in this regard can have implications across all aspects of business design.

Learning Outcomes

After studying this chapter, you will:

- Understand the need for, and the principal components of, a strategy for growth and scalability.
- Be able to create a growth plan, including financial forecasts for revenues, costs and margins.
- Be aware of the considerations of designing a team to deliver growth.
- Be aware of the considerations of designing a scalable organization.

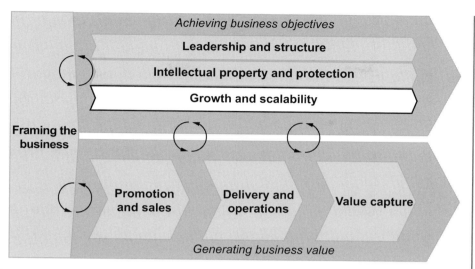

Figure 6.1 *Context of growth and scalability*

- Appreciate the funding options for growth, together with their advantages and disadvantages.
- Understand the stages of investment and the interests of different kinds of investor.
- Be able to create a business plan for a venture.

Introducing Growth and Scalability

This chapter highlights distinctions between growth and scalability, start-up and scale-up, and innovation and entrepreneurship. Importantly, it explains the need for these distinctions to be reflected in the different mindsets that are required, the differing priorities and emphases that apply, and the varying requirements for talent, capability and funding.

Business growth means increasing performance against some measure of success, which may relate to a financial measure such as revenue or profitability from sales, or to some other criterion such as increasing usage or influence across a market.

Business scalability means operating and performing *effectively* as the business grows. This includes the ability to do more at a reducing marginal cost, and the ability to accommodate increased breadth by operating in new markets, including with new propositions offered through new channels.

Scalability is different from growth, and it is possible for a venture to grow without being scalable. This can occur when the drivers of business growth are highly personality-related, or where delivery requires customization that creates unmanageable increases in cost or complexity. It can also happen where the venture is overly dependent on a scarce resource, or carries too much risk to be attractive to investors. In such cases, the performance of the venture will not increase, and may decrease, with growth. Furthermore, at some point, an unscalable venture is likely to 'hit a brick wall' in terms of its ability to continue to operate.

Likewise, a venture designed for scalability may fail to grow if no real problem is addressed, market capacity is small, or the value-capture approach

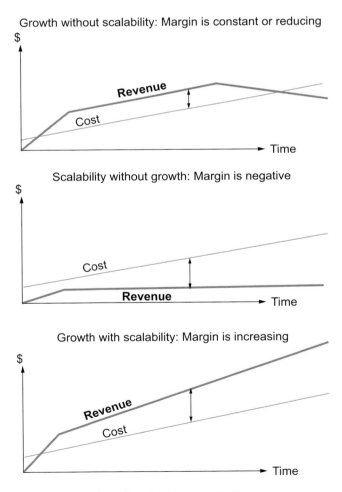

Figure 6.2 *Contrasting growth with and without scalability*

is poorly conceived or implemented. In such cases, costs will outstrip revenues, implying negative operational performance. Such ventures need to identify root causes of this failure and pivot rapidly to generate growth before a lack of confidence drains away their key resources.

By contrast, a venture that is both growing and scalable delivers increasing performance as it grows because revenue growth outstrips marginal cost increases. Consequently, the bigger the venture becomes, the more benefit it generates.

Figure 6.2 provides a simplified illustration of the three cases in respect of their implications for growth of revenues, costs and margins.

The focus of a start-up venture is typically around the generation of ideas and their exploitation through an offering and a business model into an early-stage population of customers. It is important to differentiate this from the focus of a venture in the process of scale-up, which is more around driving market consumption by larger customer populations through an organization that has been designed to operate at scale. This distinction is significant and multi-faceted, and is framed in Figure 6.3 from two complementary perspectives:

First, as a business design activity motivated by a strategy and plan for growth and scalability. The execution of the plan requires decision making and activity in respect of recruiting and motivating talent, building capability

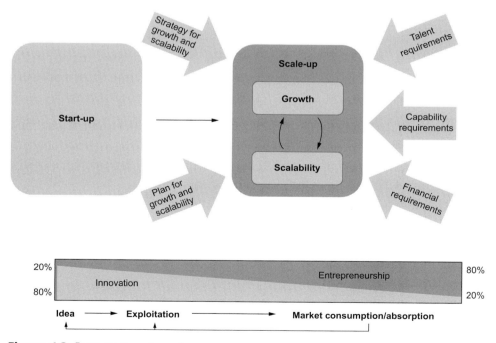

Figure 6.3 *From start-up to scale-up*

and generating or raising finance. These components can be characterized respectively as *who is needed, what does it need to be able to do* and *what funding will be needed to make it happen.*

Second, in respect of the increasing need for an entrepreneurial mindset to dominate over an initial innovation focus. Applying the Pareto principle, it may be helpful to assume an 80/20 blend at each extreme, as this enables a venture to achieve excitement across its early adopters and then to scale up to a wider customer base, while remaining alive to the needs for a level of continuing innovation.

In 1991, Geoffrey Moore, an American organizational theorist, management consultant and author, first characterized the scalability challenge using the term *crossing the chasm.* In his seminal book on the subject, Moore (2014) draws upon Rodgers (2003) to frame the scalability problem as a chasm between doing business with *early adopters* who are motivated primarily by technology and performance, and appealing to an *early majority* population of customers who are more interested by solutions and convenience. Moore notes that a proposition framed for early adopters may need to be reframed for an early majority population who can be sceptical of the advocacy of enthusiasts.

Recent empirical research by Phadke and Vyakarnam (2017) positions Moore's chasm as the third of a series of discontinuities that need to be addressed by entrepreneurs intent on scaling up. The demands of each of these are summarized in this chapter.

The multi-faceted and wide-ranging nature of growth and scalability imply a wide scope for this chapter. Furthermore, the various subjects involved overlap in implications, which means that any sequence of coverage needs to be interpreted in the context of iterative refinement. The structure chosen provides a logical coverage:

- Setting a strategy, including defining ambitions, indicators and drivers and assessing risk.
- Planning for growth and scalability, including financial forecasting, capability requirements and the implications of discontinuities.
- Creating a financial growth projection, including revenues, costs and margins.
- Designing a team for growth and scalability, including selecting and incentivizing the right mix.
- Designing scalable capability, including general drivers and capability-specific scalability.
- Assessing funding requirements and options, including organic growth and external investment sources.

- Raising external investment, where this is required.
- Consolidating a business plan that defines the venture's ambition and proposed plan.

These subjects are each addressed from the perspective of applicable considerations and techniques.

Setting a Strategy for Growth and Scalability

A strategy sets a framework for a plan to deliver the growth and scalability needed to achieve the business objectives, while managing the associated risks.
It addresses the following questions:

- What are the objectives for growth and scalability?
- What will drive growth and how will this be activated?
- What activities will be needed to mitigate or transfer unacceptable risks?

What Are the Objectives for Growth and Scalability?

Defining an Exit Ambition

As with all areas of design, addressing the development of a scalable business begins with the setting of objectives. In this context, defining exit ambitions can help clarify the motivation and risk appetite of the founders, which will in turn influence design decisions.

Broadly speaking, there are two options: to grow and scale a business that will offer a financial exit through a stock market listing, a significant investment round or a merger and acquisition (M&A) transaction; or to grow a business with the intention that it will provide a desired lifestyle over the longer term, with no guarantee of a financially rewarding exit event. The ambition may be set at a broad level, or it may be more specific in terms of the parties involved, the nature of the transaction or the time frame.

It is important for any venture that the members of the founding and investing team are open and honest about their individual ambitions, because confused or hidden ambitions can become a damaging source of conflict within the team.

Setting an ambition and acting consistently upon on it will mitigate the risk of building a business of limited market value, or a business from which founders and other investors have no exit options. From a positive perspective, setting an ambition clarifies the need and drive for growth and scalability, which in turn sets priorities and appetites for activity.

Instilling an Investor Mindset

Early consideration of exit can help to instill an *investor mindset*. Business founders are investors in their business, and need to learn how to behave and operate like the other kinds of investors that may join the venture as it develops.

There are significant differences of perspective between the mindsets, and hence the priorities and behaviours, of investors and employees:

- Investors are motivated by growing business value, whereas employees are motivated by recognition and reward for performing their role well.
- When an investor takes a risk, they may need to put at stake years of effort, resources and reputation, whereas an employee usually risks only their current role.
- Investors need to be able to take decisions on the grounds of what will benefit the venture beyond the short term, even if this means sacrificing short-term benefits.

Continuing awareness of this distinction is necessary to ensure real and sustainable growth.

Setting Objectives and Indicators

It is important to ensure that growth and scalability enhance the value of the venture to its founders and investors, and to prospective future investors and acquirers. This cannot be assumed to occur by default because, for example, the relentless pursuit of rapid revenue generation can actually be counterproductive to a venture's longer-term ambitions. This is borne out by research reported by EY Poland (2014), which concludes that 'short-termism results in insufficient attention being paid to the strategy, fundamentals and long-term value creation'.

This point underlines the need to focus explicitly on value when setting a strategy for growth and scalability. The following kinds of objectives can be adopted to *bake value into the business* such that continuing growth will translate into enhanced business value:

- Proving market demand by generating revenues.
- Proving the potential to generate cash by generating profits.
- Evidencing demand by capturing market share.

- Achieving competitive success to create friction and attract attention.
- Customer satisfaction to prove market understanding and successful engagement.
- Indicate strategic potential through independent market endorsement.
- Proving a viable and scalable delivery capability through active channel partners.

A venture's strategy might prioritize a balanced collection of such objectives as its means of demonstrating growth in value. Those adopted will be recorded as key objectives, associated with KPIs by which achievement can be tracked.

The KPIs selected will be driven by business objectives and market norms. Assessing the latter requires market research on the measures that are highlighted by competitors or by comparable businesses operating in the same market. The following examples suggest norms for three different markets:

- For a retail sector business with the objective of achieving a high valuation from an investor within 12 months, suitable indicators might be fast growth in monthly recurring revenues and a profitability that increases with growing user numbers.
- For a business that monetizes online content for content creators, channel providers and publishers, suitable measures might include the ratio of customer lifetime value to customer acquisition cost.
- For a business that offers a software platform service, suitable measures might include gross margin and operating margin to demonstrate scalability through growth.

The accuracy of any data that is used or reported must be beyond question, so collecting and calculating data for the selected indicators needs systematic planning.

What Will Drive Growth and How Will This Be Activated?

The strategy must express clearly what will drive and sustain market appetite and activity.

There are two necessary preconditions for growth:

1. The business model must be able to deliver and sustain a real perceived benefit, or return on investment, for its targeted customers and for other relevant ecosystem players such as channel partners.

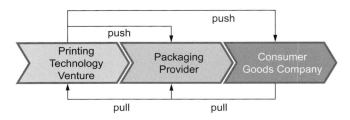

Figure 6.4 *Illustrative growth strategy*

2. The value-capture approach adopted by the venture must deliver its objectives in terms of revenues, customer retention and future commitment, plus
   market confidence and reputation.

Given these preconditions, existing customers will be retained, new customers will be
attracted and the value captured will contribute directly to the venture's success.
However, analysis of growth drivers needs to go further than this: it needs to
understand how growth can be stimulated, influenced or controlled.

With some ventures, growth needs to be driven proactively: it needs to be
pushed through targeted promotional and channel activities. With other businesses, growth can be reactive or pulled by a market that is attracted to a
compelling and affordable solution to a problem.

Most ventures grow by achieving a mix of push and pull from the market by
means of a programme of promotional activities, including targeted advertising,
pricing manipulation or engaging the kinds of market influencers described in
Chapter 3.

In addition to these, it can be helpful to consider how the dynamics of the
ecosystem might be used to benefit the venture. Figure 6.4 provides an example
of how this can work.

The example relates to a hypothetical venture that offers an innovative printing
technology for providers of packaging materials for consumer goods companies.

As a growth strategy, the venture might push its promotional activities at
packaging providers, while simultaneously engaging directly with consumer
goods companies to generate a demand pull for the innovative technology on
their suppliers. The effect of this strategy will be to energize the venture's push
activities by creating a parallel pull on its offering in response to the new
demands placed on packaging providers.

Exploitation of the ecosystem is central. Channel partners that are engaged
for promotional or delivery activities can be motivated to accelerate growth and
so multiply the effectiveness of the venture's in-house initiatives. An ideal

situation is where a snowball effect is created within a customer segment such that, as more customers commit to an offering, its attractiveness to others increases.

What Activities Will Be Needed to Mitigate or Transfer Unacceptable Risks?

Growth and scalability are subject to several risks, including the following:

- The risk that the appeal of the offering proves more limited than anticipated and so demand fails to grow at the projected rate. This can arise because of poor choice or segmentation of market, poor packaging of the offering to customers, unanticipated competition or simply because the innovation does not address a sufficient need. Mitigating this risk can involve revised market targeting, or reframing aspects of the business model, depending on the specific cause.
- The risk that the business model works and customer demand grows, but the planned supply chain or channels to market do not scale sufficiently to satisfy this demand, prompting a loss of customer and market confidence, or the need to accept additional unanticipated costs. This is an *external process risk*. The mitigation is to monitor, identify and diagnose the problem rapidly, such that replacement or additional partners can be engaged.
- The risk that the business model works and customer demand grows, but the processes within the business fail to scale to meet demand, prompting additional costs and a risk of losing confidence. This is an *internal process risk*. It may relate to product development velocity or to the effort needed for product manufacture and testing to an acceptable quality. As with external process risks, the mitigation is to monitor, identify and diagnose the problem rapidly such that internal resource constraints can be lifted, or external partners engaged.
- The model works and customer demand grows, but co-adoption or co-innovation assumptions fail to scale to meet the venture's needs. This can arise when a component supplier fails to produce a version that will support enhanced customer demand. The principal mitigation is continuing research for alternative partners that can be substituted in the event that existing players fall short of what is needed.

The growth and scalability strategy should include an assessment of such risks and an anticipation of the mitigations that may be required.

Case Study: SportMagenta

Strategy for Growth and Scalability

The founders agree on a mutual ambition of growing the venture to a point at which it can be floated on the stock market either in the UK or the USA within the next three to five years. They acknowledge that M&A activity is likely to happen along the way.

Their plan for baking value into the business starts with the three-month period of pilot engagement with clubs from a major chain to validate the ROI and demonstrate the potential for revenue generation. Thereafter, the venture will pursue rapid growth of market share and revenues over a twelve- to eighteen-month period to attract the attention of digital marketing companies and event-related system integrators who will offer new global routes to market. Such partners will be motivated by the prospect of additional scalable revenues through a platform with potential to deliver additional services.

The founders believe that growth for their venture will be driven by a combination of a compelling case for revenue share, and the enthusiastic adoption of the offering by sports club members and visitors.

The risk of underachieving against the plan will be mitigated by targeted promotion to club users plus a generous initial business case for clubs and promoters.

The risk of insufficient growth capacity will be mitigated by pilot proving of capacity and process requirements, adoption of standard technologies and methods, and automation of support processes.

Planning for Growth and Scalability

A plan forecasts the shape and time frame of the growth curve based on assumptions and decisions about the talent and capabilities that will be needed. Future sections address techniques to create the components of the plan.

This section provides background material relating to financial forecasting, business capability requirements and the implications of addressing commonly experienced discontinuities. It emphasizes the iterative nature of the planning process.

Financial Forecasting

An overview of the terminology used in financial forecasting is provided for readers with little or no previous experience of the subject.

Orders, revenues, costs and *margins* are the principal items that need to be understood and applied consistently with normal market interpretations.

Orders

An order is a contracted purchase from a customer. At a minimum, it has a description of the products and services to be purchased, the amounts to be paid, and a time frame for delivery and payment.

Revenues

Revenue is income received by a business from its normal business activities, such as satisfying customer orders for products and services. Revenue is also referred to as *the top line*, or *sales*, or *turnover*. The calculation of revenue is based on an accounting policy such as the International Financial Reporting Standards (IFRS) or in the USA the Generally Accepted Accounting Principles (GAAP).

The policy adopted is important as it defines when revenues can be *recognized*. In general, revenue may be recognized only when it has been earned, which means that in the case of an order for a six-month service, the associated revenue will be recognized monthly over that period, and not at the point of receiving the order. This can affect the periodic reporting of revenues.

Figure 6.5 illustrates the recognition of revenues from a collection of orders received over a six-month period. The orders assumed in the example combine *pure product* orders that are earned immediately at the point of the order; *service orders* that are earned monthly; and *blended orders* that combine product and service in which product-related revenues are earned at the point of order, and associated service revenues are earned over the relevant time frame.

Costs

Two categories of cost are usually acknowledged.

Indirect costs are independent of output. These are the underlying costs needed to keep the venture operating. They may relate to the support of multiple products. Indirect costs can further subdivide as follows:

- Fixed overheads, such as upfront purchases of equipment or licences.
- Recurrent indirect costs, such as:
  - Staff salaries and contracts.
  - Property rental and services.
  - Power, communications, hosting services.
  - Professional fees, including accounting, bookkeeping, legal or insurance.
  - Promotion charges, including costs of advertising or sponsorships.

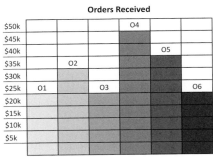

Order Details

O1 $25k order for a five-month service at $5k per month, starting in month 1

O2 $35k pure product order with no service component

O3 $25k order comprising $10k pure product plus a three-month service contract at $5k per month, starting in month 3

O4 $50k order for five-month service at $10k per month starting in month 4

O5 $40k order comprising $20k pure product plus a four-month service at $5k per month starting in month 5

O6 $25k pure product order with no service component

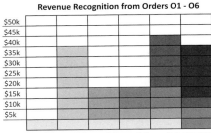

Figure 6.5 *Illustration of revenue recognition from orders*

Direct and variable costs are those associated with product development and sales. Direct costs are those that relate to delivery of an offering to customers, typically including staff and equipment. Variable costs are those that vary with the volume of sales, typically including materials, packaging, channels and external services, such as hosting.

A structure and process for creating a budget for cost control is addressed by Chapter 8.

Margins

A margin is a measure of the ratio between revenues and costs. Two margins are commonly used: gross margin and operating margin.

Gross margin measures the percentage of sales revenue that is retained after accounting for the direct and variable costs associated with the goods and services sold.

$$\text{Gross margin}(\%) = (\text{revenue} - \text{cost of sales}) / \text{revenue}$$

The higher the percentage, the more the business retains on each dollar of revenues. For a scalable venture, the cost of sales will increase at a lesser rate than revenues, hence the gross margin will increase with higher revenues. Consequently, the gross margin for a venture provides an indicator of the scalability of its capabilities for promotion and sales and for delivery and operations.

Operating or profit margin measures the proportion of revenue that remains after paying for all operating costs.

$$\text{Operating margin}(\%) = (\text{revenue} - \text{opex}) / \text{revenue}$$

Where *opex* includes all operating costs (indirect, direct and variable) associated with the functioning of the venture.

For a scalable venture, operating costs increase at a lesser rate than revenues, hence the operating margin will increase with higher revenues; consequently, the operating margin for a venture provides a good indicator for the scalability of a venture as a whole.

Business Capability Requirements

A capability is an abstraction comprising processes and controls together with the people, assets and resources needed to achieve an outcome. The concept of capability is independent of organization structure, and therefore can provide an objective and resilient basis for designing what is needed for the venture to grow and scale. The mapping of capability design onto an organizational structure will evolve with the venture.

Figure 6.6 illustrates a model comprising four generally applicable capabilities that are needed for a venture to grow and scale.

A later section of this chapter addresses design considerations and techniques for developing capabilities that will scale. This section focuses on the principal requirements of those capabilities that are needed.

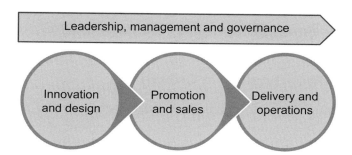

Figure 6.6 *Capabilities required for growth and scalability*

Leadership, Management and Governance

From a growth and scalability perspective, this capability is responsible for delivering the venture's strategy and objectives. This includes identifying, recruiting, shaping and motivating the talent that is required; identifying and establishing the processes, resources and assets required by other capabilities; determining and accessing sources of funding; and tracking and directing the venture's progress over time.

Innovation and Design

This capability is a key driver of growth. It is responsible for delivering continuing innovation through the design of a business model that offers a strong value proposition into an active ecosystem.

The business model must be able to deliver and sustain a real perceived benefit for customers and other ecosystem players, including channel partners. Equally, the value captured by the venture must align with the venture's ambitions.

Promotion and Sales

This capability is critical to both growth and scalability. It is responsible for the effective targeting, promotion and sales of the offering through scalable channels and competent market engagement.

Delivery and Operations

The processes for productization and delivery of the offering are critical to a venture's scalability. These determine the quality of the offering, the customer experience, the robustness of the development roadmap, and the effectiveness of the delivery mechanisms and the supply chain.

This capability is responsible for ensuring scalability of development, production, delivery and support, and the targeted prioritization of a forward roadmap to enable the development velocity needed to meet customer demand. It is also responsible for providing the processes, systems, equipment, data, security and premises required to enable the venture to operate effectively.

Addressing Discontinuities in Growth

Empirical research reported by Phadke and Vyakarnam (2017) identified three commonly experienced discontinuities in the development of a business. Drawing on the terminology of Moore (2014), they refer to these as *chasms* that need to be crossed. Their research identifies those capabilities (referred to as *commercialization vectors* in their work) that are most significant in crossing each of these chasms. Their findings can be summarized against the four broad capabilities introduced above.

Crossing the First Chasm

Chasm one is the challenge of developing an idea into a working prototype. This can be characterized using the technology readiness framework introduced in Chapter 4 as achieving TRL3: *experimental proof of concept.*

The capabilities that enable this chasm to be crossed are:

- Innovation and design, to frame the business proposition within its ecosystem.
- Delivery and operations, to develop the initial technology offering.

Crossing the Second Chasm

Chasm two is the challenge of creating a fully functioning product or service offering with a sustainable business model. This can be characterized as achieving TRL8: *system complete and qualified.*

The capabilities that enable this chasm to be crossed are:

- Leadership, management and governance, to secure the required funding and manage the venture's IP.
- Innovation and design, to develop and test the business model.
- Promotion and sales, to define the initial target customer market.
- Delivery and operations, to synthesize a sustainable offering.

Achieving a fully functioning offering requires development maturity, not only in terms of functionality, but also in terms of delivery, integration, security, support and the various other topics addressed in Chapter 4.

Crossing the Third Chasm

The third chasm aligns with that addressed by Moore (2014). It relates to the progression that occurs at TRL9 from sales to *early adopters* to acceptance by a larger *early majority* population of customers.

The capabilities that enable this chasm to be crossed are:

- Leadership, management and governance, to recruit, shape and motivate the required talent.
- Promotion and sales, to prioritize target customer markets.
- Delivery and operations, to establish delivery channels and effective supply chain management.

In terms of a strategy for crossing this chasm, Moore (2014) provides the following succinct advice to B2B ventures:

- The approach should be market-led, not sales-led: determine a vertical market with sufficient size and a real problem that is solved by the offering.
- Focus on the needs of that market in respect of messaging, pricing, distribution and so on.
- Analyse the market landscape in terms of the applicable forces, and create a plan to dominate the market and mitigate the applicable risks.

Having dominated one vertical market, the venture would prioritize additional markets and apply the same approach.

Although his focus is on B2B ventures, Moore suggests the following approach for B2C ventures:

- Acquire traffic – become visible and active.
- Engage users – build up the community.
- Monetize engagement – determine how to translate engagement into revenues.
- Enlist advocates – to extend reach and build reputation.

There are several further implications of crossing this chasm to access a significantly larger market.

The first of these can affect the venture's initial framing and promotional approach. A conflict can emerge between the inherent enthusiasm of early adopters and the pragmatism of the early majority. This may mean that the latter are not impressed by references from the former, who are likely to describe their motivation and experiences in terms that do not give comfort to pragmatists. For this reason, new reference customers may need to be developed, and the proposition may need to be reframed from being a *state-of-the-art* technology to being something more like a *reliable industry standard.*

The second implication affects the venture's processes for development and release. Early adopters tend to be technically confident and hence may be predisposed to accept a product that requires a degree of integration or customization, or that is not packaged with comprehensive support. This cannot be assumed to be true with other types of customer. Such considerations can be very significant to the later majority group of customers, who tend to be conservative and cautious, but it can also be true with early majority customers, especially in a B2B context with larger customer organizations. In this context,

Davidow (1986) introduces the term *whole product* and embeds it in his strategic principle that 'marketing must invent complete products and drive them to commanding positions in defensible market segments'. Planned development activities need to take this *whole product* requirement into account if larger customer populations are to be accessed successfully.

The third implication relates to the mix of people that is needed in the team. In its early days, a venture needs innovators to develop ideas and notions of how they can be brought to market. As the offering matures and the supported customer base grows, in parallel to continuing development, it becomes important to ensure that the team comprises the right mix of operators and innovators. Having too many innovators can risk losing the confidence of an increasing population of pragmatic and technically cautious customers, whereas having too many operators can risk ossifying product development in a way that threatens to lose customers' interest and the venture's competitive edge.

A fourth implication refers to the co-innovation assumed of other organizations for the offering to work and to be sustained. This can include providers of components and technology platforms such as networks, operating systems or graphics engines. It can be important to consider the appetite of the growth market for installing version upgrades, including the likely frequency with which updates will need to be released, and the corresponding effort required, both by the venture and by the customer. Some larger customer organizations limit the ability of their suppliers to apply upgrades, and hence it may be necessary to continue to use earlier versions of technologies for some considerable time. The strategy needs to consider any implications of this on any co-innovation assumptions and arrangements.

The fifth implication relates to co-adopters, those parties from which some form of product or service contribution is needed for an offering to be made available to the customer in an acceptable form and at the scale that is needed. Co-adopters can include external providers of support, and distribution partners that can deliver at scale. In his book on the subject, Adner (2013) characterizes the need to motivate co-adopters as a 'tug of war between innovation and the status quo'. A case in point is when issuing a product upgrade requires activity from a partner, but provides them with no additional benefit. Addressing such questions may require a review of the applicable financial arrangements to ensure that required actions are incentivized. A growth strategy needs to identify such requirements and assess any related opportunities or mitigations needed.

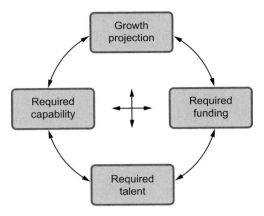

Figure 6.7 *Iterative development of a plan for growth and scalability*

Elements of a Plan

A plan combines a financial growth projection with assumptions and decisions about the talent, capability and funding needed to support it. As these elements are closely interrelated, they need to be developed iteratively, as illustrated in Figure 6.7.

The nature of this iteration can be indicated by the following simple example. Suppose that initial growth projections are deemed to be too slow or cautious, and that it is decided to create a revised plan with more optimistic assumptions and hence a steeper growth curve. These revised assumptions might imply a need for additional technical roles in the team and for scaling of delivery through new channel partners. The growth projection will then need to be reworked to include the costs of new personnel and channels, which will impact margin calculations. Additionally, assumptions of required funding will need to be reviewed.

The following sections address these elements in turn in respect of relevant techniques and considerations. An iterative application of these is assumed throughout.

Creating a Growth Projection

Growth projections are typically expressed in terms of revenues, costs and margins. This section provides and illustrates a method for projecting these quantities. Projections based on other growth indicators can be developed using a comparable approach.

Revenue Projections

A revenue projection is a forecast of the earnings a venture will generate during a specific period. It sets a target for the amount of revenue that will be recognized during that period.

When creating any forecast, it is necessary first to make a collection of assumptions relating to the performance of sales channels and the effectiveness of the process whereby prospects will become revenue-generating customers. In the case of revenue projections, these assumptions can be informed by addressing questions such as the following:

- How many *prospects* are expected to be *qualified* as viable customers within a time period?
- How long will it take to *close* a sale; that is, for a qualified customer to place their first order?
- What are the projected average sizes for first and subsequent orders?
- What is the capacity of the channel to handle multiple prospects and customers?
- What is the probability of winning a contract for which a competitive bid is required?
- What is the expected customer retention rate?
- What is the likely repeat order frequency?
- What is the projected customer lifetime value?

The answers assumed to questions such as these need to be documented explicitly in any forecast model. Over time, the model will be validated and tuned through experience.

As far as possible, these assumptions should be grounded in market facts, such as actual experiences or the experiences of other comparable ventures, market size projections and the results of specific market research activities.

Based on the assumptions made, revenue projections can be calculated over a forecasting period. This is usually up to one year and may be extended up to three years with a lower degree of confidence.

It can be useful to create multiple projections, each of which reflects a future scenario based on a set of assumptions. Typical scenarios include:

- A conservative projection that assumes low performance of marketing and sales channels, difficulties in scaling to handle volume and pessimistic performance of product development.

- A more aggressive projection that assumes strong channel performance in qualifying and closing sales and in handling sales volumes, and a product development and release process that can keep pace with demand.

If the conservative and aggressive scenarios prove to be far apart, then it may be helpful to create additional intermediary projections.

A venture that is seeking investment to fund its growth plan might create several groups of projections, each of which demonstrates the benefits of investing at particular levels. One group of projections might relate to organic growth without investment, another with assumed investment at a moderate level and a third with a higher level of investment.

Revenue projections can be central to the discussion with potential investors, who will use them together with margin projections to assess their likely returns in respect of how much and when, and with what risk.

Case Study: SportMagenta

Revenue Projections

Assuming a twelve-month planning horizon, the founders decide that two scenarios will be sufficient for their planning purposes. A conservative projection will assume a modest revenue share of the increased sales that are achieved by clubs during the pilot activity, and a relatively slow take-up of the offer by additional clubs following the pilot activity. A more aggressive projection will assume increases in the percentage of revenue share achieved and in the speed of take-up by clubs after the pilot.

Sonny computes these projections as follows, based on the assumed performance of the five three-month (twelve-week) pilot projects that have been agreed with a chain of sports clubs:

Conservative Scenario

Assume that the five clubs achieve on average a 5 per cent increase in revenues against a \$200,000 weekly baseline, and assume that each club shares 10 per cent of that increase with SportMagenta.

This would mean that the revenue generated for SportMagenta over the pilot period would be

(12 weeks × 5 clubs × 5% revenue increase × \$200,000 revenue × 10 per cent share) = \$60,000.

Following the three-month pilot projects, suppose that a six-month (twenty-four-week) roll-out phase attracts five further clubs, and that each again achieves on average a 5 per cent increase in its revenues per week, and shares 10 per cent of that increase with SportMagenta. Assume also that the five clubs engaged as initial pilots continue to perform at the same level.

This would mean that the revenue generated for SportMagenta between months four and nine would be

(24 weeks × 10 clubs × 5% revenue increase × $200,000 revenue × 10 per cent share) = $240,000.

Finally, suppose that during the final three months (twelve weeks) of the year, five further clubs are engaged on the same basis. Assuming that all fifteen clubs achieve and share the same levels of increased revenues, this would mean that SportMagenta's revenues would increase by

(12 weeks × 15 clubs × 5% revenue increase × $200,000 revenues × 10%) = $180,000.

In summary, Sonny's conservative revenue projection for the year would be ($60,000 + $240,000 + $180,000) = $480,000.

Aggressive Scenario

Assume that the initial three-month pilots achieve the same increased revenues as with the conservative projection, but agree to share 12.5 per cent rather than 10 per cent of the increased revenues achieved. The revenue generated for SportMagenta would increase to $75,000.

Assume that the six-month roll-out attracts ten further clubs rather than five, and that each of these (including the five initial pilot clubs) achieves a 10 per cent increase in revenues and shares 12.5 per cent of this increase. The revenue generated for SportMagenta during this phase would increase to $900,000.

Finally, assume that during the final three months of the year five further clubs are attracted, each of which (and the fifteen existing clubs) achieves a 10 per cent increase in revenues and shares 12.5 per cent of this increase. The revenue generated for SportMagenta during this phase would increase to $600,000.

In summary, the aggressive revenue projection for the year would be ($75,000 + $900,000 +$600,000) = $1.575 million.

By judging the likely phasing of revenues received by the venture, Sonny plots line graphs forecasting the revenues to be generated under each of the two projections. Two representations are generated: that above shows the forecasted pattern of revenues to be received during the year; that below shows a projection of the cumulative revenue forecast for the year.

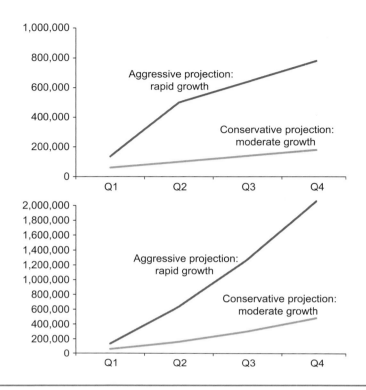

Cost Projections

A cost projection can be set out as a quarterly tabulation of the indirect, direct and variable costs associated with achieving a revenue projection, covering people, services, licences, commissions, materials and rentals. A cost projection will be created for each scenario envisaged.

In assessing the likely costs of personnel required, a useful rule of thumb suggested by Y Combinator's Geoff Ralston (2016) based on current Silicon Valley norms at that time is that an engineer is likely to cost about $15,000 per month. Consequently, the cost of an eighteen-month planning horizon with a team of five engineers would be in the order of $15,000 × 5 × 18 = $1.35 million.

Margin Projections

Gross and operating margins can be calculated from revenue and cost projections for each scenario. A wide disparity between conservative and aggressive scenarios would indicate the need for an additional midway scenario.

Norms for gross and operating margins vary across sectors and types of offering. In general, pure software offerings generate higher margins because of the relatively low marginal costs, whereas service-intensive offerings have lower margins. It is advisable to validate margin projections against industry norms before presenting anything to a knowledgeable party.

Case Study: SportMagenta

Cost and Margin Projections

Zara estimates that delivering a reliable and performant product will require a development team of at least three competent software engineers. Against this assumption, the founders estimate the likely costs associated with the twelve-month period of piloting and initial roll-out activities to be as follows.

Indirect costs, independent of output and applicable to both conservative and aggressive projections, comprise:

Fixed overheads: none	
Recurrent indirect costs:	
Employment of two, growing to three, operational people:	$100,000
Property rental and services:	$ 16,000
Power, communications and internet:	$ 8,000
Professional fees:	$ 4,000
Promotion, including advertising and sponsorships:	$ 16,000
Which suggests a total indirect cost base of	$144,000

Direct and variable costs relating specifically to product development and sales comprise:

Direct costs (conservative projection):	
Employment of three, growing to four, developers:	$195,000
Variable costs (conservative projection):	
Hosting of customer activities:	$ 12,000
Cost of sales (conservative projection):	($195,000 + $12,000) = $207,000
Operating costs (conservative projection):	($144,000 + $207,000) = $351,000
Direct costs (aggressive projection):	
Employment of three, growing to six, developers:	$270,000
Variable costs (aggressive projection):	
Hosting of customer activities:	$ 20,000
Cost of sales (aggressive projection):	($270,000 + $20,000) = $290,000
Operating costs (aggressive projection):	($144,000 + $290,000) = $434,000

The founders recognize that the detail of the direct costs will vary according to the timing of new joiners through the year, and make what they consider to be reasonable assumptions quarter by quarter, as shown below. The graph above shows the forecasted pattern of costs to be incurred over the year; that below shows a projection of the cumulative cost forecast for the year.

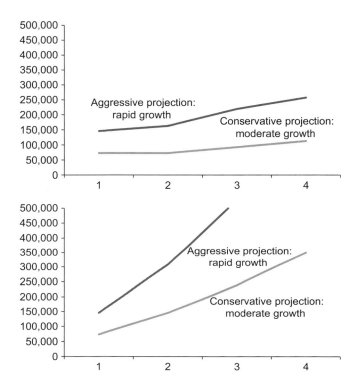

From these cost assumptions, they calculate the gross and operating margins for each of the growth scenarios.

Gross margin = (revenue − cost of sales) / revenue
Conservative GM% = (480,000 − 207,000) / 480,000 = 57 per cent annual
Aggressive GM% = (1.575m − 290,000) / 1.575m = 82 per cent annual
Operating margin = (revenue − operating costs) / revenue
Conservative OM% = (480,000 − 351,000) / 480,000 = 27 per cent annual
Aggressive OM% = (1.575m − 434,000) / 1.575m = 72 per cent annual

The founders recognize that their aggressive growth assumptions lead to high margin projections and a relatively small difference between operating and gross margins, which together indicate that they are projecting a very high gearing of the business.

Effectively, this means that the marginal cost of delivering additional growth is assessed to be very small, which will make the business highly attractive if the forecast can be achieved. They recognize too that their conservative growth assumptions lead to much lower margin projections for the first year, and acknowledge that results such as these would likely fall short of objectives and hence prompt a review of business.

Designing a Team for Growth and Scalability

There are three parts to this consideration:

- Determining the talent required, including size and shape of the team.
- Selecting the right people to achieve and sustain the venture's competitiveness.
- Setting the right incentives and rewards to motivate and retain people.

Determining the Talent Required

For a planning horizon of, say, eighteen months, it is possible to determine the roles and likely numbers required to meet the assumptions of the growth forecast. Broadly speaking, the roles required within a scalable venture can be assessed against the set of required capabilities illustrated in Figure 6.6.

In early ventures, it is often the case that individuals will play multiple roles. For the purposes of this exercise, it is useful to question such assumptions, because growth can demand clarity of focus and purpose. One aspect of *thinking like an investor* is recognizing that the team needs to be capable of scaling, which implies a need for leadership.

The time frame for introducing new people can also be significant because introducing new members to a team can be time-consuming and demanding. In the early days of a venture, each new person brings a significant change to team dynamics and introducing too many new people too quickly can prove disruptive. As the venture matures through the introduction of structure, process and culture, the introduction of new people has lower impact. For this reason, phasing can be important. However, it is important to acknowledge that finding and recruiting the ideal person can take between three and six months, especially when taking account of a notice period with an existing employer.

It is common for the initial assessment of required personnel to change during hiring because the impact of new people often prompts questions about the working of the plan. One scenario is where a highly competent new developer is able to pull forward the planned release date for a new and more powerful offering, which in turn brings forward the need to expand the sales role. Under another scenario, the same developer may have demonstrated that the previous plan was overly optimistic, and that additional development resource will urgently be needed in the short term.

Likewise, the initially expected balance of required roles can be questioned by applicants that combine required skills in unanticipated ways. For these reasons, it is important to keep a focus on business objectives and retain flexibility over how these will be achieved.

Skills shortfalls can be met using associates or contractors to fill required roles. This approach can have the benefit that these are often experienced professionals who will establish the role to the required standard; the costs, however, can be considerably higher than for full-time employees. Tapering out of contractors as newly recruited employees join can have beneficial training and continuity benefits.

Selecting the Right People to Achieve and Sustain Competitiveness

Each person brought into the venture needs to be considered in terms of their individual qualities and their contribution to the required mix.

Assessing a Candidate's Suitability for a Role

Some generically useful considerations to be tested at interview include:

- Will the person perform and excel as a member of the team?
- Is the individual an *innovator* or an *operator* (a *pioneer* or a *settler*), and which of these is needed for this role?
- Will the person fit within the existing team in terms of culture and values?

These considerations can be expressed more pithily as: will they be able to do the job; will they love doing it; and will we be able to tolerate working with them?

Some larger organizations use personality type analysis to assess an individual's likely fit into a team. This is unusual with smaller ventures, which are more inclined to be personal in their assessment of the individual and their likely fit.

Assessing a Candidate's Contribution to Competitiveness

To contribute to the competitiveness of a venture, each person in the team should enable the business either to exploit an opportunity or to mitigate a

Table 6.1 Use of the VRIO technique

Valuable?	Rare?	Costly to imitate?	Exploited by the organization?	Competitive implication
Yes	Yes	Yes	Yes	Sustained competitive advantage
Yes	Yes	Yes		Unexploited competitive advantage
Yes	Yes			Temporary competitive advantage
Yes				Competitive parity
				Competitive disadvantage

threat. This applies both to existing personnel and to those being considered for recruitment.

These qualities can be assessed using a technique proposed by Barney (1995), called VRIO analysis. This assesses the competitive potential of the team through analysis of each person in respect of the following four criteria:

- *Value*: does the person help to exploit an opportunity or neutralize an external threat?
- *Rarity*: does the person provide a scarce expertise or knowledge?
- *Imitability*: how difficult or expensive would it be to imitate what this person offers?
- *Organization*: how ready is the venture to be able to exploit the value offered?

Table 6.1 shows the working of the technique. As shown by the matrix, if a person is *valuable* because they help to exploit an opportunity or neutralize a threat, then they contribute competitive parity to the venture; if they are also *rare* because they provide a scarce expertise, then they contribute a temporary competitive advantage, at least until the competition also have access to their own scarce resource; and so on.

This technique enables the venture to assess the value of current or potential team members in terms that align with the objective of growing business value.

Setting the Right Incentives and Rewards to Motivate and Retain People

The wider topic of compensation and benefits for employees is addressed in more detail in Chapter 8. In this section, the focus is on designing additional mechanisms whereby individuals are motivated to deliver a planned programme of growth.

Motivating people to work to a particular goal means making them feel like stakeholders in the plan. This can be achieved through offering a shareholding, an attractive remuneration package or a combination of the two.

Use of Shares or Share Options

One option is for the venture to issue an equity share to purchase buy-in from an individual. Sometimes referred to as *sweat equity* or *equity compensation*, this approach can be used instead of other remuneration methods for a venture with limited cash.

Sweat equity usually assumes that, on successful delivery of the growth plan, there will be some form of transaction that crystallizes the value of stock through an investment or acquisition, and by which the sweat equity holders will benefit financially. The benefit of this approach to the venture is that the shareholder shares the risk of the plan such that if the plan fails, then no cost is incurred.

For the sweat equity holder, if a crystallization event occurs, they will be satisfied with their investment of effort. If it does not, however, either because the plan failed or because the market did not respond as anticipated, then the equity holder may feel bitter towards the venture.

An alternative approach is for the venture to remunerate the team at a reasonable level, and additionally to commit to an issue of shares (or share options) on the achievement of the plan, or perhaps on meeting intermediate targets. The difference between shares and options is addressed in detail in Chapter 8. This approach is commonly used as an incentive for valuable team members to stay with the venture.

With any issue of any shares or options, there are important considerations:

- Issuing new shares dilutes the holdings of existing shareholders, and issuing significant numbers of new shares may impact the majority decision-making power in the business. This can be mitigated by limiting new motivational shares as non-voting shares. It is important whenever considering the issue of new shares to ensure a clear majority control is retained where it is needed. Retaining a 75 per cent voting majority for investors ensures that they have the legal power to pass a special resolution, should that be required.

- Issuing too many shares to early employees can bring later problems over fairness or parity, as those joining later may need to be offered smaller packages so as not to risk over-dilution. This recommends the early agreement to a future plan for share allocation that takes account of the needs of investors and new personnel that will join.
- An issue of shares is associated with a share agreement. Each class of shares has its own agreement that sets out the rights and obligations of the shareholder. Importantly, together with the company's articles of association, it will set out conditions on the shareholder leaving the business. This latter point can be particularly important as the prospect of people with significant shareholdings leaving a venture brings a range of risks that may affect the appetite of future investors.
- When using shares, or share options, as a motivational device, it is important to have a realistic expectation for when the implicitly promised value will be realized. This can occur either through a business transaction such as an investment, acquisition or flotation, or by means of dividend payments. If no such rewards are forthcoming, or likely, then those who were originally motivated may become more cynically inclined.

Use of Salary and Bonus Schemes

For ventures with sufficient financial security, a preferred means of securing buy-in by the team may be through the offer of a competitive salary, with the option of bonus payments on the achievement of targets.

The benefit of this approach, where it is feasible, is that it separates the considerations of equity holding from those of team motivation. This gives more scope to use the venture's equity to secure necessary investment while retaining reasonable shareholdings for founders.

Case Study: SportMagenta

Team Requirements and Assessment

The founders review the details of the shape and size of the team that will be needed to support their growth projections over the forthcoming year. These are determined to be as follows:

Direction and management:

Sonny and Zara, the founders; rewarded by dividend payments.

Innovation and design:

> No dedicated staff; this role will be met initially by the founders working closely with their technical colleagues.

Promotion and sales:

> A specialist influencer and networker; funded by a sweat equity arrangement aligned with objectives.
>
> Additional sales person to join later in the year; modest salary plus bonus against objectives.

Delivery and operations:

> Three to six technical developer roles; salaried and recruited in response to demand. Three operational roles responsible for accounting, planning, resources and infrastructure; salaried.

The founders propose a bonus scheme that will reward all employees on the achievement of the venture's growth objectives during the year. They also promise to introduce a share option scheme for all employees, to be established before the end of the year.

A VRIO analysis (table below) assesses the proposed recruitment plan and confirms its competitive advantage.

Role × no.	Valuable?	Rare?	Costly to imitate?	Exploited by the organization?	Competitive implication
Technical × (3–6)	Yes	Yes	No	Yes	Temporary competitive advantage
Influencer × 1	Yes	Yes	Yes	Yes	Sustained competitive advantage
Sales role × 1	Yes	No	No	Yes	Competitive parity
Operational roles × 3	Yes	No	No	Yes	Competitive parity

Designing Scalable Capabilities

As described earlier in this chapter, the principal capabilities required to achieve scalable growth by a business include the following:

- Leadership, management and governance.
- Innovation and design.
- Promotion and sales.
- Delivery and operations.

Specific businesses may need additional capabilities, but these four are universally applicable, and so are adopted as the focus here. The operation of each of these involves process, people, assets and resources. This section addresses considerations relating to achieving scalability of the venture through the design of these capabilities.

A capability is an abstraction and not an organizational structure. It may be that a one-to-one mapping exists between a venture's capability model and its team structure, but this is not necessarily the case. As noted in the previous section, capabilities are here adopted because they provide an objective and widely applicable basis for making design decisions. There is a need, though, to translate capability design decisions into their implications for team structures and responsibilities.

General Drivers of Capability Scalability

The following four principles drive scalability across all capabilities:

1. **Standardize** as far as possible without compromising the business model. Adopting formal or industry standards can have a positive impact on the availability of required sub-components, technologies, skills and methods; on any interfaces that need to be supported or provided; and on the choice of communications and deployment infrastructures.

   This use of standards de-risks the purchasing decision for customers, increases options for alternative channels for supply and distribution, widens recruitment options and opens options for outsourcing of components or processes.

   Standardization also applies in respect of internal activities, such as the processes for handling customers and suppliers, the scheduling of work and the setting of budgets. This use of standards minimizes internal errors and conflicts and gives an opportunity for skilled operators to optimize the way in which things work.

2. Build a **flexible workforce**, whereby as many employees as possible are able to perform a variety of different roles. The benefits of this include having the capacity to cover in the event that some people become unavailable, and having the ability at short notice to concentrate additional capacity on an activity.

Achieving such flexibility comes at the cost of a cross-training pro-gramme, but can be highly beneficial in a fast-growing business where unpredicted events can occur.

3. As far as possible, **automate** the processes within the business, and between the business and its customers and partners. In addition to speeding up processing times, this will help to standardize the way in which things work and hence contribute to reliability and scalability.

4. Invest in a **scalable systems and information infrastructure** for the venture. Poor information management can cost a venture dearly in terms of wasted time and accidental breaches of confidentiality or other commitments. Modern cloud platforms and SaaS applications make this much more achievable for ventures than in former times, when bespoke development could be a significant distraction from doing business.

   Such infrastructures do not negate the need for setting policies for information management and security. In some respects, the ease with which information can be shared can introduce or exacerbate the risks to the venture.

Capability-Specific Scalability Considerations

In addition to the above general approaches for designing scalability into the venture's capabilities, there are also specific approaches that can be taken to increase the scalability of the core capabilities relating to product design, promotion, sales and delivery.

Designing Scalability into Innovation and Design

The following considerations enable maximum scalability of this capability:

- Minimize the use of assumed product or service customizations that might impose additional cost or effort on product or services upgrades. The need to dedicate significant effort to each particular customer for every upgrade that is released can lead to an escalating *technical debt*.
- Prioritize the functionality that is provided by the offering such that development and support effort can be directed towards features that contribute to achieving the venture's objectives. It is easy to be beguiled into incorporating a range of extra *pet features* that do not contribute significantly to the value achieved by the customer, but which impose a growing maintenance cost within continuing development, testing and support.

Designing Scalability into Promotion and Sales

The following considerations enable maximum scalability of this capability:

- The promotional channels by which visibility is achieved across a wider market can provide the potential for highly scalable generation of demand. As with delivery channels (with which promotional channels can overlap), it may be important to plan for a range of channels for access to different geographies and vertical markets.
- Knowing the cost of customer acquisition through the various channels available can enable a business to operate at scale by dropping those that are uncompetitive. In its early days, it is normal for a venture to sustain multiple channels in the spirit of learning what works and at what cost. Achieving scalability with growth requires the venture to be more calculating about this and to invest only in those channels that are most economic. A useful measure for evaluating channel effectiveness is CLV or customer acquisition cost (CAC).

Designing Scalability into Delivery and Operations

The following considerations enable maximum scalability of this capability:

- The partner channels through which the offering is delivered to the market can provide the potential for highly scalable distribution. Planning for a range of channels can open scalable access to different geographies and vertical markets. With some ventures, developing and managing channel relationships can consume significant management effort. Such channels do, however, give access to a majority market that may be inaccessible without them.
- The design of the supply chain can be critical to scalability for ventures with complex needs. Decisions about outsourcing and contractual arrangements can make the difference between a business being able to operate at scale or being limited to a *cottage industry*.

Funding Growth and Scalability

Achieving growth and scalability needs money to pay for the people, equipment, assets, services and resources required. This money comes from a mix of revenues and investment.

Assessing the Funding Requirement and Options

A venture needs to know the current length of its *runway*. This is a measure of how long the business can operate with its current resources and commitments before it runs out of cash.

For example, the runway for a venture that has $100,000 in the bank, no projected revenues and a spend, or *burn rate*, of $10,000 per month will be ten months.

For early-stage ventures, the runway sometimes combines company and personal resources.

As explained in the previous section, a plan for growth and scalability makes revenue and margin projections that take account of the costs required to acquire the talent and build the capabilities needed to achieve these. This plan, together with a knowledge of the current runway, enables a calculation to determine whether the growth and scalability objectives can be achieved in the projected time frame using the venture's own resources, or whether external sources of finance will be needed.

If the plan cannot be delivered through the resources available within the existing runway together with forecasted revenues, then the venture has a choice:

(a) Revise the plan to reduce the cost profile to a level at which it becomes affordable. This is likely to involve slowing the speed of growth or reducing potential capacity by compromising on aspects of scalability. Under this option, the venture determines to fund its growth and scalability through its own revenues. Investment may be raised at a later point following demonstration of growth potential.

    or

(b) Determine to raise investment to fund the growth plan. Having taken this option, the venture may continue to fund its growth by securing successive rounds of investment or, after achieving an ability to generate revenues, it may determine to fund continuing growth through its own revenue generation.

This choice can be obvious for ventures with rapid growth ambition, or which need significant upfront money, such as where there is a need to fund long periods of trials before revenues can be earned. In many cases, this is a conscious and important choice, and the considerations below can help to inform that choice.

In cases where a plan can easily be met through its own revenue projections, the level of ambition of the objectives may be questionable, unless the venture's ambition is to provide a lifestyle for its founders.

Irrespective of its future intentions, the first choice a venture faces is whether to fund growth and scalability through revenue or investment. The relevant considerations of each are addressed below.

Funding Growth and Scalability through Revenues

This approach is often called *organic growth*. It involves launching an offering at an early stage and driving this to generate revenues. The profits are reinvested to fund continuing development, growth and scalability.

There are two significant benefits and two significant disadvantages associated with this approach.

The first benefit is that control can be retained over company equity. There need be no external influence over decision making, and the founder-investors retain complete ownership of the business.

This flows into the second benefit, which is that, should investment be sought at a later stage, say, to scale the business into a new market, then a better valuation can be achieved, because:

- There will be a demonstration of business value through existing revenue and profits.
- The case for investment to scale an existing business into a new or wider market is much lower risk than the case for investment to grow a business from nothing.

The first disadvantage is the flip side of the first benefit, in that the venture does not benefit from the experience and network that can be provided by early-stage investors. This disadvantage can be offset by mentors and business friends who may be engaged through accelerator hubs or local business networks. Ventures that elect to grow organically can benefit significantly from connecting keenly through such networks, at least in the early stages.

The second disadvantage of organic growth is the difficulty of funding step-changes out of incremental revenues. A steady revenue stream can cover steady-state costs over a modest growth curve, but where the business has a need or opportunity to invest in a major new product development or the opening of an operation in a new territory, the available funds can be limiting. This situation can be addressed by a loan, so long as a compelling case can be made to the lender that the venture can afford to fund the repayment plan with interest.

Funding Growth and Scalability through Investment

Throughout this section, the term 'investment' is used as a generalization for both debt- and equity-based approaches. Debt-based investment refers to a loan, normally associated with a period of time and an applicable interest rate, whereas equity-based investment refers to funds provided in exchange for a share of the equity, or ownership in the venture.

Two important questions should precede any consideration of investment:

- Why is the investment needed?
- Is the venture ready for investment?

Defining the Investment Requirement

It is important that a venture knows why it needs the investment before making any serious approach to investors. Without rational answers to this question, either the investor will quickly determine that the approach is premature, or the venture will negotiate a poor deal that will not meet its real needs.

A poor investment deal is one that severely damages a venture by giving away so much equity that the founders are no longer motivated to continue, or by accepting more cost than the venture can bear, or by setting targets that are more ambitious than can realistically be achieved. Any of these outcomes will be to the detriment of all parties.

The principal questions to be addressed by the venture before making any approach to an investor are as follows:

- What will the investment be spent on? This seems such an obvious question, but it is surprising how many ventures approach investors without a clear plan for growth and scalability to justify the need for investment and the corresponding benefits that will accrue to all parties.
- How much investment is needed and when? Both the total magnitude of the investment and its phasing over time need to be justified by the growth plan that underpins the investment case.
- What is the venture prepared to offer in return for investment? This will usually include an expected equity range, based on a *pre-money valuation*, one or more board positions, plus other guarantees that may be requested.
- What special benefits can the venture offer to the investor? This may relate to the potential of a strategic advantage in a particular market, or a tax benefit such as pre-approval for SEIS in the UK.
- What kind of investor is required? As the following section outlines, there are several kinds of investor. An important consideration is whether the investor

is expected to be able to bring more than money. Other expectations might include market knowledge or influence, or a network of relevant contacts.

- How will the venture go about getting investment? This includes a plan for when to start and how to go about engaging candidate investors. It also includes considerations of any help that may be needed. Help can be given via accelerator hubs, local business networks or brokers. The latter are businesses that can be engaged to seek and conclude investment deals, and which are usually recompensed through a mix of upfront fees and a percentage of the investment proceeds achieved. Brokers bring market knowledge and an ability to shape the venture towards meeting its investment objectives.
- What if the venture does not get investment in the required time frame, or if it gets only part of what's needed? This is an important question for the venture. Is there a *Plan B* for a period of organic growth ahead of a further approach to the market at a later date? Or will the case need to be re-formed and replayed based on learning achieved?

Investment Readiness

A good way for a venture to frame and classify itself ahead of investor conversations is to test its readiness level.

Chapter 4 introduced a scheme of technology readiness levels to enable a venture to indicate the maturity of its offering. Here, by comparison, a scheme of investment readiness levels (IRLs) is introduced by which a venture can indicate its maturity for investment.

The investment readiness scheme was first proposed by Steve Blank, co-author of *The Startup Owner's Manual* (Blank (2012)). It has been modified here as Figure 6.8 to serve as a general-purpose checklist and indicator for ventures ahead of engaging with investors.

The higher the venture's IRL, the lower the risk to the investor, and hence the better the valuation that is likely to be achieved.

Raising Investment

The raising of investment is a significant subject. For a more comprehensive coverage, the reader is referred to Draper (2012), Romans (2013) or de Vries (2016).

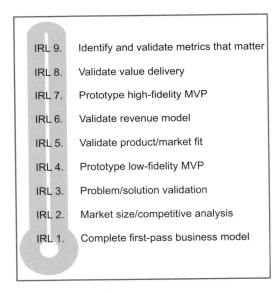

IRL 9.	Identify and validate metrics that matter
IRL 8.	Validate value delivery
IRL 7.	Prototype high-fidelity MVP
IRL 6.	Validate revenue model
IRL 5.	Validate product/market fit
IRL 4.	Prototype low-fidelity MVP
IRL 3.	Problem/solution validation
IRL 2.	Market size/competitive analysis
IRL 1.	Complete first-pass business model

Figure 6.8 *Measuring investment readiness*

This section summarizes the principal considerations for entrepreneurs of digital ventures:

- A synopsis of the investment stages and the types of investor that participate in each.
- A summary of the investment process, including negotiating a term sheet and the implications of delaying valuation on investment.

Investment Stages and Types of Investor

It is important to determine the right kind of investor to satisfy the venture's requirements at each stage in its development. Each investor has a defined space within which they operate, and it is important for a venture to qualify suitable candidates and to understand their interests before making any approach. An investor's interests can usually be summarized in terms of:

- The technologies in which they invest (such as AI, VR or advanced materials).
- The markets in which they invest (such as *Fintech, Autotech* or *Medtech*).
- The specific sizes and kinds of business in which they invest. This may be expressed in a number of ways, such as 'those with less than $2m valuation', or 'those offering taxation advantages', or 'those with market potential greater than $5bn', or 'those with potential for rapid revenue-generation'.

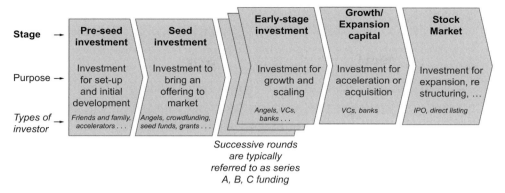

Figure 6.9 *Investment stages and associated types of investor*

A widely used process and terminology of investment stages is illustrated in Figure 6.9, which locates the respective interests of the principal types of investor.

The types of investor are elaborated below in relation to their respective involvement in stages of investment.

Pre-Seed Investors

- **Friends and family.** This term refers to personal sources of investment which may be gifted, loaned or more formally constructed. Such investors are common in early-stage ventures. It is important to future-proof any such arrangement because they are usually closely connected with individual people, and peoples' circumstances and relationships can change.
- **Seed, start-up or tech accelerators.** These organizations are early-stage investors which usually operate via fixed-term (three months) cohort-based programmes that include mentorship and educational components, and which culminate in a public pitch event or demo day. An accelerator will usually make a small pre-seed investment in a venture in exchange for a small equity share. At the end of the programme, a venture will usually seek to close a seed investment.

Seed Investors

Seed investment provides finance for early development and growth and can come from many sources, as described below.

- **Angel investors.** Angels are individuals who provide investment capital to early-stage ventures, usually in exchange for equity ownership and sometimes through some form of convertible debt scheme. In the UK, convertible debt schemes do not qualify for tax relief and so advanced subscription agreements (ASAs) are growing in popularity; such agreements pay no interest, but offer little or no downside protection.

Angels usually invest through equity crowdfunding or through angel networks or *syndicates* that share research and pool investment capital. An important additional benefit of angels can be their past experience as entrepreneurs and their close involvement and input into the business, including through market access.

- **Crowd-funding**, or peer-to-peer consumer lending. This is a means of raising investment for a venture or a specific project by taking funds (typically of small size) from a large number of people. A range of exchange offerings are used, including charitable giving, advance access to products or equity. This route to investment is more suited to B2C offerings, where consumers can share in the motivation and benefits of the initiative.
- **Grants**. Grant funding may be provided by public or private bodies to support specific research and development initiatives. Such funds are not usually repayable, but their use will be monitored by the awarding body to ensure that its investment is used as it intended. In some cases, contribution funding may be required by the venture to match some proportion of the grant provided.
- **Seed funds**. These are equity-based loans offered by organizations, including *micro-VCs*, universities, corporate seed funds (from Google, for example) and by those VCs that choose to invest earlier in the development of ventures.

In Silicon Valley, a typical seed round might seek to raise between $500,000 and $1.5 million, in exchange for perhaps 20 to 25 per cent of the company's equity. According to Glasner and Teare (2016) writing in CrunchBase, the size of the average seed round in the first half of 2016 was $1.14 million, up from $947,000 in the same period during 2015.

Where investments are made by a syndicate or group of investors, it can be advisable to use a *nominee service*. Under such an arrangement, the shareholdings of investors are managed by an independent organization (the nominee) under a declaration of trust whereby the nominee acts as the shareholder in the company's register, but holds the shares on behalf of the various shareholders. Individual shareholders can claim any tax benefits such as SEIS or EIS in the UK, but the company does not need to manage and administer multiple relationships with investors, including the need to monitor and enforce their rights.

The nominee service offered by the crowd-funding platform Seedrs is widely used by investors, including some start-up accelerators. At the current time, the Seedrs business model involves charging a fee of 7.5 per cent of returns achieved over and above the original amount invested. This aligns the interests of the nominee with those of the investors.

An alternative approach is adopted by the CrowdCube platform, where individual shareholders each directly hold their own shares and the company will be expected to manage relationships with each. The advantages of adopting this approach are that the investors do not need to pay fees, and there is not a single nominee that consolidates the interests of all of the shareholders.

Early-Stage Investors

This usually relates to the first round of venture capital (VC) financing. Under the usual convention, a *series A* investment is the first significant equity transaction following those relating to founders, employees or angel investors. Subsequent rounds are then referred to as *series B, C, D* and so on.

- **Venture capital (VC) investor.** VCs invest in early-stage businesses with high growth potential. The moneys invested are held within VC funds, which may combine investments from multiple sources. VCs usually have *sweet spots* in terms of the kinds of businesses that they favour, and this may include preferred size, performance, market sector or geography. A VC may cooperate with a bank to assemble an investment that combines equity and debt.
- **Bank.** Investment from banks for the medium to long term is usually provided by way of loans, or debt finance: the provision of money against an agreed repayment schedule, including an interest component. A loan may be secured against an asset or it might be unsecured. A *senior bank loan* is a legal claim to the venture's assets above all other debt obligations if the business fails. The advantage of using debt finance is that the business has no need to dilute its equity; it must, however, be confident of being able to cover the required repayments.
- **Corporate investor.** A corporate investment is money provided by an established company that has a strategic interest in the business. Many large corporations use this approach to establish close connections with relevant emerging technology businesses. The approach can bring significant benefits to an early-stage venture by way of access to markets and to deep market knowledge. In some cases, the initial approach is through a co-development agreement that establishes a working relationship ahead of an investment

dialogue. In many cases, an investment leads towards an acquisition of the business as an enhanced capability. This approach can speed access to market for businesses with complex or expensive production processes, or where established markets are difficult to penetrate. It can, however, limit future options for development and partnerships, especially where the corporate investor takes a controlling share.

Growth or Expansion-Stage Investors

This stage of investment usually applies to ventures that have been operational for more than three years and where significant revenue growth is demonstrated from mature product or service offerings.

Growth-stage investors can be VCs, corporate investors or banks. At this stage, an investor may offer *mezzanine financing*: debt capital that gives the lender the right to convert to an equity interest if the loan is not paid back in time.

Stock Market Investors

A venture can choose to *go public* and achieve a listing on a stock exchange. This means that the company's shares would be traded according to the rules of that stock market.

A public company can continue to raise capital by selling additional equities. Additionally, a well-performing publicly traded company will usually be treated favourably by other types of investor when additional capital is needed.

The Investment Process

The investment process for a venture can be long and tortuous. Negotiation topics can be demanding in terms of future objectives and projections, financial plans, the business model and team, the security of the IP involved, the trading history and past relationships.

Detailed negotiations usually occur through a process known as *due diligence*, normally conducted under exclusivity and non-disclosure terms. This process usually assesses financial, technical, IP and people-based considerations of a proposed investment. For ventures with a substantial trading history, this can be especially time-consuming, because the scope to be scrutinized will also include such things as taxation, pension and infringement liabilities, treatment of former employees and previous stock transactions. Several iterative rounds of negotiation can be involved, in each case with the potential investor requesting additional information for analysis.

In such negotiations, the critical point is often the agreement of a valuation of the venture's equity. This determines the amount of the venture's equity that will be acquired by the investor in exchange for their funding. Approaches to this calculation are summarized in Chapter 5.

An alternative approach to basing an investment on an agreed equity valuation is for the venture to offer a *convertible note* or *advanced subscription association* (ASA). Under these approaches, the company valuation is delayed until the occurrence of some future event, typically a future equity deal or an insolvency. At that time, the debt will convert to equity, usually at a discount on the share price set by the next round of investment. Convertible notes charge interest on the loan in the meantime and offer a degree of downside protection. These latter benefits are not usually offered by ASAs.

In the UK, convertible notes do not usually attract SEIS or EIS tax relief, whereas ASAs can attract such relief if established carefully. In addition to avoiding the need to agree on a valuation, such schemes can be more rapid and less costly to establish. They also avoid the need to agree on the formal structure of the shareholding until a later date. This can be helpful in buying time for ventures that are not yet ready to commit to detailed future plans.

When negotiating an investment, the normal process is to agree first on a *term sheet*: a simplified agreement that defines the principal parameters and conditions of the deal. The term sheet informs and guides lawyers when constructing the formal legal documentation. A term sheet may be interpreted and treated as being legally binding on the parties involved. This point can be important: if that is not to be the case, then the document should explicitly say so.

A term sheet usually includes at least the following terms:

- The agreed valuation of the business.
- The agreed investment.
- The agreed future share structure and options.
- The agreed board composition.
- Shareholder agreements.
- Agreement on priorities in the event of liquidation.
- Agreed warranties provided by the venture.

After reaching agreement on a term sheet, the formal legal agreements are created and signed to close the deal and release the initial tranche of cash to the venture.

Creating a Business Plan

A business plan can encapsulate all the topics addressed by this book; it can be a substantial document with significant detail, especially in relation to finances and projections.

There are several reasons why such a plan might be required, and the type and level of detail contained tends to vary for differing requirements:

- A plan may be created by and for the founders of a venture to provide a clear description of their business and its future projections for the purposes of agreement and common communication within the team. The detail included in such cases will depend upon the priorities of the founding team, but this will usually be at a summary level.
- At the other extreme of detail, a plan may be created for potential investors to make and support a case for investment. Although a summary may be sufficient for the first pass of an investor discussion, any further interest usually demands substantial detail. The investor may provide a template of headings that are required. As the plan will need to be explicit in its detail of past and future customers and partners, any sharing of detailed business plans outside of the team will be subject to a non-disclosure agreement (see Chapter 7).
- A plan of some sort may also be requested by prospective customers, potential channel partners or by other parties such as banks, lawyers or accountants, to give confidence in the credibility of the venture. Such plans will be much less detailed than those required by investors and are likely to be required to focus on summary information about business strategy and financial stability. Any such plans would only be shared under non-disclosure agreement and it can be advisable not to disclose unnecessary detail, including current customers.

Before investing effort producing a business plan, it is important to understand its purpose so as to determine the required content and level of detail, and an appropriate means of sharing and protecting the confidential information that will be included.

Business Plan Headings

A business plan might include any combination and sequence of the headings provided in the template suggested below, which reflects the typical content of a plan for a digital business. As noted above, the headings and level of detail provided will reflect the purpose and readership of the plan.

In all plans, the one-page *executive summary* should be sufficient to enable the reader to grasp the principal elements of the business. It can sometimes be useful to unpack and elaborate the executive summary to an additional level of detail in an *overview* section before diving more deeply into the respective areas of detail. Executive summary:

- The business in summary, including an *elevator pitch* of its background, motivation and mission, plus a brief synopsis of the target market, the innovation and distinctiveness that is offered, financial projections, team size, future potential and plan.

Overview of the business:

- The motivation for the business, including the problem it addresses, its mission and its objectives.
- A summary of the customer value proposition and the initial and future potential target markets.
- A summary of the KPIs by which growth will be demonstrated, including current trends.
- A summary of the distinctiveness of the offering and the underlying innovation.
- A summary of the personnel involved, their backgrounds and expertise.
- A financial projection of the short- and medium-term potential for development and growth.

Proof points and experience:

- Current customers and other market engagements, including case studies.
- Revenues generated and margins achieved.
- Pipeline of prospective future business.
- Customer endorsements and feedback.

The business model:

- The value proposition(s), in the context of the business ecosystem and relevant value chains.
- The proposed approach to creating brand visibility in the market.
- The proposed channels and routes to market for delivery, including the customer journey.

- The proposed means of value capture and the underlying rationale.
- Analysis of how demand will be driven to fuel business growth.
- An assessment of any blockers that may inhibit growth, and how these will be countered.

Market analysis:

- Summary of market research conducted by the business or available in the public domain.
- A characterization of the current market landscape, segmentation and size.
- An analysis of the competitive environment, including potential for collaboration.
- The proposed promotional channels and how their effectiveness will be measured.

The product or service offering:

- A description of the distinctiveness and power of the innovation.
- A description of how the offering will be developed and sustained.
- A development roadmap with assumptions of dependencies and required assets.
- A summary of intellectual property developed and plans for licensing and protection.

Operational plan:

- An analysis of any applicable legal and regulatory considerations.
- The required supply chain and options for in-sourcing and outsourcing.
- The key measures of success and the targets against which these will be assessed.
- The plan for scaling the business's key capabilities.
- A proposed plan of activities for the forthcoming twelve months.

Financial plan:

- Current costs, cash flow projection and runway.
- Growth forecast for the next year, including detailed projections of revenues, costs and margins.
- Summary growth forecast for the medium-term horizon and indicative trends beyond that.
- Options for speeding growth and the associated scaling and resource dependencies.

Team and shareholding:

- The size and make-up of the current team and of the team required to deliver the plan.
- Additional personnel required and the recruitment plan.
- Current and proposed shareholding structure for the business.

Opportunity for investors:

- Resources and funding needed to deliver the business plan, and why and when it will be needed.
- A projection of the benefit that may be achieved by the investor.

Risk analysis:

- A register of the principal risks facing the business, plus tolerances, mitigations and transfers.

Associated Communications Materials

A business plan should be self-sufficient as a document. However, in most situations, its content will first need to be presented in some form to orientate the investor to the principal points. Any such presentation is very different from a sales presentation, although there may be some overlap in respect of customer case studies and endorsements.

It can be helpful to prepare three levels of communication alongside a business plan:

- A thirty-second *elevator pitch* that summarizes the core value proposition and distinctiveness of the offering, for the purposes of attracting and intriguing people. It is useful for everyone in the team to know this pitch and to be able to communicate it confidently.
- A three- to five-minute *pitch deck*, which may be spoken, or may comprise a few slides or a short video, essentially covering the material in the executive summary. This should focus on creating interest and motivation for further engagement. It would typically be used at events and exhibitions, including angel syndicate meetings. It may be offered as a webinar.
- A full-length presentation of the business plan that covers all sections. Its purpose is to support a detailed promotion of the business to investors or strategic partners. The need for this level of presentation sometimes means that a presentation tool is used for the creation of a business plan.

Each of these should be developed and presented to a professional level. The quality of a presentation can set an expectation for the strength of a market proposition: if it looks impenetrable or is delivered in a haphazard way, then the recipient is likely to make similar assumptions about the viability of the business.

Summary of Growth and Scalability

This chapter has addressed the need for both growth and scalability. These topics are separate but overlapping, and demand different considerations for the entrepreneur intent on progressing from start-up to scale-up. Underlying the material addressed is the need for a revised balance of entrepreneurship and innovation in the leadership required. This is reflected in the need for a different mindset with revised priorities and emphases, and a plan to address the needs for additional people, structure and finance.

The scale-up mindset needs to be motivated by exit ambitions without which there can be no clarity over the decisions needed. This ambition drives a strategy and a detailed plan. Underlying the strategy is an understanding that growth alone does not create scalability and that scalability needs to be designed into the core capabilities of the venture through strategic intentions that will bake value into the business.

The key points addressed are summarized below.

- **A growth and scalability strategy** comprises a set of assumptions, principles and requirements that will together enable the development of a plan for delivering the growth and scalability needed to achieve the business object-ives, while managing associated risks:
  - Setting an ambition for growth clarifies the need and drive, which in turn sets priorities and appetite for activity.
  - It is important to determine how growth will be driven, including by a mix of push and pull from the market.
  - The risks associated with growth and scalability need to be assessed in terms of required mitigations or transfer activities.
- **Planning for growth and scalability** is about forecasting the shape and time frame of the growth curve based on assumptions and decisions about the team and capabilities needed, and how discontinuities will be addressed:

- o Orders, revenues, costs and gross and operating margins are commonly used as growth indicators, and a plan for growth usually includes multiple projections of these over a time horizon.
- o Four generally applicable capabilities are required and these must work together effectively for a venture to grow and scale.
- o Three discontinuities or chasms are commonly experienced in the growth process, and crossing each of these poses maturity and performance requirements of the venture's capabilities.
- o A plan combines a financial growth projection with assumptions and decisions about the talent, capability and funding needed to support it.
- **Creating a growth projection** forecasts the shape and time frame of the growth curve according to an assumed business design by which this will be achieved:
  - o A revenue projection is a forecast of the earnings that will be generated during the period. Multiple projections may be created to reflect future scenarios.
  - o Cost projections are tabulations of the indirect, direct and variable costs associated with revenue projections.
  - o Gross and operating margins can be calculated from revenue and cost projections for each scenario.
- **Designing a team for growth and scalability** considers the size and shape of the team, plus how to judge the right people and align these with the right incentives:
  - o For a planning horizon, it is possible to determine the roles and likely numbers required to meet the assumptions of the growth forecast.
  - o Each person in the team should enable the venture either to exploit an opportunity or to mitigate a threat.
  - o Motivating people to work to a particular goal means making them feel like stakeholders in the plan.
- **Designing scalable capabilities** considers the scalability of performance of each core capability needed by the venture's operations:
  - o The application of four general principles can drive the design of scalability into all capabilities: *standardization, flexible workforce, automation* and *scalability of infrastructure.*
  - o Specific approaches can be taken to increase the scalability of each of the principal capabilities.
- **Funding growth and scalability** is about how the venture will pay for the people, equipment, assets, services and resources required:

- o An important choice is whether initial growth will be funded through revenue generation or by raising investment.
- o Funding through revenues, or organic growth, means launching an offering, driving this to generate revenues and reinvesting the profits.
- o Funding through investment needs clarity over what investment is needed and whether the venture is ready for investment.
- **Raising investment** means identifying the right kind of investor to satisfy the venture's requirements at each stage in its development:
  - o There is widely used process and terminology of investment stages within which the interests of the principal types of investor can be located.
  - o The investment process for a venture can be long and tortuous and the critical point is often the agreement of a valuation of the venture's equity.
  - o When negotiating an investment, the normal process is to agree first on a term sheet: a simplified agreement that defines the principal parameters and conditions of the deal.
- **Creating a business plan** can mean a need to encapsulate all of the topics addressed by this book into a substantial document with significant detail, especially in relation to finances and projections:
  - o Before producing a business plan, it is important to understand its purpose and to determine the required content and level of detail, together with an appropriate means of sharing and protecting the confidential information that will be included.
  - o A one-page executive summary should enable the reader to grasp the principal elements of the business.
  - o It can be helpful to prepare three levels of communication alongside a business plan: a thirty-second elevator pitch, a three- to five-minute pitch deck and a full-length presentation.

ANALYSIS EXERCISES

The table below lists a collection of digital businesses to be used as subjects for the exercises that follow.

Business	Focus	Website
Darktrace	Cyber security	www.darktrace.com
EventBright	Event promotion and management	www.eventbrite.co.uk

Business	Focus	Website
Fitbit	Health, fitness and performance	www.fitbit.com
JustEat	Online takeaway food	www.just-eat.co.uk
Reposit	Property rental	www.getreposit.uk
Snapchat	Social media	www.snapchat.com
Sorry as a Service	Customer services and retention	www.sorryasaservice.com
SwiftComply	Regulation and compliance	www.swiftcomply.com

On the basis of information available in the public domain, address the questions below for at least one of the businesses listed.

1. The business's customer(s):
   (a) Who is the customer(s) for the proposed innovation?
   (b) Who are the principal players in the business ecosystem?
   (c) What are the principal value exchanges with these players?

2. Growth and scalability strategy:
   (a) What might be the business's strategic ambition?
   (b) What drives growth for the business?
   (c) What are the principal risks that the business faces as it grows?

3. Growth plan:
   (a) What indicators might the business use to measure growth?
   (b) What margins did the business achieve during the latest reporting period?
   (c) How do these margins compare with those of two other businesses that operate in the same sector?

4. Designing for growth and scalability:
   (a) Choose two roles that are needed by the business and suggest how each might be incentivized to contribute to business growth.
   (b) Suggest two capabilities of the business that need to be scalable for the business to grow.
   (c) Suggest two risks that could inhibit the business's growth.

5. Funding growth and scalability:
   (a) Is the business funding growth through revenues, through investment or by a combination of both?
   (b) If the business is investor-backed, then what stage of investment currently applies?

DESIGN EXERCISES

The design exercise at the end of Chapter 1 encouraged identification of a business idea to be developed incrementally by specific design exercises through subsequent chapters of the book. That activity commenced in Chapter 2 with the framing of the selected business idea using the elements introduced in that chapter. This was extended in Chapters 3, 4 and 5, with reference to the additional considerations and decisions introduced.

Extend your current design through the following tasks:

1. For each aspect of business growth and scalability covered in this chapter, perform an assessment and analysis of your business. This should include at least one growth forecast expressed in terms of revenue, cost, gross margin and operating margin. If using the Business Design Template, summarize the resulting considerations in the left-hand cell of the *growth and scalability* section.

2. Extract from your considerations the set of key decisions relating to business growth and scalability by your business. If using the Business Design Template, document these in the right-hand cell of the *growth and scalability* section.

3. Review the extended design of your business for consistency, and address any issues that arise.

4. Capture separately any of the following:
   (a) Key points learned from the exercise.
   (b) Outstanding issues or uncertainties.

7 Intellectual Property and Protection

Focus of This Chapter

Figure 7.1 illustrates how the material addressed by this chapter fits within the framework of considerations for business design.

The considerations addressed here elaborate upon the decisions made during business framing in the context of the question *what are the risks?*

The categories of risk addressed by this chapter arise throughout the life of a venture, from its inception through to mature operation. Consequently, considerations relating to its protection can be prompted by activities relating to any of the other chapters, and the decisions made in this context might impact any other aspect of business design.

Learning Outcomes

After studying this chapter, you will:

- Understand the general risks that face any venture, and the available means of protection.
- Be aware of the internationally applicable legal mechanisms for protecting IP.
- Appreciate the need and options for protecting confidentiality, know-how and trade secrets.
- Be aware of the principal risks inherent in licence, service and delivery agreements.

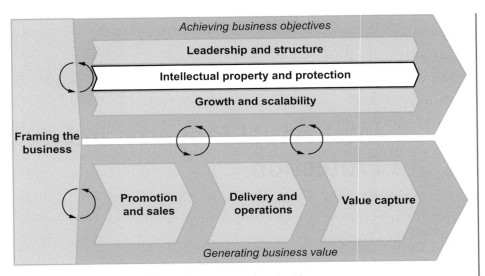

Figure 7.1 *Context of intellectual property and protection*

- Appreciate the important relationships between managing security and managing people.
- Be able to determine an appropriate business response to applicable legal requirements.

Introducing Intellectual Property and Protection

This chapter is about ensuring that the venture maximizes the value inherent in its intellectual property (IP) and manages the risks that can arise through deliberate and accidental activity.

With effective protection of its assets and reputation, a venture can enjoy the benefits of its capabilities and investment. On the other hand, failure to protect effectively against risk in the fast-moving digital world can rapidly lead to damage and disruption, both financial and reputational.

Chapters 2, 3, 4 and 5 address the core sequence of decisions and actions needed for an offering to be developed, promoted and delivered into a market such that business value is generated. Other than competitive and negotiating pressures, the material provided within those chapters assumes a benign and uninterrupted operating environment.

However, the world in which any venture operates is not benign. There are many *actors* that may seek to steal or damage a venture's assets, whether for simple financial gain or for more sophisticated purposes, and unfortunate events can have a negative impact on a venture and its operations. Such considerations apply across all the topics addressed by previous chapters, and are factored out into this chapter as a parallel set of business design considerations.

Chapter 2 describes the need to determine, for any identified risk, whether it can be tolerated and, if not, then how it will be mitigated or transferred. This chapter addresses a collection of generally applicable risks together with relevant mitigation and transfer options, to inform the production of a plan to protect the venture's assets and reputation. Any such plan must be managed and communicated effectively across the team to ensure that its provisions are comprehensively and consistently applied. This usually means embedding the plan within a business environment whereby progress on its activities can be reviewed on a continuing basis.

This chapter is structured around the kinds of protection illustrated in Figure 7.2. For each of these, the associated risks are illustrated and examined, and the applicable protective mechanisms are described to enable a reasonable assessment of the options available and their respective implications.

The section addressing protection of IP is significantly larger than the other sections, because of the crucial double importance of IP for digital businesses:

• Internationally recognized legal protection mechanisms such as trademarks, registered designs, patents and copyright can be used to establish and crystallize the value of IP. Effective use of such mechanisms turns risk into significant opportunity.

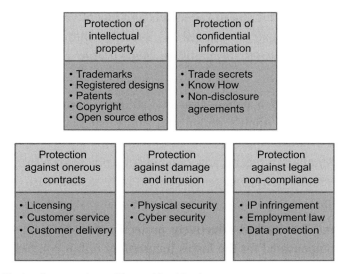

Figure 7.2 *Kinds of protection addressed in this chapter*

- These same mechanisms can be used to protect IP from theft or abuse by granting the venture legal powers to prohibit uncompetitive practices and pursue claims for damages.

The section that addresses protection against onerous contracts refers to three appendices of relevant contractual terms and their implications for the venture.

Many of the topics introduced in this chapter vary geographically in terms of legal treatment. This includes, for example, the rules for what can be patented, and the provisions of employment and data protection legislation. In such cases, as far as is reasonably possible, relevant principles and approaches are described, and important differences are highlighted.

This chapter references legal matters regarding topics such as the protection of IP, contractual liabilities and requirements for legal compliance. This is not an authoritative legal textbook, and as such matters are also changeable over time, the reader is strongly advised to seek relevant professional advice before committing to any course of action relating to legal matters.

Throughout the chapter, references are made to real-world examples and studies and, where it is helpful, the SportMagenta rolling case study is developed.

Protection of Intellectual Property

Risks Relating to Theft of IP

The theft of IP can lead to loss of actual or potential revenue, additional costs of recovery, and an undermining of the means and incentives for entrepreneurs to innovate. Protection against such risks is available through a range of internationally applicable legal mechanisms. High-profile examples include the following:

- In 2012, the jury in a patent case in California found that Samsung had infringed several of Apple's design and utility patents with a variety of its devices, and awarded Apple more than $1 billion in damages against Samsung.
- In 2013, a Manhattan federal jury ordered Nintendo to pay Tomita Technologies over $30 million in damages in a patent infringement case concerning 3D technologies.

Both Apple and Tomita had effectively protected their IP in these cases, and hence were compensated for the losses incurred by unfair competitive activity.

Defining IP and the Benefits of Protection

IP is about creations of the mind. From a legal perspective, a piece of IP is something unique that has been physically created using skill and judgement. There is no property in an idea, a thought or any other purely cerebral creation: the creation must be physically fixed or created. An idea for a book or for a consumer product would not be IP, but the words within a book would be protectable as a piece of IP, as would a fabricated product, however crude. Designs, whether on paper or held electronically, are IP, as is software code, a logo, a manufactured fragrance or a purpose-designed colour.

There is a set of internationally recognized legal mechanisms whereby IP can be protected, including trademarks, registered designs, patents and copyright. Each of these has a different scope, with relevant international authorities, and works in its own distinctive way.

IP is a tangible asset that can be licensed, sold or mortgaged, just like other forms of property. Unlike some other forms of property, however, its value is determined to a large extent by the diligence with which it has been defined and the effectiveness with which it is exploited and protected from abuse.

Protecting its IP gives a venture an opportunity to benefit from its use by other parties through licensing agreements for software products and patent rights. The mechanisms for protection can be used to secure exclusive exploitation rights, with the confidence of being able to achieve legal redress should the IP be used without permission. A third benefit is the ability to evidence a tangible and unique asset to provide confidence to an investor. These benefits, however, come at a cost of both effort and financial commitment.

An important distinction is drawn between registered and unregistered rights:

- Registered rights are lodged with a relevant authority through a defined process, and give the owner legal protection amounting to a monopoly over the use of those rights. The applicable registration process, cost and time frame for achieving registered protection varies across the different legal mechanisms.
- Unregistered rights are held by the IP owner as an automatic consequence of IP creation. These give some legal protection to the owner, especially against copying without permission, but infringement can be more difficult to prove, and hence damages claims can be more difficult to pursue.

In respect of IP protection, the important decisions for business ventures are which IP to protect, which mechanisms to adopt for its protection and whether this protection should be registered.

If a venture does not take steps to recognize and protect its IP, then others may be able to use it for their own purposes with no benefit to its inventor. In an extreme case, a party might adopt and exploit IP developed by someone else, and even be able to stop the original inventor from exploiting it themselves.

Consequently, there is an important decision: invest in the cost and effort of protection, or tolerate the risks associated with other parties being able to exploit it for their own benefit.

There are situations under which a business might choose to tolerate these risks:

- The market to which the IP applies is so fast moving that any protection activity will be obsolete before it becomes effective. This is often argued to be the case with fast-changing B2C software offerings. In such cases, the venture may be confident that it can exploit its IP to capture its target market and achieve a dominant position before anyone else has chance to copy; and in any case, by the time someone else has copied it, the original business will have progressed its offering to a new level.
- The venture decides upon an open-source strategy. This approach is not really a case of unprotected IP, but of IP that is shared with a community as an aspect of the business model. Open-source material is protected by an open-source agreement (as addressed in a subsequent section), which ensures that its further exploitation by other parties accords with the intentions of the inventor. For example, Microsoft ASP.NET is now available as open source, with the intention of 'building and leveraging' an extensible ecosystem of developers. Also, as noted in Chapter 5, open source need not mean zero cost.

Even where a decision has been made not to protect IP in any formal way, it may be important to protect underlying confidential information and trade secrets such as designs and coding. This topic is addressed further in the following section.

The remainder of this section addresses in turn each of the set of internationally recognized legal mechanisms whereby IP can be protected, with reference to both registered and unregistered forms.

Trademarks

According to the World Intellectual Property Organization (WIPO), a trademark is a sign capable of distinguishing the goods or services of one enterprise from those of other enterprises. A trademark can comprise a name, a word, a phrase, a logo, a symbol, a design, an image, a sound, a shape, a signature, a fragrance, a colour, or some combination of one or more of these.

Because of the investment typically required to develop and promote a venture's name and associated brand identity, these are usually protected as a trademark that comprises some combination of a name, a graphic and possibly a colour combination. The principal decision is whether to register the mark. This decision is driven by the following considerations:

- The venture's capacity and appetite for spending time and money on registration.
- An assessment of the risk of – and damage that could be caused by – the mark being copied by someone else before the venture gains significant traction in the market.
- An assessment of the risk of a claim for damages from someone else if the mark infringes an existing trademark. Note that this risk can also be mitigated by a trademark search before investing in any proposed new mark.
- The venture's international ambitions for operation using the same mark.

Trademarks are a form of IP protection that can be registered, and the considerations relating to both registered and unregistered forms are addressed below. The relationship with internet domain name registration is also included for completeness.

Trademark Registration

In the European Union (EU), trademarks for member states or for the EU are registered through the EU Intellectual Property Office (EUIPO). The UK has its own Intellectual Property Office (UKIPO), and in the USA the comparable organization is the US Patent and Trademark Office (USPTO). Registration for a granted trademark is initially for a ten-year period, after which it can be renewable indefinitely on payment of renewal fee. A registered trademark is denoted using the ® symbol against the trademark or one of its components.

The ® symbol indicates that the mark has been registered and that action may be taken in the event of its unauthorized use by another party. There is a statutory duty upon trading standards officers to act against those using unauthorized trademarks. To be able to protect a trademark effectively, it is important to be able to show evidence of previous use and enforcement.

The process of registration within a single territory usually takes three to four months, although in the USA the process can take between six months and a year.

According to the WIPO Trade Marks Act of 1994, a trademark must meet a number of criteria to be accepted for registration, including:

- Being capable of distinguishing the goods or services of the registering business.
- Not being common or indistinct; it cannot be a simple statement like 'we are the best'.
- Not being in any way misleading.
- Not being offensive by containing indecent language or pornographic images.
- Not describing the goods or services it will relate to; the word *software* cannot be a trade mark.
- Not looking too similar to state symbols such as flags.
- Not conflicting with existing trademarks.

Registered trademarks are classified according to their applicability. There are thirty-four applicable classes of goods and a further eleven applicable classes of services, including, for example:

Class 1 (relating to goods) covers 'chemicals used in industry, science and photography ... tanning substances; adhesives used in industry'.

Class 9 (relating to goods) covers 'scientific, nautical, surveying ... calculating machines, data processing equipment, computers; computer software; fire-extinguishing apparatus'.

Class 35 (relating to services) covers 'advertising; business management; business administration; office functions'.

Class 42 (relating to services) covers 'scientific and technological services and research and design relating thereto; industrial analysis and research services; design and development of computer hardware and software'.

The trademark registration process involves choosing which of these classes are applicable. This is important in limiting the scope of protection needed, and also the cost of registration. Two apparently similar trademarks do not conflict if their respective classes do not overlap.

Classes 9, 35 and 42 are commonly adopted for trademarks in digital businesses.

Trademarks can be registered across multiple territories. If a business only registers its trademark in one country, then others may use the same mark in other countries without infringing their rights.

Applications for trademark protection can be made to the relevant body within each country for which the business intends to operate. In most cases, an initial application is made in a single territory, after which further applications are made for the mark in other territories. Any further applications made within six months can benefit from the date of the original filing, providing those further applications are for the same mark in respect of the same goods and services.

The need for multiple national applications can be avoided using the provisions of WIPO's Madrid Protocol, which provides an efficient and cost-effective way of securing international trademark protection in the 114 countries which currently subscribe to the protocol, including those within the EU, the USA, Japan and China. The procedure starts with registration of a *home* application in a single country of origin.

A familiar and widely used form of protective words for trademarks that apply to multiple territories is along the lines: '® X and Y are either registered trademarks or trademarks of Z Corporation in the United States and/or other countries'.

Unregistered Trademarks

An unregistered or *common law* trademark is declared simply by using the symbol ™ against the claimed mark. As its legal validity has not been tested, and it is not known and registered by any legal body, such a mark has less power than a registered trademark when it comes to enforcing a claim that the mark has been copied or stolen by someone else.

UK law can protect unregistered trade marks against *passing-off* actions, where a business falsely encourages customers to believe that their offerings are those of another, so long as there is sufficient evidence of use and goodwill attached to the trademark. This means that unregistered trademarks can only really be protected where relevant goods or services are being sold, and hence there is sufficient goodwill that can be damaged.

Domain Name Registration

The choice and registration of internet domain names has become an important business decision, and it is important for a venture's brand image that its domain name(s) fit with its other marks.

Registering a domain name is not, however, equivalent to registering a trademark, and the ownership of a domain name will not protect a business against another company that owns a conflicting registered trademark.

If a registered domain name conflicts with a registered trademark owned by another party, then the resulting action can lead to loss of the domain name and a liability for the owner's legal costs. This ruling has been important in defeating so-called *domain name pirates*, who register domain names for established trademarks and then try to sell them to the relevant businesses at high prices.

Consequently, a domain name is in some ways comparable to an unregistered trademark.

Case Study: SportMagenta

Trademark Considerations

The founders recognize that they will be investing considerably in the SportMagenta brand, and so are keen to protect themselves from the potential loss and disruption from any deliberate or accidental *passing off* by another party.

Consequently, they decide to register SportMagenta as a trademark, citing classes 9, 35 and 42. Because of their international ambitions, they determine to apply the provisions of the Madrid Protocol and register the mark in the UK (initially) and subsequently in the USA and the EU.

They register the internet domain www.sportmagenta.com.

Design Rights

A design right, also called an *industrial design right* by WIPO, and a *design patent* in the USA, protects the *look* of a product, including its appearance, physical shape, configuration (how different parts of a design are arranged together) and decoration. More formally, according to WIPO, it is a two- or three-dimensional pattern used to produce a product, industrial commodity or handicraft.

Design rights can be used to protect a user-interface design or the shape of a physical product or a pattern, so long as it is unique. The *function* of the affected entity is not protected: that is the purpose of a patent.

Design rights can be registered. Unregistered design rights are recognized by some countries.

Design rights apply to those offerings for which the *look* is distinctive and significant to the value proposition. In such cases, significant effort may be required to develop that look, and hence there will be a desire to ensure that the look cannot simply be copied by competitors. The decision of whether to register the design is driven by the following considerations:

- The venture's capacity and appetite for spending time and money on registration.
- An assessment of the risk of – and damage that could be caused by – the design being copied, or co-invented, by someone else before it gains significant traction in the market.
- An assessment of the risk of a damages claim from someone else if the design infringes an existing registered design. Note that this risk can also be mitigated by a search of the current registers before investing in any proposed new design.
- The venture's international ambitions for the design, and hence the need to protect the design in multiple territories.

Registered Designs

Design registration can complement the protection given by a registered trademark where that mark has a distinctive graphic element.

The specific rules and procedure for registration vary between countries, but in general for a design to be registered, it must:

- Be novel: differ from any design that has already been made available to the public.
- Have *individual character*: the overall impression it produces must differ from that of any previous design.
- Not be offensive.
- Be owned by the applicant.
- Not make use of protected emblems or flags.

There are three benefits of registering a design:

- **Longevity**: although the initial registration is for five years, in the UK and the EU, a registered design can be secured for up to twenty-five years, whereas unregistered designs have much shorter duration.
- **Stronger protection against infringement**: it is not necessary to prove that a design has been copied to establish infringement, only that another design infringes the registered design.
- **Breadth of jurisdiction**: registered designs are recognized widely across the world, whereas unregistered rights are limited outside of Europe.

For ventures operating in EU countries, EUIPO is the body responsible for granting what it refers to as *registered community designs*. In the USA, design rights are registered through the USPTO, and in the UK the comparable organization is the UKIPO. It takes three to four months to register a typical UK or EU application, providing no opposition is received.

As with registered trademarks, designs must be registered in all the territories for which protection is needed. Costs vary in different countries, but tend to be much lower than patent protection.

Apple's claim in 2012 that Samsung had infringed its registered design when designing the Galaxy tablet provides an illustration of the application of registered design rights. According to BBC reporting at the time, Apple's case was rejected by the US Court of Appeal on the grounds that:

- Samsung's logo on the front of its devices distinguished them from Apple's design, which said that there should be 'no ornamentation'.
- The sides of Apple's design – which featured a *sharp edge* – were significantly different from the tabs in Samsung's design.
- Samsung's designs were 'altogether busier' with a more varied use of colour on the rear of devices and the inclusion of a thicker section to house a camera.

A further example that illustrates the need for care in selecting the images used when registering a design is the Trunki case reported in 2016 by the Chartered Institute for Patent Attorneys. In this case, the UK Supreme Court ruled that Kiddee Case, a rival product to the Trunki ride-on suitcase, was different enough in appearance for Trunki maker Magmatic not to be able to prevent its sale. In this case, the allegedly infringing product was judged to give a different impression to the computer-generated design images used in the registration. Consequently, although the Trunki and the Kiddee Case products actually look very similar, the design registered by Trunki didn't look like the product that was manufactured for sale.

Unregistered Designs

In the UK, an unregistered design is an automatic right given to a designer when producing a new design, whereas in the EU the right only exists after the design is made available to the public. UK law provides protection for up to ten years after disclosure; in the EU protection lasts only for three years.

The usual purpose for claiming an unregistered right is to gain some protection where a design has been copied. However, the principal difficulty when enforcing such a right is the necessity to prove that the other party has actually copied the design, rather than having independently created something very similar.

Unregistered design rights in the UK only protect designs with regard to their shape or configuration. EU rights also protect the appearance of the product, including colours, shape, texture, materials and decoration.

As noted above, unregistered design rights are not widely recognized outside of the UK and the EU.

Case Study: SportMagenta

Design Right Considerations

The founders recognize the need for a distinctive user interface (UI) for their B2C component to attract and retain users' attention in a lively and active environment. Their ambition is for a design that sets the app apart from others by its use of colour and layout, with minimal text.

Zara's UI design ideas impress early users during market research. The founders know that their ideas might easily be copied by competitors, and so determine to register a set of designs relating to the principal screen layouts that will be adopted. As with the SportMagenta trademark, all design rights will be registered in the UK, the USA and the EU.

Patents

A patent, also referred to in the USA as a *utility patent*, to distinguish it from a *design patent*, is an exclusive right granted for an invention that enables its owner to decide how – or whether – the invention can be used by others. In exchange for this right, the patent owner publishes technical information about the invention with sufficient clarity and completeness for it to be understandable by someone *skilled in the art*.

In the UK, the EU and the USA (for filings after 1995), a patent gives a twenty-year monopoly right to the inventor. Its description, which is openly published eighteen months after its initial date of filing, fully describes the invention.

A patent gives powerful protection: its owner has exclusive rights to exploit, and to prevent others from making or selling something that infringes the patent; and infringement can be met with an injunction, a damages claim or an order for destruction of infringing articles.

For smaller ventures, filing a patent can be a significant investment of time and effort, and so there needs to be good reason for doing so. The cost for an initial filing, using a professional patent attorney, is typically in the region of $2,000 to $3,000; in the UK, an initial filing can cost as much as $6,000.

As noted earlier in the chapter, some innovations and markets are so fast moving that any patent application is unlikely ever to keep pace with the rate of change of the underlying idea and its applications. However, for an offering that meets the criteria below, the option should be considered seriously, as patent filing can yield important benefits, including:

- Having monopoly rights over its exploitation, including the right to license exploitation by other businesses and the ability to take legal action against infringing parties.
- Being able to cite an existing patent application (*pat pending*) can be a powerful promotional message that demonstrates confidence, ability, seriousness of purpose and uniqueness.
- Gaining the attention of larger organizations that are inclined to respect the inventor of a new and potentially powerful invention.
- Demonstrating to potential investors that the venture has serious IP and that this is unique and protectable.
- Potentially deterring copycat activity by the implied threat of a legal response.
- For larger businesses, patents give bargaining power in an environment with multiple legal cases, as with Apple and Samsung.

Patent Criteria

The conditions to be met for a patent to be granted are commensurate with the power it brings:

- It must be **eligible**, in that the subject matter is permissible for patent protection. The laws of nature, for example, are ineligible for patent protection.
- It must be **novel**, in that it is not already part of the *state of the art* at the time the application is filed. This rule means that it is important to file a patent application before any publication or demonstration that would bring the invention into the state of the art.
- It must be **non-obvious**, in that it constitutes an *inventive step* that is not obvious to someone who is *skilled in the art*. This is a reference to a fictional person who is considered to have the normal skills and knowledge in a particular technical field; if it would have been obvious for this fictional

Table 7.1 Eligibility of Subject Matter

Subject matter of patent application	UK	EU	USA
New and non-obvious compounds and apparatus	✓	✓	✓
New and non-obvious methods or processes	✓	✓	✓
New business methods – ways of doing business	✗	✗	✓
New software, except for automation of existing practice	✗	✗	✓
New software with the potential to cause a technical effect	✓	✓	✓

person to come up with the invention while starting from the prior art, then the particular invention is considered not patentable.

- It must be **useful**, in that it is amenable to industrial application, which prohibits patenting of pure scientific discoveries that have no conceivable application.

The eligibility rules vary across territories, as indicated in Table 7.1.

For many digital technology businesses, the subject of an application involves either a new business method and/or a new software-based artefact, both of which can be difficult to patent in the UK and the EU. To achieve a patent for a software-based or software-driven invention, the critical requirement is for it to create a *technical effect* that is measurable in some tangible way, such as by increasing the speed or changing the operation of a physical device. Consequently, when applying for patents in the UK and the EU, it is important to assert not only the novelty of any embedded software algorithm, but also the novelty of its technical effects upon the wider system within which it will execute.

In the USA, the rules relating to software patents have been stricter since the so-called 'Alice case' in 2014. This refers to a case in which Alice Corporation claimed that CLS Bank was infringing a patent embodied within its electronic financial trading service. However, the US Supreme Court judged that the claims in the patent related to an abstract idea, and that the implementation of those claims on a computer was not enough in itself to transform the idea into patentable subject matter.

Patent Application Process

There is no concept of an unregistered patent: protection is only available through formal application through a recognized national organization such as the UKIPO, the USPTO or the European Patent Office (EPO).

A first application is usually filed through a national office. This establishes a *priority date* for the patent, which may be important in resolving future infringement cases. If protection is required in additional territories, then further applications will need to be made for each. Importantly, if these are filed within a year of the priority date, they can count as if they too had been filed on the priority date.

The specific details of the application process are available through individual offices. The principal steps are as follows:

- Filing of an informal patent application: this establishes a priority date.
- After twelve months, this is replaced by a formal application, including a list of specific claims. These claims form the principal substance of the patent by defining the limits of exactly what the patent does, and does not, cover.
- After eighteen months, the application is published. At this point, the full details of the invention are publicly available.
- After publication, there is a variable-length period of examination, challenge and response, which may last several more years, at the end of which the patent is either granted or rejected. In the UK, the minimum time for patent grant is four years; in the USA, it can be less.
- After patent grant, annual renewal fees are payable to the relevant territories.

The process of international filings is significantly eased by the Patent Cooperation Treaty (PCT), an agreement administered by WIPO covering most industrial countries. The PCT system provides two useful functions for those seeking to achieve patents in multiple territories: it helps with assessing the likelihood of achieving patents in other territories; and it enables the filing of a single PCT application that takes the place of the many individual applications that would otherwise have been required. Each of the resulting individual patent applications is then progressed through the respective offices to obtain individual granted patents. Afterwards, in a period referred to as the National/Regional Phase, a PCT application is converted into individual patent applications for each territory in which protection is to be sought.

As of 2018, the EU is expected to recognize a new unitary patent (UP) process that will have effect across the twenty-five European countries that have so far signed up to the scheme. Significantly, a single renewal fee will be payable annually across all participating countries. Alongside this, a new UP Court (UPC) will handle relevant litigation and actions, including where these apply to applications and patents processed through the current scheme and which have not specifically opted out of the UPC.

Case Study: SportMagenta

Patent Considerations

The founders intend to differentiate the B2B aspect of their software by innovating smart algorithms that apply AI techniques to infer users' likely interests from aspects of their personal characteristics, together with their previous associations and purchases. They consider that submitting a patent to protect this innovation may deter copycat activity from competitors, while demonstrating distinctiveness to potential partners and investors.

Being aware of the limitations of patenting software, the founders recognize that neither their software nor the algorithm that it deploys can reasonably be associated with a technical effect that will satisfy patent examiners, and so they dismiss any hope of gaining patent protection in the UK or Europe. They do believe, however, that their innovative business method, implemented using leading-edge software techniques, will be patentable in the USA, and hence determine to file an application ahead of any exposure of this software component into the public domain.

Copyright

Copyright is the right of the owner of a work to control its use for a fixed time, usually seventy years after the death of its originator (in the USA, the EU and the UK). It applies to a range of types of work: literary, artistic, musical, graphical and software code.

Copyright only protects the owner from the literal copying of their work; it does not give any protection from theft of ideas expressed in it. The latter needs to be protected through one of the mechanisms described earlier in this section.

Although a wide range of works can be protected by copyright, any enforcement will require that the originator is able to show that they applied skill, labour and judgement in the creation of the work. Under special provisions, a limited part of any work may be copied for private study, research or review without infringing the owner's copyright.

In the UK and the EU, copyright is automatic on creation of a piece of work, and the originator needs only to mark their work with ©, together with their name(s) and the year of creation. In fact, whether the work is marked or not does not affect the level of protection, but may assist in demonstrating the rights of the originator.

Copyright gives exclusive right to its owners to protect against exploitation of material by copying or reproducing, adapting, distributing, selling or renting, broadcasting or public performance. In addition to the normal legal copyright claim, a longer form is sometimes used, such as 'all rights reserved' or 'not for distribution without express consent'. These forms can be useful in reinforcing the owner's intention to control their works.

Infringement of copyright can be addressed by legal injunction against the perpetrator to forbid related sales and a claim for damages against lost earnings.

In the USA and some other countries, copyright needs to be registered using the internationally recognized Copyright Witness Service. Known in the UK as the UK Copyright Service, this supports international copyright protection by securing independent evidence of ownership that helps to prove originality and ownership in any claims or disputes.

Database Rights

Database rights are a form of aggregate copyright, where the owner claims protection for their skill and judgement in compiling a set of works, although not necessarily in any of the constituent parts. These rights might apply to a literary anthology, a marketing list or a related collection of legal statutes. The level of creativity required is low: the requirement on the owner is to be able to show that they had some discretion and made some choices in what to include or how to organize the various works.

In the EU, databases can be protected under the Database Directive, which aims to protect the intellectual creativity involved in the selection and arrangement of the database. In this respect, the Directive is similar to copyright protection in the USA, where databases are protected as compilations.

Case Study: SportMagenta

Copyright Considerations

The founders recognize that the source code of both B2C and B2B components of their software can be protected by copyright, and so establish a discipline of copyright marking in all code headers. They appreciate that the protection offered by this is not of itself very strong, and recognize the need to combine this policy with considerations of trade secret protection.

They acknowledge that the same considerations will also apply to all documentation and marketing materials that they create, and that those that they consider to be confidential or trade secrets will need additional protection as such.

The Open-Source Ethos

Copyright gives the owner of a work the right to control their property in any way that they wish. This right can be exercised to limit further copying or modification of the work by others, but equally it can be exercised to grant others the rights to distribute copies and modified versions of the work within an *open-source ethos.*

The open-source ethos usually provides free access rights to copy and modify a work, subject to the constraint that the same rights are preserved in all modified versions that are created. This provides a general method for making a creative work freely available and distributable.

Copyleft, or Share–Alike

Copyleft, or *share-alike*, is the application of copyright law to foster and encourage the right to copy, share, modify and improve creative works, usually with the objective of building collaborative communities that share and improve those works. It is sometimes denoted with a ☺ to align it with and distinguish it from copyright.

Copyleft is usually implemented using one of the copyleft licence forms, such as the GNU General Public Licence (GPL) or the Creative Commons Attribution Share Alike Licence (CC).

In the context of software code, these licences also require that the information necessary for reproducing and modifying the work must be made available to recipients of the executable code. The source code files will usually contain a copy of the licence terms and acknowledge the author(s).

Sponsored by the Free Software Foundation, GPL (currently at v3), provides the user or developer of an open-source software product with the following *freedoms*:

- To use the software for any purpose.
- To change the software.
- To share the software with others.
- To share any changes made.

Importantly, whenever someone creates or modifies software covered by GPLv3, they must provide every recipient with permission to apply any patent that is needed to exercise the rights that the software gives them. This means that users and developers can work with GPLv3 software without worrying about being sued for patent infringement.

The CERN Open Hardware Licence (CERN OHL) is a comparable licence that has been created specifically for use with hardware.

Adopting the Open-Source Ethos

Open source essentially means placing designs, frameworks, code, documentation and all other related materials in the public domain, usually using one of the copyleft licence forms with the object of growing a community of developers and users that will together share and improve the offering.

The approach is currently applied to:

- Software, such as the Linux operating system (known as GNU/Linux by the Free Software Foundation) and the Apache web server (from the Apache Software Foundation).
- Hardware, such as Facebook's Telecom Infra Project (TIP), which comprises a range of wireless broadband technologies, and the various offerings on CERN's Open Hardware Repository.
- Frameworks, such as TOGAF, The Open Group's Architecture Framework and its associated architecture modelling language, Archimate.

It is important not to confuse open source with zero cost: both open-source and proprietary (or closed-source) products can have associated charges, or be offered at zero cost.

The open-source ethos is about enabling unlimited modification and sharing by a community of users who, therefore, in the words of the Free Software Foundation, have the freedom to 'run, copy, distribute, study, change and improve' the offering. In the context of the open-source world, *free software* means software that in some way gives freedom to its users.

As a business approach, a venture usually adopts the open-source ethos in the development, distribution and protection of its offerings for one of the following reasons:

- The business model benefits from encouraging a community of developers to extend the market.

- It seeks a philosophical fit with the marketplace ethos, such as in a public service or research world.
- Its aim is to maximize adoption of the product across a marketplace as a platform for sales of related support and services.

Choosing the open-source route is usually a binary decision for a venture. Although it is possible to succeed with a combination of open- and closed-source approaches, this needs careful management, both of technology and of licensing. A successful example of so-called *dual-licensing*, where both open-source and proprietary versions of an offering are made available, is Oracle's MySQL database. In this case, a *community version* is available at zero cost under an open-source licence, alongside a range of more functionally extensive commercially licensed offerings.

Where the open-source ethos is not adopted by a venture, it is normal for investors, and even strategic partners, to require assurances of freedom from open-source materials. This is because of the viral nature of some open-source licences, which require that any *derivation* of the work must also be distributed under that same licence. Consequently, as noted in Chapter 4, it is crucially important, when considering the use of a third-party component that originates from the open-source ethos, to determine the consequence of the relevant licensing arrangements. An example of such a consequence would be the implicit waiving of all patent rights in the product, as provided by GPLv3 licence.

Easy Access IP

Aligned with the open-source ethos, Easy Access IP is an arrangement whereby an international collective of universities and research institutions provides free access to some of their IP to benefit society and the economy. The approach does not replace traditional routes for exploitation of higher-value opportunities, but enables a rapid means whereby institutions can offer selected IP to a community for exploitation.

It applies a simple one-page agreement whereby the licensee:

- Demonstrates how they will create value for society and the economy.
- Acknowledges the licensing institution as the originator of the intellectual property.
- Reports annually on the progress on the development of the Easy Access IP.

- Agrees that if the IP is not exploited within three years, then the licence will be revoked.
- Agrees that there will be no limitations on the licensee's use of the IP for the university's own research.

Easy Access IP can be a beneficial route for IP exploitation by an institution in cases where:

- It offers a hook to leverage other industry interactions; in this way, it can be aligned with the *freemium* pricing approach.
- It provides a practical means to handle the outputs of collaborative research.
- It can facilitate beneficial social and student enterprise.
- There is a desire for a convenient means to return IP to its inventors.
- It can benefit the institution by stimulating local SME engagement.
- It provides an opportunity to align exploitation with an ethos of achieving impact and of capturing this activity; in this sense, the Easy Access IP brand can be a valuable marketing tool for an institution.

Case Study: SportMagenta

Open-Source Considerations

Sonny and Zara consider the option of taking an open-source route with the SportMagenta software. They recognize that the approach may bring benefits in terms of motivating a community of developers to innovate the product and its application, potentially creating demand for an ecosystem of ventures that could supply associated business services for training, integration and support. For the founders, this would be a significant change to the business model initially framed; the venture would become part of a community of cooperating and competing service providers.

The founders review the objectives set for their business and determine that these are less likely to be met through an open-source route. Furthermore, they acknowledge that there is currently no open-source ethos in the leisure services sector. Consequently, they take the view that their product, although offered at zero cost to its users, will remain proprietary to SportMagenta.

Protection of Confidential Information

Risks Relating to Theft of Confidential Information

The theft of confidential information and trade secrets can lead to losing the revenues and rewards of market advantage, and sometimes also to the additional costs of recovering from reputational damage. Protection against such risks is available through a range of procedural and legal mechanisms. High-profile examples include the following:

- Facebook is being sued in the USA by BladeRoom Group, a UK business that claims its trade secrets and IP for data centres have been stolen. As reported in February 2017, the case will go to court despite Facebook's assertions that the defendants did not own the trade secrets in question and did not make reasonable efforts to protect their information.
- Waymo, the Alphabet subsidiary responsible for Google's self-driving car project, sued Uber after one of its former employees allegedly stole 14,000 confidential registered design files before resigning from the company to found a start-up that was later acquired by Uber for $680 million. The case concluded with Uber agreeing to pay a 0.34 per cent equity stake, worth roughly $245 million, and committing not to use Waymo's technology.

These cases illustrate that legal mechanisms for protecting IP may not be sufficient to defend a venture's market advantage, and that further measures may also be required.

Confidential Information and Trade Secrets

Early-stage ventures and SMEs can be vulnerable when engaging with larger customer or partner organizations: the other party might take their ideas and replicate them using their own resources. This can be particularly acute where potential partners offer complementary products or services, or operate in a related market.

The term *confidential information* covers documents, templates, software source code, database designs, financial plans, ROI calculations, market strategies and any other materials that are valuable to a business, and that it would not wish to be available without strict controls governing use and further distribution. With such materials, copyright is not helpful, as it gives protection only from actual copying, and not from theft of any constituent ideas or information.

According to the 2013 European Commission study on trade secrets and confidential business information in the internal market: 'A consensus among economists has emerged that trade secrets play an important role in protecting the returns to innovation and that trade secret protection is an integral and important part of the overall system of protection available to EU firms to protect their intangible assets, like patents and copyrights.'

In the words of WIPO: 'any confidential business information which provides an enterprise with a competitive edge may be considered a trade secret'. Hence, the terms *confidential information* and *trade secrets* are broadly synonymous. However, legal treatment of these terms does vary across territories.

In the USA, trade secrets are considered to be a subset of confidential information, and are protected under the Uniform Trade Secrets Act. Since 1996, it has been a federal crime to misappropriate trade secret information, with heightened penalties if the misappropriation was intended to benefit a foreign entity. However, in the USA, most trade secret enforcement occurs through civil suits under state law.

In many EU countries, including the UK, trade secrets are only legally protected in instances where someone has obtained the confidential information by illegitimate means (such as spying, theft or bribery). Furthermore, in the UK, as trade secrets are not classed as property, there is no criminal sanction, hence civil suits need to be brought to enforce claims for damages and legal injunctions.

On a worldwide basis, to qualify for any such remedies a business needs to apply the criteria of the World Trade Organization's Agreement on Trade-Related Aspects of Intellectual Property Rights (TRIPS Agreement): the information concerned must not generally be known or readily accessible; it must have commercial value; and it must have been subject to reasonable steps by the rightful holder of the information to keep it secret.

Comprehensive protection of confidential information usually involves the use of a range of mechanisms, including:

- Clear decisions on the trade secrets that need to be protected, as it is not practicable to protect everything. These decisions need to be communicated across the team to avoid accidental or inadvertent sharing.

- Careful management of information and sharing, including the marking of confidential information as such, and the use of non-disclosure agreements (NDAs) – covered in more detail below – when working with other parties.
- Effective security from unwanted intrusion to mitigate the risks of damage from theft and any unauthorized access to, or use of, confidential information.
- Enforceable contractual obligations on employees, while employed and afterwards.

Know-How

Know-how is the practical knowledge, often tacit, of how to accomplish something. Its tacit nature often makes it difficult to record or to transfer to another person using conventional written or spoken language forms.

As an economic asset of a business and a category of confidential information, know-how needs to be respected, valued and protected. For a venture that produces a product with a significant software component, the know-how surrounding the coding and configuration of the software is valuable, and failure to protect such know-how would expose the company to several risks:

- If a competitor had access to this know-how, they may be able to use it themselves to their competitive advantage against the company's interests.
- If a malicious agency had access to the know-how, then they may be able to use it to identify potential security breaches and hence damage the company or its reputation.
- If the company were to lose that know-how – for example, by employees leaving – then it is likely that additional costs would be incurred in reconstructing it.

The third of these risks needs to be mitigated by effective management and forward planning of the workforce. In the early days of a venture, it is often the case that individuals hold in their heads significant information which, if unavailable, would severely damage the venture's operations. One mitigation is diligent back-up of the work of such individuals; another is a priority plan to introduce new people who will be encouraged to learn from those *high-risk individuals*, and hence provide continuity in the event of accident or departure.

Confidentiality or Non-Disclosure Agreements

The most common way for a venture to protect its interests when it needs to share confidential information with another party is to enter into a confidentiality or non-disclosure agreement (NDA) that confirms the parties' mutual intention to protect and respect each other's confidential information. A joint development agreement (JDA) is a similar form that is more usually associated with joint research activities. The points below apply equally to NDAs and JDAs.

Any agreement of this kind will normally provide the following:

- The reason for provision or sharing of confidential information. In many cases, this will be to enable exploration of the benefits of doing business together.
- The period of time for which the agreement will apply, with some provisions continuing for a longer period.
- The remedies that will be available to the parties in the event of a breach by the other.

Additional topics that may also be covered include:

- Non-compete clauses relating to mutual interests in specified market(s).
- Non-poaching of staff during the period of the agreement.

NDAs are sometimes mutual and sometimes asymmetric, according to the situation. In cases where the purpose for sharing relates to joint development or exploration, it is reasonable to expect full mutual treatment of parties' confidential information, even though one may be much larger than the other. In such cases, the larger party will usually insist on using their own standard form of agreement.

It is important always to ensure that no other unintended rights are granted by an NDA, especially any transfer of ownership or long-term exclusive commitments.

Case Study: SportMagenta

Confidential Information Considerations

The founders set a policy of marking all confidential documents, designs, models and agreements as trade secrets, and establishing a secure storage area within which they will be kept. This policy will be enforced and shared with all future employees.

In the early days, the founders know that their venture will be vulnerable to loss of know-how through personal accident. They set an intention to ensure that as the venture grows, critical know-how is continually distributed as widely as possible across the workforce.

A further policy adopted is for a mutual NDA to be established ahead of any dialogue with a potential customer or partner. No confidential information will be shared without NDA.

Protection against Onerous Contracts

Risks Relating to Onerous Contracts

Entering into an onerous contract can lead to punitive liabilities or open-ended responsibilities beyond the venture's control, and to claims for damages and associated costs. Protection against such risks is available through a range of procedural and legal mechanisms.

The case of global security business G4S and its contractual difficulties with the UK 2012 Olympic Delivery Authority provides a high-profile example. The case hit the news when G4S admitted two weeks before the Olympic opening ceremony that it would be unable to meet its contractual commitments. The company was forced to pay out £88 million ($115 million) and its reputation was severely damaged by a public description of its performance as 'unacceptable, incompetent and amateurish'.

Protecting a venture against such risks requires care and diligence with all contractual relationships. Many kinds of agreement have the potential to cause harm by imposing onerous demands or by limiting future activities and opportunities. The focus of this section is on the following three kinds of agreement that apply commonly to digital businesses:

- Licence agreements for product usage.
- Customer service agreements.
- Customer delivery contracts.

Other kinds of agreement can also bring unacceptable risk. This applies to property leases, joint venture and product distribution agreements, and contracts for purchase of goods or services. The principal topics and considerations addressed within the context of the three kinds that have been selected here also apply generally to the other kinds encountered.

Product Licensing Agreements

A licence is a permission given by the owner of IP rights (the licensor) to someone wishing to use those rights (the licensee) to do something which the owner could otherwise prevent. Importantly, the product or service that is licensed remains the property of the licensor. In the world of software, the term *end-user licence agreement* (EULA) is commonly applied.

A good licence protects both the venture and its IP (its product offering) by defining the terms on which the product may be used, and specifying bounds on what is permitted and what risks are tolerated.

Conversely, a poor licence can damage the venture by granting rights that limit future sales or imposing punitive liabilities on the business. If there is no licence agreement, then there is no clarity over terms, and hence sales of its product may expose a venture to a host of risks, including lost revenues, IP theft and damages claims.

For businesses operating within the open-source ethos, one of the family of copyleft licences will usually be selected and offered, together with the source code of the product. Consequently, the following considerations apply only to the provisions of a licence for closed-source, or proprietary, offerings.

A normal approach to licence distribution is for it to be bound or wrapped into product packaging and as such not to be open to negotiation. Large customer organizations may, however, expect to negotiate specific licence terms. As far as possible, this should be resisted because it will add legal costs and possibly lead to a more complex licence management environment in which different customers operate different licences. Investors are likely to be concerned at any suggestion of multiple varying licence terms. A halfway approach that can sometimes be acceptable to larger customers is the offer of a side-letter, signed by both parties, which clarifies a small number of terms for the purposes of interpretation against their intended usage.

For products comprising a software component that will be delivered using an online mechanism provided by a third party such as Apple or Google, there are published conditions that affect the form of licence offered. With Apple, this includes the requirement that 'the license granted to the end-user for the Licensed Application must be limited to a non-transferable license to use the Licensed Application on any iPhone or iPod touch that the end-user owns or controls and as permitted by the Usage Rules set forth in the App Store Terms of Service'. The comparable text from Google is 'you grant to the user a non-exclusive, worldwide and perpetual licence to perform, display and use the Product on the Device'.

If one of these mechanisms is intended to be used for software distribution, it is important that the relevant licence embodies and is consistent with the required conditions.

Although the legal treatment of some matters varies across territories, there is a collection of generally applicable licence terms that it is particularly important to consider. These are addressed in Appendix A: Principal Terms of Product Licensing Agreements. This gives explanations, cautions and, in some cases, optional forms of words for each of the principal licence terms. It is important to note that the specific wording adopted may need to be reviewed in the light of applicable legal territories.

Customer Service Agreements

A customer service agreement is a contract between a service provider and a service user, or customer, under which the provider will deliver a specified collection of services over a prescribed time frame. It sets out the specifics of the services to be delivered, and describes relevant aspects of their quality, performance and availability. It also scopes out the set of responsibilities and obligations on each of the parties involved.

Broadly speaking, there are two kinds of customer service agreement:

- **Those framed around the provision of a service.** Sometimes referred to as service level agreements (SLAs), this form is widely adopted for cloud-based offerings including SaaS and platform as a service (PaaS). They are self-standing agreements that define a service that will be provided to the customer. Services will be associated with a pricing approach that is typically charged at a regular recurring rate, such as a monthly fee.
- **Those framed around an insurance model.** Sometimes referred to as customer care agreements (CCAs), this form is associated with a related product. The customer purchases the assurance that a required level of product support will be provided as and when it is needed. In such cases, services are not costed with regard to effort or output, but at a level commensurate with the benefit of mitigating the risk of non-availability. With this kind of agreement, it can be important to ensure clear referencing and consistency between the CCA and the product licence to avoid any potential for conflict or confusion.

As with licence agreements, a good service agreement protects both the venture and the products and services it delivers. When designing a service, it is important to decide what commitments can be made and what will be the continuing cost of delivery. For example, if 24/7 service is to be offered on a worldwide basis, then it is necessary to calculate the operational cost of staffing and managing this, or of purchasing additional cover from a third party. This also means assessing the likely volume of service usage, and the potential impact of peaks and troughs in demand. Such considerations need to inform the commitment made to service performance levels.

As with licence agreements, a standard form of agreement is preferable, with an option of a side-letter to clarify any particular priorities or requirements of larger customer organizations. In some situations, the customer service agreement is wrapped into a product licence agreement or a customer delivery contract. Irrespective of whether it stands alone, or as part of another contract, the important considerations that apply will be the same.

Although the legal treatment of some matters varies across territories, there is a collection of generally applicable terms relating to this kind of agreement that it is particularly important to consider. These are addressed in Appendix B: Principal Terms of Customer Service Agreements. This gives explanations, cautions and, in some cases, optional forms of words for each of the principal terms to be included. It is important to note that the specific wording adopted may need to be reviewed in the light of applicable legal territories.

Customer Delivery Contracts

This kind of agreement applies to quite a wide range of situations, including:

- **Pilot or proof-of-concept projects**, where the venture is contracted to work with a customer or partner to demonstrate a benefit case or prove the effectiveness of a product within an operational environment. The outcome of the project may be an agreed framing for a **delivery project** or **customer service agreement**.
- **Delivery projects**, where the venture is contracted to create and deliver a collection of defined outputs or outcomes within a defined budget and time frame. The outcome of the project may be an operational digital system or platform.
- **Joint development projects**, where the venture works with a potential customer or partner to develop a case for future collaboration by, say, demonstrating integration potential or evidencing market demand. The outcome of the project may be an agreed framing for a **delivery project** or **joint venture agreement**. In this context, the customer role may be played by the partner organization or by the putative joint venture.

Each of these has its own specific considerations, and all of them have much in common with product licensing and customer service agreements.

A good contract can be critical to the success of a project. It is possible for a venture to win and deliver a good project result while severely damaging its longer-term prospects by compromising its future options for IP exploitation, or by burdening itself with onerous long-term liabilities that expose it to continuing risks that deter investors.

These kinds of agreement can be subject to extensive negotiation. In cases where one party is much larger than the other, the larger party will usually expect its contractual framework to be adopted. When entering into such a negotiation, it is crucially important for a venture to decide what can be offered and accepted, and what cannot.

Although the legal treatment of some matters varies across territories, there is a collection of generally applicable terms relating to this kind of contract that it is particularly important to consider. These are addressed in Appendix C: Principal Terms of Customer Delivery Contracts. This gives explanations, cautions and, in some cases, optional forms of words for each of the principal terms that usually apply. It is important to note that the specific wording adopted may need to be reviewed in the light of applicable legal territories.

Protection against Damage and Intrusion

Risks Relating to Damage or Intrusion

An unwarranted intrusion, physical or electronic, that involves theft or damage can bring disruption, reputational harm, fines and additional costs for recovery and future insurance. Protection against such risks is available through the purchase of appropriate equipment and insurance, and the implementation of procedural controls. High-profile examples include:

- In 2015, a cyber-attack was launched on Sony by a group called *Guardians of Peace*, with the aim of making the company cancel its publication of a comedy film. According to Sony Pictures' Senior General Manager Kazuhiko Takedato, the attack cost the company up to $35 million.
- An attack on TalkTalk during the same year was reported to have cost the company $60 million plus a fine of £400,000 from the UK Information Commissioner's Office for failing to protect customers' information.

Sony's insurance against cyber-attacks enabled the company to recover a significant portion of the costs it incurred, but the reputational damage to TalkTalk caused it to lose more than 100,000 customers.

Every venture is vulnerable to accidents and deliberate attacks, and the effects of both can range from minor inconvenience to catastrophe. Even for a small business, the range of potentially damaging events will be too broad to permit a detailed risk analysis of each, but it is nonetheless possible to compile a list of things that could destroy or severely damage the venture, and hence put in place reasonable mitigation and transfer measures.

The principal and most severe risks usually have a financial, reputational or personal effect on the venture, irrespective of whether they are triggered by fire, burglary, cyber-attack, accident or tragic personal circumstance. Mitigating and transferring such risks typically involves a combination of:

- Investment in physical mechanisms, such as alarm systems, door and window locks, hard disk encryption and safes for storage of valuable or protected materials.
- Policy, procedures and training on security matters, both physical and cyber.
- Insurance cover for property, equipment and people, to transfer certain risks and enable business continuity.

For ventures that operate in certain sectors, such as national security, there may also be legal or customer requirements that mandate the use of additional security precautions.

Although physical and cyber security overlap significantly, it is important that each is given mature consideration by the venture, and hence they are addressed here separately.

Establishing Physical Security

Physical security is about protecting business premises, equipment and personnel from accident or attack, including fires, burglaries or malevolent activity by staff.

At a physical level, common mitigation measures include secure locks on doors and windows, fire alarms and fire-fighting equipment, and mechanisms for secure safe keeping of physical materials and documents.

More difficult are the personnel-related mitigations. Theft and disruption caused by current or past staff, potentially working with outsiders, can pose a significant threat to any venture. This can be mitigated by a combination of the following measures:

- Vetting of staff during recruitment, including being diligent about references from previous employers.
- Allocating passes and key cards to staff, to control who has access to which physical areas of buildings.
- Establishing a code of conduct that covers acceptance of gifts from customers or suppliers.
- Developing and enforcing policies and procedures for visitors to the venture's premises to ensure that only trusted visitors are given *freedom to roam.*
- Developing and enforcing governance regimes, including checks and inspections, and procedures to protect against fraudulent or illegal behaviour.

This final point can be the most difficult to implement and enforce, but it is particularly important. Research reported by entrepreneur and commentator Eric Sikola (2013) writing in *Business News Daily* revealed that employee theft and fraud is a major drain on US businesses, with $50 million stolen annually by employees, and 75 per cent of employees admitting to stealing on at least one occasion from their employer. And the seriousness of this risk is underlined by the finding that about one-third of business bankruptcies are the result of employee theft.

Mitigating this risk implies the need for a policy of process audits, typically addressing expense reclaims and company purchases, to ensure that all members of the team are behaving in the venture's interests, and that nobody is in some way defrauding the venture or exposing it to unacceptable risk. With new and fast-moving ventures, such audits rely to a great extent on a strong bond of trust between team members.

Establishing Cyber Security

The 2013 cyber-attack on US retailer Target involved the theft of the personal data and payment card details of more than 40 million customers. This tarnished the company's reputation and, according to Fadilpašić (2015), cost the company $162 million. Although the thieves were outsiders, they gained entry to the company's systems using the credentials of an insider who was, according to Upton and Creese (2014), one of the company's refrigeration vendors.

In 2016, a medium-sized UK vehicle hire company, MNH Platinum, suffered after one of its members of staff clicked a link on an email. The consequence was the activation of a virus that encrypted over 12,000 files on the company network. A ransom demand followed, offering to decrypt the company's files in exchange for around $5,000. According to Mark Smith (2016) writing in *The Guardian*, the company had no choice but to pay up. Ransomware attacks are becoming more widespread: in May 2017, the *WannaCry* virus was reported to have infected more than 230,000 computers in more than 150 countries.

According to the Hiscox Cyber Readiness Report (2017), cybercrime cost the global economy over $450 billion in 2016 through damage and destruction of data, lost productivity, post-attack disruption, forensic investigation and reputational harm. More than half of businesses in the USA, the UK and Europe have experienced an attack over the past year, and 40 per cent of businesses have had to cope with two or more attacks.

The financial impact of cyber-attacks is disproportionately high for smaller companies. In the UK, the Cyber Streetwise report (2016) addressed small ventures and found that 60 per cent of those surveyed had experienced a cyber breach and, of those, 89 per cent reported a negative impact, including brand damage, loss of clients and a struggle to win new business.

The scale of this risk seems not, however, to be fully appreciated, as only 29 per cent of the 1,000 ventures surveyed considered reputational damage from a cyber-attack to be important.

The examples above illustrate that businesses of all sizes are under attack from threat actors applying a wide range of *attack vectors*, many of which, such as USB-looking devices, are commercially available at affordable prices.

A safe assumption is that every venture will at some point be the target of a cyber-attack, and all must therefore take reasonable precautions to defend themselves by at least applying the following three precautions:

1. Apply physical security measures, such as those addressed previously, to control access by untrusted persons. It should not be possible for someone to attach a USB-like device to any network point. This is the approach that was used to compromise Target, as reported above.
2. Conduct a programme of education and training in cyber hygiene for all staff. This should at least address the need for procedural requirements such as regular password changes, and provide an awareness of the *social engineering* techniques used by threat actors to trick people into clicking on malicious links or revealing information that can be used in an attack.

The Ponemon Institute (2016) reports that more than half of companies attribute a security incident or data breach to a malicious or negligent employee, with the top two insider risks being data breach caused by an employee exposing sensitive information, and an employee succumbing to a targeted phishing attack.

Related to this is the use of blackmail as an attack vector for recruiting insiders. Data breaches such as the 2015 Ashley Madison attack can be used to reveal information that can help attackers to identify and target potentially vulnerable individuals in their workplaces.

To be effective, any programme of education and training will require clear policies for transfer and sharing of information, plus regular monitoring and strict enforcement.

3. Implement controls for at least basic-level protection. The *cyber essentials* programme published by the UK government (2014) recommends the following:
    - The use of firewalls and internet gateways to prevent unauthorized access to or from private networks.
    - Ensuring that systems are configured in the most secure way for the needs of the organization.
    - Ensuring that only those who should have access to systems have access, and at the appropriate level.
    - Ensuring that virus and malware protection is installed and is up to date.
    - Ensuring that the latest supported version of an application is used, and that all necessary patches supplied by the vendor have been applied.

Cyber essentials certification is a requirement for ventures to bid for certain categories of UK government contracts. It can also reduce cyber-related insurance premiums, and is claimed to reduce the risk of cyber-attack by up to 80 per cent.

Depending on the nature of the venture, and the demands of its customers, additional measures that may also be required include:

- Encryption of devices.
- Management of the wider network, including ensuring security and passwords on all connected devices.
- Safeguarding against any risk of intrusion through the supply chain.

A related risk of online damage comes from malicious reviews or criticisms. According to research carried out by the reputation management company Ignyte and reported in *The Telegraph* by Rebecca Burn-Callander (2015), more than half of UK companies acknowledge that they have experienced unfair reviews or had been targeted by *trolls* posting inflammatory remarks online.

The research found that the problem has cost one in five organizations as much as $35,000 to put right. This is a growing problem, and in response, an increasing number of businesses are creating roles specifically responsible for tracking and responding to reviews and online content.

Protection against Legal Non-Compliance

Risks Relating to Legal Non-Compliance

Infringing other parties' IP, or failing to comply with legal requirements, can lead to damages claims, legal costs and reputational damage. Protection against such risks is available through registration with required bodies, purchase of appropriate insurances, and the establishment and enforcement of policies and procedural controls. High-profile examples include the following:

- Napster was a peer-to-peer file-sharing network launched in 1999 to make music freely available to its users. The company was sued for infringement of copyright, with the result that it was forced to shut down in 2002 after making a public apology and paying $26 million in damages.
- In 2017, online gambling firm 888 was ordered by the UK Gambling Commission to pay £7.8 million ($10 million) for failing to protect vulnerable customers. The Commission is reported to have identified 'significant flaws' in the business's social responsibility processes.

In both of these cases, the businesses involved suffered significant reputational damage. In the case of Napster, the remedy was so severe that the venture was forced to close.

Compliance risk, or integrity risk, is the risk of a business incurring legal penalties, reputational damage or material loss when it fails to act in accordance with industry laws and regulations, or prescribed best practices. There are many ways in which a venture can become exposed to such risks, and ignorance of legal requirements is never a good defence.

This section addresses three areas of particular relevance to digital technology ventures:

- The potential for infringement of another business's IP.
- The potential for infringement of employment legislation.
- The potential for infringement of data protection legislation.

In each of these areas, it is important that a venture understands the legal requirements for compliance across its operating territories, and sets up simple policies to avoid any inadvertent breach. The principal mitigations for these risks are knowledge and a proactive attitude.

Relevant legislation varies significantly across territories. This section indicates areas where knowledge may be required, and stresses that it is the responsibility of each venture to determine its particular requirements. This task is assisted by government portals such as www.usa.gov/business in the USA and www.gov.uk/browse/business in the UK, both of which provide access to government services and information to help businesses to comply.

Avoiding Infringement of Other Businesses' Intellectual Property

An earlier section of this chapter addressed the options for protecting IP using trademarks, design rights, patents and copyright. Other sections address the related topics of the wording adopted within licences, service agreements and delivery contracts. The other side of these considerations is the risk of accidentally infringing the IP of, or of breaching an agreement with, another party. Failing to avert this risk can expose the venture to damages claims, injunctions, reputational damage and disruption.

The key to avoiding this risk is awareness. This means educating the wider team and ensuring a degree of diligence, especially in respect of the following:

- Across promotional and development activities, the need to conduct market research to identify any existing registered IP that potentially overlaps with the offering or its description.
- Specifically within development activities, the need to assess licence agreements relating to all products or product components that are adopted for use, whether for internal operation within the venture, or for incorporation into an offering.
- The need to conduct all activities with customers, suppliers, partners and other players with an awareness of the terms set out in relevant contractual arrangements, including liabilities, obligations and confidentiality requirements.

It can be difficult to anticipate accidental infringement of patent applications, as details are not published until eighteen months after application. Searching for published patents globally is supported by Espacenet (www.epo.org), supported by the European Patent Office. The risk of infringing an unpublished patent can be transferred by insurance, and policies are available to cover damages incurred even after an infringement case has been brought.

A related risk is where a member of the team, or perhaps a former member, accidentally or deliberately discloses confidential information relating either to the venture or to another party. Although employment or engagement contracts may allow damages claims in the event of wrongful use or disclosure of confidential information, such action and compensation may be too little too late if the knowledge underpinning a competitive advantage has been disclosed to competitors. Furthermore, it can be difficult to trace or to prove the source of a confidential information leak.

The most effective way to mitigate this risk is to ensure the following:

- That all confidential information belonging to the business and to its customers and partners is marked as such and is stored securely.
- That such information is only disclosed to employees and other associates when it is strictly necessary to their role, such that they have a *need to know.*
- That those team members with whom such information is shared are made aware of its importance and the liabilities on them and the venture.

Avoiding Infringement of Employment or Regulatory Requirements

Employment law imposes a range of requirements on businesses that employ people. These can vary significantly across territories, as illustrated below.

In the USA, federal law requires most employers to post a number of employee notices, including:

- Employee Polygraph Protection Act (EPPA).
- Fair Labor Standards Act (FLSA).
- Family Medical Leave Act (FMLA).
- Occupational Safety and Health Administration (OSHA).
- Uniformed Services Employment and Reemployment Rights Act (USERRA).

Failure to comply with these requirements could lead to citations and fines during an inspection or audit, ranging from $210 up to $10,000. In total, a business can face a combined fine of up to $17,000 per location. The situation could be exacerbated if an employee files a lawsuit over the violation of their workplace rights, because failing to post can undermine a *good faith* defence.

In the UK:

- Most employers need employers' liability insurance, proof of which must be displayed.
- Ventures that employ five or more people must display a health and safety poster, or provide each worker with a copy of the equivalent pocket card.
- Ventures have a duty to take reasonable care for the safety of their employees.
- Employers are liable for the acts of their employees if committed during their employment.

Failure to comply with these requirements can have serious consequences, both for the business and its directors. Sanctions include fines, imprisonment and disqualification.

Across the developed world, employment legislation includes statutes for a very wide range of topics, including disability rights, safeguarding of children, equality and discrimination at work, unfair dismissal, flexible working rights, maternity and paternity leave, working-time regulations, wages, equal pay, health and safety at work, monitoring and surveillance, union membership, data protection rights, disciplinary and grievance procedures, time off for dependents and others.

An early-stage venture cannot reasonably be expected to create and manage policies and procedures for such a plethora of topics. What can be expected, though, is that when an issue arises relating to one of these areas, the venture's response includes establishing the current legal position and acting within it. Information and guidance is readily available online for each jurisdiction.

Failing to comply with, say, maternity rights or an employee's claim for unfair dismissal is likely to lead to personal upset, additional costs, disruption of operations and a risk of reputational damage in the market.

Avoiding Infringement of Data Protection Requirements

Personal information means any detail about a living individual that can be used on its own, or with other data, to identify them.

Data protection legislation exists in most European countries, plus many others in Latin America, Asia and Africa. Such regulations need to be taken seriously by businesses operating in the digital economy because they set rules governing the handling of personal information relating to their own personnel, and that of their customers and other external parties.

In the USA, the Privacy Act of 1974 regulates the collection, use and disclosure of many types of personal information. However, as shown by a report from the European Parliament Directorate General for Internal Policies (2015), the provisions made in Europe and the USA differ widely.

The UK Data Protection Act (DPA) requires any business that processes personal information to register with the Information Commissioner's Office (ICO), unless it is exempt. To be exempt, a business must process personal information only for:

- Staff administration, including payroll.
- Advertising, marketing and public relations for its own activity.
- Accounts and records.

For any venture that is in doubt about the need to register, a self-assessment toolkit is available on the ICO's website at www.ico.org.uk. In any case, due to the sensitivities of some customers about the handling of their personal information, it can be advisable to create and share a privacy policy.

For UK businesses that satisfy the conditions for exemption, it remains important to adhere to the principles of the DPA and understand best practice for managing information, including fair use, accuracy, adequacy and the reasonable retention period. For ventures that are unsure about their exemption or which opt to future-proof their activities, there is an option for voluntary registration.

In the EU, the General Data Protection Regulation (GDPR) is intended to strengthen and unify data protection for individuals within the EU, including in relation to the export of personal data outside of the EU. Its provisions are stronger than those of the current UK regulations and so are the punishments: in the event of a data breach, the maximum penalties will increase from $625,000 to more than $20 million (€20 million), or 4 per cent of total annual worldwide turnover. Calder (2016) provides a pocket guide to the provisions of the GDPR, and comprehensive coverage is provided by the IT Governance Privacy Team (2017).

The potential impact of the act can be illustrated with reference to the 57 million Uber passenger and driver records that were hacked in October 2016, an event that was covered up for more than a year after the company paid hackers not to release the stolen data. As GDPR regulations will apply to any EU citizen's data, if some of the stolen data had related to EU citizens, then GDPR may have been applicable to punish Uber to the full extent available.

The GDPR will apply in the UK from 25 May 2018. Due to the risks of incurring high penalties and the likely reputational damage from publicity, businesses need to be aware of the applicable provisions. That awareness will inform the need to register with the relevant authority. In the UK, this activity is not arduous for SMEs: it involves a small payment and an online self-certification.

Larger organizations commonly employ a data protection officer with responsibility for protecting the business from the associated risks. This role is described from a professional standpoint by Lambert (2016). The leadership and management teams of smaller ventures need to assign such responsibilities to a competent member of the team.

Case Study: SportMagenta

Data Protection Considerations

The founders consider their intended use of personal data relating to club members and visitors for promotional targeting of products and services. They conclude that in the UK and the EU, this is likely to require the venture to register with the appropriate authority and to abide by the applicable regulations.

As they intend initially to operate in the UK, Sonny and Zara determine to submit a voluntary registration with the UK ICO. They recognize that the use of members' and visitors' data may become a sensitive subject, and determine to be scrupulous in the way that such data is captured, stored and used by the product. This principle will need to be accepted and reflected within all agreements entered into with sponsors and product promoters.

Summary of Intellectual Property and Protection

IP protection has a critical double importance for digital businesses. On the one hand, a venture can use internationally recognized legal protection mechanisms such as trademarks, registered designs, patents and copyright to establish and crystallize the value available through exploiting its IP. Additionally, these same mechanisms enable the venture to protect its valuable IP from theft or abuse.

This chapter has addressed the need of ventures of all sizes to manage a range of generally applicable risks. The consequences of not taking appropriate action to mitigate or transfer such risks can include unanticipated costs, fines, legal injunctions, reputational damage, disruption to operations, loss of competitive position, lost or damaged assets and painful limitations over future business opportunities. Consequences such as these have been described and illustrated by real-world examples.

The chapter has presented a collection of protection measures by which mitigations and transfers of these risks can be achieved. The considerations addressed will inform the development of an activity plan to create a tolerable risk profile for the venture.

None of the activities required to mitigate or transfer the various risks addressed is especially onerous or expensive, even for a small venture, and the effort and costs involved can be trivial compared with those associated with recovering from an occurrence of one of these risks. The most important point to be stressed, therefore, is the need to give mature and diligent attention to the very real risks that surround any venture. Failure to do this means relying principally on luck.

The key points addressed by this chapter are summarized below.

- **Protection of IP** is important because IP is the core of many digital ventures; exploiting its value and protecting it from theft, copying, loss or damage are paramount concerns. The range of exploitation and protection measures have been elaborated, including the legal differences that apply to different territories:
  - *Trademarks*, both registered and unregistered, can be used to protect names and other aspects of a venture's brand identity.
  - *Design rights*, both registered and unregistered, can be used to protect a user-interface design or the shape of a physical product or a pattern, so long as it is unique.
  - *Patents* give powerful protection by granting exclusive rights for their owners to exploit an innovation and to prevent others from making or selling anything that infringes the patent.
  - *Copyright* gives exclusive rights to its owners to protect their material, including source code, against copying or reproducing, adapting, distributing, selling or renting, broadcasting or public performance.
  - Adopting an *open-source* approach means placing designs, frameworks, code, documentation and all other related materials in the public domain,

with the object of growing a community of developers and users that will together share and improve the offering.

- **Protection of confidential information** is about ensuring that those documents, templates, software source code, database designs, financial plans, ROI calculations, market strategies and other materials that are valuable to the venture are subject to strict controls that govern their availability, use and further distribution:
  - *Trade secrets* play an important role in protecting the benefits of innovation, and trade secret protection is an integral and important part of the overall system of protection.
  - A venture's *know-how* is an economic asset that needs to be respected, valued and protected.
  - *Confidentiality* or *non-disclosure agreements* are the normal way for a venture to protect its interests when sharing confidential information with another party.

- **Protection against onerous contracts** is about exercising diligence with the agreements by which products and services are licensed, used, sold and procured to avoid exposing the venture to onerous demands or limiting its future activities and opportunities:
  - A good *licence* protects the venture and its IP; a poor licence risks damaging the venture by granting rights that limit future sales or impose punitive liabilities.
  - A good *service agreement* protects both the venture and the products and services it deploys by defining and enforcing acceptable commitments.
  - A good *delivery contract* can be critical to the success of a project for a venture; a poor contract risks compromising future options for IP exploitation and burdening the venture with onerous long-term liabilities.

- **Protection against damage and intrusion** is about addressing the risks that can apply to a venture's finances, continuity, reputation and personnel as a consequence of fire, burglary, cyber-attack, accident or tragic personal circumstance:
  - *Physical security* is about protecting the business premises, equipment and personnel from accident or attack, including fires, burglaries or malevolent activity by staff.
  - It can be assumed that every venture will at some point be the target of a cyber-attack, and must therefore take reasonable *cyber-security* precautions to defend itself by at least applying basic precautions.

- **Protection from legal non-compliance** is about managing the risk of the venture incurring legal penalties, reputational damage or material loss as a consequence of failing to act in accordance with industry laws and regulations, or prescribed best practices:

  - *Infringement of other parties' IP* or *breach of an agreement* can expose the venture to damages claims, injunctions, reputational damage and disruption.

  - *Employment legislation* includes statutes for a very wide range of topics, and when an issue arises relating to one of these areas, the venture's response must respect the current legal position or risk facing significant fines and reputational damage.

  - *Data protection legislation* needs to be taken seriously because it sets enforceable rules governing the handling of information relating to a venture's own personnel, and that of their customers and other external parties.

ANALYSIS EXERCISES

The table below lists a collection of digital businesses to be used as subjects for the exercises that follow.

Business	Focus	Website
Darktrace	Cyber security	www.darktrace.com
EventBright	Event promotion and management	www.eventbrite.co.uk
Fitbit	Health, fitness and performance	www.fitbit.com
JustEat	Online takeaway food	www.just-eat.co.uk
Reposit	Property rental	www.getreposit.uk
Snapchat	Social media	www.snapchat.com
Sorry as a Service	Customer services and retention	www.sorryasaservice.com
SwiftComply	Regulation and compliance	www.swiftcomply.com

On the basis of information available in the public domain, address the questions below for at least one of the businesses listed.

1. The business's customer(s):
   (a) Who is the customer(s) for the proposed innovation?
   (b) Who are the principal players in the business ecosystem?
   (c) What are the principal value exchanges with these players?

2. Protection of intellectual property (IP):
   (a) Suggest three elements of IP that the business relies upon in its operations.
   (b) For each element of IP identified in (a), what protection options are available to the business?
   (c) What evidence of the business's IP protection is available in the public domain?
   (d) Does the business in any way subscribe to the open-source ethos?

3. Protection of confidential information:
   (a) Suggest five kinds of confidential information that the business will need to protect.
   (b) Suggest three methods that the business might adopt to protect the confidential information identified in (a).

4. Protection against onerous contracts:
   (a) Suggest three kinds of agreement that the business is likely to use.
   (b) For each of the agreements suggested in (a), suggest at least two terms that are likely to be critical to the business.

5. Protection against damage and intrusion:
   (a) Suggest three risks faced by the business in respect of managing its physical security.
   (b) For each of the risks identified in (a), suggest a mitigation or transfer approach.
   (c) In what three ways might the business be exposed to cyber-attack?
   (d) Suggest three mitigations to reduce the risk of damage to the business from cyber-attack.

6. Protection from legal non-compliance:
   (a) Suggest a scenario in which the business might be at risk of infringing another party's IP.
   (b) Suggest a scenario in which the business might be at risk of breaching an agreement with another party.
   (c) Suggest three aspects of employment legislation that will affect the business.
   (d) Suggest three ways in which data protection legislation will affect the business.

DESIGN EXERCISES

The design exercise at the end of Chapter 1 encouraged identification of a business idea to be developed incrementally by specific design exercises through subsequent chapters of the book. That activity commenced in Chapter 2, with the framing of the selected business idea using the elements introduced in that chapter. This was extended in Chapters 3, 4, 5 and 6, with reference to the additional considerations and decisions introduced.

Extend your current design through the following tasks:

1. For each aspect of business protection covered in this chapter, perform an assessment and analysis of your business. If using the Business Design Template, summarize the resulting considerations in the left-hand cell of the *IP and protection* section.
2. Extract from your considerations the set of key decisions relating to value capture by your business. If using the Business Design Template, document these in the right-hand cell of the *IP and protection* section.
3. Review the extended design of your business for consistency, and address any issues that arise.
4. Capture separately any of the following:
   (a) Key points learned from the exercise.
   (b) Outstanding issues or uncertainties.

8 Leadership and Structure

Focus of This Chapter

Figure 8.1 illustrates how the material addressed by this chapter fits within the framework of considerations for business design.

The considerations addressed are driven by the mission and objectives set within the framing of the business.

They apply at the legal creation and structuring of a venture and their relevance continues throughout its development. The decisions taken can have significant implications for all aspects of business design.

Learning Outcomes

After studying this chapter, you will:

- Understand the roles of leadership, management and governance in a business venture.
- Appreciate the requirements for financial planning and control, including cash, budgets and tax.
- Understand the kinds of legal structures that can be adopted for business entities.
- Know the contractual responsibilities of directors, employees and contractors.
- Be able to design a shareholding structure for a venture.

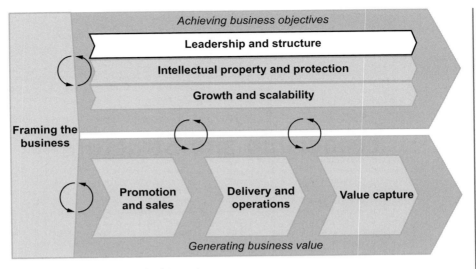

Figure 8.1 *Context of leadership and structure*

Introducing Leadership and Structure

The principal responsibility of the leadership team is to work within its legal structure to deliver the venture's business objectives. This implies three more specific responsibilities:

- To establish and sustain an organization that values, motivates and rewards its people.
- To plan and control the venture's resources, including its people and finances.
- To ensure compliance with the reporting and taxation regimes of the territories within which the venture operates.

Throughout the life of a business, it is important that the leadership team remain aware of their legal duties and of the risks that they carry with regard to those who work within the organization or who participate as investors, shareholders or providers of professional services. Without such awareness, both the business and its leaders may be exposed to legal or financial redress.

The topics covered by this chapter are subdivided into two parts, as illustrated in Figure 8.2. The first part relates to the leadership and governance

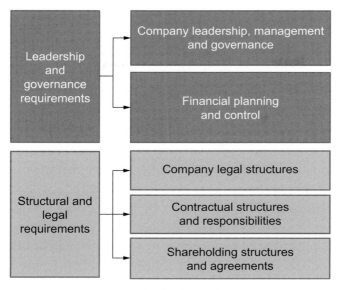

Figure 8.2 *Considerations of structure, leadership and governance*

requirements of a business, and the second to its structural and legal requirements. Both parts address material that can vary by territory.

As this is not intended as an authoritative legal textbook, the reader is expected to complement this coverage by assessing the legal situation in the relevant territories.

This chapter addresses several large and wide-reaching topics. The coverage provided aims to equip the entrepreneur with sufficient understanding of the necessary requirements, options, relevant considerations and principal decisions that are needed.

Company Leadership, Management and Governance

Leadership Requirements and Responsibilities

Apart from a handful of notable exceptions, the myth of the *hero leader* or *great man* plays a diminishing role in the modern digital world. As a general notion, this myth has been shown to be neither realistic nor effective. However, it continues to be reinforced through popular media and so it retains metaphorical power in some communities.

According to InnovateUK (2017), a strong leadership team is the most critical factor for a successful scale-up. The research discovered that in 97 per cent of cases where investors turn down requests for funding of scale-ups, the principal reason is the inadequacy of the leadership. Investors seek drive, passion and resilience, and leaders often underestimate the value placed by investors on good communications and chemistry.

Jeffry Timmons, an author and pioneer of entrepreneurship, provides a constructive characterization of leadership in Timmons (1999): 'a way of thinking, reasoning, and acting that is opportunity obsessed, holistic in approach, and leadership-balanced for the purpose of value creation and capture'. This sense of a balanced leadership is also offered by Davenport and Manville (2012), who introduce the term *organizational judgement* to refer to a maturity of decision making that is underpinned by a culture that respects analytics rather than gut feelings.

Some entrepreneurs make well-rounded leaders, but a more usual situation is for the leadership of a venture to be provided by a team of individuals, who together offer the required balance of *capabilities* and *qualities*. Both of these aspects of leadership are important.

Acknowledging the insights of Burns (2011), a leadership team requires five *capabilities*:

- An ability to articulate the venture's vision and objectives. This is not an abstract or static activity performed at the start of the venture, but a continuing and connected activity that develops with the business, providing the growing team with a sense of who they are, what they are doing and why.
- An ability to sustain a long-term strategic plan. This is about seeing beyond the day-to-day necessities and retaining the context of what's happening and why.
- An ability to communicate effectively within and outside the venture. Having the right words, metaphors and pictures can be central to being able to reinforce the venture's differentiation and confidence.
- An ability to inspire the values and culture of the business. Every individual person has inherent values and ways of behaving and engaging; they have personality. Likewise, so does a business, and an important role of leadership is to develop, inspire, tune and sometimes correct individuals to create and sustain a coherent organization.

- An ability to set and control performance towards objectives. In parallel with fixating on a long-term strategic plan, leadership needs to be able to root the business in the facts, to respect the analytics of performance and to initiate change where needed.

Three *qualities* are necessary to deliver and sustain these capabilities:

- Leaders have sufficient *adaptability* to recognize the benefit of moving away from an existing assumption, plan or objective. They can pivot where necessary without carrying regrets and blame.
- Leaders are *resilient* and do not give up when things become difficult. They have the commitment, determination and grit to *stick at it* while conviction exists.
- A leader has the *independence* of mind and an appetite for risk such that they trust their judgement rather than always following established or obvious routes and methods.

These capabilities and qualities belong to what is referred to by Drath *et al.* (2008) as the *tripod* of leaders, followers and common goals. They propose an alternative approach that reflects the trend in some social or purpose-driven ventures, towards more collaborative models of leadership. In their *DAC ontology*, the essential entities are expressed as outcomes:

- *Direction*, implying agreement in a collective on overall goals, aims and mission.
- *Alignment*, implying the organization and coordination of knowledge and work in a collective.
- *Commitment*, implying the willingness of members to subsume their own interests and benefit within the collective.

Irrespective of the model adopted, leadership differs from management, both differ from governance, and any venture needs a balance of each.

Whereas leadership is about setting direction and inspiring a team to work to that end, *management* is about obtaining, empowering and controlling the resources that are needed for this to succeed.

Governance refers to the structures, principles, rules and controls by which a venture achieves and sustains coherence, compliance with laws and regulations, and is able to operate within a known and acceptable risk envelope. As such, the considerations of governance overlap with those of both leadership and management.

Having an imbalance of roles is a common problem for early-stage ventures. A leadership team that comprises strong-minded visionaries without the counter-balancing managerial and governance capabilities needed to anchor that vision into a plan that can be delivered through a functioning organization, is unlikely to succeed. Likewise, a leadership team that focuses intently on developing detailed structures, plans, policies and procedures, with no inspiring vision of direction or purpose, is unlikely to be able to carry others along with it.

A key requirement of leadership is to achieve this balance of responsibilities in a way that is open to continuing question and change. This can sometimes imply a need to introduce external people.

Team Reward and Motivation

This is a topic that is commonly overlooked in early ventures, but which can be critical to motivating the performance needed for business development.

The management of a venture needs to give conscious consideration to several topics that can have a significant impact on team behaviour and motivation:

- Continuing skills development and progression within the team.
- Payment of compensation and benefits to the team.
- Using sweat equity within the team.
- The payment mechanisms used to reward the team.
- Recognition and appreciation of the team.

Continuing Skills Development and Progression within the Team

Larger businesses offer developmental opportunities for their employees, usually through a structured process of learning and advancement referred to as continuing professional development (CPD). This is important for continuing motivation and retention of staff. Smaller ventures have fewer options for this, and yet the demand from employees for an advancement route can be just as powerful. Consequently, to avoid losing good staff, it is important that managers actively identify developmental routes for individuals, and align these with skills development that is advantageous to the venture.

As a venture grows, so does the need for management, and hence managerial positions. This often brings a need to structure the development, operations and other teams with a mix of junior and more senior roles, which creates opportunities for individuals from hybrid technical or process roles to advance into roles with greater managerial responsibility.

This can be attractive as a way of retaining strong individuals, but it can also introduce problems. First, it is a poor idea for individuals who are inherently unsuitable or unwilling to manage. They will not perform well or be content in their new managerial role, and they may inflict damage on relationships across the team. It is important to consider individuals' competences and preferences carefully. A better means of retaining strong but ambitious technical staff can be through creating additional senior technical positions that enable them to continue to work to their strengths.

Second, when someone is promoted to a managerial role for which they are suited and capable, it is important to recognize a potential need for training in matters such as delegation of responsibility, project management and financial control. Such topics can be learned by experience on the job, but learning often means making mistakes, and in a fast-growing venture, these can be expensive.

Payment of Compensation and Benefits to the Team

Compensation is about how and how much employees are paid as a reward for investing their efforts in the venture. Benefits are additional elements that are offered to motivate required behaviours.

The principal questions to be considered are as follows:

- For what role is an employee being compensated? It can be important to align employees' salaries with market norms for that role in that location, such that individuals feel that their skills are respected and so are not easily tempted to look elsewhere.
- What behaviours does the venture choose to reward? This is about incentivizing loyalty and commitment through schemes that are additional to salary, including additional benefits such as private health care or company car, participation in a bonus scheme or offer of share options.

Addressing these questions separately can be helpful in identifying the right package for each employee, such that they feel content in their role in the team and are motivated to perform with commitment to their highest ability. A dissatisfied team member can be a very disruptive element within a team.

Using Sweat Equity within the Team

For an early-stage venture, the use of equity can be an attractive way to compensate people. Under this approach, employees or contractors are granted shares or share options in return for accepting salaries that are nil or lower than respective market norms. The future expectation of both parties will be for an investment, acquisition or flotation transaction that provides an opportunity for the equity holder to achieve a return, which will pay them for their effort (*sweat*) invested in developing the business.

This can sound attractive because company founders often feel as though they have lots of equity and very little cash, so if someone does not need to be paid in cash, then the approach seems ideal.

There are, however, pitfalls in using this approach, both to the company and to the potential equity holder. Before offering a sweat equity deal, it is important to consider the following:

- Is the individual able to behave like a founding partner in the longer term, in terms of their levels of determination, adaptability and resilience? If the individual does not possess these qualities, then the relationship may end badly for both parties.
- Does the individual bring something valuable, rare and inimitable that is needed for business growth or scalability? It is important to the business that its equity will not be tied up in an individual who will not provide it with real sustained competitive advantage.
- Are their objectives compatible with those of the company? If the individual expects a rapid and lucrative exit, whereas the company's founders are more inclined to a *slow burn* process of growth, then there will be conflict between the parties and this is likely to be disruptive.
- What terms will be associated with the shareholding offered? This covers all of those aspects addressed in a later section of this chapter, including the individual's voting rights, whether they will receive dividend payments, whether there is a vesting period and what would happen in the event that they leave the company for some reason.

The founding shareholders of a business need to respect that the equity in their company is precious by thinking like investors from the outset: if too much equity is distributed too early, then the options available later will be compromised. If, on the other hand, a sweat equity deal entered into with *eyes wide open* enables a venture to grow rapidly and achieve its short- or medium-term goals, then it will have been a success.

Payment Mechanisms Used to Reward the Team

Employees are usually paid a monthly salary from which taxes have already been deducted. The operation of the salary process is typically outsourced to the company's accountants or another service provider, who will ensure correct calculation of deductions.

Contractors, by contrast, are paid a fee according to the time frame set out in their contract. This might also include expenses reclaim and any applicable sales tax. With contractors, all calculation and payment of tax is their responsibility, not that of the company.

For a company with sufficient profits, the board of directors can decide to distribute some portion of the company's profits as a dividend paid to nominated classes of shareholders. A dividend applies to a particular share class and is stated as an amount to be paid per share. All holders of the relevant class of share must be offered the dividend and all will benefit proportionally to their shareholding. Dividends are taxable at rates appropriate to the territory.

In the USA, companies are required by many states to withhold at least the standard tax on a dividend, and to pay out the balance to shareholders. In the UK, however, shareholders receive their dividend in full and are responsible for declaring and paying the relevant taxes.

In the UK, company directors, at the discretion of the board of directors, can receive a director's loan from the company. The reverse is also possible: directors may loan money to a business, typically to alleviate short-term cash-flow problems. There are record-keeping requirements for such loans and, for loans received by directors, there are taxation requirements on both the company and the director. The moneys owed by the director or by the company are shown on the balance sheet in the company's annual accounts.

Recognition and Appreciation of the Team

In addition to compensation and benefits, an important motivational consideration is the publicizing and rewarding of exceptional performance or achievements by individuals or teams. This can be particularly important following an intense period of activity, such as a sales campaign or delivery push to release a new product, which has required the team to work for additional time and under exceptional stress.

Recognition can be shown through prizes of cash or goods, treats (such as vouchers for meals, accommodation or an experience) or acknowledgement in a company newsletter or blog.

Failing to acknowledge a special commitment can lead to a sense of not being appreciated, and hence reduced willingness at a future time to invest the same punishing degree of effort.

Financial Planning and Control

Effective governance of a business needs a rhythm, which is usually defined by monthly leadership or board meetings at which achievements, opportunities, obligations, performance, cash, requirements, risks and issues are reviewed, and required actions are determined and assigned. This is not to say that all decision making occurs on a monthly cycle, because at times of greater intensity, such monitoring and re-factoring of plans and budgets may need to happen much more frequently. What is important, though, is that a rhythm is established, and that objective data are available to support the decisions required of responsible directors.

The requirements of this governance rhythm dictate the structure of this section, which addresses:

- Cash management.
- Setting and balancing of budgets.
- Monitoring of company performance.
- Requirements for company reporting and taxation.

This book addresses, at a broad level, only those considerations that directly affect all ventures. Its intention is to provide just enough material to enable entrepreneurs to establish a financial governance system and to make well-informed decisions about their needs for specialist financial support. For a more detailed coverage of the wider subject, the reader is referred to Burton and Bragg (2000), Lee *et al.* (2009), Atrill (2014) or Cornwall *et al.* (2016).

Cash Management

There is a saying that 'turnover is vanity, profit is sanity, but cash is king'. Its author is unknown, but its sentiment will be understood by every entrepreneur. Irrespective of the robustness of the plan, the offering, the market analysis and everything else, if there is no cash, then a venture cannot pay its people or its suppliers, and it will be at risk of failing.

Consequently, cash management is a central requirement for any venture. For the purposes of this section, this means managing cash flows and being diligent in agreeing payment terms with customers and suppliers.

Managing Cash Flows

There is no complexity to managing the cash flow. It is simply a projection over time, usually three to six months, of the cash that will enter and leave the business and when this will happen. This is not about orders or revenues or margins – it is only about actual movements of cash.

In some cases, such as with salary and tax payments, the dates of cash transactions are fixed beforehand; in other cases, such as when a customer payment arrives, there may be a degree of variability. When creating or refreshing a cash-flow projection, all anticipated cash movements should be included; where necessary, best-guess estimates need to be made for when receipts and payments are likely to occur.

Table 8.1 illustrates the construction of a simple cash flow projection. Weekly columns are usually advised for small ventures to anticipate any problems that may occur between receipts and payments within the month. Starting with an opening balance, the projection lists the anticipated receipts and payments, concluding with an ending balance, which is carried forward to the next column.

The reason for managing projections at such a detailed level is to identify situations where there may be either insufficient cash or a surplus. It may be useful to consider moving any surplus cash into a deposit account for higher interest. If this is a regular occurrence, then such a move could be systematized on a monthly or quarterly basis.

Where the projection indicates the likelihood of a cash deficit, then action may be required. When choosing banking arrangements for a venture, it can be useful to request a provision for cash-flow overdrafts up to a certain level; a minimal charge would be made for the small negative fluctuations that can occur due to timing difficulties.

Where the projected deficit is outside of such limits, however, there are three options.

The first is to delay payments that are due to suppliers or other creditors. This will mean reaching agreement with the recipient as to when payment will be made and whether any additional recompense needs to be made. Some suppliers make an extra charge for extending terms. Delaying salary payments for staff can have a very serious effect on team confidence and morale, and should be avoided as far as possible.

The second is to accelerate receipts that are due from customers or other debtors. This usually means seeking agreement with a customer to pay earlier

Table 8.1 Illustrative Cash Flow Forecast

Weekly cash flow projection				
Period: 2017 Quarter 1				
	Jan-17			
	02–Jan	09–Jan	16–Jan	23–Jan
Starting balance for period	12,500.00	38,975.00	44,925.00	17,430.00
Receipts				
initial payment from X	3,450.00			
annual subscription from Y	23,475.00			
grant payment from Z		8,500.00		
Total cash receipts	26,925.00		0.00	
Total cash available (before payments)	39,425.00	47,475.00	44,925.00	
Payments				
salaries			17,850.00	
tax and NI			7,140.00	
materials	450.00			
expenses reclaim			2,505.00	
communications		2,550.00		
Total cash payments	450.00	2,550.00	27,495.00	
Ending balance for period	38,975.00	44,925.00	17,430.00	

than originally planned. The cost for this may be expressed as a loss of goodwill, which cannot be mined indefinitely, or by some other means, such as a special discount on future purchases. When making such a request to the customer, it is advisable to be proactive by leading with a suggested offer.

The third option is to introduce a *credit factoring* scheme to smooth cash receipts. Such schemes provide a form of insurance against the risk of delayed payments. They typically involve the provider of the service paying a percentage of the face value of an invoice immediately, and then paying the remainder, minus a commission, when the customer pays. Although they carry a cost, such schemes can increase the confidence of positive cash flow projections.

Agreeing Payment Terms with Customers and Suppliers

The payment terms within a contract define when payments will be made. Terms are usually expressed along the lines of fifteen or thirty working days following the date of an invoice.

For B2B ventures, the payment terms can be a negotiation topic that forms part of the mix when agreeing a contract. Due to internal policies, large companies may demand very long terms. Where this is the case, the risk of the payment terms causing a cash flow shortfall can be mitigated by agreeing a schedule that provides an upfront payment plus interim payments, with charges for late payment. This can be an important aspect of the sale, and may require the venture to give something in return for preferential payment terms that help with business continuity.

Likewise, when agreeing a purchase agreement with a supplier, the payment terms may be a significant topic for negotiation. It is important to anticipate cash flow implications when agreeing the terms of any contract.

Setting and Balancing Budgets

A budget is a financial plan that projects the moneys that will be required to support the venture's operations over the forthcoming period, including its plans for growth and scalability. A budget is normally created for the forthcoming year of business activities; hence budget development usually occurs around the end of one year in preparation for the start of the next.

Two aspects are addressed here: the structuring of the budget, and the processes whereby it is created and monitored.

Budget Structure

A single budget can be used to detail all of a venture's projected expenditures. Alternatively, separate budgets can be created for individual functions, together with a consolidated version that rolls these into a single headline summary. The former is attractive in that the details of all planned expenditure can be seen on a single sheet, and hence balancing considerations can be applied. This can, however, become too complex when a venture reaches a size beyond which a single sheet is manageable.

Budgets are usually subdivided by time. This can be monthly or quarterly, chosen so as to reflect the projected patterns of spend. This can be particularly important for ventures with seasonally varying markets. A seasonal pattern can emerge for any offering as a consequence of the budgeting and buying rhythms of the venture's customers. Ventures that sell into large public-sector organizations often experience spikes in demand towards the end of the tax and budget year when their customers are inclined to spend remaining moneys.

A sample annual budget, subdivided monthly and with quarterly totals, is shown in Table 8.2. In the table, major headings are subdivided into detail items and totals are provided by heading and by time period. This structure permits analysis of the relative costs of the principal headings, and hence the balancing of total spend across headings.

A draft structure for a set of budget headings and detail items can be compiled from the topics covered by the chapters of this book, as illustrated in Table 8.3. In this example, the detailed costs have been subdivided into team costs and other costs. This can be helpful to enable costs of personnel to be aligned with growth in numbers of each role, assumed compensation rates and relevant employment costs, including recruitment and taxation.

Budgeting Process

Responsibility for creating the budget falls to the board of directors. It is highly advisable for the wider team to be engaged in the process so as to create a sense of transparency and mutual accountability over costs.

A balanced budget refers to one in which the projected costs are met by projected income to the business from revenues, investments, loans and other sources of funds. Where the budget exceeds such projections, either overall or within a particular period, either additional funds need to be identified, or projected costs need to be reduced.

Responsibility for managing costs in accordance with the budget may be assigned to appropriate personnel within the business with a delegated authority to tolerate changes within defined bounds.

An annual budget needs to be reviewed periodically, and at least quarterly, by the leadership team. Such reviews will match projected costs against actuals,

Table 8.2 Sample Annual Budget, Subdivided by Month

| Heading | Detail item | Budgeted spend by time | | | | | | | | | Year Total |
		Month-1	Month-2	Month-3	Q1 Total	Month-4	Month-5	Month-6	Q2 Total	etc.	
Heading-1	Item-1	1,000	1,200	1,500	3,700	2,000	2,500	2,750	7,250	...	33,450
	item-2	150	150	150	450	175	175	175	525	...	2,475
	Total	1,150	1,350	1,650	4,150	2,175	2,675	2,925	7,775	...	35,925
Heading-2	Item-3	5,000	5,000	5,000	15,000	5,000	5,000	5,000	15,000	...	67,500
	Item-4	0	0	0	0	2,500	0	0	2,500	...	2,500
	Total	5,000	5,000	5,000	15,000	7,500	5,000	5,000	17,500	...	70,000
All headings	Total	6,150	6,350	6,650	19,150	9,675	7,675	7,925	25,275	...	105,925

Table 8.3 Sample Budget Headings

Heading	Detail items	
	Team costs	Fees, materials and other costs
Promotion and sales	Marketing, sales and customer management roles	Communications services and materials; customer community events; participation at exhibitions and conferences; promotional programmes; analyst and media engagement
Delivery and operations	Development, operations and infrastructure roles	Establishing and managing channels; equipment, infrastructure and logistics for development, delivery and support; production facilities; materials and supply chain; accommodation and transport
Value capture	Roles responsible for analysis of customer and market value	Collaboration costs; market and customer analysis services
Growth and scalability	Any specialist or incremental roles required	New operations, infrastructure and IT for scaling; assistance with pursuing and securing finance; additional accommodation and transport requirements
IP and protection	Innovation and design roles, and security specialists	IP protection fees; legal input from IP specialist; physical and cyber security; security vetting of staff and partners
Leadership and structure	Leadership and management team	Corporate legal input; taxation; bonus schemes and recognition; continuing professional development for all teams; professional services

and consider any required changes in the light of revised plans. Where necessary, the budget will be updated and rebalanced. As with the original process, the wider team may be involved in agreeing such changes to retain a sense of team buy-in.

Monitoring Company Performance

This is about reviewing achievement against targets. In broad terms, a review can determine four kinds of actions:

- If performance is above target, the team may decide to reframe their targets upwards and to review the opportunities offered.
- If performance is on target, the team may decide to continue with the current plan.

	Target	This period	Previous period	Change
Customer perspective				
indicator-1 (units)				
indicator-2 (units)				
Process perspective				
indicator-1 (units)				
indicator-2 (units)				

	Target	This period	Previous period	Change
Financial perspective				
indicator-1 (units)				
indicator-2 (units)				
Indicator-3 (units)				
Learning and development perspective				
indicator-1 (units)				
indicator-2 (units)				

Figure 8.3 *A sample layout for a balanced scorecard*

- If performance is below target, the team may decide to reframe their targets downwards or to retain existing targets and review options for improving performance.
- If performance is unclear or ambiguous because the wrong indicators are being measured or the measurements are deemed not to be reliable, the team may decide to reframe the indicators and targets and to establish the mechanisms whereby these can be captured and calculated.

The topic of key performance indicators is addressed in detail by Chapter 2. That chapter stresses the importance of choosing a blend of lead and lag indicators, together with the need to establish a balance of perspectives relating to customer, financial, process and learning considerations. An additional requirement is that the indicators selected are measurable at reasonable cost.

The indicators adopted can be evaluated periodically to inform decision making, both by the leadership team and in some cases also by other interested parties, such as investors and partners. The usual form for review is the balanced scorecard (BSC).

A BSC is a performance-monitoring approach that visualizes current performance and trends over time from differing perspectives to enable achievement to be assessed against targets, and hence to show progress towards objectives. Although Kaplan and Norton (1992) originally envisaged the BSC as a strategic planning tool, it has also proved to be useful for regular operational reporting. Many businesses combine the four perspectives into a single dashboard structure, along the lines of that shown in Figure 8.3.

When completing a scorecard for a period, it can be useful to use colour to highlight achievement or otherwise against targets. This can help reviews to focus on areas of principal concern.

Case Study: SportMagenta

Balanced Score Card for Performance Monitoring

In their initial framing of SportMagenta, Sonny and Zara defined a collection of performance indicators and associated targets, repeated here from Chapter 2 for convenience. Additional KPIs relating to CRR and CLV have been added following the analysis reported in Chapter 3.

Key performance indicators	Target	Perspective	Lead/ lag
Percentage user satisfaction with product	100%	Customer	Lead
Percentage of user base downloads	95%	Customer	Lag
Percentage of customer feedback requests satisfied per month	80%	Learning	Lead
Percentage of relevant platforms supported	95%	Process	Lag
Time required to support new platform (days)	3	Process	Lead
Percentage revenue increase by targeted clubs	5%	Financial	Lag
Percentage revenue increase by sponsors	5%	Financial	Lag
Recurring revenue growth month on month	10%	Financial	Lag
Recurring revenue growth year on year	200%	Financial	Lag
Customer retention rate average over time	85%	Customer	Lead
Gross margin growth month on month	5%	Financial	Lag
Gross margin growth year on year	150%	Financial	Lag
Customer lifetime value average over time	150,000	Customer	Lead

They work together to create a corresponding balanced scorecard and to establish the mechanisms, automated and manual, whereby actual values for each indicator can be calculated at the end of each month.

At the end of month three, following initial pilot activity, the venture's balanced scorecard is as shown below.

The founders recognize that they have some way to go with many of their indicators, but are heartened by the increases achieved over the past month. An area of concern is the number of relevant platforms supported, which has still not increased beyond 85 per cent. Zara recommends that the target for this indicator is reduced due to the significant development costs required and the negative impact of relevant activities on development priorities that more closely align with increased gross margin. The founders agree to this change.

Customer perspective

	Target	This period	Previous period	Change
Percentage user satisfaction with product	100%	80%	55%	45%
Percentage of user base downloads	95%	50%	40%	25%
Customer retention rate average over time	85%	100%	100%	0%
Customer lifetime value average over time	150,000	80,000	50,000	60%

Process perspective

	Target	This period	Previous period	Change
Percentage of relevant platforms supported	95%	85%	85%	0%
Time required to support new platform (days)	3	3	5	40%

Financial perspective

	Target	This period	Previous period	Change
Percentage revenue increase by sponsors	10%	20%	17.5%	14%
Percentage revenue increase by targeted clubs	15%	15%	12.5%	20%
Monthly recurring revenue achieved	30,000	40,000	35,000	14%
Monthly gross margin achieved	75%	60%	55.0%	9%

Learning and development perspective

	Target	This period	Previous period	Change
Percentage of customer feedback requests satisfied	80.0%	75%	50.0%	50%

Company Reporting and Taxation

The final aspect of a company's financial governance requirements addressed by this chapter relates to statutory reporting requirements and company taxation.

Although these matters vary significantly across territories, a collection of generally applicable requirements can be factored out, and a summary of these is provided here.

Statutory Reporting Requirements

These subdivide into annual reporting requirements and sales tax returns.

Annual Reporting

Most territories require companies to prepare, disclose and file annual reports on their activities, including financial performance. The specific information required varies according to the size of company and whether it is privately held or publicly listed. Financial statements are compiled in accordance with accounting practices such as IFRS or GAAP.

The information provided in annual returns may be of interest to shareholders, potential investors and other parties such as competitors and potential partners.

In the USA, publicly listed corporations are required annually to file a 10-K report plus quarterly 10-Q reports. Privately held companies are not required to file financial disclosure documents with government regulators, which means that detailed financials are not readily available to the public, other than through research organizations.

UK reporting requirements vary with company size. For small companies, there is no need for an audit, and the requirements are as follows:

- *Micro companies* (typically fewer than ten employees) need only provide a balance sheet.
- *Small companies* (typically fewer than fifty employees) need only provide a balance sheet with notes, plus the name and signature of a director.

For medium and larger companies, the UK requirement is extended to include a profit and loss account, notes about the accounts and a director's report. An auditor's report may also be required, unless the company claims exemption. Reports are available online from Companies House, for the most part at no cost.

It is important that a venture is aware of its requirements for annual filing: failure to meet statutory reporting time frames can lead to fines and wasted time.

Sales Tax Returns

Most territories apply some form of sales tax that businesses must add to the price of their goods and services, unless they can claim exemption. These taxes are collected from sales receipts by businesses and are periodically paid to the tax authorities through a *returns* procedure.

In the USA, this requirement applies to all businesses, although the details vary by state. Returns can be completed and filed online monthly, quarterly or annually.

In the UK, there is a turnover threshold above which a business must register, collect and pay UK value-added tax (VAT). The threshold is currently around £85,000 ($115,000). Returns are usually completed quarterly.

Inspections can be made by the authorities to ensure correct recording and payment of taxes, and fines can be levied in the event of delayed, incorrect or fraudulent activity.

Company Taxation

Corporation tax is paid annually by a company on its taxable profits. The calculation varies significantly by territory.

From 2018, US corporation tax (or *corporate income* tax) at the federal level has been set at a flat rate of 21 per cent. Additionally, local income taxes are payable. These vary from state to state and range between 1 and 12 per cent of taxable income.

In the UK, the normal rate of corporation tax will be 19 per cent from April 2017, and 17 per cent from April 2020. Payment is usually made nine months and one day after the end of the applicable accounting period.

A careful choice of year-end date for the company's accounting period can help to balance the treatment of tax liabilities, especially at the early stage of a venture. Territories vary in the applicable rules for setting and changing accounting periods.

Other taxes payable by companies include employment-related taxes such as:

- *Payroll tax* in the USA; referred to in the UK as *pay-as-you-earn.*
- *Unemployment tax* in the USA; comparable with *national insurance* in the UK.

These are collected monthly and paid directly to tax authorities.

It is important to determine when taxes will become payable and to assess the likely amount due, so that these costs can be anticipated in the cash flow forecast.

Company Legal Structures

Types of Business Entity

A business entity is an organization that is formed and operated to perform business activities, charitable work or other activities. Several commonly applied types of entity are recognized across the legal systems of most territories and, although their specific rules vary from place to place, the broad concept and operation of these types is similar.

These principal types of business entity are summarized below. Consistent with the purpose and scope of this book, all types of business entities are here referred to as companies: a company is the legal vehicle through which business is performed.

Sole Traders and Partnerships

A sole trader, or *sole proprietor*, is the simplest of business structures. Under this approach, the company is entirely owned and operated by an individual with no legal distinction between themselves and their business. The sole trader or proprietor is entitled to all the profits, and is responsible for all the debts, losses and liabilities.

A sole tradership or proprietorship is an individual person conducting business activities, and so is not a separate legal entity. Other than in respect of the treatment of company names, the legal treatment of these entities is similar in many countries, including the USA and the UK. No formal action is required to form a company and the business itself is not treated separately from the individual in respect of taxation.

A variation on this approach is where two or more sole traders decide to form a partnership. Partnerships in the UK must be registered with the tax authorities. However, the legal approach is similar to that for sole traders, in that the partners personally take responsibility for the business: they share the business's profits, and each partner pays tax on their share. In the USA, each state has its own statutes and common law governing such partnerships.

Private Limited Liability Companies and Corporations

A private company or *corporation* is an independent legal entity that is owned by its shareholders. Significantly, it is the company itself, and not its shareholders, that is legally liable for its actions and debts, so long as it has operated within the law. This is the usual vehicle for digital ventures with growth ambition.

Because it is a separate legal entity, the company's finances and taxation are separate from those of its founders and shareholders. A shareholder's financial liability is limited to a fixed sum, usually the value of their investment in a company. Although shareholders' liability for the company's actions are limited, they are still liable for their own activities. This can apply where personal guarantees have been provided or where laws have been broken.

In the UK, the normal vehicle is the *limited company* (denoted Ltd), which can be registered through government online services or purchased through one of several online formation service businesses and can cost as little as $20. Such companies must have a pay-as-you-earn system established for collecting income tax payments and national insurance contributions from employees. A variation on the normal limited company structure is the *private company limited by guarantee*, in which shareholders' liability is limited to a fixed amount; this form is often used by charities and social enterprise groups.

In the USA, the normal vehicle for creating such companies is a *C corporation* (denoted Inc), which needs to be formed under the laws of the state in which it is registered. Another option is an *S corporation*, which differs in that profits and losses can pass directly through to the personal tax returns of its owners.

The rules differ across European countries. In Germany, the equivalent structure is a GmbH (Gesellschaft mit beschrankter Haftung) in which shareholders' liability is limited to the total amount of legal capital, which is set at a minimum of €25,000 ($30,000).

Limited Liability Partnerships

This hybrid legal structure provides the limited liability features of a company or corporation and the tax efficiencies and flexibility of a partnership.

As with limited-liability companies, these are recognized as legal entities separate from their owners, who are referred to as *members*. In the USA, these entities are called limited liability companies (LLCs), and in the UK, they are called limited liability partnerships (LLPs). The principles are similar in both cases, although in the USA, an LLC is not technically a corporate body because its legal existence is time limited.

Unlike limited companies or corporations, LLCs and LLPs are not taxed as separate business entities: their profits and losses pass to each member, who is then responsible for reporting these on their personal tax returns. Because they are recognized as independent entities, their liabilities are joint but not several, so that one member is not responsible or liable for another's actions or misconduct.

This structure is commonly used for partnerships of professionals, such as lawyers and accountants.

Public Companies

A public company is one whose shares are listed and traded on a public stock exchange and can be bought and sold by anyone. Public companies are more closely regulated than private companies, and are governed by stronger reporting regulations. This vehicle is also treated as a separate legal entity from its owners.

A business may choose to *go public* to raise money for expansion, or to provide an exit strategy for its shareholders. The process usually involves an initial public offering (IPO), whereby an investment bank is contracted to underwrite the shares by assuming legal responsibility for them. The underwriter sells the shares to the public, with the aim of achieving a higher price than was paid to the original owners.

In the USA, a private corporation that achieves a stock market listing is referred to as a publicly listed corporation. In the UK, a listed company is called a public limited company (denoted plc), and must have a minimum share capital of £50,000 ($62,000).

Establishing a Typical Legal Structure

The process of setting up a company in the USA varies by state. In the UK, the process can be performed directly with Companies House, or indirectly through an online formation service provider.

In the UK, registering (or *incorporating*) a private limited company involves providing the following details:

- A company name, and there are rules on what this can and cannot include.
- A registered address for the company, which may be a personal address or the address of the company's accountant.
- The details of at least one director and at least one shareholder.
- A *memorandum of association*, documenting the agreement of the initial shareholders (or *subscribers*) to create the company.

- A *statement of capital* for the company, detailing its shares and their associated rights.
- *Articles of association* for the company, defining the rules about how it will
  be run.

The *articles of association* are sometimes referred to, together with the *memorandum of association*, as the company's *constitution*. Standard (or *model*) forms
of these are available and are adequate for the initial purposes of most businesses. These documents are updated over time in line with changes to the
business and its operations.

Other than choosing its name and a suitable address, a company's *statement
of capital* embraces the principal set of decisions required at the outset. This
needs to state:

- The currency in which the company will usually trade.
- The classes of shares to be issued (addressed in a later section).
- The number of shares of each class to be issued.
- The *nominal* value per share of each class (see below).
- The amount paid or due per share. If this is the nominal value, the shares are
  fully paid.
- The amount unpaid per share (where payment will be received later).
- The voting rights to be associated with each class of share.

The nominal, or *par*, or *face* value of a share is chosen independently of its
current market value. The market value of a share is usually higher than its
nominal value and the difference is called the *share premium*. If a company
intends to distribute shares to its employees, then setting a low nominal value
can make them more affordable. Also, setting a low nominal value means that a
larger number of shares will be available within any authorized limit, which will
give greater flexibility over future distributions. Shares may not be issued at a
discount on their nominal value.

The statement of capital can be very simple at the time of incorporation. For
example, the initial share capital might include 100 × £1, or 1,000 × £0.1,
ordinary shares. It is not necessary to state at the time of incorporation the
maximum number of shares that can be issued, as the requirement for such a
limit was abolished in the UK in 2006. A limit may, however, be imposed in the
articles of association to control future dilution of existing shareholders. Where
a limit is in place, the board will need to file an ordinary resolution to increase
this before issuing additional shares. If no limit applies, then the number of
shares issued can be increased at any time.

In the UK, a *certificate of incorporation* is issued by Companies House to confirm that a company legally exists. This shows its company number and date of formation.

Many ventures establish a legal structure comprising multiple entities, typically including a holding company and a collection of subsidiaries, each of which is wholly or partly owned by the holding company. Although this requires a degree of administration, it can offer several benefits, including the following:

- The flexibility of using distinct companies to pursue diverse offerings and/or sectors, each with its own board of directors and share structure.
- A structure within which to create a new subsidiary associated with a new venture, such as a JV or a new high-risk market exploration.
- There can be tax advantages from being able to manage costs across a group of companies.
- Creating a holding company that owns the venture's IP can protect that asset from the contractual risks to which operating companies may be exposed.

Joint Ventures

A joint venture (JV) is a contractual business undertaking between two or more parties. It may be established as a separate legal entity (a limited company or corporation), or as a contractual or less-formal collaboration. A JV may be limited in time or may be enduring, depending upon the nature of the collaboration.

Individuals or companies enter joint ventures to share strengths, address risks, or to increase reach or competitive advantages in a larger marketplace. The world's longest-running JV between a Japanese and an American company is Fuji Xerox, formed in 1962 to exploit the mutual strengths of the two companies in the Asia-Pacific region. With smaller businesses, such ventures can be more transient, often responding to opportunities for mutually beneficial promotion or development activities.

The parties within a JV will have rights and responsibilities over the management and control of the venture and will share in its profits or losses. Where the JV is established as a separate legal entity, it will have its own board, usually comprising members drawn from the participating parties.

Having a signed JV agreement is beneficial for clarity and performance management. This will normally define the objectives and targets of the venture, the responsibilities and duties of each participating party, and the treatment of IP and other rights. In cases where the partnership is established as a separate legal entity, the agreement may be embodied within the constitution of the JV company. In other cases, it can take the form of a legally binding contract or as a less-formal *memorandum of understanding* between the parties.

Before entering into a JV, it is important to consider the cultures and chemistry of the other parties involved, because personal frictions and different ways of working can provoke stress and frustration. Fundamentally, however, the success of a JV usually comes down to how well the JV performs against its objectives and whether there is mutual trust and respect between parties.

Situations change, and what makes sense at one time may not work so well a short time after. For this reason, it is important that any JV agreement provides for termination of the partnership. This may be permitted by mutual agreement of parties at a pre-assigned time, upon the accomplishment of its purpose, or in the event that serious disagreements between the members make its continuation impracticable.

Franchises

A franchise is not a different type of legal entity, but another means of growing and scaling. Under this approach, *franchisees* are granted the rights to use a business's brand and way of operating, usually for a limited period of time. Offering franchises avoids the investment and liabilities required by a franchiser to replicate a chain of outlets. The approach is widely used in the retail sector across many territories by, for example, Macdonald's, 7-eleven and Subway.

Franchisors are usually rewarded through a percentage of sales achieved by the franchisee and a management fee that covers:

- A royalty for use of the franchisor's brands.
- The costs of any training and advisory services provided by the franchisor.

In the USA, the Federal Trade Commission has oversight of franchising. In the UK, there are no franchise-specific laws, and so franchises are subject to the same laws that govern other businesses.

The approach is not widely used with digital businesses, although it offers a scalability option for ventures where the offering is amenable to being packaged as a commodity offering for a particular market.

Contractual Structures and Responsibilities

Contractually speaking, a company has a board of directors and a collection of employees, and it may from time to time engage contractors. Each of these has responsibilities, rights and obligations, and it is important that a venture establishes and sustains its team with appropriate structural and contractual mechanisms.

Directors may also be employees of the business with their responsibilities and reward set out in a service contract. In the USA, any officer of a company is treated also as an employee.

Employees' duties and remuneration are defined through a *contract of employment*, the details of which vary across territories. Legally speaking, if a company loses money or fails in one of its duties, then employees are not held to the same level of responsibility as directors.

Contractors differ from employees in that their roles are defined through an arm's-length service contract. Unlike employees, they are usually responsible for their own tax affairs.

This section addresses each of these three positions in respect of relevant requirements and considerations. Finally, it reviews the needs of a venture for professional services.

The Board of Directors

A director is an officer of a company or corporation who has been appointed to manage business activities and finances and to ensure that statutory obligations are met. They must act lawfully and honestly in their dealings, and their decisions must be to the benefit of the company.

The collection of directors constitutes the company's board. Once appointed, directors serve at the discretion of the board. A director can be removed by a majority vote of shareholders.

Many businesses recognize two distinct categories of director:

- *Executive directors*, who are authorized by the board to carry out certain functions, such as chief executive officer (CEO), managing director (MD), chief technology officer (CTO) or chief financial officer (CFO).
- *Non-executive directors* (NEDs), who have no executive responsibilities and whose role is more oriented towards providing wider market access, stature or credibility, or objective advice and governance.

An NED is legally a director and so carries the same legal responsibilities as an executive director. Whereas an executive director is normally remunerated with a salary, possibly plus shares and other benefits, an NED is more usually remunerated with shares, although an annual service charge may also apply. In the UK, the chairman role is often played by an NED.

From a legal perspective, in most territories, there is only one category of director, so the legal responsibilities apply irrespective of their title or actual day-to-day involvement. In the UK, company law embodies these responsibilities in the following seven requirements:

- To act within the powers granted to them in the company's articles of association.
- To promote the success of the business.
- To exercise independent judgement in all decision-making.
- To use reasonable care, skill and diligence at all times.
- To avoid or declare any conflict of interest.
- To avoid accepting benefits from third parties or using their position to make private profits.
- To declare beforehand any interest in a proposed transaction or arrangement.

Alongside these statutory duties, there is also a code of conduct for directors which requires that they consider the broader impact of any decision. Martin (2008) provides a comprehensive coverage of the role of the company director in the UK.

Additional directors' responsibilities are usually defined within the company's articles of association. These may include the following:

- Monitoring the financial position of the company.
- Timely filing of annual accounts and tax returns.
- Timely payment of corporation tax and any other tax liabilities.
- Attending board meetings.
- Appointing solicitors, accountants and auditors.
- Issuing and/or transferring shares.
- Complying with employment law.
- Complying with health and safety legislation.

Company directors are not personally responsible for business debts if they have not broken the law.

As a business develops, its directors usually assume titles to reflect their specific areas of responsibility within the board, including chairman or president, CEO, MD, CTO and CFO. Adopting naming conventions for directors has the advantage of helping customers and partners understand the level of seniority and power that attaches to the person with whom they are, or will be, dealing. This can be especially important for ventures that need to engage with larger organizations.

In the USA, certain named officers (typically president, secretary and treasurer) are usually required by the laws of the state in which the company is incorporated. It is conventional that the president takes charge of internal management of the business, while the CEO is responsible for external relations. In the UK, a conventional distinction is for the CEO to be focused on business strategy, alignment and development, whereas the MD will focus on operations and management.

Whatever naming conventions are adopted by the board of directors, the priority is to identify and assign the leadership roles that are needed to achieve the business objectives and sustain the day-to-day operations. This means distributing responsibilities across the members of the board and ensuring that the individuals nominated have the competence and support needed.

This can prove challenging as a venture grows and scales, because new requirements can emerge that challenge the abilities of the founding members. This can be a point of contention for investors, who will demand confidence in the venture's future board.

Employees

An employee is hired to provide services on a regular basis in exchange for compensation. They may have a contract of employment, and will therefore operate under the protection of the applicable employment legislation. By contrast, contractors, or associates, have a contract to provide specific services on a freelance basis. Although teams might mix employees and contractors, and their roles and contributions can overlap, it can be important to acknowledge that their legal positions differ.

In the UK, employment is treated by law as a right that gets stronger with the employee's length of service. Employees have a contract of employment that defines legal obligations and protections, and employers need a good reason to terminate employment. Such reasons can include the position becoming redundant (in which case, the employee receives notice and a lump-sum payment), or an act of gross misconduct by the employee. Amending a contract in the UK requires consultation and agreement.

In the USA, written employment contracts are not usual, except with senior management positions. Job offer letters are more normal. In most cases, employees are employed *at will*, which means that either party can terminate the employment for any lawful reason without either cause or notice, and without fear of legal action. Furthermore, an employer can change the terms and conditions of an *at-will* employee at any time. If employment is not to be on this basis, then a written contract of employment sets out the terms that are to apply.

There are additional differences between employment law in the UK and the USA, including in respect of the treatment of sick pay. In general, there is no right to sick pay in the USA, although some states have passed local laws that guarantee it. In most of the USA, if an employee cannot work, then they get no compensation from their employer. In the UK, however, most employees qualify for statutory sick pay.

Much of UK employment law originated in the EU and so the comments above also reflect legal practice across other European territories. There is, however, complexity over the decision of which specific territory's laws should apply in cases where a dispute arises from an employee who is operating in a different country from that in which their employer is based. A practice guide that addresses this situation has been published by the European Commission (2016).

In the UK, a contract of employment usually sets out employment conditions, rights, responsibilities and duties, covering at least the following:

- The venture's name.
- The employee's name, job title (or description) and start date.
- How much and how often the employee will be paid, and by what mechanism.
- The normal hours of work.
- The annual holiday entitlement (and whether that includes public holidays).
- The location at which the employee will be working.
- The handling of IP generated by the employee.
- Confidentiality and non-disclosure.
- The required notice period if the employee decides to leave.
- Any pension arrangement that is offered (employers will have to provide a workplace pension for eligible staff by 2018).

- Any other benefits to be provided, such as share options or medical insurance.
- The company's procedure for handling complaints and grievances.
- Any restrictive covenants that are to apply when the employee leaves the company, including not poaching former colleagues or approaching the company's customers within a set time frame.

It can be useful to apply a more limited form of contract during an introductory period of, say, three months. At the end of that period, the full contract provisions will come into effect. This allows for situations where the employee does not fit into the team, or where some other factors come to light that did not surface in the interview process.

A contract comes into effect as soon as someone accepts an offer of employment in the UK, even if the agreement is not written down. Both employer and employee can be disadvantaged by not having a written contract, because either party can claim a certain right or responsibility, and resolving the matter is likely to cause friction and disruption within the venture. It is, therefore, advisable for a venture to adopt a normal form of contract and to ensure that a corresponding agreement is signed by both parties whenever a new employee joins.

Contractors

Businesses usually hire contractors to perform specialist tasks or to provide a temporary increase in capacity. In some business areas, the use of self-employed or agency workers is normal, for organizational or economic reasons.

The same principle applies as with employees: a written agreement should exist between the venture and the contractor to cover the terms of their engagement. This will normally cover the following:

- The services to be delivered and the relevant time frame.
- The payments to be made, and when and under what conditions these will become due.
- Assumptions of tax handling by the contractor.
- The handling of IP generated by the contractor.
- Confidentiality and non-disclosure.
- The contractor's liabilities and any warranties provided.
- Any restrictive covenants that are to apply when the contributor leaves the service of the company, including not poaching former colleagues or approaching former customers within a set time frame.

UK tax avoidance legislation (referred to as IR35) aims to identify contractors who operate as *disguised employees*, to ensure that they pay the relevant taxes. This legislation applies particularly to contractors who work primarily for a single customer, who are controlled like employees and where no right of substitution is available in the event of the contractor's non-availability.

For this reason, it is important when hiring contractors that the venture does not expose itself to the risk of being investigated under this rule because it can also become liable. It is advisable that the form of contract is validated for compliance with applicable tax avoidance legislation.

Professional Service Requirements

The requirements for professional services vary across businesses, and also by time. The commonly used types of service and the principal considerations are as follows.

Legal Services

Services may be required to assist company set-up and registration, or for specialist input in respect of IP registration, employment, specific market regulations and legal compliance requirements.

The requirement for legal support on company start-up varies by territory and by complexity of business. In the UK, unless the envisaged business has unusual aspects, a company can be set up online without specialist support. If, on the other hand, it will be required to operate across multiple territories, or comprise multiple entities with associated IP arrangements, or adopt an unusual constitution, then seeking professional advice may be appropriate. In the USA, every state requires a registered agent to represent the company within that state if the company has been incorporated or authorized to do business there.

The need for specialist IP services depends on the IP-richness of the venture. If a patentable process or a distinctive design is central, then specialist assistance with preparing and filing relevant applications is advisable. A patent or design application produced by an expert can bring significantly greater powers of protection and enforceability. This is because the technicalities in the wording applied in such registrations can have unforeseen consequences for those not versed in the art.

The same applies for specialist employment law considerations, where the rights of employees in certain territories may differ from those assumed.

Thinking like an investor means recognizing the importance of protecting those aspects of the business that are valuable and not exposing the business to unquantified future risk. For some entrepreneurs, the need for access to a first-rate lawyer is beyond question.

Banking

Every company needs a bank account on set-up, and this will usually provide services such as online transactions and international payment services, over-draft provision for cash-flow flexibility and, where required, a company credit card for purchases.

Choosing a bank that is sympathetic to the business, and which offers a personal point of contact, can be an attractive consideration for some ventures.

Accountancy and Finance

Some ventures are fortunate to include people with accountancy skills who can establish required procedures for bookkeeping and company reporting. For ventures that do not have this advantage, several excellent online account packages are now available at minimal cost, and adopting one of these can be sufficient to enable non-financial people to handle routine transactions and tax calculations. Alternatively, the services of a professional accounting company may deliver efficiencies in terms of enabling the team to focus on its business without the distraction of questions about practice or procedure.

The requirement for professional assistance with finance and taxation grows with the venture. When choosing an accountant, it can be useful to ensure a degree of common empathy between the individuals in the accounting company and those in the venture, such that the questions that emerge from business activities can be resolved efficiently and without misunderstandings.

Insurance

In line with applicable legislation, every venture has legal obligations to estab-lish certain types of insurance such as for public and employer's liability. As addressed by Chapter 7, these requirements need to be known and complied with.

Additional to these are the risk-driven decisions about insurance offerings for professional indemnity and to cover eventualities such as damage to contents or loss of key people. Where the requirements are not trivial or of a commodity nature, it can be advisable to identify an insurance broker that can act on behalf of the venture to identify and establish appropriate policies. As the cost of a broker is usually borne by the insurance providers, the advantages of their specialist advice may be achieved at relatively little cost.

Health and Safety

The need for specialist input to health and safety depends very much on the nature of the business and especially on its need to handle potentially dangerous materials or processes. In such cases, industry-specific regulations and services may overlap with risk-driven insurance considerations.

Some territories expect a safety handbook as a minimal requirement: templates can be purchased online for customization.

Property and Investment

The impression communicated by a venture's address and premises can be significant and so needs to be considered coherently with promotional messaging.

Some ventures need premises with space for equipment and facilities for customer demonstrations and workshops; others need very little by way of physical presence. In all cases, the visitor experience needs to be designed to confirm and enhance the venture's reputation, reliability and professionalism, because small presentational issues can have a large reputational impact. A tangential anecdote from the airline industry applies here: a passenger who folds down their tray-table and finds it dirty may conclude that the airline's maintenance procedures will be just as shabby, and hence choose a different carrier next time.

Likewise, location can have a significant impact on business success: propinquity with high-performing, interesting or entrepreneurial organizations can give confidence *by association* to visitors. For this reason, siting the venture's premises on a science park or in a lively tech zone can be worthwhile, even though rental costs may be higher.

Thinking like an investor can be beneficial when considering property options, because business property can offer interesting opportunities for personal reward. If funds can be raised by the founders to purchase the premises, then the space can be leased to the venture, hence makes good use of the necessary costs of accommodation. Additionally, there can be taxation advantages in some territories. In the UK, the self-invested private pension (SIPP) scheme offers an approach to business property investment whereby rental payments by tenants can attract pension benefits. Some entrepreneurs generate significant wealth from their property portfolios by thoughtful investment of business rents that would have otherwise been paid to independent landlords.

Shareholding Structures and Agreements

A company's shareholding is a fundamental asset that needs to be designed and managed consistently with its objectives. Considerations of control, flexibility, motivation and reward can lead to the need for different types (or *classes*) of shares for different kinds of current and future shareholders.

The UK and US terminologies (*share* and *shareholding* versus *stock* and *stockholding*) can be used interchangeably.

Shares and Options

A company can be established with a single class of *ordinary* or *common* shares. In such cases, company equity holdings, voting rights and dividends paid will all simply be proportionate to the numbers of shares held. All shareholders have the same rights and enjoy the same benefits.

All companies are required to have ordinary shares as part of their stock, as defined in their articles of association, and at least one ordinary share must be issued. In addition to ordinary shares, some companies choose to issue *preference shares* and *share options* for particular purposes, as described below.

Preference shares rank above ordinary shares when it comes to payment of dividends and return of capital (say, on liquidation). Preference shares may or may not carry voting rights and are sometimes used to pay out a dividend at fixed points in the year. These properties make *prefs* attractive to some investors. They can be converted into ordinary shares.

Share option schemes are often designed to offer employees a tax-efficient way to share in the success of the company. They can be relatively easy to implement and employers have a high level of flexibility in choosing how the scheme will operate.

A share option entitles its holder to buy a share at an agreed price on a future date, with an expectation that the share will have increased in value when the option is *exercised*. The option may be associated with a *vesting* arrangement (see below), or may be subject to individual or team performance targets. The granting of options means that no purchase of shares is required by an employee until the shares have increased in value, with the intention that this increase will cover the purchase cost.

Vesting arrangements are widely applied in the USA and are increasingly used in the UK. The process works by issuing shares or options associated with time or performance-based rules whereby these can be earned. An employee's shares may be granted on a staggered basis over a period of time, or the employee may be required to hold the shares for a specified number of years. Additional rules may define what will happen to these rights in the event of an investment or IPO event. The approach is attractive because it can provide motivational incentives for employees while safeguarding the interests of the other shareholders.

In the USA, incentive stock options (ISOs) are a type of stock option that enables employees to receive advantageous tax treatment. ISOs must be held by an employee for at least one year after the date of exercise if the favourable capital gains tax is to be achieved. The scheme places a $100,000 limit on the value of ISO stock that can be exercised in any year, and applies a rule that the exercise price must match or exceed the value of the stock on the grant date. Importantly, the granting of options is not taxable, and employees pay no regular federal income tax when an ISO is exercised. Where required, ISOs can be subject to performance or time-based vesting conditions.

In the UK, the Enterprise Management Incentive (EMI) is available to companies with assets of £30 million or less, and with fewer than 250 employees. The maximum value of shares held by an option holder at the date an option is granted is £250,000, and they must be in employment and working at least 75 per cent of their time with the company.

EMI is highly beneficial in terms of taxation, as no tax is payable by the employee or the employer on the grant of an EMI option. When such options are exercised, say as part of a financial investment or other M&A transaction, capital gains tax may be payable by the employee on the difference between the exercise price and the value of the shares when the options were granted. For this reason, the valuation associated with granting of EMI shares can have a significant impact on the value of the shares to the employees, as it may determine the tax that they will pay following any transaction.

The valuation approach underlying the establishment of an EMI scheme is usually performed by the venture's auditors, who will apply the rules recommended by the relevant tax authorities. Currently, in the UK, these rules include an assessment of two valuations: actual market value (AMV) and unrestricted market value (UMV), technical terms devised by UK tax authorities. Essentially, the former is a lower value that takes account of various restrictions that may limit the value of the shares, whereas the latter ignores any such considerations.

Structuring Multiple Share Classes

When designing an equity structure for a company, it can be useful to create multiple classes of shares to provide flexibility in respect of, for example:

- Being able to pay dividends at chosen levels to particular groups of shareholders.
- Being able to provide voting or other rights to particular classes of shareholders.
- Being able to limit the voting or other rights of particular groups of shareholders.

New classes can be created and issued after a company has been established, so this decision does not necessarily need to be taken at start-up. All advanced economies recognize and support the need for this flexibility.

When issuing multiple classes, the usual convention – the *alphabet* approach – is to denote the classes as A, B, C and so on. Each class will be defined in the articles of association in terms of its voting rights, dividend-paying status, rights on liquidation and other applicable rules, such as what happens to shares when an employee shareholder leaves the company.

The structure by which these classes are defined is called a *capitalization table*, or *cap table*. This is usually a spreadsheet that shows the share classes and ownership, including ordinary shares, preference shares and options, and the various prices that have been paid for these through successive rounds of investment or restructuring.

The cap table needs to be kept up to date. Transactions such as selling or issuing new shares, or creating, granting or terminating options, can all affect the table and hence the equity holdings and voting rights of shareholders. An up-to-date and comprehensive cap table is necessary for an entrepreneur to make informed decisions on opportunities and required changes. Figure 8.4

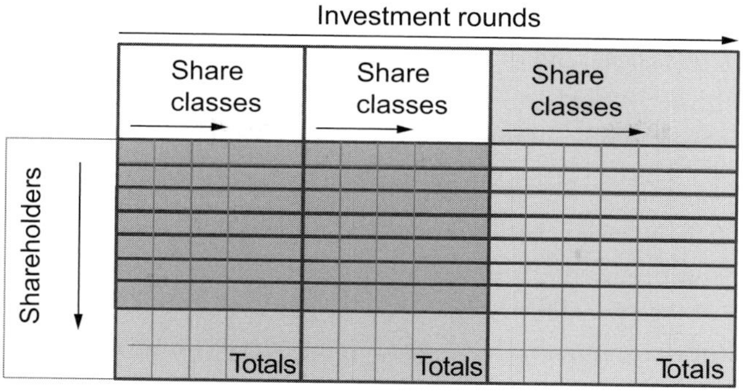

Figure 8.4 *Illustrative capitalization table structure*

provides an outline cap table structure for illustrative purposes. Templates are available on the internet.

Each round of investment restructures the cap table to reflect the requirements and interest of the investors and their intentions for the company. This can include the issuing of additional classes of shares for the following purposes:

- *Management shares*, which usually have additional voting rights to enable control of the company by particular parties.
- *Sweet equity shares*, which are issued at a lower price to motivate management.

Case Study: SportMagenta

Accounting Valuation for Share Option Creation

Because the initial market for the offering has been determined to be UK sports club chains, the founders initially establish the company in the UK as SportMagenta Limited.

At the time of creating the company, and before it establishes a trading history, Sonny and Zara decide to create a share option pool to motivate the loyalty and dedication of their employees. This means that they need to value the business for accounting purposes to ensure that a reasonable value will be associated with the options when they are granted to employees. They understand that an unrealistically low company valuation may lead to their future employees incurring large tax charges in the event of future M&A transactions.

When they establish the company, the founders decide to create two classes of ordinary shares: class 'A' and class 'B'. These will have identical rights, except that the A shares will be limited to being able to appoint a single director to the board. They will, however, come before B's on return of capital in the event that the business fails.

The company is established with issued share capital of a million shares comprising 100,000 class A ordinary shares and 900,000 class B ordinary shares. All shares will have a nominal value of £0.001, giving the company an initial capitalization of £1,000.

Sonny and Zara individually have good track records and networks from previous ventures, and between them are able to secure £100,000 from an angel investor called Paschar in exchange for the 100,000 A shares. Sonny and Zara plan to divide the B shares equally.

This means that Paschar paid £1 per share for a 10 per cent shareholding. In crude terms, therefore, this gives a market value of the company at (£1 × 1,000,000) = £1 million.

Paschar, Sonny and Zara decide to create an EMI option pool of 10 per cent of as yet unissued shares that will dilute all three shareholders equally. These will be granted to future employees who demonstrate the ability and willingness to make a significant contribution to the business. The shareholders' intention is to achieve some form of significant company transaction – a major investment, acquisition or flotation – within the next three years.

From an accounting perspective, the value of the share options to be established will be driven by the value of the investment so far made: £1 per share for 100,000 A shares.

As the new EMI shares will have fewer rights than A's, a discount of about 30 per cent might be recommended by the company's auditor, indicating an actual market value for the new shares of around £0.7 per share. The auditor might then calculate the unrestricted market value by applying a 10 per cent premium to reflect the relaxation of actual market restrictions, and hence recommend a value of around £0.77 per share. The founders understand and accept that future employee option holders may be required to pay capital gains tax on the difference between this valuation and any increased market valuation of the shares that can be achieved through the venture's activities.

Shareholders' Agreements

The structures, rights and rules applying to each class of share are defined in the company's articles of association. This is a formal legal document that may be available publicly. Due to its legal language, it can often be long, and not useful as a working document.

By contrast, a *shareholders' agreement* (or *stockholders' agreement* in the USA) is established for private use within the company. It covers and regulates the interests of all shareholders and all classes of shares, although summary versions may be created for specific classes for shareholders unfamiliar with corporate legal language. It is binding on the shareholders.

In general terms, the content of a shareholders' agreement will at least set out:

- The shareholders' rights and obligations.
- The rules for sale or transfer of shares in the company.
- The rules for appointing and removing directors.
- The rules for providing management information to shareholders.
- The protection to be provided for minority shareholders.
- The confidentiality requirements.
- The rules for paying dividends.
- The dispute resolution procedure.
- Exit provisions, including *drag* and *tag*.
- Leaver provisions for employee shareholders.
- Any restrictive covenants, including limiting shareholders for the period while they hold shares and for a period afterwards from association with a competing company, or from soliciting customers or employees.

As it is a confidential company document, a shareholders' agreement might also be used to express other issues of internal company regulation beyond those expressed in the articles, including:

- Matters relating to remuneration of directors.
- The giving of rights, or imposing of obligations, such as binding a person's shareholding to their capacity as director.
- The requirement on a long-term shareholder who leaves the company to dispose of their shares. This can be a sensitive matter because a shareholder who has invested in developing a business may feel that they have earned the right to keep their shares and so benefit from its future growth. On the other hand, the company may be concerned about loss of control over its equity, and also the potential for a non-contributor to benefit from future activities. One solution in such cases can be the issue of a special class of *capped value* shares.

Shareholders' agreements are contracts covered by contract law, whereas articles of association are constitutional documents, covered under corporate law. As the two documents typically contain overlapping material, there is a potential for conflict. Should this situation arise, it may be important to bear in mind that, for external parties, only the constitutional document will apply, and that a court will be unlikely to grant an injunction or award damages in relation to a shareholders' agreement where to do so would be inconsistent with the company's articles.

Summary of Leadership and Structure

The principal responsibility of a venture's leadership team is to establish and work within its legal structure to deliver the business objectives. This involves establishing and sustaining an organization to motivate and reward its people, plan and control its resources, and ensure that the venture complies with relevant reporting and taxation regimes.

Considerations of legal structure continue through the life of a venture, with important implications on its potential for motivating investment of effort and money. Understanding the available legal options and implications, and designing share structures that support business expansion ambitions, can contribute significantly to a venture's success. Conversely, poor structural decisions at any point in the development of a business can hamper its ability to attract investment or to retain its key staff, or even to reward its founders for their efforts.

The key points addressed by this chapter are summarized below.

- **Company leadership, management and governance** pose different requirements for personal competences, qualities and behaviours; diversity is needed, and it is important for a venture to achieve the right balance of each. An unbalanced leadership can have difficulty inspiring the confidence and commitment of a growing team in a changeable environment:
  - *Leadership* is about setting direction and inspiring the team to work to that end; *management* is about obtaining, empowering and controlling the resources needed for this to succeed; and *governance* is about establishing the structures, principles, rules and controls necessary for coherence and compliance.
  - Management considerations around *team reward and motivation* are sometimes overlooked by early-stage ventures, but can be critical in motivating the commitment and performance needed to meet business objectives.

- **Financial planning and control** is about establishing a governance regime that sets a rhythm for review of the venture's performance and obligations:
  - 'Turnover is vanity, profit is sanity, but cash is king.' If there is no cash, then a venture cannot pay its people or its suppliers, and it will be at risk of failing.
  - A balanced budget shows how projected costs will be met by projected incomes. Engaging the wider team in the budget-setting process can create a sense of transparency and mutual accountability over costs.
  - Monitoring company performance can use a balanced scorecard to visualize performance trends over time from differing perspectives, to enable achievement to be assessed against targets, and hence to show progress towards objectives.
  - It is important that a venture is aware of its requirements for annual filing of returns and payment of taxes due, because failure to meet statutory requirements can lead to fines and disruption.
- Establishing a **company legal structure** is about creating the legal business entities through which business will be performed:
  - Several commonly applied types of legal entity are recognized across the legal systems of most territories and, although their specific rules vary from place to place, the broad concept and operation of these types is similar.
  - The process for establishing a legal structure varies by territory. The typical vehicle in the USA is the C corporation; in the UK, it is the private limited company. Establishing a company involves defining an initial distribution of its equity, or shareholding.
  - A joint venture is a contractual business undertaking between two or more parties. It may be established as a separate legal entity or as a contractual or less formal collaboration.
  - The franchising approach is not widely used with digital businesses, although it offers a scalability option for ventures where the offering is amenable to being packaged as a commodity offering for a particular market.
- **Contractual structures and responsibilities** recognize the distinctions between directors, employees and contractors, and the relevant responsibilities, rights and obligations of each:
  - A director is an officer of a company appointed to manage business activities and finances and to ensure that statutory obligations are met. They must act lawfully and honestly in their dealings, and their decisions must be to the benefit of the company.

○ An employee is hired to provide services on a regular basis in exchange for compensation. They may have a contract of employment and will operate under the protection of applicable employment legislation.

○ A contractor, or associate, has a contract to provide specific services on a freelance basis, usually relating to a specialist task or to a need for temporary increase in capacity.

○ Requirements for professional services vary across businesses, and by time. Thinking like an investor can be beneficial when considering property options, because business property can offer interesting opportunities for personal reward.

• **Shareholding structures and agreements** recognize that a company's shareholding is a fundamental asset that needs to be designed and managed in a manner consistent with its objectives. Considerations of control, flexibility, motivation and reward lead to a need for different classes of shares for different kinds of current and future shareholders:

○ All companies are required to have ordinary shares as part of their stock, as defined in their articles of association, and at least one ordinary share must be issued. In addition to ordinary shares, some companies issue preference shares and share options.

○ It can be useful to create multiple classes of shares to give flexibility around the payment of dividends and a facility to provide or limit the rights of certain groups of shareholders.

○ A shareholders' agreement (or stockholders' agreement in the USA) is a contract that is binding on the shareholders and that is established for private use within the company.

ANALYSIS EXERCISES

The table below lists a collection of digital businesses to be used as subjects for the exercises that follow.

Business	Focus	Website
Darktrace	Cyber security	www.darktrace.com
EventBright	Event promotion and management	www.eventbrite.co.uk
Fitbit	Health, fitness and performance	www.fitbit.com
JustEat	Online takeaway food	www.just-eat.co.uk

Business	Focus	Website
Reposit	Property rental	www.getreposit.uk
Snapchat	Social media	www.snapchat.com
Sorry as a Service	Customer services and retention	www.sorryasaservice.com
SwiftComply	Regulation and compliance	www.swiftcomply.com

On the basis of information available in the public domain, address the questions below for at least one of the businesses listed.

1. The business's customer(s):
    (a) Who is the customer(s) for the proposed innovation?
    (b) Who are the principal players in the business's ecosystem?
    (c) What are the principal value exchanges with these players?

2. Company leadership, management and governance:
    (a) Suggest three responsibilities of the business's leadership team.
    (b) Suggest three management responsibilities within the business.
    (c) Suggest three governance responsibilities within the business.

3. Financial planning and control:
    (a) What would you consider to be the three most significant costs for the business?
    (b) Suggest three performance indicators that are likely to be on the business's BSC.
    (c) Suggest two statutory reports or returns that the business will need to file.

4. Company legal and contractual structures:
    (a) What can you learn about the legal structure of the business?
    (b) How many directors are on the board?
    (c) How many people does the business employ?

5. Shareholding structures and agreements:
    (a) What can you learn about the shareholders of the business?
    (b) Suggest two groupings of shareholders that might usefully be assigned shares of different kinds or classes.

DESIGN EXERCISES

The design exercise at the end of Chapter 1 encouraged identification of a business idea to be developed incrementally by specific design exercises through subsequent chapters of the book. That activity commenced in Chapter 2, with the framing of the selected business idea using the elements introduced in that chapter. This was extended by subsequent chapters with reference to the additional considerations and decisions introduced.

Extend your current design through the following tasks:

1. For each aspect of leadership and structure covered in this chapter, perform an assessment and analysis of your business. If using the Business Design Template, summarize the resulting considerations in the left-hand cell of the *leadership and structure* section.
2. Extract from your considerations the set of key decisions relating to value capture by your business. If using the Business Design Template, document these in the right-hand cell of the *leadership and structure* section.
3. Review the extended design of your business for consistency, and address any issues that arise.
4. Capture separately any of the following:
   (a) Key points learned from the exercise.
   (b) Outstanding issues or uncertainties.

9 Key Themes and Summary Points

Introducing the Key Themes

This chapter collects and reflects upon ten key themes that emerge from previous chapters.

The top ten themes are illustrated in Figure 9.1. Each provides a perspective from which a venture might be reviewed, prompting questions such as the following:

- What evidence indicates that the business has been designed to perform?

   Such evidence might be provided by demonstrating margins that increase with growth, or by the ability to penetrate a new market.
- What evidence indicates that the business is in control of its finances?

   Such evidence might be provided by demonstrating a budget process, a performance tracking rhythm and an active cashflow projection.
- What evidence indicates that the leadership team takes decisions from an investor mindset?

   Such evidence might be provided by demonstrating alignment between business objectives and the development roadmap, investment in IP protection or a plan for scalability to support growth into new markets.

For each of the ten key themes, a brief narrative summarizes its applicable contexts and picks out the principal points to be noted.

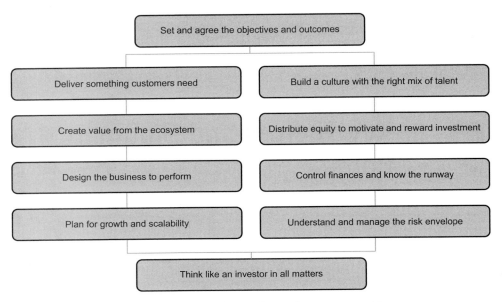

Figure 9.1 *Top ten themes of business innovation and entrepreneurship*

Set and Agree the Objectives and Outcomes

Ambitions and objectives change over the lifetime of a business. With fast-moving digital ventures, it is uncommon at the outset for the team to prepare a comprehensive plan and to assume that this will proceed in a straight line towards a prescribed conclusion. In most cases, it is assumed that the initial plan will be sufficient to propel the venture in a particular direction, and for periodic reviews of learning, progress and opportunity to recalibrate the trajectory and implications of the next phase.

However, at any point in time, it is important that the leadership team agree broadly to an ambition that is underpinned by common objectives for the business, as these can impinge strongly on many aspects of company activity.

In the broadest terms, business ambition can be expressed at an abstract level, such as:

- To provide a stable and enjoyable lifestyle over the longer term.
- To build a fast-growing venture that can generate a substantial reward within a time frame.

- To develop a stimulating business that will sustain over time and offer an exit at some point.
- To contribute to a worthy cause that delivers a personally rewarding experience.

Even a broad statement of ambition can influence the specifics of the business plan, including the way in which the market is addressed, the channel strategy and the value-capture approach. It can also influence the design of the product roadmap and the appetite for investment in IP protection, growth and scalability. It affects the design of the company's shareholding structures and the kinds of people that are recruited, and it influences the character of the business and the way in which its people engage with customers, partners and investors.

Due to its wide-ranging impact across business design, prioritization and behaviour, it is critically important that the leadership team determines and communicates an initial ambition. This can change: everyone will understand that the journey may not develop as initially envisaged.

If a venture sets an ambition to create a stimulating environment in which to work, then decisions are likely to be based on short- and medium-term interests, and opportunism is likely to be valued. However, if strongly opportunistic behaviour is evident within a venture that professes more specific objectives, then it is likely to be surmised by the team that any stated ambition is not actually held with conviction. In such cases, a range of different motivations and assumptions are usually in play, and any objectives that have been set are unlikely to be achieved.

A lack of clarity, or conflicting objectives, can be a major source of difficulty and friction for a venture, and the experience for the team will be like continually swimming upstream, or even drowning, rather than working together to develop an exciting and worthwhile business.

Deliver Something Customers Need

To create value for the business, the offering needs to create value for the customer.

Consequently, a business will not grow, and is unlikely to deliver on its investors' ambitions, unless it offers something that the customer perceives as valuable by saving them money or time, making them money or mitigating a high-impact risk. This value need not be quantifiable at the outset; indeed, it may initially be intangible, but if the need is real, then over time the business will determine how to evidence and measure the value.

An offering can achieve a degree of buy-in across a population of enthusiastic early adopters, but unless it offers something they need, this enthusiasm will be short lived, as such people will always be seeking 'the next great thing'.

Market research can be a good way to test need. When conducting such activities, it is necessary to ask the right questions and hence prompt the hard answers. These can include:

- How much will people be willing to pay?
- How often will they use the offering, and for what purpose?
- How do they currently get by without it?

An innovation that does not address a real customer need will get no real sustained traction across a market of any significant size, and hence business investment will be frustrated. Right at the outset, and at every review point, it is critical for the venture to question the value of their offering, and how best this can be expressed and quantified.

This theme plays directly into business value growth, and a further consideration here is the nature of the alignment between the value of the offering and the value of the business, including to any potential investor or acquirer:

- Is there a linear relation, such that an incremental increase in sales into a new market segment leads to a corresponding increase in business value?
- Is the relation less than linear, in that sales need to grow to sustain the same business value?
- Is it greater than linear, such that every sale accelerates the attractiveness of the business?

The answer to this question can pose a good test for the business ambition and for the investor mindset of the leadership team.

Create Value from the Ecosystem

Digital businesses vary widely in their value propositions, but every venture's business model relies on an active ecosystem of parties and value exchanges. Whether the venture forges a new ecosystem, modifies an existing collection of market dynamics or accommodates itself within an existing world, it is critically important that the following is known, for each party in the ecosystem:

- What the party needs, and how this need can be met to best advantage.
- What the party can offer, and how this can benefit the venture.
- What assumptions the venture can make about the party's motivation, including their propensity to purchase, promote, channel, co-adopt, co-innovate, collaborate, disrupt or compete.

Failure to understand the ecosystem and its real and changing dynamics can lead to problems such as:

- Customer needs being under or overvalued, or wrongly addressed.
- Difficulty in getting the expected level of traction and activity from a promotional or delivery partner.
- Difficulty in offering and supporting *the whole product* to a customer segment because the expected co-adopters and/or co-innovators do not operate as was assumed.
- Additional and unanticipated costs of supply chain or distribution due to changes in market norms or customer demand.

The ecosystem is a central construct in the design of a business and its dynamics needs to be understood, proven by market analysis and borne out by experience. An evidenced understanding gives the venture the power to maximize the benefit of its business model.

Markets can change fast in the digital world and the ecosystem map needs continually to be revised. This activity can have two complementary drivers:

- Reactive changes that respond to problems or observed needs for change. In such cases, the ecosystem may be updated to include new channel partners, customer segments or product integration partners.
- Proactive changes that provoke modifications within the ecosystem to achieve a leading market position, set a new standard and stay ahead of the curve. A proactive change can be applied to mitigate the risk of being caught out on the wrong side of someone else's change and hence avoid the need to react from a point of weakness later.

Both motivations are valid and both are needed from time to time. Clearly, both are associated with risk, as is inaction. Whenever assessing options such as these, a question that must be asked is 'what is likely to happen if we do nothing?' The worst of all situations can be getting caught out in a position of ignorance and indecision.

Design the Business to Perform

A business is a complex vehicle – a system of systems – that needs to be designed to meet its purpose.

Digital businesses by their nature tend to be highly connected into their ecosystems. This means that changes to the business world around a venture can impinge rapidly and significantly with an impact that was not anticipated. As with any complex system, it can be dangerous to assume that a business will automatically retain its ability to perform and scale as it responds to the needs for multiple changes, such as new routes to market or supply-chain partners, additional competitors, or the emergence of a new customer segment with differing needs or priorities.

Without explicit design decisions, the structure of a venture evolves tactically in response to circumstances. This means that new elements will be added to existing structures, resources will be stretched further and existing processes will be applied in differing situations. Like any system developed in this way, the venture is likely to degrade in performance. This can be evident through issues such as:

- Loss of efficiency, evidenced by reducing operating margin or development velocity.
- Reduced consistency of behaviour, evidenced by increases in errors or accidents, or the need for rework.
- Higher operating costs, evidenced by cost increases beyond budgeted levels, unexpected additional costs or decreasing cash runway.
- A difficulty in motivating people and partners, evidenced by the loss of key technical people, requests for new terms of business or pressure from investors for improved performance.

Design decisions underpin the workings of all aspects of the business, from its core proposition and ecosystem relationships, through considerations of its promotional and channel strategy, into the development of the future roadmap and supply chain, and the approach to growing business value. Scalability requires a range of design activities to address the interconnected needs for talent, capability and finance, and the future-proofing of the shareholding and governance structures.

These design activities need to be driven by requirements, and to be based on a rational assessment of options and trade-offs that can be modelled, analyzed and determined in the context of the venture's objectives.

Plan for Growth and Scalability

Growth and scalability are not the same. The following extremes are both possible:

- The venture grows without the business design being scalable; costs rise in proportion to revenues and no economies of scale are achieved.
- The venture bears the costs of operating a business designed for scale, but fails to achieve growth in revenues.

Both growth and scalability need to be addressed. This means knowing what will and can drive new business, and how to use this to generate growth over a projected time horizon. Growth can be driven proactively through promotional and channel activities, or reactively, pulled by a market that is attracted to a compelling and affordable solution to a problem.

A strategy embodies the ambition of the venture's leadership. It addresses the need to 'cross chasms' to be able to deliver an increasingly mature offering into increasingly larger customer markets, and it determines the requirements for an organization capable of performing at scale. This is embodied in a plan for growth that makes projections for revenues, costs and margins.

Achieving scalability requires talent, capability and finance, and the effectiveness of the plan can be limited by several factors, including:

- A lack of confidence or commitment within the leadership team, including cautious or slow decision making in respect of required changes.
- A lack of bandwidth within the team, including limitations on its capacity to manage relationships with a growing community of ecosystem players.
- Capacity limitations on the supply-side, including the speed, volume, reliability or cost of delivery into the venture from its supply chain and component suppliers.
- Capacity on the demand-side, including the speed, volume, reliability, licensing or cost of delivery to the customer from the venture and its channel partners.
- Product development velocity, including the effectiveness of requirement prioritization; the available talent; the productivity of any fabrication, manufacturing or testing processes; and the scalability of the product architecture and associated incremental costs.
- Product support and sustainment limitation, including unexpectedly high levels of warranty claims, or labour-intensive upgrade and configuration control processes.

- Finance availability, including reliance on lumpy revenue generation, or dependence on unpredictable investors.

In mitigating these kinds of risk, it is important to plan both for under- and over-achievement, although the latter is usually much less of a concern as it tends to be mitigated by increased revenues or investor confidence.

Any significant deviation from the plan can damage confidence and the venture's reputation – with the market and investors – which can negatively affect the motivation of the team. This indicates a need to track the progress of the plan against its projected targets and to make whatever adjustments are needed to retain control and credibility through the process.

Build a Culture with the Right Mix of Talent

Attracting and retaining the right mix of talent is perhaps the single most critical determinant of success or failure. This applies at all levels.

The compatibility (or otherwise) of founders can have profound effects on the early development of a business: how well do the individuals work together and do they complement or compound each other's abilities? This can be difficult to assess at the outset, because peoples' real qualities and abilities tend to develop and emerge as they are tested. Such tests can arise from both intensely good and intensely difficult experiences: for example, a significant customer order in the early days of a venture can prompt questions of ambition that bring to the surface unexpected conflicts between personal reward and investment in business growth.

As a venture develops and the leadership team expands to include new directors, potentially including investors, the relationships between individuals need to change from being personally rooted towards being more professionally based. This change can also prove testing in some businesses, where a close-knit team of founder-directors struggle to open up to the wider influences needed to achieve growth. In such situations, original statements of ambition may seem by some founders to have been betrayed or diluted, with a negative effect on team morale.

Any rift or friction within the leadership team has the potential to poison the wider business.

The team forms and projects the culture, or personality, of the business. Every business has a unique personality, and this has the potential to be a significant asset, in terms of attractiveness to customers and team members, or to deter people from engaging. Sensitivity to this point, informed by feedback processes, can be significant in shaping the business and its culture to meet its objectives.

The impact made by each new joiner tends to diminish as the team grows, but it can be significant in the early stages. Employment law varies across jurisdictions, and in the UK and Europe it can be difficult and expensive to remove an employee. Consequently, especially in the early days of a venture, every decision must be taken carefully, with eyes wide open. This means focusing on the competitive benefit that the new person will bring, plus an agreed requirement of what is needed by way of skills, qualities, innovator or operator, and aspects of personal chemistry between those who will need to work closely together.

On the positive side, a person can have an extraordinarily positive impact on a venture. Many ventures have recruited an individual to perform a particular role, often in a technical capacity, and then discovered that their talents extend further, even opening up new avenues of business not previously envisaged.

As a venture develops and employment processes achieve a steady state, it is important to avoid storing up future problems. This means being aware of legal requirements, and establishing enforceable contracts for all people-related engagements. A clear contract can limit the levels of risk and disruption in the event of future difficulties. Additionally, offers and allocations of equity need to be made with an investor's appreciation of its value and the potential implications.

Distribute Equity to Motivate and Reward Investment

Each of the 100 percentage points of a company's equity is precious and needs to be used to motivate and reward those who invest in its development.

Some entrepreneurs take the view that equity should remain with founders and those who invest capital for growth or extension. When that approach is adopted, employees and other contributors are rewarded with competitive salary packages and motivated through bonuses and other rewards. An alternative and increasingly widespread view in digital businesses is that equity should be shared across the wider team to create a sense of mutual ownership, such that the success of the venture benefits everyone.

Whichever of these views is adopted, the underlying principle is the same: plan a shareholding structure that aligns with the ambitions and objectives of the business.

Sharing too much equity too early in the development of a venture can limit future capacity to attract investment, or can mean that investment rounds will dilute the early investors to a level below what is needed to motivate their continuing active involvement.

When this lesson is learned too late, the original founders may discover that they have invested heavily in the development of a business for a very modest return. In some cases, the founder achieves an exit with an ownership share in low single figures. In other cases, the rewards can disproportionately benefit early joiners or other parties that seemed entitled at the outset, even though they actually contributed little to the venture's value.

In situations where equity is used to motivate employees and attract investment, a good practice is to design the capitalization table at the outset with an expectation of likely future transactions. This usually means assigning fixed pools of equity for employee shares, perhaps aligned with vesting arrangements, and then planning the timing of investment rounds such that founder directors will be able to retain sufficient equity to give them the control and motivation needed to achieve their ambitions for the business.

This can mean that the founders need to work harder on organic development of a venture ahead of bringing in investment, with the aim of achieving greater market validation to reduce the investment risk and hence increase the valuation that can be achieved.

Control Finances and Know the Runway

Irrespective of a venture's wealth, it is always important to control finances, especially costs and cash reserves, and to use available resources to build growth and scalability.

Over the past few years, disappointing results from some VC-backed technology *unicorns* that received investment at a high valuation have caused investors to limit their continuing funding. The situation has been characterized as producing 'herds of starving unicorns'.

Luke Johnson, writing in *The Sunday Times* in May 2016, observes that: 'I have met young founders of hi-tech companies who seem more familiar with financing than the actual operations of their business'. Putting this more harshly, it could be said that such founders are more familiar with, and motivated by, achieving finance from investors than they are with controlling and using it to generate revenues and profits.

One side of this is investment in real growth and scalability, as addressed by a previous theme; the other side is control over costs and cash, which are finite resources that need to be earned. Although highly valued companies may for a time have the ability to behave as though they have infinite financial resources, those that retain and grow their value are the ones that understand the need to focus on both top- and bottom-line numbers.

Whether a company is valued at $1,000, $1 million or $1 billion, the principles are the same:

- Budgets need to be set for the planning horizon of the venture, aligned with the activities and investments needed to achieve business objectives.
- Business performance needs to be measured and tracked, including the monitoring of spend against budgets and achievement against plan.
- Cash flows need to be managed, including a reasonable target for an acceptable runway.

In situations where the plan is not working, or is working at a different speed from what was expected, the second and third of these points become connected. It can take time and money to execute any change that is needed.

Cash is crucial to any venture. It is certainly difficult to operate without it, because employees and creditors need to be paid, and accommodation and other day-to-day expenses become difficult without cash. And when cash is short, achieving a good business valuation can be difficult, because the venture may have a weak negotiating position with no apparent *plan B*.

Failure to control finances can also lead to serious demotivation. If it is realized late in the day that the cash bonuses promised as rewards for exceptional performance cannot be paid, high-performing individuals may start to look elsewhere.

Understand and Manage the Risk Envelope

Every activity and non-activity carries associated risk. It is important that a venture identifies and assesses its principal risks, and then undertakes effective mitigations and transfers consistent with explicit decisions.

Every venture has a risk appetite. Those with a high appetite are more willing to tolerate the consequences of a risk than those that are more risk averse. Sometimes businesses are punished for their high-risk appetites; in other cases, they benefit. Sometimes risk-averse businesses breathe a sigh of relief through being saved by their mitigation actions; in other cases, they regret spending valuable resources guarding against something that never happened. This is a choice to be made: in part, the choice is informed by market norms; and, in part, risk appetite is a question of business personality.

It can be helpful to reflect on some of the causes of failure or severe damage to a business:

- Running out of cash, either through failure to generate earnings or loss of investment.
- Losing key customer business through competition, regulatory or reputational factors.
- Unanticipated market or ecosystem change, such as new competitors or loss of value.
- Malicious or accidental damage to business assets or resources.
- Breakdown in the team through conflict or loss of confidence.

Contemplating dire consequences such as these can help a venture to focus on those risks that have real potential to inflict serious damage. It can be useful for the leadership of a venture to reflect on how and why each of these situations might arise. Having identified such risks, the team can set its risk appetite by determining which risks can be tolerated and which cannot. For those that cannot be tolerated, mitigations and transfer mechanisms need to be identified and actioned. Where the cost of such mechanisms is judged to be too high for the venture, the venture's tolerance may need to be extended. Such situations need to be reviewed periodically in the light of changed circumstances.

This kind of risk analysis can provoke conflict in the team, especially in situations where some people are inclined to bear the cost of mitigation and others are not. This can be a hard test for a venture, especially in its early period. The way in which such matters are resolved by the team can be critical.

Some risks are inherent to all businesses, some apply to a particular market and others are specific to a particular venture at its stage of development. A useful practice relating to the first and second categories is to explore the approaches adopted by comparable businesses. Every venture builds around it a *sphere of trust*, and businesses that operate within this, which may even be competitors, tend to be willing to share their concerns and experiences.

In respect of business-specific risks, it can be advisable to anticipate the additional or increased risks inherent in a development plan, and hence to design mitigations or transfers into the activities involved. For example, if the growth plan involves promoting the offering into a territory known for IP copying or theft, then the risk of lost revenues needs to be mitigated by ensuring that developmental activities associated with copy protection are completed before the launch.

Think Like an Investor in All Matters

Of all the themes that have been addressed in this chapter, this one is perhaps the most wide-ranging. The principle is that, for a business founder or shareholder, whatever your competence and whatever your role in the business, you are also an investor.

Being an investor means continually thinking beyond any current activity or situation, and considering, from the perspective of achieving the business ambition, what is the most effective course of action. This can sometimes mean making a decision that is contrary to the short-term interest, such as turning away an offer of business that would risk distracting the team from the bigger plan, or declining to prioritize a request for a product enhancement from a key customer, because it would divert the focus of development away from the needs of the wider market.

Such decisions can demand courage and confidence in the venture and the team.

Embedding and retaining an investor mindset means establishing the business ambition and being clear what this means by way of objectives and plan. Where this is performed effectively, the implications will permeate the business, influencing decisions across market targeting, product development, stakeholder management, staff recruitment and retention, and into investor choice and management.

Thinking like an investor means accepting the consequences. This can be hard to bear in cases where the business fails to perform as planned, and this is where having that leadership quality of persistence, or grit, is important. In such cases, it is necessary to be objective and either develop a different plan, or accept that the venture cannot succeed and so end it, and invest elsewhere.

Over-success can also be demanding. If a venture grows faster or larger or with more complexity than was envisaged by its original ambition and objectives, some people may begin to feel out of their depth and to lose confidence in their ability to contribute. Again, objectivity and persistence are needed. In some cases, the right answer might be to recruit and delegate powers to more experienced people who are tasked with setting a new ambition and objectives for the next phase.

In cases like these, an investor mindset does not mean experiencing a sense of failure from the personal limitations that have been demonstrated, but of experiencing the satisfaction of having enabled a new phase of development from which to learn and benefit.

Appendix A: Principal Terms of Product Licensing Agreements

There is a collection of terms that it is particularly important to consider when producing a licensing agreement to be offered to customers. This appendix gives explanations, cautions and, in some cases, optional forms of words for the principal terms. It is important to note that the specific wording adopted may need to be reviewed in the light of applicable legal jurisdictions.

Parties to the Agreement

This needs to clarify both who is the licensor and who is the licensee. It can be important to name the licensor, as this may not be the business from which the product was purchased. In businesses that adopt a multi-company structure, it can be important to state clearly which of the group of companies is granting the licence.

The licensee may be a named individual or company, an unnamed individual, or an employee or agent of a named organization. With B2B offerings, clarifying the intended user base mitigates the risk of additional users inadvertently being licensed following acquisition of the customer company by a larger organization.

The IP That Is Licensed by the Agreement

This may refer to a specific product or to a collection of bundled products for which the licence provides access and usage. It is important to clarify the scope of IP that is covered by the licence, including any patent rights that are included and whether the licence gives source-code rights or applies only to the executable form.

Grant of Licence

It is important to clarify the nature of the licence being granted:

- An *exclusive licence* is limited in being granted to a single licensee: no other party may exploit the relevant IP except for the licensee. Exclusivity can be granted within specific named markets or territories, and may apply for a specified period.
- A *sole licence* is like an exclusive licence, except that the licensor also reserves the right to exploit the IP themselves.
- A *co-exclusive licence* is limited in being granted to a specified and limited group of licensees.
- A *non-exclusive licence* grants rights to the licensee on the understanding that the licensor may exploit those rights themselves, and also grant the same rights to additional licensees.

Independent of these options, the following clarifications need also to be expressed:

- A *perpetual licence* is one without time limit. It provides the licensor with the rights to use the licensed IP in perpetuity.
- A *time-limited licence* will specify a time horizon, such as six months, one year or three years, typically together with a renewal mechanism.
- A *transferable licence* is one that permits the licensee to reassign in some way, such as through gift or sale to another organization. Transfer can sometimes be permitted specifically within the context of specified events, such as acquisition or outsourcing of relevant activities.
- A *non-transferable licence* applies only to the specified licensee, and any proposed transfer would require the negotiation of a new licence.

The use of exclusive or transferable licences needs to be considered carefully with future implications in mind.

Restrictions

The rights granted by the licence may be restricted in various ways to protect the licensor's IP and ensure that the venture is not exposed to additional risks. Limitations typically apply in relation to the following:

- Any copying of the product without specific permission from the licensor.
- Any alteration of the product in terms of function or appearance.

- Any sub-licensing to other licensees, within the same or other organization. This effectively enables the licensor to control distribution.

Applicable Use

The use that is made of the IP may be qualified by statements of what is not applicable, such as:

- The product may not be used to infringe the IP of the licensor or any other party. This limitation would be important to protect the licensor from exposure to claims of IP infringement in the case of a product that permits copying or other reproduction.
- The product may not be used for any illegal purpose. This limitation would serve to transfer the licensor's risk of legal action as a consequence of a licensee's behaviour in the case of a communications product being used to record or convey illegal content. Even where legality is not at issue, the risk of reputational damage in such cases may be acute.

IP Rights

If the licensed product embodies a registered IP right such as a patent or registered design, then the licensor will usually wish to declare this in the licence. This can have the beneficial effect of communicating the rights that will be lost if the licence is allowed to expire, or is for some reason terminated.

Given the importance to a product-based venture of protecting its IP, it can be useful, in addition to stating what is licensed, also to spell out what is not being licensed. This may be useful, as lawyers say, *for the avoidance of doubt.*

A common form of words is to assert that no rights, other than the right to use in accordance with the other terms of the licence, are granted under the licence. Further elaboration may state that the licence provides no transfer of IP ownership.

Licensing of Any Third-Party Products

Many products comprise components that have been licensed to the business by third parties. The topic is addressed in Chapter 4 in the context of controlling product configuration, and also in Chapter 7 in the context of the potentially viral effect of open-source licensing. The important message from both perspectives is the need for diligence in reviewing the terms whereby such components may be used and distributed, and an assessment of potential limitations, additional costs or wider licensing implications. A schedule of components used, and respective licence terms, should be maintained in a form that could be made available to customers, partners or potential investors.

Additionally, it may be important to clarify the rights granted to the licensor in respect of such components, in particular to clarify:

- The licensor's position regarding any liabilities relating to or arising from those third-party components.
- Whether there is any transfer of rights in those components, beyond the rights conveyed through their contribution to the product's functionality performance or appearance.

Payments and Payment Terms

Depending on the nature of the offering, the licence may or may not include reference to the licence fee. In many situations, the fee is negotiated separately, and so will be documented in a separate form such as a purchase order or requisition request. Where fees are included in the licence, then it is important to clarify dates when payments will be due, and applicable actions if payments are delayed or not forthcoming.

Liabilities

Any contract exposes the business to liabilities which may cause the business to be vulnerable to claims for damages if, for example, products and services fail to meet quality and safety standards, or to match their specification.

It is important to incorporate appropriate terms into the licence, otherwise any attempt to limit liability may fail. It is important to consider the consequence of the licensed product causing damage or injury to the customer's assets, reputation, personnel or ability to do business. Depending on the nature of the product, this might occur through data loss or corruption, spoiled facilities, infringement of third-party IP or legal action brought under health and safety legislation. Such eventualities may also have an additional, consequential impact on the customer, including lost production or sales, non-availability of key staff or increased insurance premiums.

Liability clauses limit the exposure of the licensor to such costs. In addressing these, it is helpful to separate direct liabilities, which relate to the immediate consequence of an event, from consequential liabilities, which relate to the impact of those direct consequences on the licensee's business or operations.

In respect of direct liabilities, there are usually at least three options:

- The licensor accepts no liability for any damages suffered by the licensee that could not reasonably have been foreseen.

Under US law, this approach restates common law principles. Under EU law, however, where a defective product causes damage, the producer may be liable even without negligence or fault on their part.

- The licensor limits the maximum value of liability for a damages claim at a reasonable amount.

Note that under many jurisdictions, including the UK, it is not possible to limit or exclude liability for death or personal injury caused by negligence or fraud, and attempting to do so could make the whole clause unenforceable.

- The licensor excludes liabilities for losses relating to specific aspects of the product or its use.

This approach may apply where the licensee has accepted such a condition within the agreed pricing, or the product has been developed specifically for the licensee, or in cases where such exclusions are standard in the relevant industry.

In general, licensors would be advised to avoid accepting liability for any consequential liabilities, as these have the potential to be very large, and are likely to be beyond the licensor's influence or ability to anticipate. In some consumer situations, however, there is a risk that attempting to avoid such liabilities could be held to be unfair and unreasonable if a claim reached a court of law.

Jurisdictions vary in respect of what is considered to be included within consequential loss.

Warranties and Disclaimers

A warranty is a limited promise made by the licensor regarding the quality, performance, durability, applicability or reliability of the licensed IP. It can be important to express such limits clearly to avoid claims that the product is somehow defective.

It can be helpful to specify a fixed-term warranty period during which the product will conform substantially to its description. Another common approach is to make exceptions for problems that are not caused by defects or are beyond the licensor's control.

The language of warranties introduces the notion of *remedies*. A licence may provide a remedy for cases where the product can be shown to be defective by offering either to refund the licence fee or provide a replacement product. It is generally good practice for such remedies to be exhaustive and to preclude any other remedies, such as financial compensation for loss and damage suffered by the licensee.

The purpose of a *disclaimer* is to deny any warranties which may otherwise apply to the product. Many licences contain disclaimers that exclude all other potentially implied promises regarding the quality or applicability of the software. A common form of disclaimer states that there is no guarantee that the product will be fit for a particular purpose, or meet any particular requirement. In the USA, many states permit implied warranties to be disclaimed by simply indicating that the product or service in question is provided *as is*.

Termination

Depending on the nature of the licence granted, there may be a fixed term, with conditions for renewal, or the licence may be perpetual. In both cases, it is advisable to make provision for termination in the event of a breach of the terms of the licence or unauthorized use of the product. Associated with such termination, there will usually be stated actions to be performed, such as returning all copies of the product and associated materials to the licensor and removing or destroying all copies.

Jurisdiction

Where a product is to be distributed internationally, it is important to state under which jurisdiction its licence is to be interpreted. This can be significant because even a small difference in legal rules can have an effect on the rights and obligations of the licensor and the licensee. Where appropriate, multiple licence forms can be supported.

Appendix B: Principal Terms of Customer Service Agreements

There is a collection of customer service terms that it is particularly important to consider when producing a service agreement to be offered to customers. This appendix gives explanations, cautions and, in some cases, optional forms of words for the principal terms. It is important to note that the specific wording adopted may need to be reviewed in the light of applicable legal jurisdictions.

Parties to the Agreement

This needs to clarify who is the service provider(s) and who is its user(s). This can be important as the service provider may not be the business from which any associated product was purchased. It is likely that the service user will require clarity over the party that is offering the service, and hence will be responsible for meeting its obligations.

The service user may be a named individual or company, an unnamed individual, or an employee or agent of a named organization. With B2B offerings, clarifying the intended user base may be important to contain the likely volume of service usage within acceptable bounds.

Term of the Service

The term of an agreement would usually be monthly, quarterly or annually. There may be an initial commitment to a minimum term (say, three months), followed by periodic renewals with defined conditions. It is normal for the service provider to impose a minimum notice period in the event of non-renewal. This can benefit all parties, by giving time for data migration and any other service close-down activities.

Payment and Payment Terms

Although the payment schedule is usually synchronized with the term of the service, the dates on which payments are due can vary with the nature of the service offered.

- For SLAs associated with delivery of a self-standing service, it is usual for payments to be made periodically at the start or end of the relevant period. Payment in advance is clearly preferable for the venture's cash flow. Negotiation of a larger upfront payment (say, for a year or more) can be advantageous in securing customer commitment.
- For CCAs associated with support for a product, it is normal for an annual service charge to be paid in advance, by comparison with payment of an insurance premium. Again, negotiation of multi-year arrangements can be advantageous.

Payment levels and terms are usually fixed in advance of service delivery, possibly with an option to renegotiate at specified future times, or in line with public indices. In some situations, a negotiated arrangement may adopt a fixed cost that is increased or decreased against measurable value delivery or service performance, such as where an additional charge is levied when service usage exceeds a particular threshold.

When agreeing payment levels, the related question of payment terms needs to be included. Large organizations usually have standard terms, such as *net 30* (payment thirty days after invoice date). As noted in Chapter 5, the topic of payment terms can be an important aspect of the wider pricing negotiation. It is normal practice to include a clause asserting that an interest charge at a stated percentage may be levied on late payments; similarly, a credit discount may be offered against early payment.

Defining the Services to Be Provided

It is important to define the services in sufficient detail to avoid ambiguity. There may be several distinct services, and these should be listed, in each case with sufficient descriptive text. Some examples of service definitions offered by a CCA are suggested in Table B.1.

In Table B.1, the service 'Investigation of product non-conformities with specification' makes reference to 'problem ... prioritization'. The detailed description of this service can be significant to the service provider's level of liability.

A widely used approach to limit this liability is to align a set of *severity levels* with associated *response commitments*. Significantly, response times are usually interpreted as meaning the length of time between the reporting of a problem, or non-conformity, and the commencement of investigation by a competent person. Giving actual response time commitments for fixing problems could expose the service provider to a significant liability, as the reported problem may be beyond the team's control.

It is normal to set out a series of severity levels with associated descriptions and response times, as illustrated in Table B.2.

Table B.1 Sample CCA Service Descriptions

Services offered	Description
Help desk: response to enquiries relating to a problem or to product use	A list of the available channels (web, telephone . . .), the application process and any limitations, such as a rule that the help desk may not be used as a substitute for training
Investigation of product non-conformities with specification	Explanation of the working of the process of investigation, including problem replication, prioritization and user communication
Provision of product upgrades	Elaboration of the policy for release of upgrades, in terms of time frames, forward and backward compatibility, and whether customer-specific patches will be considered
Access to online resources	Indication of the kinds of resource to be available, the benefits that they provide and frequency of update/refresh
Submitting requests for new or changed functionality	Explanation of the workings of the process for handling new functionality, including analysis, prioritization, roadmap planning and user communication

Table B.2 Sample CCA Severity Levels and Their Alignment with Response Commitments

Severity level	Description	Response commitment
1	Informational	within 8 hours
2	Minor: no user performance impact	within 8 hours
3	Standard: no user performance impact	within 8 hours
4	Critical: significant user performance impact	within 4 hours
5	Emergency: potential for significant business impact	within 1 hour

Service Provider's Obligations

Typical obligations on the provider of services include their care and competence, which implies an appropriate level of the personal and technical ability within the team, and a commitment to make *reasonable endeavours* to identify and implement a solution to every service request received.

This latter point raises a legal issue about the distinction between *reasonable* and *best* endeavours. It is widely assumed that the latter is more stringent than the former, although legal sources are not in agreement about the real extent of either. An extreme interpretation of *best endeavours* requires a party to act against its commercial interests to fulfil its obligations. Given the uncertainty over interpretation and likely differences across jurisdictions, *reasonable endeavours* presents the more acceptable wording.

Service User's Obligations

A typical obligation on the user of the services is their competence to use the service and, where appropriate, their provision of accurate and timely information to assist the service provider in analysing and assessing any request submitted.

A requirement that the service user behaves legally and with due regard for any relevant ethical or social etiquette may be helpful in transferring the risk of external censure for any bad behaviour encountered.

Additional Services

Listing those services that are additional to the agreement can be useful in demarking the services that are provided through the agreement. In many cases, these will include, for example, training, consultancy and customization services, possibly involving comparable skills sets to those required by the core services.

Such services would normally be priced independently, and a table of charges may be included in the agreement for completeness.

Confidentiality and Non-Disclosure

The activities around providing services may require either or both parties to make available confidential information, including future plans and requirements. In anticipation of this, it is sometimes useful to establish an NDA (see Chapter 7), which may be a separate and independent document referenced by the service agreement or may be wrapped into the service agreement itself. A third option is where both agreements are wrapped into a yet wider contract.

Liabilities

It can be advisable to include clauses that limit the exposure of the supplier in relation to various kinds of risks, including:

- The risk of a claim on the basis that the service did not lead to the expected business benefits.
- The risk that the user abuses the services to communicate defamatory information, or to breach third-party IP.
- The risk of a claim for consequential damages, including loss of profits or business by the user.

Service providers would be advised to avoid accepting liability for any consequential liabilities, as these have the potential to be very large, and are likely to be beyond the provider's influence or ability to anticipate. In some consumer situations, however, there is a risk that attempting to avoid such liabilities could be held to be unfair and unreasonable, if a claim reached a court of law.

In relation to direct liabilities, one of the following options can be adopted:

- The service provider accepts no liability for any damages suffered by the customer that could not reasonably have been foreseen.
- The service provider limits the maximum value of liability for a damages claim at a reasonable amount. Note that under many jurisdictions, including the UK, it is not possible to limit or exclude liability for death or personal injury caused by negligence or fraud, and attempting to do so could make the whole clause unenforceable.
- The service provider excludes liabilities for losses relating to specific high-risk aspects of the service or its use.

Warranties and Disclaimers

A warranty is a limited promise made by the service provider regarding the services and their availability, as defined in the agreement. The service provider may make exceptions for problems that are beyond their responsibility or control.

A service agreement may offer a remedy if the provider fails in its performance. This will typically involve offering to refund a proportion of the fee. It is generally good practice for such remedies to be exhaustive and to preclude any other remedies, such as financial compensation for loss and damage suffered by the licensee.

A disclaimer may be added to the effect that the service provider can make no guarantee that the service will be fit for a particular purpose, or will meet any particular business requirement.

Termination

Depending on the nature of the service definition, there may be a fixed term, or the agreement may be periodic (for example, monthly, annual), or it may start with a fixed term and then continue by a series of mutually agreed periodic renewals.

It is advisable also to make provision for termination by either party in the event of breach of the agreement or unauthorized use of the service. Associated with such termination, there may be stated actions to be performed, including refunding payment for unused service in the event of termination by the user.

Non-Poaching of Staff

Both parties to an agreement can be vulnerable to poaching or solicitation of staff by the other. Many ventures have faced the situation where a team member working at a customer site leaves the business to work directly for the customer. This situation can lead to a serious loss of competence within the team.

One solution is to include a mutual non-poaching clause in the service agreement. A better, or additional, solution is to include a non-poaching clause into the employment or engagement contracts to prevent team members, for a specified period of time after leaving, from working for clients with whom they were in contact during their employment or engagement. Anyone breaching such a restriction can personally be sued by the business.

Jurisdiction

Where a service is offered internationally, it is important to state under which jurisdiction the agreement is to be interpreted. This can be important because even a small difference in legal rules can have a significant effect on the rights and obligations of the parties. Where appropriate, multiple forms of the agreement can be supported.

Appendix C: Principal Terms of Customer Delivery Contracts

There is a collection of customer delivery terms that it is particularly important to consider when agreeing a delivery contract with a customer. This appendix gives explanations, cautions and, in some cases, optional forms of words for the principal terms. It is important to note that the specific wording adopted may need to be reviewed in the light of applicable legal jurisdictions.

Term of the Project

The term of a development or delivery contract is usually fixed and defined through a plan of the activities to be performed, with acknowledged dependencies and intermediate review points.

It can be useful to build a series of synchronization points into the plan as an opportunity to keep relevant senior stakeholders engaged, and to serve as intermediate payment points.

Payment and Payment Terms

A payment framework is usually fixed in advance of project activity. In cases where later phases of activity are not well understood at the outset, it can be helpful to agree a fixed price for the early, more definitional and scoping phases, and to leave open the specific costing of later phases to be confirmed at a defined review or synchronization point.

Another option is for pricing to be based on *time and materials*, where a schedule of day rates and reimbursable expenses is agreed within the contract. This approach is particularly appropriate with higher-risk projects, where the parties are unsighted on the likely scale of costs. In such cases, it is normal practice for the customer to set a maximum budget, and to schedule periodic reviews of cost expenditure.

In larger delivery projects, significant work may be required ahead of any cash receipts. For smaller businesses, this can present cash risks which are best mitigated by establishing an upfront payment expressed as a proportion of the total cost of the project. An agreement to upfront part-payment may be balanced by a comparable payment at the close of the project, subject to the customer's satisfaction.

When agreeing payment levels, the related question of payment terms needs to be included, and this topic can be an important aspect of the wider pricing negotiation. It is normal practice to include a clause asserting that an interest charge at a stated percentage may be levied on late payments; similarly, a credit discount may be offered against early payment.

Defining the Deliverables

It is important to define the expected deliverables in sufficient detail to avoid ambiguity. Poorly defined deliverables can lead to differing expectations between supplier and customer, which can lead to conflict and relationship damage. A useful approach is for the parties to work together to create an agreed *statement of work* that is referenced by the contract.

Supplier's Obligations

These usually include a requirement for care and competence, and a commitment to make *reasonable endeavours* to deliver the defined outputs or outcomes. The note about *best* versus *reasonable* endeavours in the equivalent section of Appendix B again applies.

Customer's Obligations

Typical obligations on the customer include the availability of appropriately skilled people, access to required materials and data, and the provision of suitable test cases by which the effectiveness of the deliverables can be demonstrated. Each of these can pose risks to the supplier if they are not forthcoming, so it is important that they are recognized contractually.

Project Management

Unless the delivery project is trivially small, it is useful to assign a project manager with responsibility to deliver the plan by prioritizing and coordinating activity, synchronizing meetings, managing documentation, reporting progress, and managing issues and changes (see below). This function may be provided by the supplier, the customer or an independent third party. When establishing the function, it is important that all parties confirm their agreement with and respect for the person appointed and their relevant responsibilities.

IP Rights

Many contracts draw a distinction between:

- *Background IP*, which is the IP that is supplied by a party at the start of the project, typically including software, patterns, specifications, designs, methods and know-how.
- *Foreground IP*, which is the IP that is created by the activities of the project, typically including operational systems, documentation and operating procedures.

In joint development projects, two additional concepts can apply:

- *Sideground IP*, which refers to IP that is relevant to the collaboration, but which has been developed independently and in parallel by one of the collaborating parties.
- *Postground IP*, which refers to IP that is relevant to a collaboration and that has been developed subsequently by one of the parties.

These distinctions and the related ownership assignment can be critically important to the value of any future exploitation of IP. In particular, if background IP rights are not retained, then there can be severe limitations on a venture's ability to license it in future. It is normal for contracts to confirm that each party will retain its background rights. Foreground rights can be more negotiable, depending upon the customer's ambitions for future exploitation. A workable approach can involve the supplier securing ownership rights in the foreground IP and granting usage rights for these to the customer.

During IP negotiations, it can be helpful to question the rights that are conveyed by *ownership* and the benefit to the customer of owning IP that has been created. This debate can sometimes be helped by separating issues of usage, confidentiality and exclusivity.

Where one party is licensing IP to the other, either for the purposes of the project, or for usage afterwards, it is important to state clearly what is licensed and on what terms, and also to clarify what is not being licensed.

The issue of know-how gained during the project can also be negotiable. This usually relates to generally applicable know-how that is gained by the supplier, and which would potentially be valuable in future deliveries with the same or other customers. Subject always to confidentiality considerations, a workable approach can be to agree that nothing in the contract prevents or restricts the supplier from developing and using any techniques, ideas, concepts, information, methods or processes of general applicability.

Confidentiality and Non-Disclosure

Development activities are likely to require either or both parties to make available confidential information. It is therefore normal to establish an NDA (see Chapter 7), either as an intrinsic part of it or as a separate and independent document that is referenced by the delivery contract.

Change Management

It is well known that 'no plan survives contact with the enemy', and the real world can easily play the role of enemy. Consequently, it is important that an agreed mechanism is established for handling changes to deliverables, time frame, parties involved or almost anything else in the contract.

A mechanism for change control will usually involve phases including:

- Analysis of the change request in terms of its motivation and rationale.
- Assessment of the impact of the proposed change, technically, financially and in terms of time frame.
- Cost negotiation to agree budget changes and impact on payment schedules.
- Agreement by parties on both sides to proceed with the renegotiated terms.
- Implementation of the change, including development, documentation and communications.

In more speculative developments where change requests are expected, the contract may make provision for handling, say, three change requests without further negoti- ation. In such cases, the supplier will have already factored the likely costs of these into the project budget. Due to the overhead that change analysis and assessment can impose, it can be desirable in some situations to refuse change requests until a particular project milestone has been achieved.

Liabilities

It can be advisable to include clauses that limit the exposure of the supplier in relation to various kinds of risks, including:

- The risk of a damages claim from the customer on the basis that the project fails to deliver the expected business benefits.
- The risk of a damages claim from the customer on the basis that the project overruns its schedule.
- The risk of a claim for consequential damages, including loss of profits or business by the user.

Suppliers would be advised to avoid accepting liability for any consequential liabilities, as these have the potential to be very large, and are likely to be beyond the provider's influence or ability to anticipate. In some consumer situations, however, there is a risk that attempting to avoid such liabilities could be held to be unfair and unreasonable, if a claim reached a court of law.

In relation to direct liabilities, one of the following options can be adopted:

- The supplier accepts no liability for any damages suffered by the customer that could not reasonably have been foreseen.
- The supplier limits the maximum value of liability for a damages claim at a reasonable amount, commonly expressed as a proportion of the total project cost. Note that under many jurisdictions, including the UK, it is not possible to limit or exclude liability for death or personal injury caused by negligence or fraud, and attempting to do so could make the whole clause unenforceable.
- The supplier excludes liabilities for losses relating to specific high-risk aspects of the project.

Warranties and Disclaimers

A warranty is a limited promise made by the supplier regarding the fitness for purpose of the deliverables. Exceptions may be made for problems that are beyond the supplier's responsibility or control.

It is generally good practice for such remedies to be exhaustive and to preclude any other remedies, such as financial compensation for loss and damage suffered by the customer.

Penalty Clauses and Liquidated Damages

A delivery contract may offer a remedy to the customer for cases where the supplier fails in its performance, including through a delay in delivery or by a deliverable failing to meet specified targets.

This will typically involve a requirement to refund a proportion of the project cost through what are called *liquidated damages*. Such damages can be expressed in a time-related manner, such as repayment of an amount of money or a percentage of the project cost every month until the failure has been remedied.

Any sum payable under liquidated damages must be a genuine estimate of the loss to the other party, otherwise the remedy would be interpreted as a *penalty clause* and therefore potentially be unenforceable in law in the USA, the EU and the UK.

Termination

A delivery project will usually have a fixed term, aligned with the project plan.

It is advisable to make provision for termination by either party in the event of breach of any terms in the contract. Associated with such termination, there may be stated actions to be performed, including total or partial refunds, plus return of equipment and materials.

Non-Poaching of Staff

Both parties to a delivery contract can be vulnerable to poaching or solicitation of staff by the other. One solution is to include a mutual non-poaching clause in the delivery contract. A better, or additional, solution is to include a non-poaching clause into the venture's employment or engagement contracts to prevent team members, for a specified period after leaving, from working for clients with whom they were in contact during their employment or engagement. Anyone breaching such a restriction can personally be sued by the business.

Assignment

In the case of longer delivery projects, an issue can arise where one party merges with or is acquired by another organization, or where one of the parties outsources the relevant function and team to a third-party organization. This may be significant in cases where the acquirer is a competitor of the other party or has connections with an unacceptable territory.

When anticipating such eventualities, it is unusual for either party to give blanket approval for reorganizations or reconstructions, and more normal to agree not unreasonably to withhold permission.

Jurisdiction

It is important to state under which jurisdiction the contract is to be interpreted. This can be important because even a small difference in legal rules can have a significant effect on the rights and obligations of the parties.

Glossary

Actor In general, a person, organization or system that interacts in some way with a business. In threat intelligence, actors are external, internal or partner. See also 'Threat actor'.

Actual market value (AMV) For the purposes of UK taxation, the value of an asset, such as a share or option holding, taking into account any market restrictions that might apply. See also 'UMV'.

Adaptive customization The adaptation of an offering by a customer, perhaps by purchasing additional features, or through further development or integration activity.

Advanced subscription agreement (ASA) A form of investment that converts to shares on a future event, such as the next financing round or an insolvency. Unlike a convertible loan, an ASA has no interest rate and there is no requirement to repay the amount within a set period. As there is no downside protection, in the UK it may be eligible for SEIS/EIS tax relief.

Advertorial An advertisement that presents subjective, promotional information about a business or offering in the style of an objective work of journalism.

Agile development A generic term referring to the use of an iterative and incremental software development method, such as extreme programming, scrum, lean development or feature-driven development.

Angel investor An individual who provides investment capital to a business start-up, usually in exchange for convertible debt or an ownership stake. Angel investors invest through equity crowdfunding, or through angel networks (or syndicates) that share research and pool investment capital.

Annual return A statutory report on a company's activities throughout the year, including its financial performance. The detail required varies by territory and by company size and type.

Anything as a service (XaaS) Referring to any cloud-based service offering, including software as a service, platform as a service . . .

Application programming interface (API) A technical mechanism that provides access to the features or data of an operating system, application or other service.

Arm's length relationship A relationship between unconnected parties that owe no special obligation to each other.

Articles of association (or incorporation) A definition of the constitution of a business, including the responsibilities of its directors, the nature of the business and the rights of its shareholders. It is a public document, and a company is required by law to adhere to it. In the UK, it needs to be filed with the registrar of companies.

Artificial intelligence (AI) Technology capable of simulating intelligent behavior, enhancing or replacing intelligent human behaviour.

Attack vector A means by which a threat actor exploits system vulnerabilities to gain access to a computer or network for the purpose of achieving a malicious outcome.

Augmented reality (AR) A technology that creates a composite view of reality by superimposing a digitally generated image over a view of the real world.

Autotech A general term for disruptive technology offerings within the automotive sector.

Average revenue per user (ARPU) A performance indicator used by consumer communications and networking businesses, calculated by dividing the total revenue received by the number of subscribers.

Background IP The IP supplied by a party at the start of a project.

Balanced budget A budget in which the projected costs are met by projected income to the business from revenues, investments, loans and other sources of funds.

Balanced scorecard (BSC) A performance-monitoring approach that visualizes current performance, from differing perspectives, with performance targets and trends over time, to enable achievement to be aligned with targets, and hence assess progress towards objectives.

Barrier to entry A specialist requirement for a business to operate in a particular market.

Barrier to exit An obstacle that limits the ability of a business to leave or to be displaced from a market.

Blockchain A technology for managing decentralized and distributed digital ledgers that record transactions across a network, such that the registered transactions cannot be altered retroactively.

Brand Imagery that distinguishes and creates an impression of a business.

Brand experience People's experience of engaging with the associated business or offering.

Brand image The psychological associations of a brand.

Brand management Relating to the building of *brand recognition* within a target market, and growing brand value through positive image and experience.

Brand recognition The extent to which a business or offering can be identified solely by its brand.

Brand value The financial value due to the brand of having customers who will pay more for it.

Burn rate The rate at which a business spends cash. Usually expressed in monthly terms.

Business capability An abstraction comprising processes and controls together with the people, assets and resources that are needed to achieve an outcome. A capability is independent of organization structure.

Business-to-business (B2B) An offering serving business customers rather than individuals.

Business-to-business-to-consumer (B2B2C) An offering serving consumers through an offering that serves businesses.

Business-to-consumer (B2C) An offering serving individual customer consumers.

Business-to-government (B2G) An offering serving local or national government departments or agencies.

Business-to-knowledge (B2K) A situation where the end-user is a professional knowledge-worker who uses an offering purchased by an organization.

Business ecosystem The network of organizations – including suppliers, distributors, customers, competitors, government agencies and so on – involved in the delivery of an offering into the market, through both competition and cooperation.

Business entity An organization formed and operated to perform business activities, charitable work or other activities.

Business growth Increasing performance against some measure of success.

Business model A construct that comprises notions whereby value will be created, promoted, delivered and captured, and which is embodied in and empowered by a business structure.

Business plan A document that describes the objectives and operation of a business, including technical, financial and team aspects, for the purpose of the business itself or of a potential stakeholder or partner.

Business scalability Operating and performing effectively as the business grows.

Capital expenditure (Capex) The purchase of goods or services that increase a business's ability to generate profit. Depreciation enables spreading the cost of the purchase over its useful life, often a five- to ten-year period.

Capital gains tax (CGT) A UK tax on the profit (or gain) made on the sale of an asset that has increased in value.

Capitalization, or cap, table A table or spreadsheet that shows a company's share classes and ownership, including ordinary shares, preference shares and options, and the various prices that have been paid for these.

Channel A partner organization through which a business offering is promoted and/or delivered to customers.

Channel business A business that acts as a reseller, offering to generate demand and provide access into targeted markets.

Channel strategy A collection of ecosystem relationships responsible for creating visibility and demand for an offering and through which value can be delivered into a target market.

Churn rate See 'Customer churn rate' and 'Employee churn rate'.

Co-adoption Required adoption of an innovation by other players in the consumption/distribution side of the ecosystem.

Co-exclusive licence A licence that is limited in being granted to a specified and limited group of licensees.

Co-innovation Innovations that are required to be developed by other players, especially on the supply/enabling side of the ecosystem.

Collaborative consumption A part of the sharing economy whereby individuals rent out underused assets, such as property, time or a car. This turns an asset into a commodity and enables physical objects to be treated as services. Offerings that provide such services are referred to as multi-sided platforms.

Collateral (marketing) Documents or information designed to encourage interest in an offering, including case studies, white papers and technical overviews.

Commodity A product or service offering that is largely interchangeable with others of the same type.

Competition-based pricing A pricing approach whereby the price is set on the basis of competitors' current pricing.

Concurrent licence A licence made available to a community of users, whereby the number of actual users at any point in time is bounded by the defined *concurrency limit*.

Confidential information Documents, templates, software source code, database designs, financial plans, ROI calculations, market strategies and any other materials that are valuable to a business, and that it would not wish to be made available without strict controls governing its use and further distribution.

Consequential damage liabilities Liabilities that relate to the impact of the direct consequences on the licensee's business or operations, possibly including lost production or business, non-availability of key staff or increased insurance premiums.

Continuing professional development (CPD) Proactive learning activities that enable professionals to develop and enhance their abilities.

Convertible debt (or loan note) A loan from an investor or a group of investors that can be converted into an equity stake on some pre-agreed terms. Conversion is usually triggered by an event, and the note is usually associated with a coupon (interest rate) and a discount on the share price set by the next round of investment. The approach is used extensively in the USA, but less in the UK because the investor cannot claim SEIS or EIS tax relief.

Copyleft The application of copyright law to foster and encourage the right to copy, share, modify and improve creative works, usually to build collaborative communities that share and improve those works. Copyleft is usually implemented using a specific copyright licence, such as the GNU General Public Licence (GPL) and the Creative Commons Attribution Share Alike Licence.

Copyright The right of the owner of a work – whether literary, artistic or musical, graphical layout or software code – to control its use for a fixed time, usually seventy years after the originator's death (in the USA, EU and UK).

Copyright Witness Service Known in the UK as the UK Copyright Service, this service supports international copyright protection by securing independent evidence of ownership that helps to prove originality and ownership in any claims or disputes.

Corporation (specifically, a C corporation) In the USA, an independent legal entity owned by its shareholders. The corporation, not its shareholders, is legally liable for its actions and debts. Comparable with a limited company in the UK.

Corporation tax The tax paid by a company or corporation on its annual profits. The level of tax and time frame for payment varies by territory.

Cost per action or acquisition (CPA) A measure of the cost to the business of converting a lead into a sale. This measure can indicate the value for money of a promotional channel.

Cost per click (CPC) In relation to a pay-per-click (PPC) marketing campaign: a measure of the cost to the business of each online visit/interaction.

Cost per mille (CPM) In YouTube speak, this is what an advertiser pays to show their video 1,000 times.

Cost-plus pricing A pricing approach whereby the customer price is calculated by adding a profit margin to the cost of production and distribution.

Creative Commons Attribution Share Alike Licence (CC licence) A public copyright licence that enables the free distribution of a work, giving people the right to share, use and build upon it. CC protects the people who use or redistribute a work from copyright infringement as long as they abide by the conditions specified.

Credit factoring A scheme where the business sells to a third party the right to collect receipts from customers. Such schemes typically pay a percentage of the face value of an invoice immediately, with the remainder being paid, minus a commission, when the customer pays.

Customer An individual or community that perceives value in an offering.

Customer acquisition cost (CAC) See 'Cost per action or acquisition (CPA)'.

Customer care agreement (CCA) Relating to a product, a contract between a service provider and a service user that sets out a package of support that will be delivered for the product, and describes relevant aspects of their quality, performance and availability. It also scopes out the responsibilities and obligations on each of the parties involved.

Customer churn rate The percentage of customers that cease to subscribe or actively use the business's offering over a period.

Customer experience (CX) The impression received by a customer as a consequence of engaging and interacting with the business.

Customer journey A mapping of customer experience across the range of possible touch points with the business.

Customer lifetime value (CLV) A measure, or prediction, of the profit (to be) achieved from the relationship with a customer.

Customer purchasing option The price-packaging approach that is offered for customer purchase of a product or service. Examples include perpetual licence, monthly service charge and payment for access to a specialist asset.

Customer retention rate (CRR) A measure of how effectively customers are being retained. It is also referred to as the *churn rate* or *attrition rate* for customers.

Customization The act of extending or modifying an offering to satisfy particular needs. See also collaborative, adaptive and transparent customization.

Collaborative customization The customization of an offering where a business works jointly with its customers to determine the precise requirement.

Coopetition A term coined to describe the situation where businesses both cooperate and compete with each other.

Crowdfunding (peer-to-peer consumer lending) A means of raising investment for a company or a specific project by taking funds (typically of small size) from a large number of people. A range of exchange offerings are used, including charitable giving, products or equity.

Cyber Essentials A UK-government-backed cyber security certification scheme that sets out a good baseline of cyber security suitable for all organizations in all sectors. The scheme addresses five key controls that, when implemented correctly, can prevent around 80 per cent of cyber-attacks.

Cyber hygiene The management of online safety to mitigate the risk of damage from cyber-attack, including daily routines, occasional checks and general behaviours required to sustain *online health.*

Cyber physical system (CPS) A systems or product that integrates algorithms, networking and physical processes with feedback loops, such that physical processes affect computations and vice versa.

Data Protection Act (DPA) A UK law that controls how personal information is used by organizations, businesses or the government. Those responsible for using data must follow data-protection principles.

Database rights A form of aggregate copyright, where the owner claims protection for their skill and judgement in compiling a set of works, although not necessarily in any of the constituent parts.

Debt finance, loan or senior bank debt The provision of money against an agreed repayment schedule, including an interest component. A loan may be secured against an asset, or unsecured. A *senior bank loan* is a legal claim to the business's assets above all other debt obligations if the business fails.

Design right, also industrial design right A right that protects the look of a product, including its appearance, physical shape, configuration (how different parts of a design are arranged together) and decoration.

Development roadmap A plan that matches short- and long-term business objectives with the development activities by which they will be achieved.

Development velocity A planning method that describes the amount of development that can be completed in a time interval. Development is usually quantified using notional units of work.

Direct and variable costs Those business costs that relate specifically to product development and sales. Direct costs are those that are needed to deliver the offering to market, and variable costs are those that vary with volume of sales.

Director (of a company/corporation) An officer of a company/corporation who has been appointed to manage business activities and finances and to ensure that statutory obligations are met. They must act lawfully and honestly in their dealings, and their decisions must be to the benefit of the company.

Disruptive innovation One that brings to the market a different and new kind of value proposition, which may have the effect of changing the market's assumptions around how things work.

Dividend The distribution of a part of a company's profits to a class of its shareholders. The dividend rate is stated as an amount paid per share.

Drag provision (within a shareholders' agreement) A provision that forces minority shareholder(s) to sell their shares where required by the majority shareholder(s).

Dual licensing A licensing approach whereby an offering is made available under two alternative licences. This usually refers to the case where both an open-source licence and also a separate proprietary licence are offered for differing user communities.

Due diligence A detailed assessment of a business by a prospective investor, typically addressing financial, technical and people-based considerations.

Early adopter One of the first organizations to adopt an offering, and which often retains a special relationship.

Earnings before interest and tax (EBIT) A company's profit, taking account of all expenses except for interest and taxes. It is the difference between operating revenues and operating expenses.

Earnings before interest, tax, depreciation and amortization (EBITDA) A company's profit, taking account of all expenses except for interest, taxes, depreciation and amortization. EBITDA removes the effects of financing and accounting, so can be used to analyse and compare profitability between companies.

Easy access IP An arrangement whereby research institutions allow free access to their IP to companies and individuals, to enable development of new products and services that benefit society and the economy.

E-commerce The online (electronic) purchase and sale of goods or services, including the transfer of funds or data. Includes online markets and retail, electronic data interchange and financial exchanges. Synonymous with e-business.

Employee An individual with a contract of employment, whether or not formally expressed, and recognized rights and duties.

Employee churn rate The percentage of employees that leave the business over a period.

End-user licence agreement (EULA) A licence to use a software product.

Enterprise Investment Scheme (EIS) A UK tax relief scheme which offers tax reliefs to investors in higher-risk small companies.

Enterprise Management Incentive (EMI) A UK government employee share scheme for companies with assets less than £30 million, whereby shares can be purchased up to a value of £250,000 without paying tax. Capital gains tax may be due on sale of the shares.

Entrepreneur Someone who designs, builds, operates, manages and assumes the risks of a business.

Equity The total value of the shares issued by a business.

European Patent Office (EPO) The EU body responsible for the search and examination of patent applications and the grant of European patents.

European Union (EU) member states Austria, Belgium, Bulgaria, Croatia, Cyprus, Czech Republic, Denmark, Estonia, Finland, France, Germany, Greece, Hungary, Ireland, Italy, Latvia, Lithuania, Luxembourg, Malta, Netherlands, Poland, Portugal, Romania, Slovakia, Slovenia, Spain, Sweden, United Kingdom.

EU Intellectual Property Office (EUIPO) The body responsible for processing trademark and design applications for the EU and its member states.

Exclusive licence A licence limited by being granted to a single licensee. Exclusivity can be granted within specific named markets or territories, and may apply for a specified period of time.

FAANG An acronym for Facebook, Amazon, Apple, Netflix and Google, a collection of corporations that currently have high weightings in all major indices.

Fintech A general term for disruptive technology offerings within the financial services sector.

First-mover advantage (FMA) The potential value available to the initial player within a market or market segment.

Foreground IP The IP that is created by the activities of a project.

Franchise A franchisee is granted the right to use a business's brand and way of operating for a period of time. Offering franchises avoids the investments and liabilities involved in replicating a chain of outlets.

Free Software Foundation A non-profit organization that promotes the universal freedom to study, distribute, create and modify computer software, with the organization's preference for software being distributed under copyleft terms, such as with its own GNU General Public Licence.

Fulfilment In business (e-commerce) terms, this refers to the process of delivering an order to the customer, potentially including warehousing, and picking and shipping it to the right address, with arrangements for failed delivery and other eventualities.

Fully paid shares Issued shares for which the company receives the nominal value of the shares.

Generally Accepted Accounting Principles (GAAP) A US accounting standard from the Financial Accounting Standards Board (FASB). An international alternative is the IFRS standard from the International Accounting Standards Board (IASB). GAAP is more rules-based, and IFRS is more principles-based.

General Data Protection Regulation (GDPR) A European regulation intended to strengthen and unify data protection for individuals within the EU.

Global Data Synchronization Network (GDSN) A cross-industry standard widely applied within the retail, health-care and food-service industries. It underpins a network by which subscribing trading partners can share product data through automated data exchange.

GNU General Public Licence (GPL) An open-source licence that allows free distribution subject to the condition that further developments and applications are put under the same licence.

Gross margin The percentage of sales revenue that is retained after taking account of the direct costs associated with producing the goods and services sold. Gross Margin (%) = (revenue – cost of sales) / revenue.

Gross merchandise value (GMV) For ventures that provide an e-commerce platform across a marketplace, GMV measures the total value of merchandise sold over a given period of time.

Growth, or expansion, capital Private equity investment in a more mature business that needs additional capital – for example, to expand or finance an acquisition.

HM Revenue & Customs (HMRC) The UK's tax, payments and customs authority.

Holding company Within a legal structure, a *parent* company that wholly owns or has majority ownership of one or more *operating companies*. It will often be responsible for the protection of assets, the management of financial losses and the limitation of liability.

Horizontal innovation One that applies across industry sectors.

Hype curve An annual publication by Gartner that positions emerging technologies across a maturity time frame.

Idea An inventive step.

Ideal customer The profile of a notional business or individual customer that will be inclined (or will need) to make a purchase, and that has both the ability to pay and the authority to purchase it. Additionally, an ideal customer will be an advocate for further sales.

Incentive stock options (ISOs) A US-government-approved stock option scheme that enables employees to receive preferential tax treatment.

Indirect costs The business costs that are independent of output. These are the underlying costs needed to keep the business operating, and can potentially support multiple products. These costs include fixed overheads and recurrent fixed costs.

Industry 4.0 A description of the current trend of automated manufacturing, characterized by cyber-physical systems, the Internet of Things and cloud computing.

Initial public offering (IPO) A process by which a business can go public. It usually involves contracting an investment bank to underwrite the shares by assuming legal responsibility for them. The underwriter sells the shares to the public with the aim of achieving a higher price than was paid to the original owners.

Innovation The successful exploitation of an idea as a product or service offering.

Innovator Someone who introduces new ideas, methods or products.

Intellectual property (IP) A property or asset that is the result of creativity. It is something unique that has been physically created; an idea alone is not intellectual property. Copyright, patents, designs and trademarks are all ways of protecting intellectual property.

International Financial Reporting Standards (IFRS) An international accounting standard from the International Accounting Standards Board (IASB). A US alternative is GAAP from the Financial Accounting Standards Board (FASB). IFRS is more principles-based, and GAAP is more rules-based.

International Standards Organization (ISO) A body responsible for developing and publishing international standards, comprising representatives from national standards organizations.

Internet of Things (IoT) The use of technologies such as sensors, actuators and network connectivity to enable data sharing and intercommunication between diverse devices, including vehicles, buildings and living creatures.

Intrapreneur An innovator of profitable new offerings within a large organization.

Joint development agreement (JDA) An agreement between parties that intend to work jointly, usually on a research and development initiative, and to respect each other's confidential information.

Joint venture (JV) A business arrangement where two or more parties agree to collaborate towards achieving a common objective. A JV can be a legal entity, business contract or loose agreement.

Key objective One that is chosen to be measured and managed through being judged to be particularly informative of business achievement.

Key performance indicator (KPI) A measurable expression that indicates the effectiveness with which key objectives are met.

Know-how Practical knowledge, often tacit, on how to accomplish something.

Lagging (or lag) measure One that gives a backward look at what has been achieved, sometimes referred to as an *outcome measure*, or a *rear-view mirror*.

Leading (or lead) measure One that gives a forward look towards achievement of objectives, sometimes referred to as a *performance driver*.

Letter of intent (LOI) A confirmation from a customer organization that it intends to proceed with a proposal. An LOI is sometimes provided to enable work to commence ahead of formal contract.

Licence to use An agreement by a licensor to a licensee to use the licensed material in accordance with the terms of the licence.

Limited company In the UK, an independent legal entity owned by its shareholders. The company, not its shareholders, is legally liable for its actions and debts. Comparable with a C Corporation in the USA.

Limited liability partnerships/companies A hybrid type of legal structure that provides the limited liability features of a company/corporation and the tax efficiencies and flexibility of a partnership.

Liquidated damages A compensation arrangement typically involving a payment to be made upon breach of contract by the failing party to the party that has suffered.

Liquidation The bringing of a company's operations to an end, including the division of its assets across creditors and shareholders, according to the priority of their claims.

Machine learning (ML) An application of artificial intelligence in which a digital device is able to learn without being explicitly programmed.

Machine to machine (M2M) A reference to any channel for data communication between machines or devices, including transmission of data to personal appliances.

Madrid Protocol A mechanism for registering and managing trademarks worldwide, through one centralized system.

Management shares A class of shares with additional voting rights to enable control of a company by particular parties.

Man-in-the-middle (MITM) attack A cyber-attack where an attacker secretly interposes themselves into the communication between two parties, who believe that they are communicating directly with each other.

Market forces (M. E. Porter) A framework that combines the related considerations of competition and negotiation into a single model of five forces (here extended to include an additional sixth force).

Market pull An innovation approach driven by market experience of a business's own or another's offering. Market-pulled innovations tend to be incremental to existing offerings.

Medtech A general term for disruptive technology offerings within the medical sector.

Memorandum of association A document that defines a company to inform shareholders, creditors and other stakeholders what the company has been formed to do, and what capital it has.

Memorandum of understanding (MoU) A written agreement between two or more parties that establishes a non-legally-binding partnership for a particular purpose. An MoU is stronger than a *gentlemen's agreement*, but weaker than a legal contract.

Merger and acquisition (M&A) activity Transactions relating to the buying, selling or merging of companies.

Mezzanine financing Debt capital that gives the lender the rights to convert to an equity interest if the loan is not paid back in time. It is generally provided by banks and venture capital companies.

Micro-business In the UK, a business with any two of the following: $<$ ten employees, $<$ £632,000 turnover, $<$ £316,000 on the balance sheet.

Micro venture capital (VC) investor A VC investor offering seed investments, typically between \$25,000 and \$500,000, in early-stage ventures.

Minimum viable product (MVP) Originally: 'that version of a new product which allows a team to collect the maximum amount of validated learning about customers with the least effort'. The term is now used also to mean an immature (but viable) early release of a product.

Monopoly (market) One with one seller and many buyers.

Monopsony (market) One with one buyer and many sellers.

Monthly recurring revenue (MRR) The income that a company can reliably anticipate every thirty days. This is central to managed service and cloud services (SaaS) businesses.

Multi-sided platforms A technology that creates value by enabling direct interactions between two or more customer or participant groups, through an effect referred to as the sharing economy.

Net fee income (NFI) The income received by a venture during an accounting period after subtracting the costs of sales, expenses and taxes from the revenues generated.

Net promoter score (NPS) A customer loyalty measure derived from answers to the question of how likely it is that a customer would recommend an offering to a friend or colleague. It is claimed to correlate with revenue growth. The term is a registered trademark of Fred Reichheld, Bain & Company and Satmetrix Systems.

Nominal (or par, or face) value of shares In the UK, every issued share has a nominal or par value, which may be, for example, £1, £0.1, £0.01 or any other sum in any currency. A share cannot be issued *fully paid* at a discount on its nominal value. Some territories, including some states in the USA, permit the issue of stock with no par value.

Nominee service/arrangement An arrangement for managing the shareholdings of multiple smaller investors. An independent organization (the nominee) is the shareholder in the company's register, but the shares are held on behalf of the individual shareholders, such that they can individually claim any tax benefits such as SEIS or EIS.

Non-disclosure agreement (NDA) An agreement between parties that intend to share materials for a specified purpose, and to respect each other's confidential information.

Non-exclusive licence A licence that grants rights to the licensee on the understanding that the licensor may exploit those rights themselves, and also grant the same rights to additional licensees.

Non-executive director (NED) A director with no specific executive responsibilities, and a role more oriented towards objective advice and governance.

Non-transferable licence Applies only to the specified licensee; any proposed transfer would require the negotiation of a new licence.

Objectives and Key Results (OKR) A performance management technique that prioritizes activity against ambitious business objectives.

Offering The embodiment of an idea in the form of product or service.

Oligopoly (market) One with a small number of sellers and many buyers.

Oligopsony (market) One with a small number of buyers and many sellers.

On-demand software A software licensing approach whereby software is centrally hosted and charged on a subscription basis. Also referred to as *software as a service.*

Open innovation Loosening of boundaries between organizations to use external ideas as well as internal ideas, and internal and external routes to market.

Open-book pricing A contracting mechanism whereby the price charged is calculated by adding a predefined profit margin to the cost of production and distribution.

Open source A software or hardware product for which the design is publicly accessible so as to enable unlimited modification and sharing.

Open-source hardware Hardware whose design is made publicly available so that anyone can study, modify, distribute, make and sell the design or hardware based on that design.

Open-source software A software licensing approach whereby source code is made available under a licence by which the copyright holder provides open rights to study, change and distribute the software; see also the 'GNU General Public Licence'.

Operating company Within a legal structure, a subsidiary company that is wholly or majority owned by the holding company. It will usually be responsible for the operations of the company.

Operating expenditure (Opex) The purchase of goods and services that a business needs to run. In contrast to capital expenses, operating expenses are fully tax-deductible in the year they are made.

Operating (profit) margin The proportion of revenue that remains after paying for all variable costs of production. Operating margin (%) = (revenue – Opex) / revenue; where Opex includes all operating costs (direct and indirect).

Order A contracted purchase request from a customer. At a minimum, it has a description of the products and services to be purchased, the amounts to be paid, and a time frame for delivery and payment.

Ordinary resolution A resolution by a board approving a change to some aspect of a company, including approving a dividend payment, appointing or removing directors, or approving loans to directors. A special resolution needs a majority vote.

Ordinary or common shares The normal equity ownership in a company proportional to other ordinary shareholders. All companies are required to have ordinary shares as part of their stock, as defined in their articles of association, and at least one ordinary share must be issued.

Organic growth The process of growing a business by reinvesting profits from its revenues, rather than by investment or acquisition.

Outcome (for a customer) The benefit received from an offering, including a new capability, a financial saving or a mitigated risk.

Paradigm innovation One that brings about changes in the underlying mental model whereby people think about how something is done.

Passing off An action where a business falsely encourages customers to believe that their offerings are those of another.

Patent, or utility patent (USA) An exclusive right granted for an invention that enables its owner to decide how – or whether – the invention can be used by others. In exchange for this right, the patent owner publishes technical information about the invention.

Patent Cooperation Treaty (PCT) An agreement administered by WIPO covering most industrial countries. It assists those seeking to achieve patents in multiple countries.

Payment terms The length of time between invoice and payment, including any associated discounts or penalties.

Penetration pricing A pricing approach whereby a low initial price is set so as to achieve rapid market share.

Perfect competition (market) One with many firms, and freedom of entry for buyers and sellers.

Perpetual licence A licence that grants the licensor with the rights to use the licensed IP without any time limitation.

Personal information Any detail about a living individual that can be used on its own, or with other data, to identify them.

Pivot A significant change to an idea or to the plan by which it will be taken to market through a product/service offering.

Platform as a service (PaaS) A cloud computing service providing a platform for businesses to develop, run and manage applications.

Postground IP IP that is relevant to a collaboration that is developed subsequently by one of the parties.

Post-money valuation The valuation of a business after receiving investment or finance. The value of a business can differ before and after receiving investment.

Pre-money valuation The valuation of a business before receiving investment or finance. The value of a business differs before and after receiving investment.

Preferred or preference shares A kind of share that ranks above ordinary shares when it comes to the payment of dividends and return of capital (for example, on liquidation). Often these have no voting rights, but can pay out a fixed dividend.

Premium pricing A pricing approach that sets a higher price than competitors to reflect unique features or advantages, or a strong brand value.

Price/earnings (P/E) ratio The ratio of a company's share price to its earnings per share, calculated by the market value/earnings per share.

Price sensitivity The degree to which the price of an offering affects purchasing behavior.

Private equity (PE) investment fund Funds and investors that invest directly in private companies.

Process innovation One that brings changes to the way in which things are created or delivered.

Product innovation One that introduces changes in the things that are offered and/or in the customer experience of the offering.

Product roadmap A plan that describes anticipated development priorities and activities over time, to align relevant parties and to assess the required effort.

Promotion Also referred to as marketing, or demand generation, this is about establishing an attractive, distinctive and accessible position within a targeted market.

Proptech A general term for disruptive technology offerings within the property and rental services sector.

Public company One whose shares are listed and traded on a stock exchange and can be bought and sold by anyone. In the USA, a private corporation that achieves a stock market listing becomes a publicly listed corporation. In the UK, a listed company is called a public limited company (denoted plc).

Registered IP rights Trademarks, patents, designs or copyright that have been lodged formally with a relevant authority, and which give the owner legal protection amounting to a monopoly over the use of those rights.

Repeat business Can refer to recurring or renewal business with a customer and also to new business, comprising the sale of a new offering or a sale of the same offering to another part of the customer organization.

Research and development (R&D) The innovation, exploration and improvement of products and services.

Return on investment (ROI) A measure that demonstrates the efficiency or value created by an investment or purchase.

Revenue Income received by a business from its normal business activities, such as satisfying customer orders for products and services. Also referred to as the *top line*, or sales or turnover. The calculation of revenue is based on an accounting policy such as the Generally Accepted Accounting Principles (GAAP) from the Financial Accounting Standards Board (FASB).

Revenue per mille (RPM) In YouTube speak, this is the revenue that a YouTube channel earns from 1,000 views.

Revenue projection A forecast of the earnings that a business will generate during a specific period.

Revenue recognition As defined by an accounting policy such as GAPP, the rules defining when revenues can be recognized. In general, revenue may be recognized only when it has been earned, which means that in the case of an order for a six-month service, revenues will be recognized monthly over that period, and not at the point of receiving the order.

Risk Refers to the possibility of something untoward or negative that may potentially happen.

Risk register A tabular technique for expressing and managing the risk profile of a business.

Route to market A function or partner through which an offering is promoted and/or delivered to customers. See also 'Channel' and 'Channel strategy'.

Runway A measure of how long the business can operate with only the current resources and commitments, before it runs out of cash.

Sale A contract whereby possession, or licence of a good or property, or the entitlement to a service, is exchanged for money, or for some other value.

Sales tax (VAT in the UK) A tax that is set at a range of defined levels for goods of specified categories. Such taxes are collected by businesses, who are required periodically to complete a return form against which a payment will be taken.

Seed/start-up accelerators Fixed-term, cohort-based programmes, which include mentorship and educational components and culminate in a public pitch event or demo day. An accelerator will usually take a small *pre-seed* investment in a venture in exchange for a small equity share.

Seed Enterprise Investment Scheme (SEIS) A UK tax relief scheme designed to help small, early-stage companies raise equity finance by offering tax reliefs to individual investors who purchase new shares in those companies. SEIS is intended to recognize the particular difficulties faced by very early-stage companies in attracting investment, by offering tax relief at a higher rate.

Seed investment The first stage of venture capital financing, usually comprising a modest amount of money to finance early development and growth. A seed round will typically involve giving up around 20 per cent of equity.

Segment A market subset with common needs and priorities. Market segments can be geographic, demographic, behavioural or psychographic.

Series A investment Under normal conventions, this is the first significant equity transaction following those relating to the business's founders, employees or angel investors. Subsequent investment rounds would be referred to as series B, C, D, etc.

Service level agreement (SLA) A contract between a service provider and a service user that sets out a collection of services that will be delivered, and describes relevant aspects of their quality, performance and availability. It also scopes out the responsibilities and obligations on each of the parties involved.

Serviceable available market (SAM) Within the total addressable market, the serviceable available market (SAM) is that part of the market that could potentially be served by a business, taking into account the competition, the available routes to market, any product or regulatory constraints and so on.

Shareholders' or stockholders' agreement A contract between a company and some or all of its shareholders, defining the rules, rights and obligations relating to the issue of one or more classes of shares. It needs to be read together with the company's formal articles of association from which it derives.

Share option An option that entitles its holder (typically an employee) to buy a share at an agreed price at a future date, with an expectation that the shares will have increased in value when the option is exercised. The option may be subject to individual or team performance targets. No purchase of shares is required until they have increased in value, which will cover the purchase cost.

Share premium The difference between the market value of a share and its nominal value.

Sideground IP IP that is relevant to a collaboration, but which has been developed independently and in parallel by one of the collaborating parties.

Skimming (pricing) A pricing approach whereby a high initial price is set and reduced over time as competitors arrive.

Small business In the UK, a business with any two of the following: < fifty employees, < £10.2 million turnover, < £5.1 million on the balance sheet.

Small and medium-sized enterprise (SME) In the USA, a business with fewer than 500 employees: they account for 99 per cent of all businesses, employ over 50 per cent of private sector employees and generate 65 per cent of new private sector jobs. In the UK, an SME is a business with fewer than 250 employees. There were 5.4 million SMEs in the UK in 2016.

Smart objective One that is specific, measurable, aligned, realistic and time-related.

Social engineering In cyber-crime, the use of deception to manipulate people into giving up confidential or personal information that can be used by an attacker.

Social enterprises An organization that is driven by social or cultural values rather than by financial gain or profit.

Software as a service (SaaS) A software licensing approach whereby software is centrally hosted and charged on a subscription basis. Also referred to as *on-demand software.*

Software escrow agreement An agreement to deposit software source code with a third-party escrow agent, to provide an ability to maintain the software in the event that the business fails or becomes incapable itself of doing so.

Sole licence Like an exclusive licence, except that the licensor also reserves the right to exploit the IP themselves.

Sole trader/proprietor The simplest of business structures, where the company is entirely owned and operated by an individual with no legal distinction between themselves and the business. The sole trader/proprietor is entitled to all the profits and is responsible for all the debts, losses and liabilities.

Special resolution A resolution by a board approving a fundamental matter affecting a company, including amending its articles of association, allowing it to buy back shares or winding it up. A special resolution needs a 75 per cent majority vote.

Stakeholder (ecosystem) An organization that participates in the ecosystem of a business, including suppliers, regulators, customers, competitors and delivery partners.

Stakeholder (programme/campaign management) An individual that is in some way significant to a campaign or programme, by virtue of being a decision-maker, a purchaser, a user, a technical adviser, an influencer, an implementer ...

Statement of capital Details of a company's shares and the rights to be attached to them, as required for company registration in the UK.

Stock option See 'Share option'.

Supply chain management (SCM) The management of the flow of goods and services from their point of origin to the point of consumption. Depending on the nature of the business, this can involve movement and storage of materials, inventory management and control.

Supply chain operations reference (SCOR) A process reference model managed and developed by APICS, the world's largest unbiased non-profit supply chain organization. It is endorsed by the Supply Chain Council as the cross-industry, standard diagnostic tool for supply chain management.

Sustaining innovation One that offers improved performance into an established market.

Sweat equity The use of company equity to recompense or motivate effort, sometimes instead of full financial compensation. Also referred to as *stock for services* or *equity compensation*.

Sweet equity A class of shares issued (usually after an investment round) at a lower price to motivate management.

Tactical map A detailed mapping of the customer journey in terms of process steps and associated support requirements.

Tag provision (within a shareholders' agreement) A provision that enables minority shareholder(s) to sell their shares for the same price and on the same terms and conditions as the majority shareholder(s).

Target market The defined, or targeted, set of customers to which a venture determines to sell its products and services, and to whom it directs its promotional activities.

Target or obtainable market (TOM) The portion of the serviceable available market that can realistically be obtained by a business in a targeted time frame by executing its plan.

Technical debt The future development work implied by a design decision motivated by short-term expedience.

Technology push An innovation approach originating from a research- and technology-driven idea that has been qualified as offering the potential to be developed as a successful market offering.

Technology readiness levels (TRLs) A framework of levels (1 to 9) for describing and assessing product or system maturity.

Technology Transfer Office (TTO) Within a university, the body responsible for arranging and managing exploitation of its intellectual property.

Term sheet Ahead of a full investment contract, a summary agreement that defines the principal parameters and conditions of the deal.

Threat actor An entity, personal or organizational, that in some way threatens an organization's security.

Time-limited licence Specifies a time horizon, typically together with a renewal mechanism.

Total addressable market (TAM) Also referred to as total available market, this is the total potential demand for an offering, assuming the whole available market is achieved.

Touch point In the context of analysing a customer journey, any way that a customer can interact with a business.

Trade secret Any confidential business information that provides an enterprise with a competitive edge.

Trademark A sign capable of distinguishing the goods or services of one enterprise from those of other enterprises. A trademark may be registered or unregistered.

Transferable licence A licence that permits the licensee to reassign in some way. Transfer may be permitted specifically within the context of specified events.

Transparent customization The customization of an offering where an offering is pre-customized for a customer.

UK Intellectual Property Office The UK government body responsible for IP rights, including patents, designs, trademarks and copyright.

Unicorn A technology business valued at $1 billion or more.

Unique selling point/proposition (USP) A succinct statement of what differentiates the offering, or what makes it better than its competitors.

Unitary patent (UP) A European patent process that will come into effect in late 2017 and that will enable an application to cover up to twenty-five member states of the EU. For qualifying patents, a single renewal fee will be payable annually for the contracting states.

Unitary Patent Court (UPC) An EU court to handle UP litigation and actions, including those relating to applications and patents processed through the current scheme and which have not specifically opted out of the UPC.

University spin-out (USO) A new venture that is initially dependent upon licensing or assignment of a university's intellectual property.

Unregistered IP rights Trademarks, designs or copyright that are automatically held by the IP owner to provide protection against copying; the protection available is less effective than with registered IP rights.

Unrestricted market value (UMV) For the purposes of UK taxation, the value of an asset, such as a share or option holding, without taking into account any market restrictions that might apply. See also 'AMV'.

US Patent and Trademark Office (USPTO) The federal agency responsible for granting patents and registering trademarks in the USA.

Value Something that is perceived by one or more communities to be valuable, whether or not this value is quantifiable.

Value-based pricing An approach whereby the price is set on the basis of the value delivered to the customer by the offering.

Value capture How the business will benefit from exploitation of its offering.

Value delivery How a value proposition will be made available to its beneficiaries such that they achieve the promised value.

Value proposition A wrapping of a proposed value with a customer or beneficiary.

Value-rarity-imitability-organization (VRIO) analysis A technique for assessing individuals' contribution to business competitiveness.

Venture A business activity or initiative involving risk or uncertainty.

Venture capital (VC) fund An investment fund contributed by investors for the purpose of acquiring private equity stakes in businesses with strong growth potential.

Venture capital (VC) investor Financing provided by firms or funds to early-stage firms that are deemed to have high growth. VCs invest in companies in exchange for equity (ownership stake).

Venture debt or venture lending A kind of loan usually provided to venture-backed companies by banks or other lenders to fund working capital or expenses.

Vertical innovation One that applies specifically to a particular industry sector, such as energy, health care or retail.

Vesting A process over time whereby an employee accrues rights to shares, options or pension contributions. A vesting schedule determines when an employee will acquire full ownership of the asset or benefit.

Viral giveaway competition A competition offered across a network of existing contacts. Entrants can increase their chance of winning by promoting the competition further across their own networks.

Virtual reality (VR) Technology that generates a digital simulation of a three-dimensional world in which a person using specialist equipment can experience and/or interact.

White labelling A practice in which a product or service produced by one company is rebranded by another company to make it appear to be their own offering.

World Intellectual Property Organization (WIPO) An agency of the United Nations created in 1967 to promote the protection of intellectual property throughout the world, through cooperation among states.

World Trade Organization (WTO) An intergovernmental organization that regulates international trade.

World Wide Web Consortium (W3C) The main international standards organization that oversees the web's continued development, including protocols and guidelines to ensure its long-term growth.

Bibliography

Books

Adner R. (2013). *The Wide Lens: What Successful Innovators See that Others Miss*, revised edn (Portfolio/Penguin).

Atrill P. (2014). *Financial Management for Decision Makers*, 7th edn (Pearson).

Baker R. J. (2006). *Pricing on Purpose: Creating and Capturing Value* (Wiley).

Baker R. J. (2010). *Implementing Value Pricing: A Radical Business Model for Professional Firms* (Wiley).

Barringer B. R. (2015). *Entrepreneurship*, 5th edn (Pearson).

Bass L., Clements P. and Kazman R. (2013). *Software Architecture in Practice* (Addison-Wesley).

Bessant J. and Tidd J. (2011). *Innovation and Entrepreneurship*, 2nd edn (Wiley).

Blank S. and Dorf B. (2012). *The Startup Owner's Manual* (K & S Ranch).

Boynton A., Fischer B. and Bole W. (2011). *The Idea Hunter: How to Find the Best Ideas and Make Them Happen* (Jossey-Bass).

Burns P. (2011). *Entrepreneurship and Small Business: Start-Up, Growth and Maturity*, 3rd edn (Palgrave Macmillan).

Burns P. (2016). *Entrepreneurship and Small Business*, 4th edn (Palgrave Macmillan).

Burton E. and Bragg S. M. (2000). *Accounting and Finance for Your Small Business*, 2nd edn (Wiley).

Calder A. (2016). *EU GDPR: A Pocket Guide*, pocket edn (ITGP).

Chemuturi M. (2013). *Requirements Engineering and Management for Software Development Projects* (Springer).

Chopra S. and Meindl P. (2006). *Supply Chain Management: Strategy, Planning, and Operation*, 3rd edn (Pearson).

Christensen C. M. (2013). *The Innovator's Dilemma*, reprint edn (Harvard Business Review Press).

Christopher M. (2016). *Logistics and Supply Chain Management*, 5th edn (FT Publishing International).

Cornwall J. R., Vang D. O. and Hartman J. M. (2016). *Entrepreneurial Financial Management: An Applied Approach*, 4th edn (Routledge).

Coughlan A. T. and Jap S. D. (2016). *A Field Guide to Channel Strategy: Building Routes to Market* (CreateSpace Independent Publishing Platform).

Davenport T. H. and Manville B. (2012). *Judgement Calls* (Harvard Business Review Press).

Davidow W. H. (1986). *Marketing High Technology: An Insider's View* (Simon & Schuster).

de Vries H. (2016). *Venture Capital Deal Terms: A Guide to Negotiating and Structuring Venture Capital Transactions* (CreateSpace Independent Publishing Platform).

Dixon M., Adamson B., Spenner P. and Toman N. (2015). *The Challenger Customer: Selling to the Hidden Influencer Who Can Multiply Your Results* (Portfolio Penguin).

Draper W. H. (2012). *The Startup Game: Inside the Partnership between Venture Capitalists and Entrepreneurs*, reprint edn (Palgrave Macmillan).

Drucker P. (2008). *The Five Most Important Questions You Will Ever Ask about Your Organization*, new edn (Jossey-Bass).

Fagerberg J., Mowery D. C. and Nelson R. R. (eds) (2005). *The Oxford Handbook of Innovation* (Oxford University Press).

Fitzpatrick R. (2013). *The Mom Test: How to Talk to Customers and Learn If Your Business Is a Good Idea When Everyone Is Lying to You* (Founder Centric).

Freeman C. and Louçã F. (2001). *As Time Goes By: From the Industrial Revolutions to the Information Revolution* (Oxford University Press).

Gallouj F. and Djellal F. (eds) (2011). *The Handbook of Innovation and Services: A Multi-Disciplinary Perspective* (Edward Elgar).

Gawer A. and Cusumano M. (2002). *Platform Leadership: How Intel, Microsoft and Cisco Drive Industry Innovation* (Harvard Business School Press).

Gee S. (1981). *Technology Transfer, Innovation and International Competitiveness* (Wiley).

Gladwell M. (2002). *The Tipping Point: How Little Things Can Make a Big Difference* (Abacus).

Goffin K. and Mitchell R. (2016). *Innovation Management: Effective Strategy and Implementation*, 3rd edn (Palgrave Macmillan).

Hartmann P. (2014). *New Business Creation: Systems for Institutionalized Radical Innovation Management* (Springer Gabler).

Hersey P., Blanchard K. H. and Johnson D. E. (2012). *Management of Organizational Behavior: Leading Human Resources*, 10th edn (Pearson).

Hobsbawm E. (1999). *Age of Extremes: The Short Twentieth Century 1914–1991* (Abacus).

InnovateUK (2017). *Scaling Up: The Investor Perspective - How Innovative UK Businesses Can Achieve Sustainable Growth* (Technology Strategy Board).

IT Governance Privacy Team (2017). *EU General Data Protection Regulation (GDPR): An Implementation and Compliance Guide*, 2nd edn (ITGP).

Jeschonnek L., Mucke P., Walter J. and Kirch L. (eds) (2016). *World Risk Report 2016* (Bündnis Entwicklung Hilft and UNU-EHS).

Kondratieff N. (1984). *Long Wave Cycle*, English version (Richardson & Snyder).

Kotonya G. and Sommerville I. (1998): *Requirements Engineering: Processes and Techniques* (Wiley).

Lambert P. (2016). *The Data Protection Officer: Profession, Rules, and Role* (Auerbach Publications).

Landstrom H. and Mason C. (eds) (2016). *Handbook of Research on Business Angels* (Edward Elgar).

Lee A. C., Lee C. F. and Lee J. C. (2009). *Financial Analysis, Planning and Forecasting Theory and Application*, 2nd edn (World Scientific Publishing).

Macdivitt H. and Wilkinson M. (2011). *Value-Based Pricing: Drive Sales and Boost Your Bottom Line by Creating, Communicating and Capturing Customer Value* (McGraw-Hill Education).

Mangan J. and Lalwani C. L. (2016). *Global Logistics and Supply Chain Management*, 3rd edn (Wiley).

Martin D. (2008). *The Company Director's Desktop Guide*, 4th edn (Thorogood).

Maxwell J. C. (2007). *Failing Forward: Turning Mistakes into Stepping Stones for Success*, reprint edn (Thomas Nelson).

McLean T. (2017). *On Time, in Full: Achieving Perfect Delivery with Lean Thinking in Purchasing, Supply Chain, and Production Planning* (Productivity Press).

Millman D. (2011). *Brand Thinking and Other Noble Pursuits* (Allwoth Press).

Moore G. A. (2014). *Crossing the Chasm*, 3rd edn (HarperCollins).

Olve N-G., Roy J. and Wetter M. (2004). *Performance Drivers: A Practical Guide to Using the Balanced Scorecard* (Wiley).

Osterwalder A., Pigneur Y., Bernarda G., Smith A. and Papadakos T. (2015). *Value Proposition Design: How to Create Products and Services Customers Want* (Wiley).

Pearce J. M. (2015). *Return on Investment for Open Source Scientific Hardware Development* (Oxford University Press).

Peppers D. and Rogers M. (2016). *Managing Customer Relationships: A Strategic Framework*, 3rd edn (Wiley).

Phadke U. and Vyakarnam S. (2017). *Camels, Tigers and Unicorns: Rethinking Science and Technology-Enabled Innovation* (World Scientific).

Phillips P. P. and Phillips J. J. (2006). *Return on Investment (ROI) Basics* (Association for Talent Development).

Pink D. H. (2014). *To Sell Is Human*, main edn (Canongate Books).

Ramachandran S., Devaraj R. and Rasidhar L. (2017). *Production Planning and Control* (Airwalk Publications).

Raulerson P., Malraison J.-C. and Leboyer A. (2009). *Building Routes to Customers: Proven Strategies for Profitable Growth* (Springer-Verlag).

Ries E. (2011). *The Lean Startup: How Today's Entrepreneurs Use Continuous Innovation to Create Radically Successful Businesses* (Crown).

Rodgers E. (2003). *Diffusion of Innovations*, 5th edn (Simon & Schuster).

Romans A. (2013). *The Entrepreneurial Bible to Venture Capital: Inside Secrets from the Leaders in the Startup Game* (McGraw-Hill Education).

Rushton A., Croucher P. and Baker P. (2014). *The Handbook of Logistics and Distribution Management: Understanding the Supply Chain*, 5th edn (Kogan Page).

Sarasvathy, S. D. (2009). *Effectuation: Elements of Entrepreneurial Expertise* (Edward Elgar).

Schilling M. A. (2016). *Strategic Management of Technological Innovation*, 5th edn (McGraw Hill).

Schumpeter J. (1994). *Capitalism, Socialism and Democracy*, revised edn (Routledge).

Schwartz M. and Kim G. (2016). *The Art of Business Value* (IT Revolution Press).

Shultz M. and Doerr J. E. (2014). *Insight Selling: Surprising Research on What Sales Winners Do Differently* (Wiley).

Tidd J. and Bessant J. (2013). *Managing Innovation: Integrating Technological, Market and Organizational Change*, 5th edn (Wiley).

Timmons J. A. (1999). *New Venture Creation: Entrepreneurship for the 21st Century* (McGraw Hill).

Toffler A. (1981). *The Third Wave* (Pan Books).

Trott P. (2016). *Innovation Management and New Product Development*, 6th edn (Pearson).

Westland J. C. (2017). *Global Innovation Management*, 2nd edn (Palgrave Macmillan).

Wheeler A. (2013). *Designing Brand Identity* (Wiley).

Wind Y. and Findiesen Hays C. (2016). *Beyond Advertising: Creating Value through All Customer Touchpoints* (Wiley).

Journal Articles

Aven T. (2016). Risk assessment and risk management: Review of recent advances on their foundation. *European Journal of Operational Research* 253(1): 1–13.

Barney J. B. (1995). Looking inside for competitive advantage. *The Academy of Management Executive* 9(4): 49–61.

Bass F. M. (1969). A new product growth model for consumer durables. *Management Science* 15 (5): 215–227.

Bessant, J. (2005). Enabling continuous and discontinuous innovation: Learning from the private sector. *Public Money & Management* 25(1): 35–42.

Bhuiyan N. (2011). A framework for successful new product development. *Journal of Industrial Engineering and Management* 4(4): 746–770.

Boer H. and Gertsen F. (2003). From continuous improvement to continuous innovation: A (retro) (per)spective. *International Journal of Technology Management* 26(8): 805–827.

Doran G., Miller A. and Cunningham J. (1981). There's a S.M.A.R.T. way to write management's goals and objectives. *Management Review* 70(11): 35–36.

Drath W. H., McCauley C. D., Palus C. J., Velsor E. V., O'Connor P. M. G. and McGuire J. B. (2008). Direction, alignment, commitment: Toward a more integrative ontology of leadership. *The Leadership Quarterly* 19(6): 635–653.

Garcia R. and Calantone R. (2002). A critical look at technological innovation typology and innovativeness terminology: A literature review. *The Journal of Product Innovation Management* 19(2): 110–132.

Hinterhubera A. and Liozub S. M. (2014). Is innovation in pricing your next source of competitive advantage? *Business Horizons* 57(3): 413–423.

Hossain M., Islam Z., Sayeed M. A. and Kauranen I. (2016). A comprehensive review of open innovation literature. *Journal of Science and Technology Policy Management* 7(1): 2–25.

Karray A. and Sigue S. P. (2016). Should companies jointly promote their complementary products when they compete in other product categories? *European Journal of Operational Research* 255 (2): 620–630.

Lok P., Hung R. Y., Walsh P., Wang P. and Crawford J. (2005). An integrative framework for measuring the extent to which organizational variables influence the success of process improvement programmes. *Journal of Management Studies* 42(7): 1357–1381.

Marin-Garcia J. A., Aznar-Mas L. and Ladrón de Guevara F. G. (2011). Innovation types and talent management for innovation. *Working Papers on Operations Management* 2(2): 25–31.

Peres R., Muller E. and Mahajan V. (2010). Innovation diffusion and new product growth models: A critical review and research directions. *International Journal of Research in Marketing* 27(2): 91–106.

Tonnessen T. (2005). Continuous innovation through company-wide employee participation. *TQM Magazine* 17(2): 195–207.

van der Panne G., van Beers C. and Kleinknecht A. (2003). Success and failure of innovation: A literature review. *International Journal of Innovation Management* 7(3): 309–338.

Chapters in Edited Books

Braam G. J. M. (2012). Balanced scorecard's interpretative variability and organizational change, in C.-H. Quah and O. L. Dar (eds), *Business Dynamics in the 21st Century* (InTech).

De Cleyn S. H. and Braet J. (2010). What determines the number of spin-offs generated by European universities? in M. Fink and I. Hatak (eds), *Current Research on Entrepreneurship and SME Management* (European Council for Small Business and Entrepreneurship), pp. 4–28.

Business and Technical Reports

Anthony S. (2016). Kodak's downfall wasn't about technology. *Harvard Business Review* (15 July) (online).

BEIS (2016). Higher education – business and community interaction survey 2014–15 (Higher Education Funding Council for England).

BEIS (2017). Business incubators and accelerators: The national picture, Research Paper No. 7 (Department for Business, Energy & Industrial Strategy, 20 June).

Bello-Perez Y. (2016). Number of new UK startups increased 4.6% in 2015. *Techcitynews* (13 January).

Blank S. (2012). It's time to play moneyball: The investment readiness level. Blog post of 25 November.

Boretos G. A. (2012). S-curves and their applications in marketing, business, and the economy. *Marketing Research Association Alert! Magazine* (February).

Burn-Callander R. (2015). Bad reviews and online 'trolls' cost UK businesses up to £30,000 a year. *The Telegraph* (29 May).

Cook J. (2016). Chandeliers and unpaid wages: How Crowdmix blew through £14 million before going bankrupt. *Business Insider UK* (21 July).

Cyber Streetwise with KPMG (2016). Small business reputation and the cyber risk.

Deloitte (2015). Global survey of R&D incentives (Deloitte Touche Tohmatsu, October).

Denning S. (2012). What killed Michael Porter's monitor group? The one force that really matters. *Forbes online* (November).

DTI (2004). Succeeding through innovation: Creating competitive advantage through innovation: A guide for corporates and business organizations (Department of Trade and Industry).

European Commission (2016). Practice guide – jurisdiction and applicable law in international disputes between the employee and the employer.

European Parliament Directorate General for Internal Policies (2015). A comparison between US and EU data protection legislation for law enforcement (European Union).

EY (2016). Top 10 risks in telecommunications revisited: Operator risk mitigation strategies in the digital era (Ernst & Young Global).

EY Poland (2014). Short-termism in business: Causes, mechanisms and consequences (EYGM).

Fadilpašić S. (2015). The true cost of Target's 2013 cyber attack. *ITProPortal* (February).

Gartner Inc. (2016). Gartner's 2016 hype cycle for emerging technologies identifies three key trends that organizations must track to gain competitive advantage. Gartner Press Release (August).

Germany Trade & Invest (2014). Industrie 4.0 – smart manufacturing for the future (1 July).

Glasner J. and Teare G. (2016). CrunchBase sees rise in average seed round in 2016, *CrunchBase* blog post of 7 September.

Govindarajan V. (2011). Innovation's nine critical success factors. *Harvard Business Review* (5 July).

Griffith E. (2014). Why startups fail, according to their founders. *Fortune Magazine* (September).

Griffith T. (2017). Co-innovation as a form of open innovation (North Carolina State University Centre for Innovation Management Studies).

Hewitt-Dundas N. (2015). Profiling UK university spin-outs, European Research Council Research Paper No. 35 (July).

Hewlett S. A., Marshall M. and Sherbin L. (2013). How diversity can drive innovation. *Harvard Business Review* (December).

Hiscox (2017). The Hiscox cyber readiness report.

Johnson L. (2016). Animal spirits: unicorns that belong in the land of make-believe. *The Sunday Times* (8 May).

Kaplan R. S. (2010). Conceptual foundations of the balanced scorecard. *Harvard Business Review*, Working Paper 10–074 (March).

Kaplan R. S. and Norton D. P. (1992). The balanced scorecard – measures that drive performance. *Harvard Business Review* (January/February).

Lemberg P. (2016). Which is better: New customers or repeat business? *Business Know-How*.

OECD (2015). Science, technology and industry scoreboard.

OECD (2016). G20 innovation report 2016, report prepared for the G20 Science Technology and Innovation Ministers Meeting, Beijing, China, 4 November.

OECD (2017). Measuring tax support for R&D and innovation, 2016 edn.

O'Hear S. and Lomas N. (2014). Five super successful tech pivots. *TechCrunch*.

Palmer K. (2016). Record 80 new companies being born an hour in 2016. *The Telegraph* (12 July).

Ponemon Institute (2016). Managing insider risk through training and culture.

Porter M. E. (1979). How competitive forces shape strategy. *Harvard Business Review* (March).

PwC (2013). Breakthrough innovation and growth, PwC report (September).

Ralston G. (2016). A guide to seed fundraising. *Y Combinator* blog (7 January).

Royal Academy of Engineering (2016). Managing intellectual property and technology transfer, submission to the House of Commons Science and Technology Committee (15 September).

Sikola E. (2013). Protect your business from employee fraud. *BusinessNewsDaily* (13 February).

Smith M. (2016). Huge rise in hack attacks as cyber-criminals target small businesses. *The Guardian* (8 February).

Sondergaard P. (2013). Gartner symposium keynote (Gartner Inc.).

UK government (2014). Cyber essentials scheme: Requirements for basic technical protection from cyber attacks (Department for Business, Innovation and Skills, June).

UK Office for National Statistics (2017). International comparisons of UK productivity (ICP), final estimates: 2015.

Upton D. M. and Creese S. (2014). The danger from within. *Harvard Business Review* (September).

Index